THE

SOCIABLE;

OR,

ONE THOUSAND AND ONE

Home Amusements.

THE

SOCIABLE;

OR,

ONE THOUSAND AND ONE

𝕳𝖔𝖒𝖊 𝕬𝖒𝖚𝖘𝖊𝖒𝖊𝖓𝖙𝖘.

CONTAINING

ACTING PROVERBS; DRAMATIC CHARADES; ACTING CHARADES, OR
DRAWING-ROOM PANTOMIMES; MUSICAL BURLESQUES; TA-
BLEAUX VIVANTS; PARLOR GAMES; GAMES OF AC-
TION; FORFEITS; SCIENCE IN SPORT, AND
PARLOR MAGIC; AND A CHOICE COL-
LECTION OF CURIOUS MEN-
TAL AND MECHANI-
CAL PUZZLES;
&c., &c.

ILLUSTRATED WITH

NEARLY THREE HUNDRED ENGRAVINGS AND DIAGRAMS,

THE WHOLE BEING

A FUND OF NEVER-ENDING ENTERTAINMENT.

By the Author of
"THE MAGICIAN'S OWN BOOK."

APPLEWOOD BOOKS
BEDFORD, MASSACHUSETTS

The original edition used for this reprint was
published in 1858 by
Dick & Fitzgerald of New York.

Thank you for purchasing an Applewood Book.
Applewood reprints America's lively classics—
books from the past that are still of interest
to modern readers. For a free copy of our
current catalog, write to:
Applewood Books
P.O. Box 365
Bedford, MA 01730

ISBN 1-55709-560-4

Library of Congress Control Number: 2001097595

1 3 5 7 9 10 8 6 4 2

PREFACE.

————o————

ALTHOUGH a volume of this kind requires little by way of Preface, we have a few remarks to make, concerning the fruit of so ardent but pleasurable a task as we have found its preparation to be.

No pains nor expense have been spared that could render the Sociable a complete and perfect *repertoire* of the Amusements of Home, while the greatest care has been taken to exclude everything that might possibly be objected to by the most rigidly fastidious.

Most of the recreations, here described, are entirely new, having been prepared expressly for this work by competent writers. The majority of the Parlor Theatricals are from the pens of Messrs. Frank Cahill and George Arnold—gentlemen of deserved literary popularity.

The Games of Action, Forfeits, and Ruses or Catch Games, will prove exceedingly pleasant for the younger members of the social circle; while those departments comprising Games requiring Memory and Attention, Wit and Intelligence, the Puzzles, and the Parlor Magic, are well worthy the attention of those "children of a larger growth," who are sensible enough not to be above being amused.

The Tableaux Vivants may be new to many of our readers, although they have been popular for some years, in polite society, both in Europe and this country, and especially in the South. These Tableaux are easily understood and arranged by persons of taste, and form one of the most refined recreations that a mixed party can indulge in.

We have striven to make this volume a hand-book of interesting and agreeable amusement for family circles, for schools, for pic-nic parties, for social clubs, and, in short, for all occasions where diversion is appropriate; and we would express an earnest hope that our endeavors may meet with the favor and appreciation of which we have tried to render them in every way worthy

INDEX.

Fireside Games for Winter Evening Entertainment.

Puzzles and Curious Paradoxes.

Answers to Puzzles and Paradoxes.

PARLOR THEATRICALS.

FEW amusements will be found more agreeable for small parties, than Parlor Theatricals. They have long held a favored place among the more cultivated circles of the old world, and only need to be more widely known, to gain equal popularity here.

As an educational agent, the amateur drama can hardly be too highly esteemed; for it teaches the young performer elocution, gesticulation, ease of manner, and a certain knowledge of the emotions and passions of humanity, which can rarely be acquired elsewhere.

For private performances, "Acting Proverbs" and "Dramatic Charades" are decidedly the most appropriate. They are necessarily short, and as the audience is expected to guess, from the plot of the piece, the proverb, or word they illustrate, a double interest is engendered. The "Tableaux Vivants" (*Anglicé*, "Living Pictures") are better known in most of our schools and family circles, and afford great scope for the exercise of artistic knowledge and taste, in their arrangement.

1 *

The Pantomime, or Acting Charade, is a description of amusement well suited to Christmas time, and often affording scope for the exercise of considerable wit and ingenuity. A word is to be chosen, the separate syllables of which may be rendered into some kind of lively performance; and the whole word must be capable of a similar representation. Then, the plan of action being agreed upon, old coats and hats, aprons, gowns, etc., etc., are looked up for the occasion, and speedily converted into a variety of grotesque costumes, suited to the representation to be made. The two most celebrated performers of the party choose "their sides," and, whilst the one group enacts the charade, the other plays the part of audience. At the conclusion of the drama, the guessing begins on the part of the audience. If they are successful, they in their turn perform; if not, they still remain as audience.

In the Proverbs, Charades, and Tableaux, which will be found in this volume, care has been taken to avoid anything that would be difficult, or inappropriate to the large majority of families and schools. Although the means and contrivances required are few and simple, it may be well to give some little instruction, for the benefit of those who have never seen or participated in such representations.

The first thing to be looked to, is the stage, which may be constructed at a trifling expense, so as to be taken up and laid down in a few minutes, and at any time. All that is necessary is a number of stout boards, such as flooring is ordinarily made of, three or four beams of sufficient strength to support the actors, furniture, etc., and twice as many boxes as beams. These boxes should be made for the purpose, of thick plank, and should be from one to two feet in height, according to the size of the room—the larger the room, the higher the stage, of course. Place the boxes firmly, so as to support the ends of the beams; lay the floor-boards evenly upon them, and when these are covered with a carpet, the stage is complete. To conceal the opening, underneath, and to hide the front boxes, a strip of some dark muslin may be tacked upon the edge of the boards, and allowed to fall to the floor.

The cut represents the appearance of the stage, when laid, where only two supporting beams are required. This would, however, be rather narrow.

The next thing of importance, is the curtain, behind whose friendly expanse the young comedians may arrange their scenes, and which may close silently upon their histrionic triumphs. This should be made of some soft stuff —the heavier the better—and should, if possible, be of the classic color, green, so long considered sacred to stage-curtains.

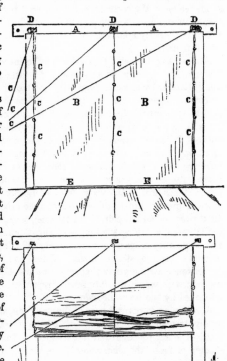

Although much has been said in favor of draw-curtains, for school purposes and private theatricals generally, the drop-curtain is much the best, and the easiest to arrange. A light wooden frame should be made, tolerably firm at the joints, and just as wide as the stage, to the front part of which, it should be attached. This frame is merely three sides of a square, and the curtain is to be strongly nailed to the top piece. A stiff wire should be run along the lower edge of the curtain, and a number of rings be attached to the back of it, in squares—say three rows, of four rings each, extending from top to bottom. Three cords are now fastened to the wire, and, passing through the rings, are run over three pulleys, on the upper piece of the frame.

BACK OF THE CURTAIN.

A A—Top of the Frame.
B B—Curtain.
C—Cords.
D D—Pulleys.
E E—Wire.

This may seem a little complicated, but the annexed cuts will show its simplicity.

The ends of the cords may be gathered together, and held by the person who officiates as prompter. On pulling them, if the pulleys and rings are properly adjusted, the curtain will be found to rise easily, in lateral folds.

Almost any household contains a sufficient variety of furniture and "properties," for any indoor scene, and a little ingenuity will produce a fair theatrical wardrobe from very common material. These things, of course, depend upon the piece to be performed, the taste of the actors, and other circumstances. The costume of Cordobello, the brigand, in the proverb of "Honor among Thieves," may be gotten up without difficulty, although it is one of the most picturesque. A common black felt hat, with the left side fastened up by a showy buckle, holding a black ostrich plume—a short velvet or woollen jacket with brass buttons (easily sewed on for the occasion)—a gay scarf bound several times around the waist, with a large knot and long ends, and a brace of pistols thrust in it—a pair of knee breeches (made by cutting off the legs of an old pair of pantaloons), with a knot of red ribbons at the knees, and long stockings—a pair of pumps, with metal buckles, and a quantity of paste jewelry, chains, etc., make a very respectable brigand's costume, at the expense of next to nothing. This is merely one instance among many that might be mentioned, and will illustrate the ease with which the "tinselled fascination of the stage" may be mimicked by the home fireside.

A still more important part of dramatic preparation is what is technically termed the "making up" of the characters, and one which requires some practice and observation. This is the painting and shading of faces, the adaptation of wigs, etc., to make the young look old, the plump lean, etc.

For the "making up" of any variety of different faces, a box of good water-colors, a little fine chalk, some camel's-hair pencils, and dry rouge, are wanted. If a comical expression is required, mix a reddish brown tint with the water-colors, stand before a mirror, assume the desired "broad grin," and trace the wrinkles produced, with a fine brush of the brown tint. This will fix the line which your face requires, to give it the expression, much more naturally than you could do it by following any of the rules current among artists. The same may be done with frowns, smirks, simpers, scowls, and all other marked contortions of feature.

Rouge should be applied with the forefinger—a much better imple ment than the traditional hare's-foot—and should be softly graded off upon the cheek. Chalk should be very sparingly used. Burnt cork is very effective for black eyes, or for representing leanness, by applying a very faint tint underneath the eyes, on the sides of the cheeks, and under the lower lip. A strong mark running from the corner of the nose down towards the corner of the mouth, on each side, is a good sign of age or emaciation, but these points are best learned by observing different faces. Moustaches and beards, when slight, should be made with India-ink and a fine pencil. A few sets of false ones, of real hair, however, as also a few wigs of various colors and patterns, will be found a great addition to the wardrobe. In the tableau of the "Drunkard's Home," in this work, there is great scope for the art of "making up," and a good effect may be produced on the faces and arms of the women and children, by deepening the shadows with cork or India-ink, and heightening the prominent features with chalk. For the man, a flushed color, with a few purplish spots on the cheeks and nose, will be appropriate.

One of the most imperative of all rules which we can lay down— and one which applies to professional, as well as amateur performers— is, "learn your parts *thoroughly*." Without this, no proverb nor charade can be well acted, or interesting to the audience. Each performer should write out his own part, with the "cues" or words which come directly before his own speeches, and should commit *every word literally*. The following example, from "No Rose without Thorns," will explain the "cues" and their use.

The performer who takes the part of Rose, should copy out and study the last words of Kate's and Jack Upson's parts, thus:

Enter KATE.

ROSE.   Katie, child, go to my room, and bring down the guitar.
(*Cue, from* JACK's *part.*)   Sing dear?
ROSE.   Oh, anything.   All your songs are sweet, to *me.*
(*Cue.*)   Like best?
ROSE.   Do you know, "I love but Thee?"
(*Cue.*)   To hear it!
ROSE.   No, no!—I mean the song of that name!
(*Cue.*)   The instrument.

And so on. When the performer hears the words of the cue, knowing them by heart, they instantly suggest the speech to follow.

The exits and entrances will be found somewhat difficult of management, in some rooms, and windows, or even closets, will occasionally have to be used—the latter, especially, for very short absences from the stage. A simple way of making one door serve for two exits, is by placing a screen in front of it, at the back of the stage, and retiring behind, or issuing from, the ends of it. This screen will be found very useful in many pieces, and we would suggest that where such entertainments are popular, it is worth while to have one constructed. It is simply made of wooden frames, some six feet high by three wide, hinged together and covered with cloth or wall-paper.

The initials for the different portions of the stage are:

L. Left.	R. Right.
U. E. Upper entrance.	L. E. Lower entrance.
C. Centre.	Etc.

The following words will be found suitable for either Pantomime or Dialogue Charades:

Air-gun,	Grand-child,	Mend-i-cant,	Sweet-heart,
Arch-bishop,	Great-coat,	Milk-maid,	Tell-tale,
Band-box,	Heir-loom,	Nap-kin,	Tow-line,
Bride-cake,	Horse-chest-nut,	Night-cap,	Up-braid,
Bull-rush,	I-dol,	Out-rage,	Up-shot,
Court-ship,	I-rate,	Out-pour,	Vat-i-can,
Cross-bow,	Jack-pudding,	Pack-cloth,	Watch-man,
Dice-box,	Jew-el,	Pop-gun,	Waist-cord,
Dog-rose,	King-craft,	Quarter-staff,	Way-bill,
Eye-glass,	Key-hole,	Rain-bow,	Water-fall,
Fag-end,	Leap-frog,	Rope-yarn,	Young-ster,
Fan-light,	Love-apple,	Sauce-box,	Zeal-ot.
Game-cock,	Mad-cap,	Sea-shell,	

With these brief instructions, which, sketchy and general as they are, the writer hopes may prove of some utility, we will proceed to some examples of the style of performance best suited to amateur dramatic talent and convenience. Though they are slight and simple, they contain good characters, healthy sentiments, and a briskness of dialogue which is necessary to short, lively pieces. In taking leave of the subject, we would only say, that amusement and instruction are the grand objects, and it is evident that the more perfect the acting, the better are these aims accomplished.

PROVERB I.

"WHEN THE CAT'S AWAY, THEN THE MICE WILL PLAY!

BY GEORGE ARNOLD.

Characters.

PATRICK O'HOLOHOOLAN, *a Coachman.*
BRIDGET FOLEY, *a Cook.*
MEHITABLE COFFIN, *a Chambermaid.*
BOB, *a Page, in buttons.*
MR. GARNETT, *a wealthy housekeeper, master of the above servants.*
MRS. GARNETT.
MIKE HENNESSY, SANDY M'CULLODEN, MRS. RAFFERTY, MISS DOLLOP
and other servants belonging to neighboring families.
A POLICEMAN.   A THIEF.

SCENE—*A drawing-room in* MR. GARNETT'S *house.*

PATRICK, BRIDGET, *and* BOB.

PAT.   Shure, thin, Miss Foley, an' it's a good time we'll be afther
navin' wid our par*hy.   Things is comed round convaynient intirely

BRIDGET. Yis, honey. It's mesilf was thinkin' that same, jist. Troth, an' I was mighty afeared that the master an' missus would niver be afther a-goin' in the counthry. Shure it's the only vacation pore servants has, when the fam'lies is out of town.

PAT. Bob, have yez given out all the invites?

BOB. Yes. They're all coming, 'cept the two Flanagans.

PAT. Bad luck to them. It's common folk they are, thin, an' onfit for the company of daycint people. I'm glad they're not comin'.

BRIDGET. An' it's the blessed thruth ye're tellin'. Them Flanagans nain't got no manners, and in consekence, no eddication. Go see what time it is, Bob.

BOB. Don't you wish I would!

PAT. What d'ye mane, ye spalpeen, talkin' to yer betthers afther that fashion? Where's yer manners, ye little roosh-light!

BOB. I don't care. I ain't the servants' servant. Master's away now, and I'm jest as good as anybody. I only went round with the invitations 'cause you promised me some of the ice-cream.

BRIDGET. Did I iver see sich an upstart! Go at onst, sir, an' see what time it is!

BOB. (*mockingly, making a face at her.*) Ya-a-a.

[Runs off, with PATRICK after him.

PAT. (*coming back.*) Shure, the imperence of these underlings is awful, Miss Foley! (*Bell rings.*) There's the bell—some of the company must be afther arrivin'.

BRIDGET. Yis, machree; jist step an' let 'em in. That gossoon will niver answer the bell.

PAT. Well, Miss Foley, I don't think it's quite the coachman's place to be runnin' to the doore.

BRIDGET. No more it isn't the cook's.

PAT. But shure, ma'am, it's more of a woman's bisness than a man's.

BRIDGET. Misther O'Holohoolan, I'm dressed for the parthy, sir, an' I decline agoin' to the doore, if it isn't opened to-night.

[Bell rings.

PAT. Och, smithereens! Here, Bob. *[Calling.*

Enter BOB.

BOB. What d'ye want?

BRIDGET *and* PAT. Don't yez hear the bell, shure?

BOB. Yes, I hear it.

BRIDGET. Well, it's the company.

Bob.   Oh, is it!

Pat.   Yis, an' they wants to come in.

Bob.   Oh, does they?

Bridget.   Go to the doore, Bob, there's a honey!

Pat.   Go to the doore, ye thafe of the world!

Bob.   Do you want the door opened, you two?

Pat *and* Bridget.   Av coorse!   [*Bell rings.*

Bob.   Well, you'd better open it, then.   [*Runs off.*

Pat.   Shure an' I see I'll have to be afther bemanin' my station by openin' the doore mesilf. (*Looking reproachfully at* Bridget.)   Some folks is too mighty proud intirely.   I won't open it agin, though.

Bridget.   *I'll* niver tend a bell.

Pat.   Shure thin, I'll jist lave it ajar, an' when they rings agin, I'll tell 'em to come right in, of thimselves.   [*Exit.*

Enter Mehitable Coffin.

Mehitable (*pertly*).   Ah, Miss Foley, hasn't nobody come yet?

Bridget.   Yes; Misther O'Holohoolan is gone down to let 'em in. Is the wine iced, Miss Coffee?

Mehitable.   Miss Coffin, if you please, marm.   I don't know anythin' about the wine, marm, I never was brought up to use spirituous things.

Bridget.   Och, darlint, an' it's a mighty dale of good a little dhrop does, now an' thin.

Mehitable.   I wouldn't tech a glass for the world, marm.   I knowed two very likely young fellers, down to hum, in Kennebec, who commenced with wine, marm, and drinked theirselves into their grave, in ten years, marm.

Enter Patrick, *with* Mike Hennessy *and* Mrs. Rafferty.

Pat.   Mike, this lady is Miss Coffin—one of our family.

Mike (*bowing awkwardly*).   My respects to yez, Miss Muffin.

Mehitable.   Miss Coffin, if you please, Mr. Mike.

Mike.   Mr. Hennessy, if you plaze, Miss Coffin.

[*During this introduction,* Mrs. Rafferty *shakes hands with* Bridget, *and takes off her bonnet and shawl, which she throws on a chair.*)

Bridget.   Good evenin' to yez, Misther Hennessy—how is the childher?

Mike.   Comf'able, mum, bad luck to 'em (Pat *introduces* Mehitable *and* Mrs. Rafferty, *at back of stage, where they stand talking*), barrin that little Joe has the fayver, and Cathrun stuck a fork in her fut, yis-

terday   Och, mum, it's hard work it is, intirely, to take care of the
poor orphlings, an' I think I'll have to be lookin' afther another wife,
shure!   [*Bell rings.*

BRIDGET.   Patrick—Misther O'Holohoolan—there's some   one
ringin' !   [PAT *goes to window, puts his head out, and shouts.*

PAT.   Come right up, shure. The doore's left ajar for yez !

   [BRIDGET *and* MIKE *retire to back of stage, talking, and* MEHITABLE
      and MRS. RAFFERTY *come forward.*

MEHITABLE.   Yes, marm, I'm uncommon fond of parties. The gals
and fellers allers has great times down in Kennebec, to corn shuckin's
and parin' bees.

MRS. R.   Och, honey, ye should jist be over in the ould counthry,
onst, and have a taste o' Donnybrook Fair ! Shure, that's the place
for coortin', an' dancin', an' singin', and fightin', and gittin' comfortably dhrunk !

Enter SANDY McCULLODEN *with* MISS DOLLOP.

PAT.   Ah, it's you, is it, Misther McCulloden ? How are yez ?
                                         [*Shaking hands.*

SANDY.   Weel, I canna say I'm in sic bad health as I ha' seen. Miss
Dollop, Mr. O'Holohoolan. Miss Dollop is the chambermaid at our
house.

MISS DOLLOP (*looking savagely at him*).   I attend to the dormitories,
and I hope I'm not ashamed to say so.

PAT.   Troth, it's all one. Sandy's fren's is my fren's, an' I'm glad
to see 'em.

SANDY.   Hoot, girl! ye need na fly aff the handle sae! It's na
disgrace to ken how to mak' a bed or hantle a broom! Gang yonder
to Miss Foley, an' let her tak' aff yer duds.

   [MISS DOLLOP *goes to* BRIDGET, *and takes off things.* MEHITABLE *and*
      MRS. RAFFERTY *join them, and they talk apart.* SANDY *sits down*
      on MRS. R.'s *bonnet without seeing it, and taking out a pipe, fills it.*
      PAT. *and* MIKE *also get pipes, and sit down with* SANDY.

MIKE (*looking suspiciously at* SANDY's *chair*).   Troth, Mr. McCulloden,
I think ye're afther a-sittin' on something.

SANDY (*getting up and holding smashed bonnet out at arm's length*)
Ay, fecks! I think I ha' doon some damage!

   [*The women come forward, and* MRS. RAFFERTY *sees the bonnet.*

MRS. R.   Och ! murther ! look at me hat—me bran-new hat ! It ·
kilt and spiled entirely ;· ochone, wirristhroo ! an' all along of that
great awkward baste of a Scotchman ! ochone !

MEHITABLE. Law sakes! you might know *she* wasn't brought up to havin' good clothes! she takes on more about a bunnet than I would about a silk gownd!

SANDY. Tush, woman, dinna mak' sic a hue-and-cry. I'm sair fashed aboot it!

[MRS. R. *snatches the bonnet, and threatens* SANDY *with her fist; all crowd about, and all speaking at once, a terrible confusion ensues.*

PAT. (*speaking at the top of his voice.*) Be quiet, will yez! (*Jumps up on chair, and shouts to the party.*) Och, be quiet, I say, an' we'll hush the matther up, over a bottle o' wine or sperits! We'll have something to drink! I say! D'yez hear! (*They suddenly become silent.*) There, thin, I knowed I could settle the difficulty, aisy enough. Come out o' the way, Sandy, for a minnit, an' help me bring in the refreshments. [*Exit, with* SANDY.

MISS DOLLOP. I guess no man wouldn't sit on my hat more than once!

MEHITABLE. Nor on mine; but I wouldn't get so cantankerous, and raise Cain so, about no cheap bonnet like that 'ere!

MRS. R. Bad luck to ye, do ye call that a chape bonnet, when it cost me five shillin's sterlin' in ould Ireland, an' I haven't worn it but two year come next Michaelmas will be a month!

BRIDGET *and* MIKE. Now, thin, don't be afther worryin' anny more.

Enter PAT. *and* SANDY *with trays, bottles, etc., which they place on table.*

PAT. Now fall to, good luck to yez all! Mrs. Rafferty, will ye thry a little bog-poteen? Miss Foley, plaze do the hanners of the table.

BRIDGET. Thank ye, sir, I'm not a waiter.

PAT. Och, wirra! an' it's mighty unobleegin' yez are, to be shure. (*Takes glass, and tries to fill it from bottle, but finds it empty.*) Shure, somebody's bin at the refreshments! (*Lifts cover from dish, and finds it empty also.*) Och, an the ice-crame's all gone, too! [*Runs out.*

MRS. R. This is a mighty pretty parthy, now, isn't it, Mike Hennessy, where a body's things is spiled an' ruined intirely, an' there's nothin' to ate or dhrink, barrin' empty bottles' an' dishes?

BRIDGET. Good enough for the likes of you, Misthress Rafferty!

[*Another confusion begins to arise, when* PAT. *appears, dragging* BOB *by the collar.* BOB *has his mouth full, a very red face, and drops apples, cakes, etc., all over the stage.*

PAT. Ochone! Haven't I caught ye, now, ye murtherin' little

chafe o' the world—ate up all the ice-crame, an' poun' cake, an' dhrink all the sherry—will ye?

BOB. (*trying to talk with his mouth full.*) Blob-blob, glob, glog, blog-lob

MIKE. Shure, now—

SANDY. Hoot, mon!

MRS. R. Well, now—

MEHITABLE. Law sakes! du tell.

BRIDGET. Och! the gossoon!

MISS DOLLOP. Deary me!

> [*They all run to table, and examine dishes. BOB slips away and runs out. All talk at once, louder and louder, till nothing can be heard but a perfect uproar.*

Enter BOB, *with his face pale, and his hair on end, looking much terrified.*

BOB. Thieves! thieves! help! murder!

> [MISS DOLLOP *throws herself into* SANDY'S *arms, and pretends to faint.* MRS. RAFFERTY *throws herself upon* MIKE, *and nearly upsets him. The rest stand back alarmed.*

PAT. Thaves? Where?

BOB. Somebody's carried off the spoons from the dining-room, and a whole lot of things!

ALL. Oh! oh!

BRIDGET. It was all along of your lavin' the front door open, Pat. Shure, it's jist like yez!

> [*While all stand aghast, the door opens, and* MR. *and* MRS. GARNETT *enter.*

MRS. G. Whew! faugh! tobacco smoke!

MR. G. What's all this? By Jove, here are pretty goings on! Patrick!

PAT. (*looking very sheepish.*) Yis, sir.

MR. G. Bridget!

BRIDGET. Yis, sir.

MR. G. Who are all these people, carousing and smoking here in my drawing-room?

PAT. Shure, sir, an' they're only a few fren's as dhropped in to—

MR. G. *Dhropped* in, did they? Well, they can *dhrop* out again now, the sooner the better. Do you hear, you people? Go—leave— vanish! [*All draw back towards the door.*

MRS. G. Oh! my poor carpet is ruined.

MRS. RAFFERTY. Och, mum, an' so is me poor hat!

Enter POLICEMAN, *holding* THIEF *by the arm.*

POLICEMAN. Mr. Garnett!

MR. G. Hallo! who have you got there, Brown?

POLICEMAN. A well-known hall thief, sir, and he had a lot of spoons marked with your name. I caught him just around the corner here, sir, and thought I'd see who he had been robbing.

[*Gives spoons to* MRS. GARNETT.

MR. G. You are a good officer, Brown; here, take this (*giving him money*), and help me to clear these wretches out of the house.

ALL. Oh! oh!

MR. G. Go, every one of you! Patrick, you and Bridget may pack up your things as soon as you can, for I can tell you that you shall not stay another day in my service. Now, Brown, clear the room!

[*The* POLICEMAN *draws his club, the party make a rush for the door, and tumble out in confusion.*

POLICEMAN. They're a nice set, sir. It's a mercy they hadn't burned the house down before now.

MRS. GARNETT. Just to think of such a company drinking and smoking in my parlor!

MR. GARNETT. My dear, it is always the way. These people, are never to be trusted, only when one's eyes are upon them. I will leave it to any of our matronly friends here (*turning to audience*), if their servants do not " worry the lives out of them."

When we're at home, they're steady as you please—
But when we go away, they take their ease;
My coachman's faithless—

MRS. GARNETT.   So are cook and maid—
  I'm out of patience!

MR. GARNETT.   And our proverb's played!

CURTAIN.

PROVERB II.

"IT NEVER RAINS BUT IT POURS."

BY FRANK CAHILL.

Characters.

PAUL SMITHERS.
JACK THOMSON, *his friend.*
MR. SIMPSON, M.C.
MRS. BOBBIDGE.
POSTMAN, WAITER, *etc.*

SCENE.—*An attic bedroom. A table, R.C., upon which are a quantity of MS., an inkstand, letters, etc.*

Enter PAUL SMITHERS, *shabbily attired, examining a large rent in the side of his coat.*

PAUL. Just my luck! must go and tear my coat coming up those confounded stairs.—I never saw such a tear.—I haven't any needle and thread, neither have I any money to get it mended. I am an unlucky fellow! Hallo! here are one or two letters that have been left during my absence in search of money. I wonder what my creditors have to say to-day. (*Takes up letter and opens it.*) Ah, the old story—wants his money. I'll be bound he don't want it any more than I want to pay him. Its no use reading any more, they're all alike, I know,—yet I may as well look over the signatures, and see who they are from. (*Opens three letters.*) Let me see, Packer, that's my tailor,—you can go there (*throws it into waste-paper basket that is at side of table*). Benson,—eh, he's my bootmaker, you can go there (*throws it into waste-basket*). Now for the last,—who's this? Smith,—Smith, I don't know anybody of the name of Smith. I'll read the letter.

"Sir:—Some time ago you recommended a friend of yours to me as a boarder; no doubt you will recollect it; telling me at the time that you would be responsible for his board. Now, sir, he has gone away in my debt, amounting in all to fifteen dollars. Will you please forward it to me, or shall I call upon you? Yours obediently,

"JOHN SMITH.

"P.S.—Your friend's name was Jackson."

Did you ever see anything like it? I have not spoken to Jackson for fifteen months, and now Smith comes down upon me for fifteen dollars:—charged a dollar a month for not seeing a fellow! (*A knock heard at the door.*) Come in.

Enter JACK THOMSON.

JACK. Hallo! Paul, how goes it?

PAUL. Shocking.

JACK. Sorry to hear it. Things are pretty bad with me just now. I say, old fellow, can you lend me five dollars?

PAUL. Do what?

JACK. Lend me five dollars. I have got into a deuce of a scrape,—must get it somewhere.

PAUL. I'm surprised at you.

JACK. Where should I go to borrow money, if not to you?

PAUL. You misunderstand me, old boy. I'd lend it you, if I had it; but I haven't a penny in the world.

JACK. It's always the way, whenever I want to borrow money, I never can get it.

PAUL. It's the same with me I've been half over town to-day, and couldn't raise a red. I am nearly worried to death. I haven't been so hard up for months.

JACK. You don't say so?

PAUL. But I do say so; and I'm being dunned for money hourly.

JACK. You must expect that; you know, misfortunes never come singly.

PAUL. Yes, indeed; misfortune must be married, and have a numerous family, if I can judge by the number of times she and hers have visited me, for I am sure she would be tired out with the number of calls she makes at my abode.

JACK. Can't we raise the wind somewhere?

PAUL. I've got nothing.

JACK. More have I—only some collars, and they won't lend anything on half worn-out collars.

PAUL. I say, Jack.

JACK. What?

PAUL.   Ain't it a pity that we haven't a rich old uncle, somewhere or other, who would turn up just now—like they do in plays—give us a lot of money, say "Bless you, be happy!" and make us marry his rich ward?

JACK.   Ah, don't I wish I had such an uncle! But I must be off. I've got to raise that money before two. Good bye.

PAUL.   Good bye—good luck to you!

JACK.   Hope so. Keep up your pluck; I'll call again shortly.

[Exit JACK.

PAUL.   No news yet from that article I sent on to the *Pacific Monthly* the other day; anybody else would have had the money by this time, and have spent it. Well, this won't do; I must go to work, anyway. (*Goes to table, and begins to arrange papers.*) It's fortunate that I have some ink and paper left; if I hadn't those, I should be in a plight. (*Knocks inkstand over.*) Goodness gracious! how careless! There, it's going all over my papers. No, it's no good—I can't get any of it up. That's nice paper to write on (*shows paper covered with ink*). Now I'm in a nice condition : no ink, no paper, and no money to buy any with. I've half a mind to—(*a knock is heard at the door*)—Come in.

Enter MRS. BOBBIDGE.

MRS. BOBBIDGE.   Mr. Smithers, I've come for my rent.

PAUL.   I am very sorry, Mrs. Bobbidge, but I can't pay you to-day.

MRS. BOBBIDGE.   But I must have my money.

PAUL.   I haven't any money, Mrs. Bobbidge.

MRS. BOBBIDGE.   If you haven't any money, what made you take my room?

PAUL.   When I took your room, I had money; you know I paid you regularly for the first six months.

MRS. BOBBIDGE.   You haven't paid me regularly for the last three.

PAUL.   I shall have a lot of money soon, then I'll pay you.

MRS. BOBBIDGE.   I want my room, Mr. Smithers; and if you don't pay me to-day you must leave.

PAUL.   How unreasonable you are, Mrs. Bobbidge. A man must live somewhere, and I may just as well run into your debt as anybody else's.

MRS. BOBBIDGE.   It don't make much difference to you, but it does to me; so, if you please, Mr. Smithers, get a room elsewhere.

PAUL.   But, Mrs. Bobbidge——

MRS. BOBBIDGE.   Don't Mrs. Bobbidge me, if you please, sir. If you don't let me have the room to-night, I'll lock up the door to-morrow, mind that. [*Exit* Mrs. Bobbidge.

Paul. Was there ever such an unfortunate fellow! Where's that penny,—here it is. I'll toss up and see whether I shall kill myself or not. It's no use living; I shall never have any good fortune again. Here goes. Heads—death; tails—live. (*He tosses penny up in the air, and catches it, at that moment a knock is heard at the door.*) Come in.

Enter a Waiter.

Waiter. Is this Mr. Smithers' room?

Paul. Yes; are you from the restaurant, across the way?

Waiter. Yes, sir.

Paul. Where's that dinner I ordered?

Waiter. If you please, sir, master says, he can't let you have any more, till you pay up.

Paul. What!

Waiter. Master says, he can't let you——

Paul. I know what your master said. Go away, you make me hungry to look at you.

Waiter. Very well, sir. [*Exit* Waiter.

Paul. Was there ever,—no matter, what do I want with a dinner, when I'm going to kill myself. Let me try again. Heads—death; tails—live. (*He spins penny again, a knock is heard at the door*). Confound that door! Come in.

Enter Postman, *with rather a large letter in his hand.*

Postman. Mr. Paul Smithers.

Paul. That's me.

Postman. Two cents to pay.

Paul (*offering to take the letter*). I'll owe it you.

Postman. No, you don't. You owe me twenty-four cents already.

Paul (*giving him penny*). There's a penny on account, now let me have it.

Postman. No, I shan't, till you give me the other penny.

Paul (*aside*). It's a large package, I shouldn't be at all surprised if it contained a remittance from the *Pacific Monthly*. (*Aloud.*) Postman, I must have that letter.

Postman. But you shan't till you pay me the other penny.

Paul (*turning up the sleeves of his coat*). Postman, give me that letter.

POSTMAN. I'll call again to-morrow with it (*going*).

PAUL (*seizing him by the coat-tail*). Stay! I am sure that letter con-tains money; let me open it, then I'll pay you.

POSTMAN. I won't.

PAUL. You won't! then I'll take it. (PAUL *and the* POSTMAN *struggle. The* POSTMAN *drops letter,* PAUL *picks it up triumphantly*).

POSTMAN. Very well, you, Mr. Smithers, I'll have you up for rob-bing the United States Mail. [*Exit* POSTMAN.

PAUL. Confounded rascal! wouldn't leave the letter without the money, but I've done him this time. Now, then, for the contents. (*Begins to open letter.*) I'm sure it contains money. It must be from the *Pacific Monthly*. Hullo! what's this,—my letters to Julia,—what can be the meaning of this;—here's a letter, perhaps that will explain it.

[*The letter contained a package of letters, which he holds in his hand; he opens one.*

"SIR: Herewith you will receive the letters that you have, from time to time, addressed to my daughter Julia. You will oblige all of us by not sending any more, till you hear from us again. I remain, yours obediently, JOHN JONES." That's a nice letter to receive, instead of money! So Julia is lost to me for ever. Oh! fickle, cruel-hearted Julia! No matter. Where's that cent? Heads—death; tails—live. Dear me, where can it have got to? I remember now, that wretched postman has taken it, and I have not even the mournful satisfaction left me, of tossing up a copper for life or death. (*A knock is heard at the door.*) Come in.

Enter SIMPSON.

SIMPSON. Is your name Smithers—Mr. Paul Smithers?

PAUL. It's no good your coming here; I have no money.

SIMPSON (*smiling*). But——

PAUL. I tell you it's no good.

SIMPSON. My dear sir.

PAUL. I can't pay you; I haven't any money.

SIMPSON. I do not want—

PAUL. You are the most indefatigable man I ever saw in my life. It's no use dunning me; I'll pay you when I have the money.

SIMPSON. Will you listen to me?

PAUL. Yes, I'll listen to you, but you're wasting your time; I haven't any money.

SIMPSON. I don't want any money.

PAUL. Why didn't you say so before? I am extremely glad to see you. [*Shaking him by the hand.*

SIMPSON. I have come on a more pleasant errand, I assure you.

PAUL. Indeed! well, anything for a change.

SIMPSON. I have come from my friend, Mr. Elliott, whom you know, I believe.

PAUL. Then you want that money he loaned me.

SIMPSON. On the contrary, I have come to offer you a situation under government.

PAUL. You don't say so?

SIMPSON. Mr. Elliott has such a high appreciation of your talents, that he has obtained for you the position of secretary to the ambassador of Otaheite.

PAUL (*delighted*). My dear sir—

SIMPSON. Will you accept it?

PAUL. With pleasure. [JACK *pokes his head in at the door.*

JACK. Can I come in?

PAUL. Yes, certainly.

JACK (*entering*). Well, I've been successful. Bateman lent me the money, and he gave me this note for you (*hands note to* PAUL). He has been out of town, and only returned this morning.

PAUL. Excuse me, Mr.—Mr.—

SIMPSON. Simpson. Certainly.

PAUL. (*Opens letter.*) Hurrah! Bateman has sent me the twenty dollars, and apologizes for not sending it before. Bateman's a brick!

JACK. Isn't he?

PAUL. Fortune has changed, Jack. Mr. Simpson has just offered me a situation under government.

JACK. Bravo! I congratulate you.

SIMPSON. I hope Mr. Smithers will find it pecuniarily to his advantage. [*A knock is heard at the door.*

PAUL. Come in.

Enter MRS. BOBBIDGE.

MRS. BOBBIDGE. If you please, Mr. Smithers,——

PAUL. I know what you want,—you want your money.

MRS. BOBBIDGE. I should like it, but here's a letter for you.
[*Gives letter.*

PAUL. Another letter,—a dun I suppose. (*Opens letter and reads.*) Hurrah! Mrs. Bobbidge, let me hug you. (*Attempts to embrace* MRS. BOBBIDGE, *who repulses him.*) Congratulate me, Jack. Mr. Simpson,

you're a trump; no, I beg pardon, you're a,—you're a,—I don't know
what you are.   [*Shakes hands with them violently.*

JACK.   What's the matter, old boy?

PAUL.   The Pacific has accepted my story, and has sent me on a
draft for a hundred and fifty dollars.   Hurrah!

[*Waves draft about, and dances frantically about the stage.*

SIMPSON.   You seem to be fortunate, Mr. Smithers.

PAUL.   Fortunate!   This morning I thought I was one of the most
unfortunate men in the world; now I think I am the most fortunate.

JACK.   Well, you're in luck, old fellow.

PAUL.   In luck!   I should rather say I was.   It reminds me of the
old adage.   It —— what is it, do you know?   I have forgotten it.

JACK.   No,—yes,—let me see.   It——oh, I don't know it.

PAUL.   Do you know the proverb, Mr. Simpson?

SIMPSON.   No, I do not.

PAUL.   You know it, Mrs. Bobbidge?

MRS. BOBBIDGE.   No, Mr. Smithers, it is such a long while since I
went to school, that really I do not remember it.

PAUL.   What shall we do? none of us remember it.   Oh!   I have
it.   (*To audience.*)   We must leave it to these ladies and gentlemen.
And, if any here remember the proverb, we shall only be too happy
for them to tell us it.

PAUL *and* MR. SIMPSON *centre.*   JACK *right.*   MRS. BOBBIDGE *left.*

CURTAIN.

PROVERB III.

"HONOR AMONG THIEVES."

BY FRANK CAHILL.

Characters.

ALONZO DI CORDOBELLO, *a brigand.*
LANDLORD.
CHARLES VANE.
ALICE VANE, *his wife.*
MRS. BEAUMONT.
MASTER CLARENCE, *her son.*
LADIES, GENTLEMEN, *etc.*

SCENE—*A parlor in an Italian hotel—a window at back.*

Enter LANDLORD, *bowing, and walking backwards, followed by* MR. *and* MRS. VANE.

LANDLORD. This way, Signor—mind the step, my lady—this is the room, Signor—hope you are satisfied, my lady?

ALICE. Yes; this seems a very pleasant room.

LANDLORD. Glad it meets your approbation, my lady. Would you like some refreshments, Signor?

CHARLES. None at present—we dined on the road.

LANDLORD. Thank you, Signor. If Signor will graciously permit me, I will retire. [*Bows himself towards the door.*

ALICE. Oh! landlord.

LANDLORD. My lady.

[*Advances hurriedly towards* ALICE *and bows.*

ALICE. There is a writing desk in the carriage—will you bring it me?

LANDLORD. Certainly, my lady. [*He bows himself out.*

ALICE. So, Charles dear, we are in delightful Italy at last. The land of sunny skies, poetry, and romance. (*Goes to window, and looks out.*)   See what a charming view from this window; isn't it lovely?—such a beautiful sky, too!

CHARLES.   Enthusiast!

ALICE.   But isn't it splendid, Charley?

CHARLES (*laughing*).   Let me see.   Delightful, charming, lovely, beautiful, splendid—take care, take care—what an extravagant young woman you are!

ALICE.   Extravagant! how?

CHARLES.   Why, in the use of adjectives.   Hallo! look at those soldiers.   [CHARLES *and* ALICE *both look out of window.*

Enter LANDLORD, *with writing desk, which he places on table.*

LANDLORD.   I beg your pardon, Signor, but they'll have him now.

CHARLES.   Indeed! but who is it they are going to have?

LANDLORD.   Is it possible Signor cannot have heard?   Why, Alonzo di Cordobello, to be sure.

CHARLES.   And who is Alonzo di Cordobello?

LANDLORD.   He is the celebrated brigand, whose depredations are the talk of Italy.

ALICE (*clapping her hands*).   A real live brigand!   Do tell us about him.   Is he handsome?—is he young?   How I should like to see him!

LANDLORD.   So they say, my lady; but I have never seen him.

CHARLES.   And those soldiers, we saw in the court-yard, just now, are going in search of him?

LANDLORD.   Yes, Signor.   Prince di Costello was waylaid last night, and robbed, so government has determined to catch this Cordobello, dead or alive.

ALICE.   How romantic!

LANDLORD.   Yes, my lady.   He only plunders the rich, and frequently gives money to the poor.   Last year, when the worms destroyed Baptiste's grape crop, and he could not pay his rent, Cordobello sent him the money to do it with.

CHARLES.   Quite a Robin Hood, I declare.

LANDLORD.   Robbing?   Yes, indeed; he robs everybody he comes across.   But will Signor come and enter his name, as the police are very strict about that?

CHARLES.   Certainly.   Where is the book?

LANDLORD.   If Signor will come with me I'll show him.

  [*Goes to door, holds it open for* CHARLES *to go out, bows as he passes, turns to* ALICE, *bows to her, and exits.*

ALICE (*goes to table, and sits down*). A brigand! How delicious! Oh! if I could only see him! When we return to New York, how delightful it would be to be able to tell my friends I had seen a brigand —a real live brigand! (*As she is speaking,* CORDOBELLO *enters the room, through the window.*) I am sure I shouldn't be a bit frightened.

[CORDOBELLO, *who is in brigand's costume, comes down, and stands before* ALICE, *who screams, and shrinks from him, covering her face with her handkerchief.*

CORDOBELLO. Pardon my unceremonious entrance (*looks at her left hand*), madam. [*Takes off hat, and bows.*

ALICE. What—what do you want?

CORDOBELLO. Hearing of your arrival, politeness made me call.

ALICE. I will call my husband, sir. [*Moves towards door.*

CORDOBELLO (*intercepting her*). Nay, do not trouble yourself. Allow me to offer you a chair. [*Takes her hand, and leads her to a chair.*

ALICE (*with forced calmness*). To whom am I indebted for this visit?

CORDOBELLO. You must excuse my breach of etiquette in not sending up my card; my name is Alonzo di Cordobello.

ALICE. The brigand! [*Suppresses a scream.*

CORDOBELLO (*bowing*). At your service. Nothing is more agreeable to me than a *tête-à-tête* with a lady, especially an American lady.

ALICE (*aside*). He certainly is very handsome.

CORDOBELLO. I have heard of your country, lady, where the sky is almost as clear and as blue as our own. What a pretty bracelet: allow me to examine it. [*Takes the bracelet off her arm.*

ALICE (*timidly*). Sir,—that,—that bracelet was a wedding gift.

CORDOBELLO. A wedding gift! Really the donor must have had exquisite taste. [*Puts bracelet in his pocket.*

ALICE (*aside*). Does he mean to rob me?

CORDOBELLO. Your bays too, are very fine, are they not? Have you seen our far-famed Bay of Naples?

ALICE. Yes.

CORDOBELLO. It used to be called the finest in the world; but I have heard that some of your American bays almost exceed it in beauty. But, pardon me, I am afraid that I am exceeding the time that society allows for a call. Would you oblige me with the hour?

ALICE (*looking at watch*). It is now half past——

CORDOBELLO (*interrupting her*). Nay, I could not think of troubling a lady. Allow me to see for myself.

[*Takes chain, with watch attached, from her neck.*

ALICE (*rising*). This rudeness, sir——

CORDOBELLO. Now you are unjust (*drawing himself up proudly*) Alonzo di Cordobello is never rude to a lady.

ALICE. Then return me my watch and bracelet, and leave me.

CORDOBELLO. Pardon me; whenever I meet a lady, I always like to keep something in remembrance of her.

ALICE. Your impertinence is charming.

CORDOBELLO. I am happy that I charm, madam (*bows*). A desk too (*tries to open desk*), and locked : might I trouble you for the key ?

ALICE. I haven't it with me. I will fetch it for you. [*Going.*

CORDOBELLO. I couldn't think of troubling you. See, I can do without it. [*Forces desk with dagger.*

ALICE (*pettishly*). You have spoiled my desk.

CORDOBELLO. I am not such a clumsy workman. See,—it is uninjured. (*Takes things out of desk.*) What have we here,—letters,—those we will pass. I never interfere with the correspondence of a lady.

ALICE. Well, that's considerate.

CORDOBELLO. A miniature! and set round with diamonds.

ALICE Oh, do not take that.

CORDOBELLO. Pardon me, I must; miniatures are my especial weakness. (*Aside.*) Particularly when they have diamond settings.

ALICE. Take the setting,—take anything else I have in the world; but give me back my miniature. It is the likeness of my mother,—the only one I have,—so pray, pray, give it me.

CORDOBELLO. Ladies never ask a favor of Alonzo di Cordobello in vain. [*Tries to take miniature out of setting.*

ALICE. Then you will not take it?

CORDOBELLO. (*Aside.*) Pshaw! I cannot get it out of the setting (*Aloud.*) I am afraid I shall be obliged to take it.

ALICE. Oh! do not, I implore you.

CORDOBELLO. Lady, I promise you, on my honor, that you shall be in possession of the painting again in less than an hour.

ALICE. Pray, pray, do not take it.

CORDOBELLO. Madam, my word is passed. I never break my word. In an hour you shall hear from me. Allow me to take my leave (*bows*). Stay ! would you favor me with that ring you have upon your finger? It would keep me from forgetting you. (ALICE *takes off ring and gives it to him.*) Madam, once more farewell. (*Goes to window and gets out.*) Pardon, I forgot, not farewell, *au revoir.* (*Kisses his hand to* ALICE *and disappears.*)

ALICE. Thank goodness! he has gone. How agitated I feel.—I

wonder if he will return the miniature. (CORDOBELLO *appears again at window.*) I wonder where Cha——

CORDOBELLO. Hist! Lady!

ALICE (*starting*). Here, again.

CORDOBELLO. Pardon my return; but I have forgotten one thing.

ALICE. What is that?

CORDOBELLO. If you want your miniature restored to you, you must promise not to tell anybody of my visit here.

ALICE. I promise.

CORDOBELLO. Madam, I thank thee. Once more, *au revoir.*

[*Bows and exits.*

ALICE. What have I done?. Promised not to tell anybody I have been robbed. How absurd! And thus let the thief escape. What a tremor I am in! Hark! somebody is coming. I am so confused that I cannot meet them, so I will retire to my dressing-room, and compose myself. [*Exit* ALICE.

Enter LANDLORD, *followed by* MRS. BEAUMONT *and* CLARENCE. MRS. BEAUMONT *is leading* CLARENCE *by the hand.*

LANDLORD. This way, madam; this is Mr. Vane's room. Will you please take a seat, and I will tell Mrs. Vane's servant that you are here.

MRS. BEAU. Thank you, my good man. Give her that card, will you? (*Gives card,* LANDLORD *bows and exits.*) Now, Clarence, mind that you are a good boy, and behave in your best manner, will you?

CLARENCE. Guess so.

MRS. BEAU. There's a darling! Come and kiss me.

CLARENCE. Give me sixpence!

MRS. BEAU. What! does my boy want to be paid for kissing his mother? Oh, fie! (*Enter* ALICE *and* CHARLES.) Ah, Mr. Vane, and my dear Alice, how do you do? You are looking charming, I declare.

[*They shake hands,* ALICE *and* MRS. BEAUMONT *kiss.*

CHARLES. We are glad to see you, Mrs. Beaumont. How long have you been in Italy?

MRS. BEAU. We have only just arrived from Paris. Seeing your name in the registry, I thought we would call upon you, and see how you were.

ALICE. How kind, to be sure!

MRS. BEAU. Not at all. This is my son; you remember my son, Alice. Clarence, this is Mr. and Mrs. Vane; you know them, don't you?

CLARENCE. Yes

2*

CHARLES. And how has Clarence been, all this long while?

[CLARENCE *hangs back, sucking his thumb, in a timid and shy manner.*

MRS. BEAU. Why don't you speak to Mr. Vane, Clarence?

CLARENCE. How do?

CHARLES. Well, I thank you. How are you?

CLARENCE. First-rate.

MRS. BEAU. There's a dear. Now speak to Mrs. Vane.

CLARENCE. I don't want to.

MRS. BEAU. Yes, you do. Tell her you are glad to see her; you are glad, are you not?

CLARENCE. No.   [CHARLES *and* ALICE *laugh.*

MRS. BEAU. He is such a dear, artless creature, he always says what he thinks. I am sure you wont be angry with him.

ALICE. Indeed, no. Pray be seated, Mrs. Beaumont. (MRS. BEAUMONT *and* ALICE *seat themselves.*) You are not going, Charles?

CHARLES. Yes, if Mrs. Beaumont will excuse me?

MRS. BEAU. Certainly.

CHARLES. I have a lot of things to look after, and I know you ladies have ever so much to talk about.   [*Exit* CHARLES.

ALICE. How do you like Paris, Mrs. Beaumont?

MRS. BEAU. Oh, it's a delightful place for shopping. I have bought such a number of dresses.

ALICE. How I long to get to Paris! But Charles would come to Italy first.

MRS. BEAU. What do you think, dear? I have been presented to the Emperor.

ALICE. Oh, how nice! What did you wear?

MRS. BEAU. Well, I wore a grey moire-antique dress, trimmed with white tulle, and a—

[*During the above conversation,* CLARENCE *has been doing all manner of things about the room; jumping over chairs, pulling things about generally; opened the desk, and looked over some of the letters. Finally, he goes to the window, and stretches himself out, as though reaching for something.*

MRS. BEAU. (*giving a slight scream, and starting up.*) My boy! my precious darling! He will kill himself! (*Runs to the window, and drags* CLARENCE *in.*) What are you doing? How you have frightened your poor mother!

CLARENCE (*beginning to cry*). Now then, why can't you let a fellow alone? I want the grapes. Boo—oo—oo—

MRS. BEAU. What grapes, darling?

CLARENCE. Those just out of the window. *[Still crying.*

MRS. BEAU. There, there, don't cry any more, and mamma will give you money to buy some. (*Gives money.*) Now sit down, and be a good boy, and don't worry mamma any more. (CLARENCE *sits on chair, takes an apple out of his pocket, and commences eating it.*) Well, as I was saying, Alice, I wore a moire antique—

Enter CHARLES.

CHARLES. Oh, I beg pardon, Mrs. Beaumont; but as I was in the court-yard just now, I saw the Fentons and the Grays drive up; so I thought I'd come up and tell Alice.

ALICE. I suppose we shall be honored with a call.

Enter LANDLORD.

LANDLORD. If you please, Signor—

MRS. BEAU. Ah! goodness gracious!

[Seeing CLARENCE *eating an apple, she runs to him and takes it from him.*

CLARENCE. Give me back my apple. *[Endeavors to snatch it away.*

MRS. BEAU. You naughty boy! you shan't have it. You'll make yourself ill; you have eaten nine already. I beg your pardon, Mr. Vane.

CHARLES. Pray, don't mention it. What were you saying, landlord?

CLARENCE (*aside*). I don't care, I have another one in my pocket.

[Takes apple out of pocket, and begins eating it, surreptitiously.

LANDLORD. I was saying, Signor, that some ladies and gentlemen are down stairs, and they desired me to bring up their cards.

[Presents cards on salver.

CHARLES (*takes them*). Show them up. *[Exit* LANDLORD.

ALICE. Who is it, Charles?

CHARLES. The Fentons and the Grays.

MRS. BEAU. Clarence.

CLARENCE (*with his mouth full*). Yes, ma.

MRS. BEAU. What are you eating?

CLARENCE (*swallowing hastily*). Nothing.

MRS. BEAU. There are some ladies and gentlemen coming here, now behave like a good boy, will you?

CLARENCE. Yes, ma. *[Goes back to chair and resumes his apple.*

Enter LANDLORD, *followed by four or five Ladies and Gentlemen.* CORDO-
BELLO *enters with them, in evening costume.*

LANDLORD. This is the room, Signors.

[*He holds the door open for them to enter. Bows and exits.*

CORDOBELLO (*aside*). Oh, I know the room.

[CHARLES *and* ALICE *shake hands with the ladies and gentlemen.*
ALICE *then introduces them to* MRS. BEAUMONT, *who introduces them
to her son, who is remarkably shy and backward.*

CORDOBELLO (*to Charles*). Could I say a few words to you?

CHARLES. Certainly.

CORDOBELLO. You do not know me?

CHARLES. I have not the pleasure. Are you not a friend of——

CORDOBELLO (*interrupting*). Never saw the good people before in
my life.

CHARLES. Then, who are you, sir?

CORDOBELLO. I am Count Fuseli. Having a great regard for the
American people, I have taken the liberty to call on you, which I hope
you will pardon.

CHARLES. Not another word, I beg of you. Allow me to introduce
you to my wife. Alice. [ALICE *comes forward.*

ALICE. Yes, Charles.

CHARLES. My dear, this is Count Fuseli. Count Fuseli, Mrs.
Charles Vane.

[*They bow.* CHARLES *walks up the stage, and talks with* MRS. BEAU-
MONT, *and company.*

ALICE (*aside*). Surely I have seen that face before.

CORDOBELLO. Madame, I am pleased to have the honor of your
acquaintance. [ALICE *courtesies.*

ALICE. Have you ever been in America, Count?

CORDOBELLO. I have never had that pleasure.

ALICE. Have we not met before?

CORDOBELLO. We have.

ALICE. I thought I remembered you. Where?

CORDOBELLO. Here. Allow me to return the miniature. (ALICE
takes it.) You see I have kept my word.

[ALICE *screams.* CHARLES *runs forward, and catches her in his
arms, just as she faints. Everybody runs about for restoratives.
The* LANDLORD *enters; seeing what is the matter, he runs off, and
returns with a glass of water.* CLARENCE *is in ecstasies, he runs
about, as though it were the funniest thing in the world. In the
confusion* CORDOBELLO *escapes through the window.*

CHARLES. See, she is coming to.

ALICE (*faintly*). Where is he?

CHARLES. Where is who?

ALICE. He—he—Count Fuseli.

CHARLES (*looking round*). I don't see him here. I suppose he must nave gone.

ALICE. Count Fuseli is Cordobello.

ALL (*except Clarence*). What! Cordobello the brigand?

ALICE. Yes.

CHARLES. How do you know?

ALICE. Listen. (*They all crowd round her.*) This evening, about an hour ago, he came in through that window, and robbed me of my watch, bracelet, ring, and the miniature of my mamma.

CHARLES *and* } The scoundrel!
LANDLORD.

ALICE. I implored him not to take it. He said he must, for the setting, as it was bordered with diamonds, but promised to return the miniature, uninjured, in an hour.

CHARLES. Why did you not tell me?

ALICE. He made me promise not to. I thought he would keep his word, so I kept mine. You see he has.   [*Shows miniature.*

CHARLES. The bold rascal! But come, landlord, let us start in pursuit.

ALICE (*clinging to him*). Nay, nay, Charles, do not go. You may be injured.

LANDLORD. I am afraid it is of very little good, trying to catch him now; he has had five minutes start.

CHARLES. What shall we do?

ALICE. Do? Let us put up with our loss, and (*to audience*) hope that all present will keep their word as inviolable as the brigand.

CURTAIN.

CHARLES *and* ALICE *in centre.* MRS. BEAUMONT *and* CLARENCE *left.* LANDLORD *right.* *Ladies and Gentlemen ranged in half circle at back.*

PROVERB IV.

"ALL IS FAIR IN LOVE AND WAR."

BY FRANK CAHILL.

Characters.

LIEUTENANT GRAY, U.S.A.
LIEUTENANT RAYNOR, U.S.A.
MR. WILLIAMSON.
KATE WILLIAMSON, *his niece.*
MARY, *a lady's maid.*

Costumes.

LIEUTENANT GRAY *and* RAYNOR, *in undress uniform, as officers in the U.S.A. The rest, modern.*

SCENE—*A parlor.*

Enter GRAY *and* RAYNOR.

GRAY. Isn't she charming?

RAYNOR. Charming! Charming isn't the name for it. She's lovely, beautiful, divine!

GRAY. I told you, you'd be captivated.

RAYNOR. Was there ever a more magnificent creature? I suppose during the last three weeks you have been laying siege to her heart.

GRAY. Now really, Raynor——

RAYNOR. You rascal! But I am not surprised, I have only been here three hours, and you have been here as many weeks, yet I am deeply in love, so what must you be?

GRAY. Upon my word, Raynor, this is absurd.

RAYNOR. Absurd, or not, I intend entering for the prize; so I give you fair warning.

GRAY. I—I understand Miss Williamson is already engaged.

RAYNOR. No matter. At West Point we were taught that strategy was allowed in war. Love is much about the same thing, I take it. So, whoever is the favored swain must look out, for I'll win her, if I can.

GRAY A pleasant prospect for the gentleman in question.

RAYNOR. I hope he'll think so. But, excuse me, I have a short letter to write. I'll meet you in the garden, in a quarter of an hour.

[*Exit* RAYNOR.

GRAY. Confound that Raynor! Just as I was getting on so nicely, he must come here, and in the coolest manner possible, tell me he'll cut me out, if he can.

Enter MR. WILLIAMSON.

MR. WILLIAMSON. Ah, Gray, where's Kitty?

GRAY. I don't know, I think she is in the garden.

MR. WILLIAMSON. Gray, why don't you marry?

GRAY. Upon my word, sir, I—I——

MR. WILLIAMSON. Now there's my niece, as nice a girl as you can find in a day's march,—why don't you marry her?

GRAY. Really——

MR. WILLIAMSON. I have known you a long while, Gray, and your father before you, and nothing would give me greater pleasure than to see you united to my niece.

GRAY. My dear Mr. Williamson, I am pleased to have your good opinion.

MR. WILLIAMSON. Not at all,—have you any objection to making my niece Mrs. Gray?

GRAY. To tell you the truth, I have already fallen a captive to Miss Williamson's charms, and am trying very hard, I assure you, to make her change her name.

MR. WILLIAMSON. Ha, ha, ha! you sly dog;—you shall have my help in the matter, I'll warrant you.

GRAY. How can I thank you, sir?

MR. WILLIAMSON. By not saying a word about it. Kitty is walking in the garden, let us see if we can find her.

GRAY. With pleasure. [*Exeunt* WILLIAMSON *and* GRAY.

Enter KATE *and* RAYNOR.

KATE. There is no believing you men.

RAYNOR. Some men, I grant you, but who would have the temerity to——

KATE (*goes to table, and takes up portfolio*). Are you fond of pictures, Mr. Raynor?

RAYNOR. I am delighted with them.

KATE. This is a view of our house, with the Hudson in the distance.

RAYNOR. Charming! Are you the artist?

KATE. No, Mr. Gray drew that.

RAYNOR (*aside*). Confound Gray. (*Aloud.*) Here's a sketch of your head.

KATE. Do you think it like me?

RAYNOR (*examining sketch*). Yes, it's a bold vigorous sketch, but I do not like the mouth.

KATE. I can't alter my mouth.

RAYNOR. Pardon me,—it is not like it. If it were like the original it would be impossible to find fault with it.

KATE. How pretty! where do you learn all those nice speeches?

RAYNOR. Nowhere. When I look upon the beautiful, they come by inspiration.

KATE. A truce to these compliments. (*Shuts up portfolio.*) Is there anything new in New York?

RAYNOR. Nothing, absolutely nothing, save that somebody has walked off with a million and a half of dollars from the city treasury; but that's nothing new.

Enter GRAY.

GRAY. Oh, here you are!

RAYNOR. Yes; if I am not very much mistaken, we are here.

KATE. Where's uncle?

GRAY. In the garden, looking after his cucumbers. They are the finest I have ever seen. He ought certainly to take the prize at the next horticultural show.

RAYNOR. Does Mr. Williamson take a pride in large cucumbers, early peas, etc.?

KATE. Oh, yes. Have you not seen his tomatoes?

RAYNOR. No; I have not had that pleasure.

KATE. Will you come with me? I'll show them to you.

RAYNOR. Most happy.   [*Going off.*

GRAY. I will accompany you.

RAYNOR. You are very kind, but I can't allow you to put yourself to so much trouble.

GRAY. No trouble——

RAYNOR. You're tired—you know you're tired. Rest yourself a bit; we'll soon return.

KATE. Do not fatigue yourself, Mr. Gray, I beg of you.

GRAY. Indeed, I am not tired.

RAYNOR. What a polite fellow you are, Gray. Do you know, Miss Williamson, that it is politeness makes him want to come with us? You know you're completely used up.

KATE. If that is the case, I can't think of allowing you to accompany us. (*With mock dignity.*) So I command you to stay here. Come, Mr. Raynor.

RAYNOR (*aside to Gray*). Strategy, my boy—strategy.

[*Offers his arm to* KATE, *and exit.*

GRAY. What cool impudence! Never mind, I will be even with him yet. I'll go and watch them (*going*); no—I won't be a spy. (*Hesitates.*) Yes, I will. "Strategy, my boy—strategy." [*Exit.*

Enter WILLIAMSON *and* MARY.

MR. WILLIAMSON. So you don't know who it is, that has been at my peaches?

MARY. No, sir. I saw some boys prowling about last night. I dare say they took them.

MR. WILLIAMSON. The rascals! If I had caught them, I would have shot them. My favorite peaches, too!

MARY. It's always the way, sir. The favorites are sure to go; at least, it was so in my case. [*Sighs.*

MR. WILLIAMSON. Where's my niece—in her room?

MARY. No, Sir; she has gone with Mr. Raynor, to look at your tomatoes.

MR. WILLIAMSON. Oh, tell her I wish to speak to her.

MARY. Very well, sir. [*Exit* MARY.

MR. WILLIAMSON. Now, then, let me nerve myself for the task. I will tell Kitty that she will please me by marrying Mr. Gray. She owes me some obedience, and I have no doubt, in this case, she will do as I desire.

Enter KATE.

KATE. Did you want me, uncle?

MR. WILLIAMSON. Yes, my dear; come here. I have always been very kind to you—have I not?

KATE. Indeed you have, uncle.

Mr. Williamson. I have tried to be so. When your poor father my brother, died, he placed you in my care.

Kate. Yes, uncle.

Mr. Williamson (*abruptly*). It is time you thought about marrying, Kate.

Kate. Oh, uncle!

Mr. Williamson. Yes, my dear, if you love me, you will be as agreeable to Mr. Gray as you can. I have spoken to him about it, and he loves you dearly. Nothing would give me greater happiness than to see you and the son of my old friend, married.

Kate. This is so sudden, uncle. I—I—hardly know what to say.

Mr. Williamson. Don't say anything, my dear; only do as I wish, and please your old uncle. I must go now, as my lawyer is waiting in my study to see me. (*Aside.*) I really think I managed it nicely.   [*Exit.*

Kate. Oh, dear! oh, dear! what shall I do? Uncle wants me to marry, and I'm sure I don't want to—at least I don't think I do, unless it's to that heroic person I dreamt of. Oh! if Mr. Gray would only get those flowers! What shall I do? I don't want to disobey my uncle! I have half a mind to have a good cry, that I have. I'm so miserable.   [*Sits down at table in a melancholy and dejected manner*

Enter Mary.

Mary. If you please——lor! Miss, what's the matter?

Kate. I'm unhappy, Mary.

Mary. I'm sorry to hear that, Miss. What makes you so?

Kate. My uncle wants me to marry.

Mary. Well, there's nothing very shocking in that.

Kate. He wants me to marry Mr. Gray.

Mary. You don't say so, Miss? Mr. Gray is not so bad looking.

Kate. It's not that, Mary; but I've had a dream.

Mary. Oh! do tell me about it. Was it a nice one?

Kate. I will tell you, Mary.

Mary. Thank you, Miss.

Kate. For the last two days I have noticed growing on a projecting rock half way down the Palisades, some beautiful wild honeysuckle. Directly I saw it, I longed to have some of the flowers.

Mary. Yes, Miss, we always long for what we can't get.

Kate. Last evening I dreamed that a venerable-looking man, with a long grey beard, dressed in white, came to my bedside, and held up a large mirror before me.

MARY (*looking uneasily around*). My goodness! Go on, Miss.

KATE. In that mirror I saw the very place where the honeysuckle that I have taken such a fancy to is growing. At that moment a man emerged from the brushwood, and began climbing the rocks, at the peril of his life; for you know at that part it is considered inaccessible.

MARY. Yes, Miss.

KATE. After an amount of exertion, he gained the spot where the honeysuckle was, and plucked some. The next moment his foot slipped, and he fell to the bottom of the rocks.

MARY. How shocking!

KATE. I tried to scream out, but could not. The next instant the whole scene changed, and I found myself standing in our parlor, with the man kneeling at my feet, presenting to me the honeysuckle.

MARY. Who was it? Did you see his face?

KATE. No,—at least I cannot remember his face. The venerable-looking man who was holding the glass, said, "That man will be your husband."

MARY. How strange!

KATE. The next instant I awoke.

MARY. Oh, my!

KATE. I do not generally attach much importance to dreams; but look upon that one as an omen, on which depends my future happiness. Whoever brings me some of those flowers shall be my husband.

MARY. Why don't you tell Mr. Gray? Let him get some, and then marry him.

KATE. No, Mary; it appeared to me that the person learned that I wanted them, intuitively. The man must find out of his own accord, or not at all.

MARY. Well, Miss, all I can say is, that it is a most extraordinary dream.

KATE. That it certainly is, Mary. But come to my room; I want you to fix some dresses for me.

MARY. Very well, Miss.   [*Exeunt* MARY *and* KATE.

Enter RAYNOR *and* GRAY.

RAYNOR. So, Gray, it's war to the knife, is it?

GRAY. If you mean I won't give up my pretensions to the hand of Miss Williamson, yes.

RAYNOR. All right, then. I shall know how to act. By the way, I had quite forgotten my appointment with Mr. Williamson; he is going to show me some superb melons. I must be off. (*Going.*) One word, Gray, have you proposed to Miss Williamson ?

GRAY. Yes,—no,—that is,—not exactly.

RAYNOR. What do you mean by no,—yes,—not exactly ?

GRAY. I have her uncle's consent.

RAYNOR. You want to marry the niece, and pop the question to her uncle. What a strange fellow you are, Gray! Good bye,—I must find Mr. Williamson.   [*Exit* RAYNOR.

GRAY. I wish that Raynor had not come here just yet. If he had only waited another week, I shouldn't have cared. But why should I fear him? I have Mr. Williamson's consent, and Kate herself does not look unkindly upon me.

Enter MARY.

MARY. Oh, Mr. Gray, I am so glad you're here.

GRAY. Are you ?

MARY. Can you keep a secret ?

GRAY. Keep a secret! Why do you ask ?

MARY. Because I have one that I must tell somebody.

GRAY. Well, if you must tell it, let me hear it.

MARY. You're sure you won't tell anybody ?

GRAY. If you say not, certainly.

MARY. You,—you,—excuse me, sir; but you are in love with Miss Kate ?

GRAY. What has that to do with my keeping a secret ?

MARY. A great deal, sir.

GRAY. How ?

MARY. I'll tell you, sir. You know the Palisades ?

GRAY. Yes. But what has that to do with Miss Williamson ?

Enter RAYNOR.

RAYNOR. Where can Mr.—— (*Stops on seeing* GRAY *and* MARY. *Aside.*) What's that about Miss Williamson ? "Strategy, my boy, strategy."   [*Retires up stage.*

MARY. I'm telling you. In the centre of the Palisades some wild honeysuckle is growing.

GRAY. Well ?

MARY. Well, Miss Kate has had a dream; and in that dream she saw a man climb up there, and get some of that honeysuckle.

GRAY (*impatiently*). What has that dream to do with me ?

MARY. Don't be so impatient—a good deal. Well, she told me that whoever brought her some of those flowers, she'd marry.

GRAY. You don't say; but it is impossible to climb the Palisades.

MARY. If it is impossible, you will never marry Miss Williamson.

RAYNOR (*aside*). I'll see if it is impossible.

GRAY. I'll do it.

MARY. Mind, you mustn't tell Kate that I told you.

GRAY. No, I will not. Do you know the exact spot where the honeysuckles are?

MARY. Yes.

GRAY. Come and show me, will you?

MARY. Certainly, sir. Come along.   [*Exit* MARY *and* GRAY.

RAYNOR (*coming down*). I'll also—with your leave, Mr. Gray, or without it, for that matter—see the precise locality. [*Exit* RAYNOR.

Enter MR. WILLIAMSON *and* KATE.

MR. WILLIAMSON. Was there ever anything so annoying?

KATE. What's the matter, uncle?

MR. WILLIAMSON. Matter! Some scoundrels have been robbing my melon patch. Oh! If I could only catch them, I'd—I'd pitch them into the Hudson.

KATE. What, for taking a few melons?

MR. WILLIAMSON. A few melons! The best that were on the vine! Where's that confounded gardener of mine? I'm sure he don't keep half watch enough. I'll go and talk to him about this.

[*Exit furiously.*

KATE. What a dear, kind, cantankerous old fellow my uncle is! He wouldn't harm a worm; yet he is always talking of killing or shooting somebody. I wonder whether Mary has finished that dress yet. I'll just go up-stairs and see.   [*Exit* KATE.

Enter RAYNOR.

RAYNOR. Glorious! I've seen the spot, and, as Gray said, it is impossible to climb up there. However, I think I've hit upon a plan. I'll knock off a few of the flowers with my gun, and pluck some honeysuckles that are rather nearer the bottom of the Palisades. Now for my gun. There is certainly nothing like strategy.   [*Exit* RAYNOR.

Enter KATE.

KATE. Where can Mary be? She has not touched that dress, and she knows that I want to wear it this evening.

Enter GRAY.

GRAY. I have come to—I have come to——Are you fond of flow·
ers, Miss Williamson?

KATE. Exceedingly.

GRAY. I have just seen some honeysuckles growing on the Palisades; they seem very beautiful, so I am going to pluck some for you.

KATE. Oh, thank you. (*Aside.*) How pleased uncle will be! The
man of my dream!

GRAY. In a few minutes I will return with them. (*Aside.*) I
wonder she don't persuade me from going; I shall certainly break my
neck. (*Aloud.*) Well, good bye.

KATE. Good bye.

GRAY. If I should kill myself in the attempt, you will sometimes
think of me.

KATE. That I will.

GRAY (*aside*). How cool she is! (*Aloud.*) Farewell, perhaps for
ever, farewell!

    [*Imprints a kiss upon her hand, and runs off. As he goes off,* RAYNOr
    enters with a gun in his hand and a bunch of honeysuckles.

RAYNOR. Hollo, Gray! where are you going to in such a hurry?
He's off. Ah, Miss Williamson, will you accept these flowers?

    [*Offers flowers.*

KATE. Thank you. Where did you get them?

RAYNOR. As I was walking under the Palisades this morning, I saw
these honeysuckles growing upon a rock about half-way up. How
they got there I don't know.

KATE (*aside*). What will my uncle say? The man of my dream!
(*Aloud.*) And did you risk getting these for me?

RAYNOR. What would I not risk for you? Oh, Miss Williamson,
believe me that I love you—love you to distraction!

KATE. Oh, sir, consider——

RAYNOR. I can consider nothing, but that I love you—madly,
fondly. Will you—will you give me one word of hope?

KATE. Well then—you are—you are—you are not indifferent to
me.

RAYNOR (*seizing her hand and covering it with kisses*). A thousand
thanks.   [*They retire up stage.*

Enter MR. WILLIAMSON, *dragging in* GRAY.

MR. WILLIAMSON. What do you mean, sir, by endeavoring to break
your neck in that manner?

GRAY. I was only going to pluck some flowers.

MR. WILLIAMSON. Pluck some flowers! Only going to kill yourself, you mean. What do you think, Kate? Mr. Gray, here, was trying to climb the Palisades, only I caught him at it, and saved him from breaking his neck.

KATE. There is no occasion for Mr. Gray getting those flowers now, for Mr. Raynor has saved him the trouble.

GRAY. What! Raynor got them!

RAYNOR. Yes, Raynor has got them. And Raynor would ask Mr. Williamson's consent to his union with his niece.

MR. WILLIAMSON. How's this? Are you in love with Mr. Raynor, Kate?

KATE (*softly*). Yes, uncle.

GRAY. But, Mr. Williamson, you promised her to me.

MR. WILLIAMSON. I did promise her to you, but a man who risks his neck by climbing up perpendicular rocks, is hardly safe to be trusted with her. I don't want my niece made a widow too soon. Raynor, take her, and be happy.   [RAYNOR *takes her hand.*

RAYNOR. You have made me the happiest of men.

GRAY. And me the most miserable.

KATE. And me the happiest of women. (*Aside.*) Henceforth I shall believe in dreams.

GRAY. I say, Raynor, how did you manage to get those flowers?

RAYNOR. "Strategy, my boy, strategy." (*To audience.*) If any here should condemn my conduct, I can only refer them to the old adage. Guess it, if you can.

RAYNOR *and* KATE *centre.* WILLIAMSON *right, and* GRAY *left.*

CURTAIN.

PROVERB V.

" 'TIS AN ILL WIND THAT BLOWS NOBODY GOOD.'

BY FRANK CAHILL.

————————•◦•————————

Characters.

> JOHN BONIFACE, *landlord of a country hotel.*
> MICHAEL, *an Irish waiter.*
> MR. CRŒSUS.
> PAUL EDMONDS.
> MRS. MYRTLE.
> FANNIE MYRTLE, *her daughter.*

————————•◦•————————

SCENE—*A parlor in a hotel on the Hudson.   Window at back.*

BONIFACE *discovered looking out of window.*   MICHAEL *dusting chairs, &c.*

BONIFACE.   Hullo! there's another pleasure party landing.   Of course they're not coming here.   Oh, no, there's a carriage waiting for them.   Of course they're going to the Belle Vue House, top of the hill, nobody ever comes here.   Well, there's one consolation, we're going to have a shower soon, and as it's an open carriage, they'll get wet through before they get there.

MICHAEL.   And who'll be afther gettin' wet, sur?

BONIFACE.   Those carriage folks.   Yes, there it goes along the road, past my house of course.   Michael, you may as well shut up the house, nobody ever comes here.

MICHAEL.   Aisy now about shuttin' up the house;—do you think I'd be afther losing my place now?   Git out wid you.

BONIFACE.   Here it is at last: bless me how it comes down.   Did you ever see such rain?   Michael, go and shut the up-stairs' windows.

MICHAEL.   An' shure I will, sur.   [*Exit* MICHAEL.

BONIFACE.   Well, here I am, with ruin staring me in the face.   There never was such an unlucky fellow.   I've tried all manner of dodges to draw customers. I've had sea serpents, and wild women out of number, yet they won't draw. I've half a mind to open a free hotel, and get rid of my stock that way.

Enter MICHAEL, *hurriedly.*

MICHAEL. I knew they'd be afther comin' this time, anyhow.

BONIFACE. Who's coming?

MICHAEL. Why them folks, who passed by just now, here in a carriage.

BONIFACE. What! coming here?

MICHAEL. Yis, an' didn't I till yez so intirely?

BONIFACE. Here they are; now, Michael, bustle about, and get things in order. I'll go out and receive them. [*Exit* BONIFACE.

MICHAEL. Sure now, it's a mighty nice bit of luck that shower was, that's bringin' those jintale paple here, where there's plinty, and niver a bit of stint.

Enter BONIFACE, *followed by* MR. CRŒSUS, PAUL EDMONDS, MRS. MYRTLE, *and* FANNIE. *The gentlemen have their coat collars turned up. The ladies have their handkerchiefs over their bonnets.*

BONIFACE. This way, ladies.

CRŒSUS. What a sudden shower! I am afraid you have got wet, ladies.
[*The ladies brush the rain off their clothes; the gentlemen do the same.*

MRS. MYRTLE. Not very! It was fortunate we were so near shelter.

PAUL. Exceedingly so. Can I assist you, Miss Myrtle?

FANNIE. Thank you.
[*Hands* PAUL *her handkerchief, with which he wipes her mantilla.*

MRS. MYRTLE (*taking the handkerchief from* PAUL). Don't trouble yourself, Mr. Edmonds,—I'll assist my daughter.

BONIFACE. There's a dressing-room up stairs—would the ladies like to go to it?

MRS. MYRTLE. Yes, if you please.

BONIFACE (*calling off*). Mary, show these ladies to the dressing-room.

MRS. MYRTLE. Come, Fannie. [*Exeunt* MRS. MYRTLE *and* FANNIE.

CRŒSUS. I say, Edmonds, we may as well lunch here,—eh?

EDMONDS. It was merely a passing shower—see, it is holding up already.

BONIFACE. We have every accommodation, sir.

MICHAEL. Sorra bit of a lie is that.

CRŒSUS. This seems a comfortable place, and we shall have another shower directly, so I think we had better stay where we are.

MICHAEL. My sintimints to a T.

4

EDMONDS.   As you like.   I am agreeable to anything.

CRŒSUS.   Landlord, can we have lunch here?

BONIFACE.   Certainly, sir.

CRŒSUS.   Well, then, prepare us a nice lunch for four.

MICHAEL.   Good luck to ye.   May the hair of your head be hung with diamonds.

BONIFACE.   Come with me, Michael, I shall want your assistance.

MICHAEL.   Arrah, now, an' aint I the boy to help you?

[Exeunt BONIFACE *and* MICHAEL.

CRŒSUS *(looking out of window)*.   They seem to have nice grounds here.   It has left off raining—let us take a stroll round.

PAUL.   Well, I've no objection.   *[Exeunt* PAUL *and* CRŒSUS.

Enter MRS. MYRTLE *and* FANNIE.

MRS. MYRTLE.   It is of no use talking, Fannie; I am exceedingly angry with you.

FANNIE.   But, mamma!

MRS. MYRTLE.   I have noticed it, all the way from New York.   You let Mr. Edmonds pay you a great deal too much attention.

FANNIE.   But I can't help it, mamma.

MRS. MYRTLE.   Yes, you can; you ought not to receive them.   The idea of letting Mr. Edmonds wipe your mantilla.   Why didn't you let Mr. Crœsus do it?

FANNIE.   Mr. Crœsus never offered to.

MRS. MYRTLE.   Well, then, why didn't you make him?   You know that Mr. Edmonds hasn't a penny in the world, and that Mr. Crœsus is as rich—as—as—oh, you know he is ever so rich; yet you go on in this way.

FANNIE.   I am sorry, mamma, and I'll try not to let Mr. Edmonds wipe my mantilla again.

MRS. MYRTLE *(kissing her)*.   There's a good child.   Now, go and see if you can find Mr. Crœsus in the garden, and be agreeable to him.

FANNIE.   Very well, mamma.   *(Aside.)*   Oh, what will Paul say?

[Exit FANNIE.

MRS. MYRTLE.   Now, if Fannie only plays her cards well, she will, in all probability, be Mrs. Crœsus, and ride in her own carriage.   Of course, I shall live with her.   Yes, that's settled—I'll live with her.

Enter CRŒSUS.

MRS. MYRTLE.   Ah, Mr. Crœsus, have you seen Fannie?

CRŒSUS. No, I have not.

MRS. MYRTLE. She this moment went into the garden. Ah, Mr. Crœsus, you have no idea what a good girl she is.

CRŒSUS. I am extremely happy to hear it.

MRS. MYRTLE. I hardly know what I shall do when I lose her; for I suppose some of you naughty men will be soon robbing me of her.

CRŒSUS. When daughters are handsome, Mrs. Myrtle, we must expect such things.

MRS. MYRTLE. She is so kind, so considerate, she never gives me a moment's uneasiness. (PAUL *and* FANNIE *are seen through the window crossing the stage, talking earnestly together.*) (*Aside.*) With that Mr. Edmonds again! I must put a stop to that. (*Aloud.*) There goes my dear child. Excuse me for a minute, Mr. Crœsus.

[*Exit* MRS. MYRTLE.

CRŒSUS. Strange woman that; what in the world can she be driving at? However, I'll go and see how the landlord is getting on with the lunch.   [*Exit* CRŒSUS.

Enter PAUL.

PAUL. Confound that Mrs. Myrtle. I can't be alone with Fannie a moment but she must poke her stupid old head in, and spoil our *téte-à-téte.* I've half a mind to—no, I hav'n't—yes—no——.

[*Rests his chin upon his hand, as though lost in meditation.*

Enter CRŒSUS, *who walks up to* PAUL *and taps him on the back.* PAUL *starts.*

CRŒSUS. What's the matter, Edmonds, my boy? What are you dreaming about? Are you in love or in debt, which?

PAUL. Ah! yes—no. Excuse me.   [*Walks off rapidly.*

CRŒSUS. Hullo! what's the matter with the man, I wonder? He's in love, I suppose; but it's nothing to do with me. There's one consolation though—lunch is coming on finely. Really that fellow has a capital idea of what's good. We must patronize him for the future.

Enter MRS. MYRTLE *and* FANNIE.

MRS. MYRTLE. You here, Mr. Crœsus? I thought you were in the garden. Fannie and I have just been taking a walk round the grounds

FANNIE. Yes, and we have seen such a dear little lot of pigs. Such tiny ones, no bigger than kittens.

CRŒSUS. Indeed! they must be interesting. But where is Edmonds have you seen him in the garden?

MRS. MYRTLE (*aside*). A good excuse to leave them together. (*Aloud.*) I will go and see if I can find him.

FANNIE. Shall I come too, mamma?

MRS. MYRTLE. No, my dear; the ground is damp, and you may catch cold. I shan't be long.   [*Exit* MRS. MYRTLE.

CRŒSUS. We are going to have——by the way, I had nearly forgotten it; I must mix the salad myself. Excuse me, Miss Myrtle.

[*Exit* CRŒSUS.

FANNIE. I wonder where Paul can be; he has kept away from me all day. I'll be quite angry with him when I see him, and tell him that mamma says I am to have nothing more to do with him.

Enter PAUL, *with his hands in his pockets, looking extremely dejected. On seeing* FANNIE, *he runs forward, takes her by the hand and shakes it.*

PAUL. My dear Fannie!

FANNIE. There, there, that will do; you need not shake my hand off, sir. Where have you been all this while, sir?

PAUL. I have been looking for you, Fannie.

FANNIE. A pretty excuse, indeed! You could not have looked very far.

PAUL. Do not be angry, Fannie.   [*Endeavors to take her hand.*

FANNIE. Leave my hand alone, sir. You have shaken hands with me once already.

PAUL. Why are you so cool, Fannie? Why do you speak this way to me?

FANNIE. Mamma says I must not talk to you so much.

PAUL. Oh! I see how it is: I'm poor; Mr. Crœsus is rich.

FANNIE. That is an unkind remark, sir. Hush, here comes mamma.

PAUL. May I hope?

FANNIE. While there's life there's hope.

Enter MRS. MYRTLE.

FANNIE. Ah, mamma.

MRS. MYRTLE. Where's Mr. Crœsus?

FANNIE. He just this moment left the room.

PAUL. Yes, he left the room this moment.

Enter MICHAEL.

MICHAEL. Where will ye be havin' it laid, here or in the garden?

MRS. MYRTLE. Having what laid?

MICHAEL.   Shure, an' aint it the tablecloth I mane?

PAUL.   Oh! you mean the tablecloth?

MICHAEL.   Wisha, now, d'ye see that? As though ye did'nt know it.

PAUL.   What do you say, ladies?

MRS. MYRTLE.   What does Mr. Crœsus say?

PAUL (aside).   Confound Mr. Crœsus.

MICHAEL.   He bade me ask the ladies; and bless 'em! says Michael O'Grady.

FANNIE.   Let us lunch here, mamma; this is a very pleasant room.

MICHAEL.   Pleasant! by the powers, it's a perfect paradise, now your ladyship's in it.

PAUL.   We can dispense with compliments, my good fellow; so look sharp, and lay the cloth.

MICHAEL.   Yes, sur, I'm the boy that'll do it immadiately.

[*Exit* MICHAEL.

FANNIE.   What a strange man he appears to be.

PAUL.   Yes; if he hadn't a brogue, I should have known him for an Irishman, by the compliments he paid you, ladies.

Enter CRŒSUS.

CRŒSUS.   Well, lunch is nearly ready, and really, I must beg your pardon, ladies, but I have countermanded your order, and lunch will be served in a room overlooking the river. A much pleasanter room, I assure you.

MRS. MYRTLE.   Anywhere you like, Mr. Crœsus.

PAUL.   Suppose, while we're waiting for lunch, we pass the time with a dance.

FANNIE.   Oh, that will be nice.

CRŒSUS.   A capital idea. Mrs. Myrtle, will you allow me the pleasure?   [MRS. MYRTLE *courtesies, and he takes her for partner.*

PAUL.   Fan—I beg pardon, Miss Myrtle, will you honor me with your hand.   [*She gives it.*

MRS. MYRTLE.   Sir!

PAUL.   For the dance, I mean.

MRS. MYRTLE.   Oh!

[*The music strikes up, and they form themselves for a quadrille. As they are dancing,* MICHAEL *enters, with a tray of plates, dishes, etc. He looks at them a minute, then drops the tray, rushes into the midst of them, and begins an Irish jig. They disperse in confusion.*

Enter BONIFACE, *who, on seeing* MICHAEL *dancing, runs up to him, and after some slight difficulty stops him.*

BONIFACE.   What are you doing? what do you mean by this conduct?

MICHAEL.   Mane, is it?   Aint I entertainin' the illegant company for you?

BONIFACE.   You rascal! if you don't finish setting that table, I'll discharge you this instant.

MICHAEL.   Och! be asy now, an' aint it miself, that's going to do it?
                                          [*Picks up tray and broken crockery, and exit.*

BONIFACE.   I hope, ladies and gentlemen, you are not offended at my servant's rudeness.

CRŒSUS.   Not at all, at least I am not.   But I certainly should advise you to get a waiter who wasn't quite so eccentric.

FANNIE.   Shall we finish our dance?

PAUL.   By all means.   Come.

Enter MICHAEL.

MICHAEL.   If ye plaze, leedies and jintilmen, lunch is ready.

BONIFACE.   This way, if you please.

   [BONIFACE *leads the way,* CRŒSUS *offers his arm to* FANNIE.   PAUL *offers his arm to* MRS. MYRTLE, *and exeunt.*

MICHAEL.   Faith, and troth, it's an illegant company we've here to-day.   Och! mavourneen, what a purty face the young ledy has, an' her bright eyes do you good to look on 'em.

BONIFACE (*calling off*).   Michael, Michael, where are you?

MICHAEL (*calling*).   Isn't it here I am?

BONIFACE (*calling off*).   Come here.

MICHAEL.   Yes, sur, I'm comin'.   [*Runs off.*

Enter FANNIE.

FANNIE (*looking about stage*).   Where can my handkerchief be, I wonder?   I am sure I had it when I was dancing.

Enter PAUL.

PAUL.   What are you looking for?

FANNIE.   My handkerchief.

PAUL.   I have also lost something.

FANNIE.   What?

PAUL. My heart!

FANNIE. Your heart?

PAUL. Yes, Fannie, my heart. Oh! Fanny, I cannot—cannot go on this way any longer. Tell me,—pray, tell me,—yea, I implore you to tell me that I am not indifferent to you.

FANNIE. Who said you were?

PAUL. Nay, do not trifle with me.

FANNIE. Well then,—well then,—you are not indifferent to me.

PAUL. What rapture!

MRS. MYRTLE (*calling off*). Fannie,—Fannie!

FANNIE. Hush! here's mamma. I wonder where my handkerchief an have got to?

[PAUL *and* FANNIE *look about the stage, anxiously.*

Enter MRS. MYRTLE.

MRS. MYRTLE. What are you doing, Fannie? Lunch is waiting.

FANNIE. I am looking for my handkerchief, mamma.

Enter CRŒSUS.

CRŒSUS. Here you all are,—eh? I have come to look after you. Lunch has been waiting for you this last quarter of an hour.

Enter BONIFACE, *followed by* MICHAEL.

BONIFACE. Really this is too bad; as a man who takes an interest in his business, I protest against it. Here, the lunch has been waiting more than twenty minutes, and everything is getting cold.

MICHAEL. Yis, an' so is the champagne.

CRŒSUS. We can understand your feelings upon the subject, Mr. Boniface, and appreciate the manner in which you have attended to us. So much so indeed, that for the future, we shall always come here, and recommend our friends to do the same.

BONIFACE. If the shower has robbed the Belle Vue House of some customers, it has done me some good.

CRŒSUS. How?

BONIFACE. Did it not drive you here for shelter, and have you not promised me your patronage for the future?

MICHAEL. Arrah! good luck to the shower, that sent ye here.

PAUL (*aside*). And so say I; I have gained a wife by it.

FANNIE (*aside*). And mamma has lost a daughter.

CRŒSUS. Come, let us give the lunch another trial.

[Boniface *goes off, followed by* Paul, Fannie, Crœsus, *and* Mrs.
Myrtle.

Michael *(to audience.)*   Leedies and jintilmen, would ye oblige
me, by laving me your address.   Long life to you, I know ye will.
The rason I wants to know, my darlints, is, in case I should lave this
situashun.   For isn't it thrue to all of ye, that I make a fust rate sar-
vent, an' any of ye would employ me ?

CURTAIN.

* * *

PROVERB VI.

"THERE IS NO ROSE WITHOUT THORNS."

BY GEORGE ARNOLD.

* * *

Characters.

Jack Upson, *a wealthy young lawyer.*
Rose Thorne, *a young lady engaged to* Jack.
Mr. Thorne, *father to* Rose.
Kate, Rose's *waiting-maid.*

* * *

SCENE—*A parlor in* Mr. Thorne's *country house on Staten Island.*

Jack Upson.   Rose Thorne.

Jack.   I say, my dear, it is too bad.   The boat is all out of order—
leaks dreadfully—torn sail—pump broken—everything topsy-turvy !
We can't have our sail this afternoon, that is plain.

Rose.   Oh ! never mind it, Jack.   You shall stay and read Tennyson to me, instead.

Jack.   I was afraid you had set your heart upon the sail, and would
be angry.   I might have known better, though, you're always so kind
and good-natured.

Rose.   How could you think I would ever be angry with *you ?*
Now, Jack, go and bring Tennyson, and read aloud to me by this window

JACK. Umph! My dear!

ROSE. What is it?

JACK. I'm afraid——

ROSE. Of what?

JACK. It is too bad that you should be disappointed again!

ROSE. Disappointed! How, dear Jack?

JACK. Why, I left my volume of Tennyson in the city last night. I took it up to the office to show Paul a passage we were disputing about, and when I returned I was in such a hurry that I forgot all about it.

ROSE (*pettishly*). Dear me. (*Very blandly.*) Well, well, I'm sorry, but it cannot be helped. We will find some other amusement.

JACK. Oh! you are so good-tempered! Shall I sing you a song?

ROSE. Yes, do; and accompany yourself with the guitar.

[*Rings bell.*

JACK. I am a little hoarse to-day, but I guess I can sing something.

Enter KATE.

ROSE. Katie, child, go to my room and bring down the guitar.

KATE. Yes 'm. (*Aside.*) How mighty soft-spoken she is before her husband that is to be. He said he was "a little hoarse," but I think he's a little donkey if he marries her. [*Exit.*

JACK. What shall I sing, dear?

ROSE. Oh! anything. All your songs are sweet to *me*.

JACK. But which do you like best?

ROSE. Do you know, "I Love but Thee?"

JACK. Well, I didn't *know* it positively, but I'm very glad to hear it.

ROSE. No, no! I mean the song of that name.

JACK. Oh! no. I never heard it; but here is Kate with the instrument.

Enter KATE, *with guitar.*

KATE. Here it is 'm.

ROSE (*with affected sweetness*). Give it to Mr. Upson, Katie, child.

KATE (*aside*). Oh, my! Butter wouldn't melt in her mouth.

[*Gives guitar to* JACK, *and exit.*

JACK (*trying guitar*). Oh! it is terribly out of tune.

[*Begins tuning it, and breaks string.*

ROSE. Oh! How that frightened me!

JACK. Too bad again, I declare! The E string has snapped, just in the middle! The ends are too short, and that is the end of our music!

3*

Rose (*aside*). How awkward! (*Aloud.*) What a pity! Well, I suppose we must find something else to pass away the afternoon.

Jack. Yes. I'll go into the garden for some flowers, and you shall arrange a bouquet.   [*Exit.*

Rose. The stupid fellow! I have no patience with him! Here are three disappointments within an hour, and all his fault. I could almost cry.

Enter Mr. Thorne.

Thorne. Well, Rosie, I have a pleasure for you.

Rose (*pouting*). I don't want any pleasures!

Thorne. You don't. You're a strange girl!

Rose. I'm not a strange girl!

Thorne. Don't be foolish, Rosie. I have got some tickets for the Academy of Music, to-night. Don't you want to go with Mr. Upson and myself? We can take the six o'clock boat, and get to the city just——

Rose. No! I won't go! I hate the opera! I hate Mr. Upson!

Thorne. But, my dear child, you must not be so unreasonable. What has happened?

Rose. Nothing has happened! I'm not unreasonable! Mr. Upson has insulted me—he won't do anything for me—he won't take me out sailing, and he won't read to me, and he won't sing for me, and I don't care a pin for him. I believe he is ashamed to be seen with me, because my bonnet is so old! There now!

Thorne. Nonsense! He is too sensible a young man for that, and besides, I have just brought your new bonnet from the milliner's. You shall wear it to-night. Here, Kate!   [*Calling.*

Enter Kate.

Kate. What, sir? Did you call?

Thorne. Yes. Bring the bandbox from the sitting-room table.

[*Exit* Kate.

Now then, here are the tickets for the opera—Lucia di Lammermoor is to be performed.

Rose. I won't go!

Thorne. Then Mr. Upson and I will go alone, and you may stay at home!

Rose. I won't stay at home! You shan't go away and leave me!

[*Snatches tickets, and tears them to pieces.*

Thorne. Rose! What do you mean? You ought to be ashamed of yourself!

Enter KATE *with bandbox in one hand and a bonnet in the other.*

KATE.   Oh! it is *such* a beauty, mum—a real love of a bonnet!

ROSE.   Give it to me, this instant! What right have you to open my bandbox, and handle my new bonnet with your great coarse paws?

[*Seizes bonnet from* KATE.

THORNE.   Daughter! I am really ashamed of you!

ROSE (*looking at bonnet*).   There's a pretty thing, now, isn't it? Why, I wouldn't be seen in such a miserable, cheap affair! It looks like a coal-scuttle!

THORNE.   Cheap! It cost thirty dollars! I guess if you had to earn your own money, you would be very glad to get as good a one! Try it on, and say no more about it.

ROSE.   I won't try it on. I won't be seen in it! It isn't half so nice as Miss Jones's bonnet, and she is only a poor school-teacher.

THORNE.   I wish to goodness your temper was half as good as Miss Jones's! But I tell you, you shall wear that or your old one. I'm determined to give you a good lesson. Do you hear?

ROSE.   I'll never wear it as long as I live! I'll tear it to pieces first!

THORNE.   I command you to wear it, you ungrateful girl!

ROSE.   And I say I won't!

[*Tears bonnet to pieces, and tramples it under foot.*

THORNE.   Stop! Here, Rose, you—— (*She runs off, sobbing.*) Was there ever such a frightful temper in the world?   [*Exit.*

KATE.   Goodness gracious me! What a flighty creature? Now how much better it would have been to have given *me* that bonnet! (*Picks up the torn bonnet.*) Just to see—the flowers all torn out of it —was there ever!—the crown all jammed in. Who would think, to look at her—hallo!

Enter JACK UPSON, *with bunch of roses.*

JACK.   What's that you're saying?

KATE.   Nothing, sir, only Miss Rose seems to be a little out of humor—she is troubled about something.

JACK.   Poor soul! she has had enough disappointments to vex a saint. It is a wonder to me how she keeps her temper!

KATE.   Yes; but she *can't* keep her temper!

JACK.   I don't know how you can say that. To me, she seems the most unwaveringly good-humored girl I ever saw.

KATE. Yes, sir; that's very likely, *to you.*

JACK. What do you mean?

KATE. Hush! here she is—I must go.   [*Exit* KATE.

Enter ROSE.

ROSE. Dear me! I declare I never was so put out in all my life I could—(*seeing* JACK). Oh! my dear Jack! what a beautiful bouquet you have got!

JACK. Yes, dear; but what were you saying when you came in?

ROSE. Nothing. I was only speaking to Kate.

JACK. Here, take these roses, and arrange them. Put this white one in your hair. (*She takes the roses, and admires them.*) Did you see your father? I met him in the garden a moment ago, as he came up from the boat.

ROSE. No—yes—that is, yes, I saw him only a moment.

JACK. Did he tell you that we were all going to the Opera to-night?

ROSE (*aside*). What shall I say? What a fool I was to destroy the tickets! (*Aloud.*) Yes, he told me; but I cannot go.

JACK. You cannot? How is that?

ROSE. I—I don't feel well enough. I think I have a headache.

JACK (*half laughing*). You *think* you have? Don't you know?

ROSE. I mean I am afraid I shall have one. (*Aside.*) What does he mean by laughing at me? Never mind! when we're once married, I'll let him laugh, if he feels like it then!

JACK. Well, well; make up your bouquet, and if you feel like it, we will go. Now excuse me a moment—I wish to see your father.

[*Exit.*

ROSE (*sitting down and spreading flowers out on her lap*). Let me see—I want some thread to tie up these roses. (*Rings bell.*) If I could only keep my temper until I am Mrs. Upson, I wouldn't care, but these odious people do provoke me so that I don't know what I'm doing. The idea of papa buying me that horrible bonnet, and then expecting me to go to the Opera in it! (*Rings bell with great violence.*) Where is that huzzy Kate, I wonder? She never answers the bell!

Enter KATE.

KATE. Did you ring, mum?

ROSE (*mimicking her*). Did you ring, mum? Of course I rang? Why can't you attend to your duties? What are you hired for, I should like to know?

KATE. Indeed 'm, I came just as quick as ever I heard the bell!

Rose. I don't want you to talk—I don't want any of your impertinence. If you can't attend to my wants, I must find a girl who can. Go and get me some thread—some white thread.

Kate. Yes 'm.   [*Goes towards door.*

Rose. Here, Kate!

Kate (*stopping*). What 'm?

Rose. Go, this instant; do you hear? (*Exit* Kate, *angrily*) Seems to me, everybody conspires to abuse and neglect me!

[*She sorts out the flowers.*

Enter Mr. Thorne, *with* Jack Upson.

Mr. Thorne. Yes, I dare say—ah, here is Rosie. Now, then, daughter, have you quite recovered?

Rose (*looking daggers at him, but speaking very softly*). Yes, papa dear, my headache is quite gone.

Enter Kate.

Kate. Please 'm, I—I can't find any thread at all, but here's some string.

[*Shows a quantity of tangled strings of all sizes.* Rose *stamps her foot and starts up, but recollecting herself, becomes calm, with an apparent effort.*

Rose. Never mind, Katie, child, I'll go and look for it myself.

[*Exit.*

Jack. I'm glad her headache is gone—we shall have a fine time at the Opera.

Thorne. Eh?

Jack. I say we will have a fine time at the Opera, to-night.

Thorne. Oh, ah!—the Opera; yes.

Jack. Certainly—didn't you tell me that you had reserved some seats?

Thorne (*much embarrassed*). Yes—reserved seats, to be sure. (*Aside.*) What shall I say? How can I tell him the tickets are destroyed? Never mind, I'll be honest, and tell him all—even if Rose should lose him for ever.

Jack. What is the matter, sir?

Thorne. Just this: I haven't got any Opera tickets.

Jack No! how is that?

Thorne. I had, but they were destroyed—torn to pieces!

Jack. Explain yourself. By whom?

THORNE. By my daughter—by Rose!

[KATE *laughs, and* JACK *looks more and more puzzled.*

JACK. I don't understand you, sir!

THORNE. My daughter, sir, has a most ungovernable temper—she is a regular virago. There, now!

KATE. There never was a truer word, sir!

JACK. But—you—you astound me! Have I not seen her undergo a dozen disappointments to-day—a dozen vexations, without a sour look or a cross word?

KATE. But ah, sir, you should have seen her pitch into me when you were away!

THORNE. Hush, Kate! It is too true, my young friend, that she has so far concealed her temper before you, for obvious reasons, but believe me, you will see it, when it is too late to avoid the consequences.

JACK. What, she, who seems so equable, so kind, so forbearing?

KATE. So fiddle-stick!

JACK. So evenly good-natured—in short, such an angel? No; I can't believe it before I see it. I beg your pardon, Mr. Thorne, for the suspicion, but I do not understand your motives for setting me against your daughter—you may have some reason—you——

THORNE. My dear boy, you do me an injustice, believe me! I have told you this for your own good, although the confession has greatly pained me. Rose is a spoiled child, and unworthy of you.

JACK. But, sir, I must not be too hasty. I have found her always the same——

KATE. When you was present!

JACK. And I never expect to find her otherwise.

KATE. It is easily tested. Step behind this window-curtain, and when she comes in, you shall hear her.

THORNE. Yes. That will prove it. I hate to humiliate my own daughter thus, but I do not wish to be responsible for your future misery.

JACK. It is hard to play the spy upon one's own betrothed, but I owe it to her and myself, so here goes.

[*Conceals himself behind curtain.*

KATE. Just in time, for here she comes!

Enter ROSE, *with thread.*

ROSE (*glancing about.*)   Where is that Mr. Upson?

THORNE. Humph,—he is—he—is——

KATE. In the garden 'm?

Rose. Ah! he is always here when I don't want him, and away when I do! I want him to help me wind this thread. (*To* Kate.) Now, then, where were your eyes? You seem to be blind as well as deaf! The thread was in my basket, on the table, right in plain sight, and anybody but an idiot would have seen it! Here, help me wind it —no, you're too clumsy for anything—go about your business!

[*Picks up flowers, and arranges them.*

Thorne. Daughter! that temper of yours is getting you into trouble.

[Kate *laughs.*

Rose. What do you want to talk to me so much about my temper for? Do you expect me to put up with everything? Now see that good-for-nothing girl laughing! Get out of my sight! Go, or I'll box your ears!   [Kate *laughs still louder.*

Thorne (*ironically*). Go on—go on! Don't mind her, Kate. You are making a very pretty exhibition of yourself, Miss Rose.

Rose (*extravagantly angry*). Do you take sides against your own daughter, with a common servant-girl? My conscience! I shall faint—hold me! (*Tears bouquet to pieces, and throws flowers at* Kate *and* Mr. Thorne.) I won't stay in the house—I won't!

Thorne. Would you like Mr. Upson to see you now?

Rose. Who cares for him? He's a good-for-nothing, hateful, odious old——

Jack (*coming from behind curtain*). Old what?

[Rose *screams and throws herself backward.* Mr. Thorne *catches her.*

Kate *and* Thorne. Are you satisfied?

Jack. Yes; and more, too. I beg leave to wish Miss Rose a very good evening, and to thank you, Mr. Thorne, for having so generously undeceived me. It was well I should know all. Good bye.   [*Exit.*

Rose (*raising her head*). Where is he?

Thorne. Gone, and for ever.

Kate. And I shall follow his example, to-morrow.

Rose (*suddenly springing up*). Well, let him go! What do I care for him? (*Looking at her hands.*) I'm only sorry that he gave me those roses; I have torn my hands all to pieces with the thorns. (*To* Kate.) What are you staring at there? Go along!

Kate (*turning to audience*). I'm wondering what all these good folks think of you?

Thorne (*to audience*). Ladies and gentlemen, you must excuse my daughter. She is a good girl at heart; but she has *such* a temper!

CURTAIN.

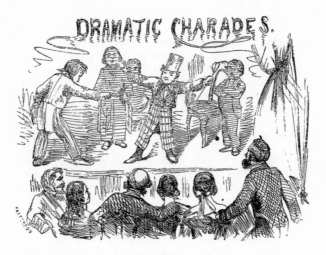

CHARADE I.

BY FRANK CAHILL.

"PHAN——TOM."

Characters.

MR. DEBIT, *a merchant.*
TOM HIGHDON, *his clerk.*
JULIUS, *a colored servant.*
MRS. REEVES.
ELLEN REEVES, *her daughter.*

PHAN—

SCENE I.—*An office in Wall street. A desk* L., *and a table* R. C.

DEBIT *is looking over some letters at table.* TOM HIGHDON *is writing at desk.*

DEBIT. Oh, Highdon!

TOM (*looking round*). Sir.

DEBIT. Did you send off those charges to Pluckem & Co.'s?

TOM. Sent them by yesterday's post.

DEBIT   That's right.   [*A pause.* TOM *resumes his writing.*

DEBIT.   Oh, Highdon!

TOM (*looking round*).   Sir.

DEBIT.   Has the "Charmer" been heard of yet?

TOM.   I called at the Underwriters' this morning, and nothing has been heard of her.

DEBIT.   Confound it!—and I am not fully insured! Has Bradbury been here this morning about that sugar?

TOM.   Yes, sir. He'll meet you on 'Change at twelve o'clock.

DEBIT.   That's right. (*A pause.* TOM *resumes his writing;* DEBIT *gets up, changes his coat, and puts on his hat.*) Copy this out in time for to-day's post, will you?   [*Gives him paper.*

TOM.   Yes, sir.

DEBIT.   I'm going on 'Change now.

TOM.   Very well, sir. (*Exit* DEBIT.) I thought he never would go out. (*Throws down pen, rises, and comes forward.*) And the advertisement says between eleven and twelve. Where's the *Herald?* (*Goes to* DEBIT'S *table, and gets newspaper.*) Let me see: "Dear Brown, call and see me. Julia." That ain't it. I wonder if Brown will go and see his Julia. "Wanted, two thousand five hundred dollars"—ah, who don't want two thousand five hundred dollars?—that ain't it. Here it is: "Found, in a Broadway stage, a lady's fan. The owner can have it by applying at No. 796 Wall street, between the hours of eleven and twelve." If I am not mistaken, the young lady who left the fan in the stage was handsome. I hope she'll come for it herself. (*A knock is heard at the door.*) Come in.

Enter MRS. REEVES *and* ELLEN.

MRS. REEVES.   Is this 796 Wall street?

TOM.   Yes, madam.

MRS. REEVES.   My daughter had the misfortune to lose a fan the other day, in a Broadway stage.

TOM.   Oh, then, you have called about that fan?

MRS. REEVES.   Yes. Seeing an advertisement in the *Herald,* to the effect that a fan had been found, and might be had by applying here, we have called to see if it is the fan that my daughter lost.

TOM.   What kind of fan was it?

MRS. REEVES.   You had better describe it, Ellen.

ELLEN.   Very well, mamma. It was an ivory fan, carved, with a landscape painted upon it, and trimmed with marabout feathers.

TOM (*goes to desk and gets fan*).   Is that it?

ELLEN. Oh, yes! How glad I am to get it back again! It was given me as a present, and I wouldn't lose it for the world.

TOM. I am happy to have been the means of returning it to you.

MRS. REEVES. Pardon me, sir, but what have we to pay you?

TOM. I paid fifty cents for the advertisement.

MRS. REEVES. Will you not allow us to pay your carriage hire as well?

TOM. Thank you, no. I left the advertisement on my way up town.

MRS. REEVES. You are very kind. Dear me, I have not my purse with me! Ellen, have you any money with you?

ELLEN. No, mamma.

MRS. REEVES. How careless of me! Really, sir, I am extremely sorry, but——

TOM. It is no matter, I assure you.

MRS. REEVES. Would it be troubling you too much to get you to call at our house?

TOM. Not at all. (*Aside.*) A capital chance to make love to the daughter.

MRS. REEVES. There is our address, sir.   [*Gives card.*

TOM. Thank you.

ELLEN. I am sure, sir, we are sorry to put you to so much trouble.

TOM. It's a pleasure, I assure you.

MRS. REEVES. Any time you are passing, we shall be happy to see you. Come, Ellen. Good morning, sir.

TOM. Good morning.

ELLEN. Good morning.   [TOM *bows, the ladies courtesey, and exit.*

TOM. What a beautiful creature! And how fascinating the mother is! Tom Highdon, you're a lucky dog! (*Strikes himself upon the chest.*) Hullo! here comes old Debit.

[*Runs to desk, sits down, and begins to write.*

Enter DEBIT.

DEBIT. Highdon.

TOM. Sir.

DEBIT. What did those ladies want that I met on the stairs just now?

TOM. They—they—wanted to know the price of cotton.

DEBIT. Strange creatures these women,—did you tell them?

TOM. Yes, sir.

DEBIT. That's right. Here, copy this out, and take it round to Jones's when it's finished.

[*Gives paper to* TOM, *then goes to table, and sits down.*
[*Scene closes.*

SCENE II.—*A parlor in* Mrs. Reeves's *house.*

—TOM.

Enter Julius.

Julius. Now, it 'pears to me dar is suffin' wrong 'bout dis house. Miss Ellen is in lub, dat's what it is. She don't eat nuffin', and am as melancolly as a rooster on a wet day. Now, when I was in lub, I felt mi'ty bad, too. My gal didn't 'have prop'ly to me at all. Dem gals do make fools of us poor cullud folks. Golly! don't dis child 'member de song she used to like to hear. I 'member,—it went dis way.

[*Sings.*

Air: "*A little more Cider, too.*"

I'll tell you all about my lub, my heart goes pity-patter;
She was as sweet as sugar-cane, her heart was soft as batter,
Her eyes was brack as eberyting—her voice as clear as nuffin',
Her har was like a blue-jay's nest—her nose was like a muffin!

CHORUS.

I lubbed Miss Dinah so,
I lubbed Miss Dinah so—
She was as gay as Chris'mas day—and—
Yah ha! I lubbed her so!

[*Kisses his hand with a loud noise.*

One day we went out walkin' by de margin ob de ribber,
De wind was blowin' kinder fresh, an' made Miss Dinah shibber;
She shibber so, I thought she'd fall, an' in my arms I caught her,
When de wind cum up an' blowed so hard, it blowed us in de water!

CHORUS.

I lubbed Miss Dinah so,
I lubbed Miss Dinah so—
She was as gay as Chris'mas day—and—
Yah ha! I lubbed her so!   [*Kisses hand.*

Miss Dinah she went in hed first, an' I went in hed foremost;
An' tho' I froze my nose an' toes, my heart was still de warmest;
We sank rite down into de waves—de people thought us drownded—
Miss Dinah she was raked ashore, but I was nebber founded!

CHORUS.

I lubbed Miss Dinah so,
I lubbed Miss Dinah so—
She was as gay as Chris'mas day—and—
Yah ha! I lubbed her so!   [*Kisses hand.*

Hello! dar's old missus a-comin'!

Enter MRS. REEVES.

MRS. REEVES. Did you leave that note I gave you?

JULIUS. Yes, missus.

MRS. REEVES. Did they give you any message for me?

JULIUS. 'Pears not, missus; nebber said nuffin' to me.

MRS. REEVES. You may go. (JULIUS *hesitates.*) Why do you stand there? You can go.

JULIUS. Beg pardon, missus, but may dis boy go out to-morrow?

MRS. REEVES. What do you want to go out for? You had a holiday last week.

JULIUS. Well, missus, Clementina,—dat gal's my cousin,—goin' to be married to-morrow.

MRS. REEVES. And you want to go to the wedding?

JULIUS. Please, missus; de party couldn't get on nohow widout Julius. I'se one of de bridesmaids.

MRS. REEVES. One of the groomsmen, I suppose you mean.

JULIUS. Yas, dat's what it is. I gibs de bride away.

MRS. REEVES. If you give the bride away, I suppose you can go, Julius.

JULIUS. Tank you, missus. Golly! won't dis boy Julius hab some fun!   [*Cuts a pigeon's wing, and exits.*

MRS. REEVES. I can hardly understand the feeling Ellen entertains toward Mr. Highdon. I must speak to her about it, and see that the connexion with that gentleman is severed.

Enter ELLEN.

ELLEN. Oh! mamma, Tom is coming here to—— ·

MRS. REEVES (*interrupting her*). Tom! who are you speaking of,—a cat?

ELLEN. Oh, no, mamma; Tom is Mr. Highdon.

MRS. REEVES. Do you know it is very improper, my dear, to call gentlemen by their Christian names?

ELLEN. But Tom don't mind it, mamma.

MRS. REEVES. I do. Mr. Highdon was kind enough to return your fan when you lost it; we would have paid him for his trouble, if he had allowed us; because he would not, I see no reason why we should be on such familiar terms with him.

ELLEN. But, mamma, Tom likes me to call him Tom.

MRS. REEVES. I do not. We must let Mr. Highdon understand that we no longer desire him to visit us.

ELLEN. But, mamma, you won't be so unkind!

MRS. REEVES. Unkind! My dear, Mr. Highdon is only a clerk, in a merchant's office down town, so it would be wrong of us to let him entertain hopes, that would ultimately have to be destroyed.

Enter JULIUS.

JULIUS. Please, missus, dat young woman dat was here dis mornin', called agin.

MRS. REEVES. Very well, Julius; I'll come and see her.

[*Exeunt* MRS. REEVES *and* JULIUS.

ELLEN. I wonder what Tom will say, when I tell him that mamma don't like him to come here. I am sure it is very unkind of mamma, just because his name is Tom, not to let him come here any more.

Enter TOM.

TOM. My dear Ellen! how do you do to-day?

ELLEN. How do you do, Mr. Highdon?

TOM. Mr. Highdon! Why don't you call me Tom?

ELLEN. Mamma says I am not to.

TOM. Why not?

ELLEN. I don't know; she says you mustn't come here any more.

TOM. Not come here! If I don't see you I shall go mad.

ELLEN. Don't go mad; I don't like mad people.

TOM. Well, then, dearest, for your sake I won't.

ELLEN. Thank you, Tom.

TOM. There's a darling; always call me Tom. I will see your mamma; tell her how much I love you, and ask her to let you be my wife.

Enter MRS. REEVES.

MRS. REEVES. You here, Mr. Highdon.

TOM. Yes, madam. I have come to ask the hand of your daughter in marriage.

MRS. REEVES (*aside*). Oh, oh! It's time I thought of putting a stop to it. (*Aloud.*) Indeed, sir, and do you love my daughter?

TOM. Most devotedly!

MRS. REEVES. And Ellen loves you?

ELLEN. Yes, mamma.

MRS. REEVES (*aside*). This has gone farther than I thought. (*Aloud.*) Mr. Highdon, will you come with me to the library; there I will speak to you upon the subject.

TOM. Certainly, madam.

[*Exit* MRS. REEVES; TOM *kisses* ELLEN'S *hand, and hurries after her.*

ELLEN. Mamma looks so cross, I am sure Tom will be disappointed, and I know I shall be. Oh dear! oh dear! why are mammas so cruel?

[*She sits upon chair, and covers her face with handkerchief.*
[*Scene closes.*

PHANTOM.

SCENE III.—*The same as Scene II.*

Enter JULIUS.

JULIUS. Nohow he can fix it—I won't let him in. He am been here two or tree times, but missus says, Julius, says she, if massa Highdon comes here, don't let him see Miss Ellen. An' dis nigger won't. (*A clock strikes twelve.*) Dar's twelve o'clock, missus can't be long, anyway.

Enter TOM, *with a sheet wrapped round him.*

JULIUS. Oh! Lor' a massy!   [*Crouches behind a chair in terror.*

TOM (*in a sepulchral voice*). Julius, Julius, Julius, I want you.

JULIUS. Go 'long; don't know you; dis man neber seed you afore.

TOM. Come here, Julius.

JULIUS. Julius am gone out.

TOM. Ha, ha, ha! Tellest thou an untruth?

[*Goes to* JULIUS, *takes him by the collar, and drags him to front of stage.*

JULIUS (*falling on his knees*). Go 'way, white man, dis cullud pussun don't know you.

TOM. Where is——

JULIUS (*interrupting him*). Where's dat sherry?

TOM (*suppressing a laugh*). Yes, where is that sherry?

JULIUS. I only took two bottles; one I gub to a yaller gal, the udder dis boy had for roomatiz.

TOM. Sayest thou so? Begone, and wait for me in the basement.

JULIUS. Lor' a massy, massa, dat I will.

[*Exit* JULIUS *in extreme trepidation.*

TOM. Ha, ha, ha! (*Resuming his natural voice.*) Love laughs at locksmiths, they say. Love laughs at negroes, say I. He was terribly frightened, but it was the only way I could get him to leave here. But how am I to see Ellen? I am almost as far from that as ever.

Enter ELLEN.

ELLEN (*screams*). What's that?

TOM (*throwing away sheet*). My dearest Ellen, it is only I.

ELLEN. Oh, Tom, how you frightened me, I took you for a ghost.

TOM. No dear, no phantom, but your own Tommy in the flesh.

ELLEN. What will mamma say, if she knows it?

TOM. But she won't know it. I have frightened Julius, thanks to that sheet, so there is no fear of his returning.

ELLEN. How indiscreet of you, Tom.

TOM. Can you expect me to be discreet, and not see you? It is impossible!

ELLEN. Did you see my letter in to-day's *Herald?*

TOM. Yes, dear.

ELLEN. Isn't it delightful that we can correspond in that way, without anybody being a bit the wiser.

TOM. It's charming. (*Aside.*) But very expensive. (*Aloud.*) I have good news for you, darling; old Debit is going to take me into partnership.

ELLEN. That's splendid!

TOM. Isn't it? Ever since your mother forbade me the house I have been indefatigable in my attention to business; so much so, that old Debit has offered me a share in the business. When that's settled we may enter into a different kind of partnership. Eh, Ellen?

ELLEN. Oh, Tom.

Enter MRS. REEVES.

MRS. REEVES. This is pretty conduct, sir, entering my house in this manner. What have you to say in palliation?

TOM. Simply, that I love your daughter.

MRS. REEVES. Nonsense! I should have thought that Mr. Highdon had more pride than to intrude himself where his presence is obnoxious.

TOM. I have reason to think, only to one person, madam.

MRS. REEVES. If I were to give you my consent, how could you support a wife ? My daughter has been used to luxuries which I am sure you, with your income, could never afford.

ELLEN. But, mamma, Mr. Debit has taken Tom into partnership.

MRS. REEV :   Is that so ?

TOM. Yes, madam, I am happy to say it is.

MRS. REEVES. Humph! (*Aside.*) Mr. Debit is one of the richest men in Wall street. (*Aloud.*) Mr. Highdon, Ellen, come here. (*Takes* ELLEN's *and* HIGHDON's *hands, and joins them together.*) Take her, Mr. Highdon, but mind, if you are deceiving me about the partnership, I shall withdraw my consent.

TOM. Then my happiness is secured.

MRS. REEVES (*ringing bell*). Now I will have a talk with Julius. You will excuse me, Mr. Highdon, but I am about to scold Julius for admitting you.

TOM. It was——

Enter JULIUS.

JULIUS. Yas, missus. (*Seeing* TOM.) Lor' a massy, dare's massa Highdon !

MRS. REEVES. Yes, and how came you to admit Mr. Highdon?

JULIUS. Dis boy neber 'mitted massa Highdon.

MRS. REEVES. How did he get into this room, then ?

TOM. I will explain that. Knowing that you had forbidden me the house, I had recourse to a lover's stratagem ; I put on that sheet, and frightened Julius into the belief that I was a phantom.

JULIUS. An' was you de spook ?

TOM (*pointing to sheet*). Yes, and there is my ghostly garment.

JULIUS (*aside to* TOM). Don't say nuffin 'bout de sherry.

MRS. REEVES. I see how it is, so I suppose I must forgive all of you.

ELLEN. If you please, mamma, and (*to audience*) ladies and gentlemen, will you be kind enough to give a helping hand to the new partnership?

ELLEN *and* TOM, *centre.* MRS. REEVES *left, and* JULIUS *right.*

CURTAIN.

CHARADE II.

CON——TEST.

BY FRANK CAHILL.

Characters.

Mrs. Lockitt.
Ada Lockitt, *her daughter.*
Charles Beauchamp.
Adolphus Sparks.
Susan, *a servant.*

CON—

SCENE I.—*A parlor.*

Enter Susan, *followed by* Adolphus.

Adolphus. I declare, Susan, you are looking positively charming.

Susan. Thank you, sir, I always do.

Adolphus. Really, now, you don't say so? But where is your mistress?

Susan. Mrs. Lockitt, sir?

Adolphus. Mrs. Lockitt! No! Miss Ada; the adorable, the incomparable Miss Ada.

Susan. She is up stairs, sir.

Adolphus. Up stairs,—eh? Susan, would you like to have a dollar given you?

Susan (*courteseying*). Yes, if you please, sir.

Adolphus. Well, then, who comes here, besides me?

Susan. Let me see,—there's the butcher, the baker, the milkman, the——

Adolphus. No, no; you misunderstand me. I mean, who visits here?

Susan. Oh, there's Miss Cann, Mrs. Staunton and her two daughters, Mrs. Jones——

4

ADOLPHUS. Stop, stop. I mean male visitors.

SUSAN. Oh, we never have any male visitors.

ADOLPHUS. None! Susan, I'm a happy man. There s a dollar for you.   [*Gives dollar.*

SUSAN. Thank you, sir. At least, none to speak of. Mr. Beauchamp comes here.

ADOLPHUS. Mr. Beauchamp! Who is he?

SUSAN. A friend of the family, sir; but he comes here so often, you can hardly call him a visitor.

ADOLPHUS. Susan, I am afraid you have got that dollar under false pretences. But, never mind, take my card up to Mrs. Lockitt.

                                                      [*Gives card.*

SUSAN. Very well, sir. (*Aside.*) Obtaining a dollar under false pretences, indeed!   [*Exit SUSAN.*

ADOLPHUS. Now, who the dickens can this Mr. Beauchamp be? Can he be a rival? If he is, I'll——

Enter BEAUCHAMP, who places his hat upon table, slowly draws off his gloves, and sits down; ADOLPHUS staring at him the while.

ADOLPHUS. That's cool.

BEAU. Eh? Did you speak?

ADOLPHUS. No, nothing.

BEAU. I beg pardon.

  [*Takes up book, and begins to read. A pause. BEAUCHAMP gives a slight cough.*

ADOLPHUS. Eh? Did you speak?

BEAU. No, nothing.

ADOLPHUS. I beg pardon.

  [*BEAUCHAMP puts down book, and walks up and down stage. ADOLPHUS does the same; finally they knock against each other.*

BEAU. *and* ADOLPHUS. What do mean, sir?

ADOLPHUS. I insist upon knowing what you mean, sir?

BEAU. Who are you, sir?

ADOLPHUS. Never mind, sir.

BEAU. There's my card, sir. Will you favor me with yours?

                                                      [*Gives card.*

ADOLPHUS (*reading card*). Charles Beauchamp!

Enter MRS. LOCKITT.

MRS. LOCKITT. Good morning, gentlemen.

BEAU. I am charmed to see you looking so well this morning.

MRS. LOCKITT. Flatterer! But you, gentlemen, do not know one another. Allow me to introduce you. Mr. Beauchamp, Mr. Sparks—Mr. Sparks, Mr. Beauchamp. [BEAUCHAMP *and* SPARKS *bow.*

ADOLPHUS. By the way, Mrs. Lockitt, why is——Do you understand cons, Mr. Beauchamp?

BEAU. Cons,—cons,—what are they?

ADOLPHUS. What an extraordinary individual you are,—don't know what a con is? Why, a conundrum, to be sure.

BEAU. Oh! a conundrum!

MRS. LOCKITT. Yes, Mr. Sparks is famous for making conundrums.

ADOLPHUS. Well, then, what article of navigation resembles an animal? (*A pause.*) Do you give it up,—eh?

BEAU. I'll give it up.

MRS. LOCKITT. And so will I.

ADOLPHUS. Why, a (s)cow, to be sure. (*Laughs.*) Isn't it good;—eh? Aint it capital?

BEAU. (*forcing a laugh.*) Yes, yes, very good. I suppose you have heard the news, Mrs. Lockitt?

MRS. LOCKITT. No. What is it?

BEAU. Mr. Bearleigh has failed for a quarter of a million of dollars.

MRS. LOCKITT. You don't say so! I wonder what his poor girls will do for dresses.

ADOLPHUS. Here is another con. Why is an oyster like a tell-tale?

BEAU. (*shrugging his shoulders.*) I'm sure I don't know.

ADOLPHUS. Do you, Mrs. Lockitt?

MRS. LOCKITT. No. You know I'm a bad hand at guessing conundrums.

ADOLPHUS. Well, then, because it is impossible to keep its mouth shut. [*Laughs immoderately.*

Enter ADA.

ADA. Good morning, gentlemen.

[BEAUCHAMP *and* ADOLPHUS *bow.*

MRS. LOCKITT. Where have you been so long, my dear?

ADA. I had a visitor.

MRS. LOCKITT. A visitor! Who was it?

ADA. How inquisitive you are, mamma. Well, it was the—the--the dressmaker.

MRS. LOCKITT. Oh!

ADA. Is there anything new at the Opera to-night, Mr. Sparks?

ADOLPHUS. Really—that is—no, I believe not. But I have a first rate con for you. Why is bacon like the asthma?

ADA. Really, I cannot tell.

ADOLPHUS. Can anybody else? No. Well, then, because smoking cures it.   [*Laughs excessively.*

BEAU. I think you have been misinformed about the Opera, sir, for Madame Solfeggio sings to-night for the first time.

ADA. How I should like to go.

BEAU. Would you allow me to be your escort?

ADA. Mamma, shall we go?

MRS. LOCKITT. As Mr. Beauchamp is so kind as to offer, I really think we will accept.

ADOLPHUS. Now, upon my word, this is too good to be lost. Why is a speechless monarch like Great Britain?

MRS. LOCKITT. I have it. Because it's great but silent.

BEAU. Really, a very good answer, indeed.

ADOLPHUS. Ah! but that's not it.

MRS. LOCKITT. No!

ADOLPHUS. No. The answer is, because it's a king-dumb. Now, that's very good—aint it?   [*Laughs exceedingly.*

BEAU. Ladies, I will now take my leave. I will call for you this evening at half-past seven.

ADOLPHUS. If you would allow me, I should like to accompany you.

MRS. LOCKITT. Certainly, With pleasure.

BEAU. Good morning, Mrs. Lockitt. Good morning, Miss Lockitt.
                    [*Bows to the ladies, and to* ADOLPHUS, *and exit.*

ADOLPHUS (*calling after him*). Mr. Beauchamp—Mr. Beauchamp— I have such a capital con to ask you. Why is a rhinoceros like a——
                    [*Runs off after* BEAUCHAMP.

MRS. LOCKITT. What an extraordinary man that Mr. Sparks is. But come to my room, my dear, I have several things to show you.

ADA. Very well, mamma.

                    [*Exeunt* MRS. LOCKITT *and* ADA. *Scene closes.*

—TEST.

SCENE II.—*The same.*

Enter ADA, *and* SUSAN *carrying a very large bandbox.*

ADA. You are sure you have packed up the right bonnet?

SUSAN. Oh yes, miss. The yellow one, with the bird of paradise feather.

ADA. That's right. Has Miss Shipton been here to-day?

SUSAN. Yes, Miss, and I gave her those dresses to alter for you.

ADA. Has Mr. Sparks called?

SUSAN. No, Miss.

ADA. When he does, I'm at home.

SUSAN. Very well, Miss.

ADA. That's all. Stay, the lace of one of my best handkerchiefs is torn, will you mend it?

SUSAN. Yes, Miss. [*Exit* SUSAN.

ADA. Heigho! How those men do torment me. I suppose I shall have to marry one of them, to get rid of the other. I know, mamma likes Mr. Beauchamp the——

Enter SUSAN.

SUSAN. Mr. Sparks. [*Exit* SUSAN.

Enter ADOLPHUS SPARKS.

ADOLPHUS. Good morning, Miss Lockitt.

ADA. Good morning.

ADOLPHUS. I am glad to find you alone.

ADA. Indeed! Why?

ADOLPHUS. Ever since I——You cannot be insensible to——Miss Lockitt, I am in love.

ADA. You don't say so? It is a very delicious feeling, is it not?

ADOLPHUS. Ecstatic! What would man be without love; his life would be a blank,—a ship without a rudder. Yes, love is the guiding star of our existence, and without it all would be chaos and confusion.

ADA. Quite poetical, I declare. I must certainly get you to write me a sonnet on love, in my album.

ADOLPHUS. With pleasure. Oh, Miss Lockitt, do you not pity me?

ADA. Pity you! I thought the feeling was delightful.

ADOLPHUS. Have you no compassion?

ADA. Compassion is pity, is it not?

ADOLPHUS. I will speak plainly. Miss Lockitt, I lo——

Enter MRS. LOCKITT.

ADOLPHUS (*aside*). Confound the woman.

MRS. LOCKITT. Ada, dear, I want you. How do you do, Mr. Sparks?

ADOLPHUS. Well, madam. (*Aside.*) Save a secret sorrow. (*Sighs.*)

MRS. LOCKITT. When you send your parcel to Miss Shipton, Ada, tell her I want to see her.

ADA. Very well, mamma. Mr. Sparks, will you do me a favor?

ADOLPHUS. With pleasure.

ADA. I want this small parcel taken to my milliner's, will you do it for me?   [*Takes up bandbox.*

ADOLPHUS (*looking aghast*). Really—upon my word——

ADA. You object?

ADOLPHUS. Oh, no; not in the least,—that is,—I'll send for it.

MRS. LOCKITT. Don't trouble Mr. Sparks.

ADOLPHUS. It is no trouble, I assure you. I'll go and get a boy to carry it, immediately.   [*Exit* ADOLPHUS.

MRS. LOCKITT. How silly of you, Ada. The idea of wanting Mr. Sparks to carry a bandbox.

ADA. It's only a little plan I have, mamma, so say nothing more about it, please.

MRS. LOCKITT. I have such a number of things to do, that I hardly know which to begin first, so I'll set to work and do them.

[*Hurries off rapidly.*

ADA. It was quite funny to notice Mr. Sparks's face, when I asked him to carry that box for me. I wonder what there can be in band-boxes that makes men so afraid of them. I am sure if I were a man, I wouldn't mind carrying one.

Enter BEAUCHAMP

BEAU. Ah, Miss Lockitt, I am so glad to find you alone.

ADA (*aside*). Here's another man glad to find me alone. (*Aloud.*) Mamma has this moment left me.

BEAU. I am pleased to hear it, Miss Lockitt; I have come to place my fate in your hands.

ADA. And what am I to do with it?

BEAU. Oh! can you not guess? For the last six months I have been miserable,—wretched,—yet happy. Happy to be in your society, —happy to be near you.

ADA. I am glad that I have been able to contribute to your happiness.

BEAU. Oh, Miss Lockitt, believe me, I know that I am unworthy.

ADA (*aside*). This is becoming serious. (*Aloud.*) Excuse me, interrupting you; but Mr. Beauchamp,—I hardly dare ask you,—will you do me a favor?

BEAU. A thousand! if you wish it.

ADA. Well, then, would you mind taking this box down town for me? [*Takes up the bandbox.*

BEAU. (*surprised.*) That box?

ADA. Yes, this box. There is nothing very extraordinary in a box, is there?

BEAU. Certainly, I will take it with pleasure.

ADA. Thank you. Susan will give you the address. [*Gives him box.*

BEAU. Before I go, let me——

ADA. No, not now; place your fate in my hands when you return.

BEAU. Well, as you wish. *Au revoir.* (*Aside.*) I must certainly get a boy to carry this confounded thing. [*Exit* BEAUCHAMP.

ADA. I knew that Mr. Beauchamp would not mind carrying it. Men make vows and protestations, but the best way to test their sincerity, is to get them to carry a bandbox. [*Exit* ADA. *Scene closes.*

CONTEST.

SCENE III.—*The same.*

Enter ADOLPHUS.

ADOLPHUS. No one here! I am determined to come to some definite understanding with Ada. I will be accepted or rejected to-day; this uncertainty will drive me mad. I was certainly foolish—yes, decidedly foolish in refusing to carry that bandbox, for it would have been so easy to have hired somebody to have carried it. Ah, stupid, stupid Adolphus Sparks!

[*Sits down at back of stage; takes up book and reads.*

Enter BEAUCHAMP.

BEAU. Precious unfortunate! Couldn't find anybody to carry that blessed bandbox, confound it! Just my luck; I met five people I knew. No matter, it has pleased Ada, I am sure; so in that quarter I am safe. (*Seeing* ADOLPHUS.) Ah! you here?

ADOLPHUS. (*Rising and coming forward.*) (*Aside.*) My rival! (*Aloud.*) Yes, sir, and why shouldn't I be here?

BEAU. I'm sure I don't know.

ADOLPHUS. No, sir, and you won't know.

BEAU. I don't want to.

ADOLPHUS. Don't prevaricate, sir

BEAU. Prevaricate?

ADOLPHUS. Yes, sir, prevaricate. Do you object to the word, sir?

BEAU. Oh, no.

ADOLPHUS. Very well, sir, I'll use it if I like, sir.

BEAU. With all my heart.

ADOLPHUS. Yes, sir. (*Walks up and down stage rapidly.*) What are you here for, sir?

BEAU. I have yet to learn that it is necessary for me to explain my actions to Mr. Sparks.

ADOLPHUS. You're another, sir.

BEAU. (*smiling*). Indeed! I am sorry to hear it.

ADOLPHUS. Yes, sir, I say it emphatically, you're another.

BEAU. Mr. Sparks, I am at a loss to know the meaning of your conduct.

ADOLPHUS. That for my meaning, sir. [*Snaps his fingers in his face.*

BEAU. Ah! If you do that again, I'll pitch you down stairs.

ADOLPHUS. No you won't, sir.

BEAU. I give you fair warning, so take care.

ADOLPHUS. That for your warning. [*Snaps fingers in his face again.*

BEAU. Ah!

[*Seizes* ADOLPHUS *by the collar, and they struggle about the room.*

Enter MRS. LOCKITT *and* ADA.

MRS. LOCKITT. What is all this noise about? What is the meaning of this disgraceful contest in my house?

BEAU. I have to apologize to you, Mrs. Lockitt, for this unseemly conduct on my part.

ADOLPHUS. Yes, it is all on his part.

BEAU. I will finish the discussion with you, sir, elsewhere. At present, I express regrets to Mrs. and Miss Lockitt.

ADA. What is the cause of this disturbance?

ADOLPHUS. He said, he didn't prevaricate.

MRS. LOCKITT. Gentlemen, I see how it is, it is some misunderstanding on your part. Let us think no more about it;—come, shake hands, and be friends.

BEAU. I have no ill-feeling towards Mr. Sparks.

ADA (*aside*). What a magnanimous creature!

ADOLPHUS. I have no objection to shake hands.

MRS. LOCKITT. That's right. Come.   (*She takes their hands, joins them together, they shake heartily.*) Now let us go to lunch.

[BEAUCHAMP *offers his arm to* ADA. ADOLPHUS *does the same to* MRS. LOCKITT. *As they are walking off, the curtain drops.*

CHARADE III

DRAM——AT(T)IC.

BY FRANK CAHILL.

————•◦•————

Characters.

LUDOVICO JONES, *a down town clerk.*
MR. LAST, *a bootmaker.*
THEOPHILUS BUCKSKIN, *a country manager.*
DR. TOURNIQUET.
MRS. JOHNSON, *a washerwoman.*
MARY WORTHINGTON.
The part of LUDOVICO JONES, *to be played in a serio-comic manner,*
bordering on burlesque.

————•◦•————

DRAM—

SCENE I.—*A parlor, comfortably furnished, with a sofa in room.*

LUDOVICO *is discovered, with his hair all tumbled, walking about the*
room, with a volume of Tennyson, open, in his hand.

LUDOVICO. How beautiful! My blighted heart throbs, as though it
would burst this mortal clay. Ha, ha! let me read that verse once
more.   [*Reads.*

> " Oh that 'twere possible
>   After long grief and pain,
>   To find the arms of my true love
>   Round me once again!"

Tennyson, I love thee. Love! ha, ha! what is love? Nothing.
There's no such thing as love! The world is cold and heartless —

> " And my heart is a handful of dust."

Oh! Gloriana Brown, why did you jilt me? You fascinated me, as

4*

the cobra di capello fascinates the little dickey-bird, and then you,—
then you,—yes,—then you wouldn't have anything more to do with me.
Ha, ha, ha!   I shall go mad!

              [*Walks up and down stage rapidly, tearing his hair.*

Enter MARY.

MARY.   Oh, Mr. Jones, what is the matter?

LUDOVICO.   Matter!   A blighted heart is the matter.   A torn and
lacerated bosom is the matter.

MARY.   Lor'!   Mr. Jones, you don't say so?

LUDOVICO.   Mary, a crushed worm will turn, and I'll be a crushed
worm.

MARY.   Very well, Mr. Jones; but hadn't you better go down town?
It's getting very late.

LUDOVICO.   Down town!   What care I for sordid wealth?   Nothing!

MARY.   What will Mr. Benson, your employer, say?

LUDOVICO.   Confound Mr. Benson!   Wall Street has no charms for
me!   My ledger's a blank, and all is misery, desolation, and woe!

MARY.   Mr. Jones, you are ill.

LUDOVICO.   Ill!   Ha, ha, ha!   Dying!   Dying of unrequited love
and crushed affections.

MARY.   I will fetch Doctor Tourniquet, who lives next door.

LUDOVICO.   Can a doctor cure a bleeding heart?   Can he extract the
dart that is rankling in this bosom?   Answer me.

MARY.   A bleeding heart, Mr. Jones?

LUDOVICO.   Yes, Mary.   I am the victim of unrequited affection, and
my bones will soon be ready for the sepulchre of the Jones's.

MARY (*aside*).   I have heard of people dying of a rush of blood to
the heart, so I'll fetch the doctor immediately.   (*Aloud.*)   Would you
like to have your breakfast brought up stairs, Mr. Jones?

LUDOVICO.   Now, listen to her.   Who ever heard of a person crossed
in love, eating?   No, Mary, I want nothing, unless it is some poison.

MARY (*aside*).   I must certainly go for a doctor.   [*Exit* MARY.

LUDOVICO (*calling after her*).   Mary! Mary!   She don't hear me.   I
wonder if she has really gone for some poison.   I hope she is not so
foolish.   Poison is such a disagreeable thing to take; in fact, it is excessively disagreeable; so dangerous, too; if a person takes too much
of it, it's apt to kill him.   Now, I hope she won't be absurd enough to
bring poison into my room; the children might get hold of it, and if
they do, there is no knowing what the consequences will be.   However, I will rest my weary limbs, and await fate. [*Reclines upon sofa.*

Enter MARY *and* DOCTOR TOURNIQUET.

MARY. There he is, doctor.

[DOCTOR *goes to sofa, and is about to feel* LUDOVICO's *pulse, when he starts up and glares at the* DOCTOR.

LUDOVICO. Who are you, sir?

DOCTOR. Ah! I see—nervous affection.

MARY. Hush, Mr. Jones, it's the doctor.

DOCTOR. Come, come, be quiet; let me feel your pulse.

[*He forces* LUDOVICO *gently upon the sofa, in a sitting posture, and feels his pulse.*

MARY. What is the matter, doctor?

DOCTOR. Humph! Have you a pain in your head?

LUDOVICO. No.

DOCTOR. Ha! I thought not. Have you any in your back?

LUDOVICO. No, none.

DOCTOR. Of course, no pain in the back. Whereabouts do you feel pain?

LUDOVICO (*in a sepulchral manner*). In my lacerated bosom.

DOCTOR. Ah! as I thought—in the region of the chest. Does that pain you? [*Sounds* LUDOVICO's *chest.*

LUDOVICO. No, mine is a secret pain.

DOCTOR. Does that pain you?

[*Hits* LUDOVICO *violently in the chest, which makes him cough.*

LUDOVICO. Ha! a blow! minion, come on!

[*Jumps up, and commences to square off at the* DOCTOR.

MARY (*laying hold of him*). Pray, Mr. Jones, don't, for my sake.

LUDOVICO. Mary, I won't. (*Aside.*) Especially as he don't seem a bit afraid. [*Sits down again.*

DOCTOR. Ah! I see what the matter is with you. You're bilious.

LUDOVICO (*aside*). What a strange old gentleman; he calls love bile!

DOCTOR. You get some magnesia, and take that.

MARY. I will go and get it for you.

LUDOVICO. How kind you are. [*Makes a wry face.*

DOCTOR. Good morning, Mr. Jones. [*Going*

LUDOVICO. How much am I to take, doctor?

DOCTOR. Take three or four drachms.

MARY. I will see you down, doctor, and get the medicine at the same time [*Exeunt* MARY *and the* DOCTOR.

LUDOVICO (*starting up*). Ha, ha, ha! A new discovery—a sovereign remedy for love—magnesia! He told me to take three or four drams, and I'll do it. (*Runs to corner of room, pulls out demijohn, and fills tumbler.*) Here's one to commence on. Oh, Gloriana Brown, this is your doing. [*As he is drinking, the scene closes.*

—ATTIC.

SCENE II.—*An attic, very meanly furnished. No carpet on the floor; a bed in one corner of the stage; one chair and a common deal table.*

LUDOVICO *is discovered, very shabbily attired, writing at table.*

LUDOVICO. Nearly finished! My great poem, that I have been at work on for weeks and weeks, is nearly completed. Those brutal and sordid editors I must try once more! My great genius is not appreciated by them. They're jealous of me, that's what it is. They're afraid that my talents will eclipse theirs, so they won't publish anything I write. Give me a chance, and then won't I astonish the world! (*A knock is heard at the door.*) Who's there? A dun, I suppose. Come in.

Enter MARY, *with bonnet and shawl on.*

MARY. Good morning, Mr. Jones. How do you feel this morning?
LUDOVICO (*rising and coming forward*). Sick, Mary—sick of the world and all its petty jealousies.
MARY. When you were engaged down town, you were not sick of the world, Mr. Jones.
LUDOVICO. Speak not to me of old Benson; he could not understand the eccentricities of genius, so I threw up my situation; or, rather, he threw me up, because he objected to my writing sonnets in the ledger.
MARY. But what are you going to do, Mr. Jones? You know you are very, very poor.
LUDOVICO. Poor! Yes—nobody understands my genius, Mary.
MARY. Don't they, Mr. Jones?
LUDOVICO. Even your mother could not. Because I owed her a few weeks' board, and couldn't pay it, and saw no prospect of so doing, she politely told me she wanted my room.
MARY. I am sure I asked mother to let you stay; but she wouldn't listen to me.
LUDOVICO. Mary, you're a good girl, and I like you very much.
MARY. Oh, I'm so glad, Mr. Jones.

LUDOVICO. Don't call me Mr. Jones; call me Ludovico.

MARY. I don't like to.

LUDOVICO. Nonsense; and I will call you Gloriana—may I?

MARY. You may call me anything you please, Ludovico.

LUDOVICO (*taking her hand*). Well then, Ludovico and Gloriana, hand in hand, will go through the world together. (*A knock is heard at the door*) Come in.

Enter MR. LAST.

MR. LAST. Good morning.

LUDOVICO. Good morning, Mr. Last.

MR. LAST. I have called for my money.

LUDOVICO. Have you? (*Aside.*) Then I sincerely hope you may get it.

MR. LAST. Yes (*handing bill*), and here's the bill—forty-five dollars and fifty cents.

LUDOVICO. Thank you. (*Folds it up carefully, and puts it in his pocket.*) I'll take care of it.

MR. LAST. Are you not going to pay me?

LUDOVICO. Oh, yes, certainly.

MR. LAST. Well then, hand over the money.

LUDOVICO. Pardon me; I'm going to pay you, but not to-day.

MR. LAST. Now look here, I can't afford to supply you with boots for nothing. When will you pay me?

MARY (*aside to* LUDOVICO). Why don't you pay him now?

LUDOVICO (*aside to* MARY). Circumstances over which I have no control, prevent me. (*Aloud.*) Mr. Last, I am now writing a poem that will immortalize me.

MR. LAST. A poem! Fiddlededee! I want my money.

LUDOVICO. You shall have it, I tell you, shortly. I don't pretend it will be equal to the Attic authors of old, but I am sure it will be successful. Genius cannot go long unrecognised.

MR. LAST (*glancing round the room*). I suppose you call yourself au attic author?

LUDOVICO. No, sir; I am an American.

MR. LAST. When can I have it?

LUDOVICO. Next week I think I can settle it.

MR. LAST. Well, I'll call then. If you don't want to be put to trouble, you'll settle it. Good morning.   [*Exit* MR. LAST

LUDOVICO. Good morning. There, Mary,—I mean Gloriana,—you see the trials and tribulations a man of genius has to go through.

must get on with my poem. Sit down, Gloriana,—I beg pardon, there is only one chair. Stand up, Gloriana, it will soon be finished; then I'll read it to you.

MARY. Oh, that will be nice.   [*A knock heard at the door.*

LUDOVICO. My mind misgives me,—anther dun. I can't see him. Where shall I hide? Oh, here. (*Runs to bed, pulls off counterpane, covers himself over with it, and crouches down in corner.*) Speak to him, Gloriana.   [*Another knock heard at the door.*

MARY. Come in.

Enter MRS. JOHNSON, *with a basket of washing.*

MRS. JOHNSON. Oh, dear me, them stairs! What makes people who calls themselves gentlemen live in attics, I don't know! (*Sits down on chair, and wipes her face with her apron.*) Is Mr. Jones in?

MARY. No,—that is,—he is,—no, you can't see him.

MRS. JOHNSON. It 'pears to me he conducts himself mighty nice for a gentleman. Did he leave any money for me?

MARY. No,—that is,—no, he didn't.

MRS. JOHNSON. Here am I, a poor lone woman, with five small children and a sick husband, who has been laid up with the rheumatiz in his joints, and I have been washing for Mr. Jones three months, and have not seen a cent of his money; and I should like to know what would become of me, that I would, if nobody ever paid me?

MARY. I am sure Ludovico,—Mr. Jones, I mean,—will pay you shortly.

MRS. JOHNSON. Give my compliments to Mr. Jones, and tell him that he shan't have any more clothes till he pays me, and that I'm sorry, but I'm a poor lone woman, and must protect myself; so I'll take these things back with me. (*Rises, takes basket, and goes to door.*) Good morning.   [*Exits.*

          [*During the above dialogue,* LUDOVICO *has been shaking his fists at* MRS. JOHNSON *in a wild and savage manner.*

MARY. Ludovico, she has gone.

LUDOVICO (*jumping up*). Thank goodness! Gloriana, I thank you. Now for the finale of my grand poem.

          [*Rushes frantically to table, seizes a pen, and commences to write* MARY *goes and looks over his shoulder.*

                              [*Scene closes.*

DRAMAT(T)IC.

SCENE III.—*Same as Scene II.*

Enter LUDOVICO *and* MARY. LUDOVICO *has a shabby hat on, and his coat is buttoned close up, as though he had no shirt on.* MARY *has bonnet and shawl on, which she takes off.*

LUDOVICO. Yes, Gloriana, we shall soon know our fate. Mr. Buckskin will soon be here to see us rehearse one or two scenes. I think it was a brilliant idea of mine, when that grand poem I wrote was not accepted, simply through the malice and enmity of editors, to turn my attention to dramatic art.

MARY. That it was; and how beautifully you do act!

LUDOVICO. Well, I flatter myself,—but why should I be egotistical? You know that geniuses can turn their minds to anything.

[*A knock is heard at the door.*

MARY. Here he is.

LUDOVICO. Yes, it must be Mr. Buckskin. Come in.

Enter BUCKSKIN.

BUCKSKIN. Is this Mr. Jones's room?

LUDOVICO. Yes, sir, and I'm Mr. Jones, at your service.

BUCKSKIN. Ah, how d'ye do? (*Shakes him by the hand.*) Is that Miss Worthington? [MARY *courteseys.*

LUDOVICO. Yes.

BUCKSKIN. You want an engagement at my theatre?

LUDOVICO. That is what we desire.

BUCKSKIN. Let me see what you can do.

LUDOVICO. Very well; we will go through a scene, of the "Lost Father, or the Found Daughter."

BUCKSKIN. Go ahead.

LUDOVICO. Now then, Gloriana, put yourself into position. You know the scene, where the daughter recognises her lost parent.

MARY. Yes. (*Aside.*) How frightened I feel.

[LUDOVICO *throws himself into a melodramatic attitude.* MARY *does the same. The following scene must be acted in a burlesque manner.*

LUDOVICO. Listen, maiden, 'tis now some twenty years ago——

BUCKSKIN (*interrupting him*). No, no, that will never do. Say it like this. (*Alters his voice to a gruff and sepulchral tone.*) "Listen, maiden, 'tis now some twenty years ago"——Do you see?

LUDOVICO. Pardon me, but I don't commence it that way. I assume that voice, as I get worked up in the scene.

BUCKSKIN. Oh, very well. Commence again.

LUDOVICO. Listen, maiden, 'tis now some twenty years ago, on a cold and stormy night, that a man might have been seen wending his way, along a rocky path, with an infant in his arms.

MARY. Oh, merciful heavens! Say not so.

LUDOVICO. He placed that baby in the care——

BUCKSKIN. Wouldn't "he placed that infant," be better than "he placed that baby,"—eh?

LUDOVICO. We mentioned just before, his having an infant in his arms. We must avoid tautology, you know.

BUCKSKIN. All right,—all right. Go on.

LUDOVICO. He placed that baby in the care of a goodly shepherd, who lived upon that mountain.

MARY. Do my ears deceive me?

LUDOVICO. He reared that child as though it were his own.

MARY (*hysterically*). Ha, ha,—go on,—go on.

LUDOVICO. Upon that child's arm was a raspberry mark.

BUCKSKIN. That's good. Raspberry mark is quite original. Go on.

MARY (*wildly*). A raspberry mark, say you?

LUDOVICO. Do you not recognise me?

MARY. It is,—ha, ha, ha! it is my father!

      [*Walks slowly up to him, and falls fainting into his arms.*

BUCKSKIN. Bravo! Bravo! (*Clapping his hands.*) That's good,— very good.   [*Goes up to them, and shakes them by the hand.*

LUDOVICO. Shall we try another scene?

BUCKSKIN. No, not the least occasion. I see you have genius. I'll engage both of you.

MARY. Both! Oh, how delightful!

BUCKSKIN. You must alter your name, Jones. Jones don't sound well upon a play bill.

LUDOVICO. I don't mind. What shall I call myself?

BUCKSKIN. What do you think of St. Clair? What's your first name?

LUDOVICO. Ludovico.

BUCKSKIN. The very thing. Ludovico St. Clair will look first rate on a show bill. Letters two feet long,—printed in red and green. Crowded houses,—sure of it.

LUDOVICO. I only hope that I shall be more successful as an actor than I was as a poet. (*To audience.*) And I furthermore hope, that all present will come and give me a helping-hand on the night of my *debut.*

CURTAIN.

CHARADE IV.

ANTI (AUNTY)—DOTE.

BY FRANK CAHILL.

Characters.

FRED. WARD, *a Medical Student.*
JOE DASHINGTON, *his friend.*
MRS. FONDLEIGH.
SUSAN, *her maid.*

ANTI—(AUNTY—)

SCENE I.—*A parlor. A sofa in room.*

MRS. FONDLEIGH *and* SUSAN *discovered.*

MRS. FONDLEIGH. Dear me! what can make my nephew so much behind time? The cars leave New York at six o'clock, now it's past ten, and they only take an hour and a half to get here. I hope no accident has happened I am getting quite fidgetty.

SUSAN. Perhaps he missed the cars, mum.

MRS. FONDLEIGH. That may be it; but the next train is due now. I really do think an accident has happened.

SUSAN. Don't you worry yourself, mum; he'll be here safe enough, depend upon it.

MRS FONDLEIGH. You know, Susan, how careless these railway people are.

SUSAN. Indeed they are, mum.

MRS. FONDLEIGH. Why, the very last time I travelled in one of those nasty cars, which is very nearly fifteen years ago, I left one of my gloves upon the seat, and the careless fellows lost it.

SUSAN. Dear me!

MRS. FONDLEIGH. Yes; and they actually refused to give me a new pair. (*A bell rings.*) There he is; run, Susan, and open the door.

SUSAN. Yes, mum.   [*Exit* SUSAN.

MRS. FONDLEIGH. Here is my very dear nephew, at last. I wonder if he is changed? How I long to see him!

SUSAN (*talking off*). Be quiet, sir. Such impudence!

MRS. FONDLEIGH. What's that Susan's saying?

Enter FRED. WARD *and* JOE DASHINGTON.

FRED. My dear aunty, how glad I am to see you.

[*He embraces* MRS. FONDLEIGH.

MRS. FONDLEIGH. My dear boy, how have you been? You're looking very well.

FRED. Aunty, I have brought my friend down with me to stay with us. Joe, this is my aunt. Aunty, this is Joe Dashington.

MRS. FONDLEIGH. Mr. Dashington, I am glad to see you. (JOE *bows.*) Are you a student?

JOE. Oh, yes; Fred. and I are room mates.

MRS. FONDLEIGH. Indeed! I hope you haven't been letting my nephew study too hard.

[FRED. *winks at* JOE, *and puts his finger to the side of his nose.*

JOE. Well, he has worked pretty hard, that's a fact. Up till two or three o'clock reading; I have often with tears in my eyes asked him to come to bed, but it was of no use—he would work.

[FRED. *struggles violently with a laugh.*

MRS. FONDLEIGH. What's the matter, Fred.?

[*Runs to him, and looks into his face anxiously.*

FRED. Nothing, aunty. It's only a tickling of the *crico-arytenoideus posticus* muscle.

MRS. FONDLEIGH (*apparently mystified*). Oh, indeed! Is it dangerous?

JOE. Not at all, I assure you; it's perfectly harmless.

MRS. FONDLEIGH. I'm so glad of that. But what made you so late? Why didn't you come by the six o'clock train?

FRED. My dear aunty, we couldn't help it. Just as we were leaving the hospital, such a beautiful case came in.

MRS. FONDLEIGH. A beautiful case, Fred.?

FRED. Yes, aunty; a man was brought in with both the *tibia* and *fibula* bones broken.

JOE (*rubbing his hands*). It was perfectly charming.

MRS. FONDLEIGH. Poor fellow—did it hurt him much?

FRED. He didn't seem to mind it. But you see, my dear aunty, we couldn't come away till his leg was cut off.

MRS. FONDLEIGH. How shocking! Surely, Fred., you didn't cut his leg off?

FRED. Oh, no, I didn't do it; Dr. Cutting amputated it. You see it was rather an intricate case—wasn't it, Joe?

JOE. Splendid, sir, splendid.

FRED. I'll explain it to you, aunty. You see, the *cotyloid ligament* of the *acetabulum* had to be severed, so as to get at the *ligamentum teres* now that's a very dangerous operation, I assure you, and requires great care.

MRS. FONDLEIGH. I suppose so.

FRED. You see it requires great nicety in handling, or else you'd injure the patient, and that would never do.

MRS. FONDLEIGH. I am so glad, Fred., you didn't cut the man's leg off. If he had died, it would have been so horrible—wouldn't it?

Enter SUSAN.

SUSAN. If you please, mum, supper is ready.

MRS. FONDLEIGH. Very well, Susan. Come, Fred.—come, Mr. Dashington, you both must be hungry after your ride.

FRED. We will be with you in a moment, aunty.

[*Exeunt* MRS. FONDLEIGH *and* SUSAN.

JOE (*laughing*). Ha, ha, ha! that wasn't bad about the fractured leg. Aunty was nicely taken in.

FRED. If she only knew that billiards detained us, I don't think she'd be so horrified.

JOE. No; but I pitched it pretty steep about your reading.

FRED. Yes, you did that capitally. But supper's waiting—come along.

JOE. All right; I'm as hungry as a hunter. Does aunty keep a sideboard?

FRED. It will do your heart good to see it. Come along.

[*Exeunt* FRED. *and* JOE. *Scene closes.*

—DOTE.

SCENE II.—*Same as Scene I.*

Enter SUSAN *and* FRED.

SUSAN. Do be quiet, Mr. Fred.!

FRED. Well, ain't I quiet?

SUSAN. No, you are not. You are trying to—to——

FRED. Trying to do what?

SUSAN. Trying to kiss me.

FRED. There's no harm in that, is there? You kissed me when I went away to New York.

SUSAN. But you've grown so much taller since then.

FRED. Just think me a little boy again; won't you, Susan?

[*Encircles her waist with his arm.*

SUSAN. Now, do be quiet, Mr. Fred.; if you don't, I'll certainly tell your aunt.

FRED. I must steal one. (*Attempts to kiss her.*)

Enter JOE.

JOE. Hullo! (FRED. *releases* SUSAN, *who looks confused.* FRED. *puts his hands in his pockets, and whistles.*) I beg pardon; don't mind me. I'm nobody. I'll look out of window.

SUSAN. Mr. Ward was just telling me that—that——

FRED. That I wanted some buttons sewn on my shirts—wasn't I, Susan?

JOE. Oh, yes; I know you're obliged to get very close to a person when you tell them you want buttons put upon your shirts.

SUSAN. I think Mrs. Fondleigh is calling me; I'll go and see.

[*Exit* SUSAN.

JOE. I've caught you, have I?

FRED. Confound you! why weren't you two or three minutes later?

JOE. Poor fellow, then—did I interrupt him, then? Ha, ha, ha! if aunty only knew!

FRED. Hush! here she comes.

Enter MRS. FONDLEIGH.

MRS. FONDLEIGH. Good morning, Mr. Dashington. How are you this morning, Fred.? Has that—that muscle you were speaking of tickled you since?

FRED. Oh! no, aunt, it hasn't troubled me at all.

MRS. FONDLEIGH. You must be careful of yourself, Fred., you know you're not strong. Do you think him strong, Mr. Dashington?

JOE. Far from it, Mrs. Fondleigh. (*Aside.*) He's as strong as a young ox.

MRS. FONDLEIGH. And I heard you coughing, too, last night. Hadn't you better see a doctor—shall I send for my family physician?

FRED. Thank you, no, I'm perfectly well

MRS. FONDLEIGH. Be careful of yourself, there's a dear. Take some gruel to-night, and put your feet in warm water; it will do you good.

FRED. Very well, aunt, I will.

JOE (*aside to* FRED.). You're a nice delicate morsel, aint you?

Enter SUSAN.

MRS. FONDLEIGH. Where have you been, Susan?

SUSAN. I've been—I've been——

JOE. Sewing some buttons upon Mr. Ward's shirts—eh, Susan?

[*Laughs.*

FRED. (*aside to* JOE.) Will you be quiet!

SUSAN. Yes, mum. That's what I've been doing.

MRS. FONDLEIGH. There's a good girl; take care of my nephew's wardrobe while he's here.

SUSAN. Very well, mum.

JOE. Oh, Susan pays great attention to Fred., I can answer for that.

FRED. (*aside to* JOE.) Confound you! (*Aloud.*) Let's take a walk.

JOE. With all my heart.

MRS. FONDLEIGH. Oh! don't go out, quite a heavy dew fell last night. You'll catch cold, Fred.

FRED. No I wont, aunt. I'll take care of that.

MRS. FONDLEIGH. Mind you wrap yourself up well.

FRED. Very well, aunt. [*Going.*

MRS. FONDLEIGH. Stay! I must see that you don't catch cold, so I'll wrap you up. Susan!

SUSAN. Yes, mum.

MRS. FONDLEIGH. Go and get Mr. Ward's overcoat, and one or two shawls.

SUSAN. Yes, mum. [*Exit* SUSAN.

FRED. Consider, aunt, it is a beautiful fall morning, and the sun is shining brightly.

JOE.   You'd better wrap up; you know you're delicate.

[Suppresses a laugh.

MRS. FONDLEIGH.   There!   You hear what Mr. Dashington says?

Enter SUSAN, *with an overcoat, a travelling shawl, and a gentleman's scarf upon her arm.*

SUSAN.   Here they are, mum.

FRED.   Surely, you don't want me to wear all those things, this hot day?

MRS. FONDLEIGH.   Yes, dear.   I don't want to have you laid up.

FRED.   But I'm not weak or sickly.

JOE.   It's always the way with delicate people, they never will own it.

MRS. FONDLEIGH.   Come now, let me help you on with this coat.

[She assists him to put coat on.

FRED. *(aside to* JOE, *and shaking his fist at him.)*   This is all your doings.   *(Aloud.)*   That will be sufficient, aunt.

JOE.   You'd better be thoroughly protected, Fred.

FRED. *(aside to* JOE.)   Will you hold your tongue!

MRS. FONDLEIGH.   There now, Mr. Dashington is a medical student, and he must know.   Susan, give me the scarf.   (SUSAN *hands scarf.* Mrs. FONDLEIGH *puts it round* FRED.'s *neck.*)   Now button your coat up.

[He buttons his coat up in an energetic manner.

FRED.   Will that do?   Come along, Joe?

JOE.   Don't you think he'd better have that shawl round his shoulders, Mrs. Fondleigh; then he'd be quite safe?

MRS. FONDLEIGH.   Perhaps that would be the safest; how thoughtful you are, Mr. Dashington!

FRED. *(aside.)*   Precious thoughtful!   *(To* JOE.)   I'll half murder you.   *[*JOE *gives pantomimic expressions of delight.*

MRS. FONDLEIGH.   Now put this shawl round your shoulders, then there will be no danger of your catching cold.   Susan, give me that shawl.

FRED.   But, aunt!

MRS. FONDLEIGH *(placing shawl on his shoulders).*   I'll hear of no denial.   Now I think you're safe.

JOE.   Are you sure you're wrapped up enough, Fred.?

FRED.   Come along.   Good-bye, aunt.   *[Goes off hurriedly.*

MRS. FONDLEIGH.   Good-bye, my dear.   Mr. Dashington, take great care of him, will you?

JOE. That I certainly will. I'll see that he don't go within a yard of a damp spot. Good morning, Mrs. Fondleigh.

[*Exit* JOE, *with difficulty suppressing a laugh.*

MRS. FONDLEIGH. Poor fellow! I'm afraid he's very delicate, Susan.

SUSAN. I hope not, mum.

MRS. FONDLEIGH. He's a good boy; I quite dote upon him.

SUSAN. So do I, mum; at least I mean it's quite natural, mum, that you should.

MRS. FONDLEIGH. Oh! I am afraid he studies much too hard for his constitution, now he is here.

SUSAN. Yes, mum.

MRS. FONDLEIGH. But come, Susan, let us go and see the cook, and tell her to prepare something nice for his dinner, for he's far from strong. [*Exeunt* MRS. FONDLEIGH *and* SUSAN. *Scene closes.*

ANTI(AUNTY)DOTE.

SCENE III.—*The same.*

Enter FRED. *and* JOE.

FRED. It's all your fault.

JOE. How my fault?

FRED. Why, making out that I was so precious delicate.

JOE. I thought it would please the old lady.

FRED. Yes, pleased her so much that she won't advance me any money to go to Newport with.

JOE. That's bad.

FRED. Bad! yes, if you had undergone what I have, you'd say it was bad. Here have I been wrapped up like a mummy, every time I've ventured outside the door.

JOE (*laughing*). Excuse my laughing, but, upon my word, your aunt takes great care of you.

FRED. A precious sight too much for my liking. What's to be done? There's Flora Myrtle at Newport, and I haven't a penny to carry me there.

JOE. Why don't you ask your aunt?

FRED. I have asked her, and she says I'm too sickly to leave her side for a moment. Have you any money?

JOE. Yes.

FRED (*eagerly*). How much?

Joe. One dollar, fifty cents, and a nickel.

Fred. Pshaw!

Joe. Do you want to go to Newport very badly?

Fred. Don't I tell you Flora Myrtle is there?

Joe. Hold on, I have an idea.

Fred. What is it?

Joe. You shall go to Newport, and be happy in the society of Flora Myrtle.

Fred. How?

Joe. Poison yourself.

Fred. Don't be absurd!

Joe. I'm not absurd. I don't mean you to take poison actually, but pretend to.

Fred. Oh, I see.

Joe. Then I'll administer an antidote, and tell your aunt nothing can save you but a trip to Newport.

Fred. Capital. Joe, you're a genius.

Joe. Here comes somebody. Stretch yourself upon the sofa, quick. (Fred. *lies down upon sofa.*) Now then, get up a countenance of intense agony. [*Joe feels* Fred.'s *pulse, who is rolling about as if in great pain.*

Enter Susan.

Susan. If you ple——what's the matter with Mr. Ward?

Joe. Don't be alarmed. It's nothing, I assure you—he has only taken poison.

Susan. Taken poison! Oh my, oh my! what will Mrs. Fondleigh say! I'll go and tell her. Mrs. Fondleigh—Mrs. Fondleigh!
[*Exit, calling.*

Joe. Here's a lark. You do it admirably, old fellow. You're a first-rate suicide.

Fred. Look here, I begin to think it's too bad to alarm my aunt.
[*Raises himself into a sitting posture.*

Joe. Newport, old boy, Newport! Hush! here's somebody coming. (*Pushes* Fred. *down upon the sofa.*) Put on the intense agony expression again.

Enter Mrs. Fondleigh *and* Susan.

Mrs. Fondleigh. Where is he?—where is my darling boy? (*Runs to sofa, and kneels down by* Fred.'s *side, who groans dismally.*) What shall we do, Mr. Dashington? Susan, run for a doctor. [Susan, *going.*

Joe. Stay, Susan. It's no good having this thing made public, I'll administer an antidote.

MRS. FONDLEIGH. Bless you! save my darling nephew. (FRED. *gives another groan.*)   Poor fellow! how he must suffer.

JOE. His suffering must be immense. Susan, go to my bedroom, you'll find a small bottle upon the mantelpiece, bring it to me.

SUSAN. Yes, sir.   [*Exit* SUSAN.

MRS. FONDLEIGH. What kind of poison do you think he has taken?

JOE. Laudanum,—judging from appearances I should certainly say laudanum.   [FRED. *groans again.*

MRS. FONDLEIGH. Dear me, what a time Susan is, and poor Fred. in this pain!

Enter SUSAN.

SUSAN. Here it is, sir.   [*Gives bottle to* JOE.

JOE. Now then, we'll soon have him right.

[JOE *uncorks the bottle,* MRS. FONDLEIGH *and* SUSAN *look on, in breathless anxiety.* JOE *pours the contents of the bottle down* FRED.'S *throat.* FRED *jumps up, aud runs to foot of stage.*

FRED. (*coughing and spluttering.*) Ugh! weugh! pish!

MRS. FONDLEIGH. Thank goodness! it has brought him to.

JOE. How do you feel now, Fred?

FRED. (*aside to* JOE.) What made you give me ink?

JOE (*looks at bottle, then bursts into a laugh.*) (*Aside.*) By Jove! she brought down the ink bottle in mistake for the brandy.

MRS. FONDLEIGH. My dear boy, are you better now?

FRED. Yes, thank you, aunt, but I feel very weak.

MRS. FONDLEIGH. What had he better do for weakness, Mr. Dashington?

JOE. Change of air, I should recommend, and the sooner the better.

MRS. FONDLEIGH. He shall have change of air. Fred., dear, there's some money. (*Gives pocket-book.*) You had better start as soon as possible.

FRED. Oh, aunt, this kindness!

JOE. Keep quiet, old fellow, you mustn't get excited, or I won't answer for the consequences.

SUSAN. Hadn't he better take some more physic?

JOE. Oh, no, he has had enough.

FRED. (*showing pocket-book to audience.*) Yes, the antidote I have already, is quite sufficient.

MRS. FONDLEIGH *and* FRED *centre.* JOE *left.* SUSAN *right.*

CURTAIN.

5

CHARADE V.

FRIENDSHIP.

———◆———

FRIEND—

Characters.

COMMUNICATIVE OLD GENTLEMAN.
DISINTERESTED INDIVIDUAL.
HACKMAN.
MOB.

———◆———

SCENE I.—*Time, past midnight*—COMMUNICATIVE OLD GENTLEMAN, *who has arrived at Railroad Station just too late for the last train, enters angrily, carrying umbrella and carpet-bag*—HACKMAN *following, holding his whip in one hand, and a something that glitters in the moonlight, in the other.*

HACKMAN. Wot's this?

OLD GENTLEMAN. Go away with you; you know well enough what it is.

HACKMAN. I never seed one afore—wot is it?

OLD G. Your fare—a quarter.

HACKMAN. A quarter! (*He examines it closely.*) So this is wot they call a quarter; well, I can't believe as how a real gen'leman ever carried such a thing about with him.

OLD G. Don't be impertinent, or I'll give you in charge of a policeman; though I am from the country, I'm not to be imposed—

HACKMAN (*who begins to exhibit a tendency to quiz*). You're from the country, are you? Well, I shouldn't have thought it; many of you down there?

OLD G. (*quite mollified, begins to give way to his natural communicativeness*). Why, yes; there's a good lot of us. There's my four brothers, myself and wife, and I've seven children.

HACKMAN. Ah! I thought you growed thick in those parts—it must be that as makes the fields so werry green.

OLD G. (*becoming aware of his mistake.*) You're an impertinent fellow—a very vulgar fellow.

HACKMAN. I aint a gen'leman—an' wot's more, I'd scorn to be one—going about giving quarters to poor honest Hackmen.

OLD G. (*giving way to passion, and threatening with umbrella.*) You, you, you bad man!

HACKMAN (*suddenly*). Stop a bit; where do you live when you're at home?

OLD G. At Roosterville.

HACKMAN. Roosterville? Well, you aint a chicken anyhow. (*He advances on* OLD GENTLEMAN, *who still threatens with umbrella.*) I tell you wot, if you don't drop that parachutte, I'll save you the expense of a first-class ticket, and knock you into the middle of Roosterville in about two minutes.

[HACKMAN *dances playfully round* OLD GENTLEMAN, *making wind-mills in the air with his fists.* MOB *suddenly appears.* OLD GENTLE-MAN *lets his carpet bag and umbrella drop, clasps his hands, and gives himself up for lost.*

MOB to HACKMAN. Pay him out, Bill!

OLD G. (*endeavoring to expostulate.*) My friends——

MOB. You aint got none. Go ahead, Bill.

[DISINTERESTED INDIVIDUAL *pushes the mob aside, and advances towards* OLD GENTLEMAN.

THE DISINTERESTED. What's all this? Here, go and fetch a police-man, some of you; stay, I see one coming out of a grocery round the corner. [*Exit* MOB, *quickly followed by grumbling* HACKMAN.

THE DISINTERESTED. The man who wouldn't help an elderly gentle-man in distress, is unworthy the name of——(OLD GENTLEMAN *exhibits signs of distress.*) You feel faint; lean upon me. Sorry I've no salts about me—left my only bottle—splendid thing—cut glass, with a gold stopper, with my uncle this morning. Never mind; lean upon me.

[*He supports* OLD GENTLEMAN.

OLD G. (*recovering*). You're very good—quite a friend in need—and a friend——

THE DISINTERESTED. In need, is a friend indeed. You may well say that: the article gets scarcer every day.

OLD G. I shall be very happy to see you at Roosterville; we're thirteen in family: my wife and myself, my four brothers, and six chil-dren Yes, there's Jack, and Tom, and Harry, and——

THE DISINTERESTED. Charming family, I've no doubt. All combining the good sense of Papa, with the beauty of Mamma. What a thing sympathy is. I feel as if I'd known you for years—lost the train—going back to your hotel, I suppose?

OLD G. Yes, I must find another carriage—and——

THE DISINTERESTED. Not far to go; there's a carriage stand round the corner. (*He picks up umbrella and carpet-bag.*) I'll carry these.

OLD G. Oh, really, I can't think——

THE DISINTERESTED. Of course, you can't. I'm young and active. and the young man who wouldn't seek to lighten the burden of old age——(THE DISINTERESTED *looking off.*) Is that a carriage? I think it is. Stop here a moment, and I'll catch it for you. (*He is running off, then stops and turns to* OLD GENTLEMAN.) Now, mind you don't move till I come back; for without a friend, one's never safe in New York.

OLD G. Certainly not; only be quick——(*Exit* THE DISINTERESTED, *with umbrella and carpet-bag.*) Good young man that!—it's lucky I met with him, or I should certainly have got into some difficulty—pity I missed the train though. My watch must be wrong; goes too slow, decidedly. (*Bell strikes the hour.*) Ah, now to test it. (*He feels for his watch, then utters a cry of alarm.*) It's gone!!! Oh, dear me, it can't be—yes, it must be—it is that vile young man, when he was supporting me; and he's got my umbrella and carpet-bag. Here, Police! Police! Police! (*He is running off.*) Oh, dear! oh dear! here's a position for an elderly gentleman, without a friend, at one o'clock in the morning.   [*He runs off.*

———

—SHIP.

Characters.

FARMER PRETZEL.
DAME PRETZEL.
MARY.
TOM TARPAULIN.
CONSTABLES.

SCENE II.—PRETZEL'S *Cottage.*

Family discovered in great grief. Two CONSTABLES *taking down inventory of the furniture.*

DAME PRETZEL (*crying*). Oh! Mary! Mary! how could you go and refuse the young lawyer?   [*She sobs.*

MARY (*crying*). Be—be—be—cause I thought Tom's ship was sure to come home; and—and—and—Tom's worth all the young lawyers in the wor—wor—world. [*She sobs.*

FARMER PRETZEL. Donner-vetter! dis 'll preak mein heart. Der crops is so pad, and der landlords so hard, dat we shall all pe zold out, pody and preeches! [*He sobs.*

DAME PRETZEL (*looking up, and justifiably shocked*). All 'as their misfortunes, and we 'as ours; but that's no occasion why you, Dan'el, should use improper expressions.

MARY. Oh! if Tom's ship would only arrive, he'd soon put everything right again,—sailors always do, you know, mother.

DAME PRETZEL. Ships is uncertain, and so is sailors,—they changes with every wind. For my part, I leans to the young lawyer.

FARMER PRETZEL (*rising from his chair, and appealing, in the true stage fashion, to the ceiling*). I doesn't care! somedings moost turn up, somehow, for der same sun as shines on der palace vor der rich, shines on der cottage vor der poor!

[*He sits down again, pours himself out a glass of beer, takes a pipe, and is evidently comfortable under difficulties. DAME PRETZEL gives herself up to grief, and MARY goes to the window.*

FIRST CONSTABLE. No beer, and no 'bacca! and they talk of farmers' hospitality!

SECOND CONSTABLE. Not even to offer us a chair! No wonder we feels no compunction in taking the lot.

FARMER PRETZEL (*starting to his feet, and appealing, as usual, to the ceiling*). Der hard-hearted lawyer as asks a honest farmer vor der rent is nicht wort *de name von man!* (*He resumes his seat, and continues placidly smoking.*) I von't make no effort. I never does. Somedings moost turn up!

MARY (*who has been looking out of window*). Mother! father! the ship! the ship! the ship!

HER PARENTS (*both springing to their feet*). Where?

MARY (*pointing*). There! there! See, they are crowding all sail! Tom knows our danger, be assured; and has persuaded the captain to hasten his return. (*She comes from the window, and also appeals to the ceiling.*) For to rescue a female in distress, what true Yankee captain would refuse the prayer of even the humblest coxswain?

[*The CONSTABLES begin to move about the furniture, when a shout is heard from without, and TOM TARPAULIN, the "gallant Yankee tar," rushes into the room. He kisses MARY, then her mother, and shakes the old man by both hands. MARY gives way to her joy, but the FARMER and his DAME eye TOM doubtfully.*

MARY. Oh! I'm so glad to see you, my dear Tom; and so are father and mother.

FATHER *and* MOTHER (*still doubtfully*). Humph!

TOM (*who is continually hitching up his trousers to prove his nauticality*). Yes, here I am, come to my moorings at last—with twenty-seven wounds—got in twenty-seven engagements!

FARMER *and his* WIFE. Humph!

TOM. But I've got lots of prize-money—enough to make all our fortunes, and to buy a cottage and garden for my dear Molly.

[TOM *is advancing towards* MARY, *when he is rushed upon and almost suffocated by the affectionate embraces of the* FARMER *and his* WIFE.

DAME (*releasing him*). I always said Tom would come home rich.

FARMER (*releasing him*). I knew somedings vould turn up!

[TOM *produces from innumerable pockets innumerable bags of money, which he throws about with reckless profusion. The* CONSTABLES *come forward, and present a paper to* TOM. *He reads it, and tears it to atoms.*

TOM. Shiver my timbers! avast heaving! strike my topsails! etc., etc., etc. What do you mean? What! ask a pretty woman for her rent, and a Yankee sailor to the fore? There! you land-sharks! (*He gives each a bag of money. Then again embraces* MARY.) And now for love and jollity. Stay, I had forgot.

[*He walks over to* CONSTABLES, *kicks first one, then the other They both bow humbly and go out.*

TOM. So that matter settled, we'll first have a dance, and then drink srecess to the Yankee tar, and the ship that brought him over.

[*The old couple and* MARY *draw aside, while* TOM, *first placing his hat on the extreme back of his head, folds his arms, and proceeds to go through the steps of a hornpipe; and the performance concluded, takes* MARY'S *hand, and bows to the applauding and delighted audience.*

———

FRIENDSHIP.

Characters.

HORATIO BROWN.
WALTER JONES.
JACK ROBINSON.
EMILY.

SCENE III:—*A Drawing-Room.* HORATIO BROWN *and* WALTER JONES *discovered seated, both in a despondent condition.*

HORATIO (*looking up*). Have you ever been in love, Walter?

[*He sighs*

WALTER (*looking up*). Have I? Ain't I in love now? [*He sighs.*

HORATIO Curious coincidence—that we should both be in love at the same time.

WALTER (*rising*). It is curious; friend of my childhood, confide in me—and I——

HORATIO (*rising*). Will do the same.

WALTER (*solemnly*). I will.

[*They embrace, then draw chairs to the front, place them close together, and sit down.*

HORATIO. It was a balmy day in June, in the year eighteen hun-dred and fifty-six, when two travellers might be seen slowly wending their way.

WALTER. You interest me.

HORATIO. Towards High Bridge. One was a handsome youth, whose graceful figure was set off to advantage by a light brown paletôt, and his chestnut hair fell in clustering curls over his high and intellectual forehead.

WALTER. Go on.

HORATIO. I will—his companion was a beautiful girl, who had scarcely numbered seventeen summers; yet upon her brow there sat an air of pensive melancholy.

WALTER (*with a slight shrug of impatience*). She was——

HORATIO (*clasping his hands and looking upwards*). My heart's adored.

WALTER. And her companion?

HORATIO. Myself.

WALTER. You astonish me. (*He sighs.*) My love was also beauti-ful; and in the year you mention, had also scarcely numbered seven-teen summers.

HORATIO. Touching coincidence.

WALTER. Affecting sympathy. [*They embrace.*

HORATIO (*resumes his seat and story*). That day I made her the offer of my hand and heart, which she——

WALTER. Accepted.

HORATIO (*wildly*). Rejected!

WALTER. My friend, be comforted. Mine were rejected too. (WAL-TER *commences his story, while* HORATIO *takes out handkerchief and weeps copiously.*) It was a wild and boisterous night in March——

HORATIO. Proceed, my friend, your story is full of interest.

WALTER. When a young girl might have been observed, seated quietly by the parlor fire.

HORATIO (*starts*). Such was Emily's constant habit; especially on such nights——

WALTER. Emily!—*her* name was Emily !!!

[*The friends gaze at each other; then suddenly move their chairs some feet apart.*

HORATIO. Her other name ?

WALTER. Nay, answer me !

BOTH (*together*). Smith!

[*They start to their feet, and advance threateningly towards each other.*

HORATIO (*laughs sardonically*). *You* to love her—insolent presumption!

WALTER (*laughs sardonically*). *You* hope to win—contemptible assurance !   [*They advance close to each other.*

HORATIO (*his eyes travelling slowly down* WALTER, *commencing at his neck-tie and finishing at his boots*). Fellow !

WALTER (*doing the same by* HORATIO, *only commencing at boots and finishing at neck-tie*). Person !

HORATIO. Resign her !

WALTER. I shan't !

BOTH (*double their fists*). Emily Smith is——

EMILY (*suddenly entering*). Here !

[*Gentlemen fall back in much confusion.*

EMILY. How do you do, cousins ? What, quarrelling, and you such friends !

BOTH (*contemptuously regarding each other*). Friends !

EMILY. Why not? What has interrupted your friendship ?

BOTH. You.

EMILY. I ! Why, it seemed to me that I interrupted your quarrelling.

HORATIO. I love you !

WALTER (*with a contemptuous laugh*). *He* loves you !

HORATIO. We love you !

EMILY (*laughing*). What are you about, declining the verb to love ? Well, I must decline it too, as far as you both are concerned.

BOTH (*one at each side of her*). Oh, say not so; decide between us !

EMILY (*still laughing*). But I can't.

BOTH. Why not ?

EMILY. I'm married !

[HORATIO *and* WALTER *each fall back into a chair, making affecting tableau.*

EMILY (*running from one to the other fanning them with her pocket handkerchief*). How foolish you are! Oh dear! oh dear! I'll call my husband

BOTH THE GENTLEMEN (*springing to their feet*). No, don't!

EMILY. He's here.

Enter third gentleman. HORATIO *and* WALTER *look at him and start.*

BOTH. Jack Robinson!

ROBINSON. Yes, my dear fellows, I'm the happy man. Sorry to have supplanted you; but when a lady's in the case, you know——

[*The two friends look sheepishly at each other.* EMILY *advances between them, and addresses the audience.*

EMILY. Ladies and gentlemen,—I am sorry that affairs, even for a moment, should have assumed so threatening an aspect; but am now happy to announce, with the concurrence of my two allies (*she indicates* HORATIO *and* WALTER), that friendly relations between the rival lovers are again resumed.

[*She joins their hands.* ROBINSON *waves his hat. And with this pleasing tableau of general reconciliation the Charade concludes.*

CHARADE VI.

BANDAGE.

Characters.

ANTEEK YELLOWLEAF, *from California.*

LILLIE
OLIVIA } *his Nieces.*

MASTERS BROWN, JONES, *and* ROBINSON, *their Friends.*

BAND—

SCENE I.—*An elegant Interior. Music Books and Instruments lying about.*

Enter LILLIE *and* OLIVIA.

LILLIE. Well, now, dearest I *am* delighted that you so cordially fall into my views. Oh! it will be charming! Dear uncle, who, as you know, arrived this morning from California, where he has spent, I'm told, more than ten years, but who was born upon this very spot, is, no doubt, passionately attached to old customs. Among these, that one of celebrating New-Year's Eve with "music," will probably be the most cherished in his memory, and delightful to his feelings.

OLIVIA. Oh! beyond question, my love; and your plan of bringing in the assistance of our friends and *beaux*, Masters Brown, Jones, and Robinson, as the musicians, is, I declare, a perfect inspiration. But you are so clever!

LILLIE. Well, I don't know that I can justly claim all the merit of the idea. You know what a perfect Jullien at concert-conducting Brown is, and how fond of getting up musical parties. It was this talent of his which suggested the notion to my mind. However, it is all settled. Master Jones is to take the drum and pan-pipes, Robinson will be trombone, and Lyte Brown will lead off with his violin.

OLIVIA. And our parts will be the easy ones of listeners in our snug warm room, while our gentlemen friends are scraping and thumping away in the cold.

LILLIE. Just so. But hark! I hear them coming. We meet in this room to make our final arrangements. (*Goes to side.*) Yes, here they are.

Enter BROWN, JONES, *and* ROBINSON, *carrying Music Books and Instruments.* They are arrayed in greatcoats, and muffled up to represent street performers. After the exchange of bows and the usual compliments,*

BROWN. Well, here we are; don't you think, ladies, that we look our parts well?

OLIVIA. To admiration. But then, you know, a musician is not usually tested by his looks.

BROWN. Oh! it's all right! we have had a jolly practice. Haven't we, boys? down yonder in an out-house, adjoining the dog kennels.

JONES. And the best of it was that, although we went twice through all our pieces, we were never discovered.

OLIVIA (*archly*). No, folks mistook your performances for the howling of the dogs.

ROBINSON. Oh! But, Miss Olivia, you are such a quiz. Come—come, time flies, let us see what has to be done?

---

* Where the real things are impracticable, it will do to substitute imitations; the performers singing in such a way as to suggest the instruments required to be used.

BROWN. Yes. Well, I think that as we have had so many previous consultations, nothing remains to be settled. After supper, we repair to our posts. You, Miss Lillie, will give the signal when all is ready, by placing your candle in the window. Is there anything else, lads?

JONES *and* ROBINSON (*together*). Nothing, I think.

OLIVIA. Except that as it is a seasonably cold night, I shall go and warm myself by roasting a few chestnuts.

OMNES. Then, mind you don't burn your fingers! Ha! ha! ha!

[*Bows and exeunt. Scene closes.*

—AGE.

SCENE II.—*An Ante-room, with a door at the back to open and shut. Dark.*

Enter as from Bedroom, ANTEEK YELLOWLEAF. *He is attired in a long dressing-gown and nightcap, and has a rather decrepid and worn-out look. He carries a candlestick, or night-lamp, in his hand.*

ANTEEK. Ugh! Ugh! (*coughing.*) Oh, dear! Oh, dear! Ugh! ugh! I'm afraid I'm not getting younger. I *can't* sleep. These relatives of mine are, no doubt, very good people, and mean well to me, but, ugh, ugh, they have put me into a room that is haunted; not with one ghost, but with a dozen. I *can't* sleep, do what I will. There's a noise in the chimney. There's another behind the wainscot. The casement keeps up a continual rattle; and the bedstead creaks like that pair of mining boots which I threw last year at the head of George Washington Boggs, Senator from Pineville, up in the mountains. Even the lamp spits and splutters as if it was a frying-pan full of dripping. And of all things in the world, I like quietness—especially of a night. I don't like to hurt the feelings of these relatives of mine, who, I've no doubt, are very good people, and mean well, or I'd ask them to let me have another room. Well, I must again try to get to sleep, for I'm as tired as a dog—as the saying is. Ugh! ugh!

[*He retires into the room while speaking.* LILLIE *and* OLIVIA *peep on from opposite corners, and then stealthily approach each other. They speak in whispers.*

LILLIE 'Tis now quite midnight, and I think our friends may approach and commence their serenade. What does your watch say?

OLIVIA (*looking at her watch*). A quarter past twelve. Yes, do, for goodness' sake, let them begin.

LILLIE. By all means. I will go and give the signal. No doubt, our good uncle is in a sound sleep. Let *us* be careful not to wake him.

[Exeunt.

ANTEEK YELLOWLEAF (*putting his head out of the door, and projecting the rays of his lamp in every direction*). I feel certain I heard something. What *could* it be? If I was not thoroughly conscious that these relatives of mine were good people, and meant well to me, I should be apt to think they were plotting to destroy my night's rest. (*He comes out.*) Ugh! ugh! ugh! I can't get to sleep. I've tried—and tried—and tried again. But, no. There I am staring, wide awake, like a wax figure. But it won't do. If I lose my night's rest I shall be ill to-morrow, and that will never do, with the amount of business on hand that I have. Here goes, then, to make another attempt. I do hope I shall be more fortunate this time.   [*Exit into bedroom.*

    [*The music is heard, at first faintly, and then louder.* ANTEEK *again appears at his door in a terrible passion. The music should now play loud enough to render his voice unintelligible.*

ANTEEK. Now, this is too bad! Some rascally musicians! What can I do to get rid of them? I'd bribe them, only I fear that that would make them play louder at the next house. Ugh! ugh! Oh, this is little short of felony. Oh, a lucky thought! (*He retires into the room, and returns with water-jug.*) I'll fling this at the head of the leader. I'll be bound that will quiet him.

    [*Goes out at side. Crash heard. Music ceases.* ANTEEK *returns, looking pale and angry.*

ANTEEK. I hope I didn't hurt him, but that's his business. To be disturbed in such a way; and at my time of life! too bad! too bad! ugh! ugh!   [*Exit into chamber. Scene closes.*

BANDAGE.

SCENE III.—*A Breakfast Parlor.* LILLIE *and* OLIVIA *seated. A vacant arm-chair near the table.*

LILLIE. Well, dearest, and what did you think of our friends' performances last night?

OLIVIA. Oh, delightful in the extreme! But, do you know, love, I am at a loss to account for one circumstance!

LILLIE. Indeed? What is it?

OL.VIA. Why, either the tunes were so sleep-inducing that I went off into a slumber before they had played five minutes, or the music came to a sudden stop.

LILLIE. How very surprising, to be sure! My own impressions exactly. But we shall see our gentlemen amateurs this morning, and receive their explanation of the circumstance. (*Bell heard.*) Ah! there is dear uncle's bell. He will be down in a moment. Let us be silent as to the serenade, until we have observed what kind of impression it may have made upon him.

Enter ANTEEK YELLOWLEAF, leaning feebly upon a walking-cane. LILLIE and OLIVIA advance eagerly to meet him, and conduct him to his arm-chair.

LILLIE. Dearest uncle, we hope that you slept well, and that your night's rest——

ANTEEK (*interrupting her*). Not a word, my dear niece, of last night —not a word. Oh dear, ugh! ugh! I didn't sleep a wink——(LILLIE *and* OLIVIA *exchange glances*). At first, from fidgettiness—and then, oh, dear! from remorse——

OLIVIA. Remorse! uncle!

ANTEEK. Of conscience! Yes, I fear that I have killed somebody, I fear—ugh! ugh!—my poor nieces—that your old uncle is a homicide!

LILLIE *and* OLIVIA (*together*). How very dreadful!

Enter a Servant, who announces MASTERS BROWN, JONES, and ROBINSON, in their usual attire. After which, enter BROWN, with a cloth tied over his head, supported by JONES and ROBINSON.

ANTEEK (*aside*). Who are these? In stature, they remind me of the musicians of last night. Pray, heaven, it may be so.

BROWN. We have intruded upon you, sir, and upon these ladies, in order to present the earliest possible apology for the disturbance— which our well-meant—but, as it would appear, ill-timed music caused——

ANTEEK (*rising*). Then you *are* the musicians of last night?

BROWN, JONES, *and* ROBINSON. We are.

ANTEEK. And I did not kill anybody?

BROWN. No, sir, only bruised in a slight degree—your very humble servant.

ANTEEK. Good! Then, 'tis I who owe you an apology; for I perceive that your excellent intention was to honor me. I am sorry that the natural irritability of a man at my time of life led me to appreciate your performances so unworthily. If you will forgive me (*they approach, and shake hands*)—we will be friends. At any rate—if I dare invite you to breakfast in a house not my own, our fair hostesses will excuse the freedom; and if our neighbors here will excuse us also, all may yet be well. While they are considering their verdict, we will sing them an old air, which will awaken memories of the past, and give to the old friends who are present a watchword for the future:—

AULD LANG SYNE.

Should auld acquaintance be forgot,
　An' never brought to min' ?
Should auld acquaintance be forgot,
　An' days o' lang syne?

CHORUS.

For auld lang syne, my dear,
　For auld lang syne;
We'll tak' a cup o' kindness yet,
　For auld lang syne.

We twa hae run about the braes,
　An' pou'd the gowans fine ;
But we've wander'd mony a weary foot,
　Sin' auld lang syne.

　　　　　　　　　　For auld lang syne, &c.

And here's a hand, my trusty fiere,
　And gie's a hand o' thine ;
And we'll tak' a right gude willie-waught
　For auld lang syne.

　　　　　　　　　　For auld, &c.

And surely ye'll be your pint stowp,
　And surely I'll be mine ;
And we'll tak' a cup o' kindness yet,
　For auld lang syne.

　　　　　　　　　　For auld, &c.

Acting Charades.

OR

Drawing-Room Pantomimes.

SWEEPSTAKES.

A CHARADE IN THREE ACTS.

Act I.

SWEEP—

Dramatis Personæ.

LITTLE SWEEP.
OLD LADY.
SERVANT.
OLD SWEEP.

SCENE I.—*Interior of Servants' Kitchen, with the screen arranged as the fire-place.*

Little Sweep, crying (outside), "Sweep, sweep, sweep!"

Enter SERVANT hastily, rubbing her eyes and yawning. She rushes to the door and beckons, when

Enter LITTLE SWEEP and OLD SWEEP, dressed in black, and carrying brooms, and dirty clothes soot bag. Their faces are also covered with soot.*

The Servant desires them to sweep the chimney, and gives the Old Man money. Little Boy draws a nightcap over his eyes, and, taking his broom, plunges into the fire-place, his master holding a cloth before the opening. The entrance is too small and he cannot ascend. Old Sweep is enraged, and lights a fire with some straw he has brought with him, to make the boy ascend.

Exeunt Old Sweep and Servant, to see whether Little Sweep has got to the top of the chimney.

SCENE II.—*The Bed-room of* OLD LADY. *Against the wall a painting of a Young Woman. In the window curtains the* OLD LADY *discovered sleeping. She snores.*

Enter LITTLE SWEEP from down the chimney. He lifts the cap from his eyes, and wipes them several times to remove the soot. On looking about him he is astonished to find that he has mistaken his chimney, and got into the wrong room. He is alarmed, and wrings nis hands in terror. He gazes wildly about the room, and by his innocent actions intimates that he will be taken up and perhaps hung.

[*He prays.*

He feels much calmer and admires the apartment. His eye rests on the picture against the wall, and he is visibly moved. He, in affecting pantomime, confesses that he has never known a mother's love, and weeps.†

Suddenly he hears the snoring of Old Lady. He is alarmed, and runs about wildly. Then, advancing on tip-toe to the bed, he withdraws the curtain and gazes on Old Lady. He intimates that there is a striking resemblance between the picture and the Old Lady, and betrays a strong wish to embrace her. He gently lifts her hand and kisses it. The Old Lady wakes.

On seeing Little Sweep she screams, and hastily draws to the curtains. Little Sweep kneels at the bed-side imploring forgiveness. He relates his mistake about the chimneys, and stating that he has never known a mother's love, appeals to her feelings.

---

* A black silk mask must be put in requisition; unless, indeed, some enthusiastic gentleman will consent to be burnt-corked.

† None but a first-rate *artiste* should undertake the part of the little sweep. The whole piece depends upon the audience being convinced that he has never known a mother's love.

Old Lady is about to drive him away, when her eyes rest upon a locket hanging to his neck. She hastily examines it, presses her forehead, seizes the boy's head, and looks intently into his affrighted eyes. Then, clasping him to her bosom, she declares herself to be his mother.*

Enter SERVANT and OLD SWEEP in search of Young Sweep. The Old Lady horrified at being discovered in *deshabille*, rushes behind the bed-curtains. Thrusting out her head and arm, points to Little Sweep as her son and heir.

GRAND TABLEAU.

Act II.

--STAKES (Steaks).

Dramatis Personæ.

STRUGGLING CLERK.
BUTCHER.
LANDLORD.
WAITERESS.

SCENE--- *Outside of* BUTCHER'S *Shop. On one side a table covered with plates of imitation chops and steaks.*

Enter BUTCHER with housemaid's blue apron on, and the knife-steel hanging from his waist. In his hand he carries the carving-knife, which he sharpens, at the same time inviting passers-by to patronize him.

Enter STRUGGLING CLERK with blue bag in his hand. His eye rests on the meat, and he stands for a moment gazing at it. Butcher advances to him and tempts him with his low prices. Clerk yields, and, approaching the table, examines the different lots. He purchases a steak, which he wraps up in his pocket-handkerchief, and gives money to the Butcher.

Exeunt Butcher and Clerk dancing.

* The interest and pathos may be greatly increased by the mother searching for the strawberry her son was marked with on the left arm. At the embrace, a splendid effect —always sure of success—can be had, by the sweep blacking his mother's gown. This is done by cunningly placing a black silk handkerchief on the white skirt during the embrace.

SCENE II.—*Coffee-room at a Tavern, with table and chairs in centre.*

Enter STRUGGLING CLERK, who rings the bell, when

Enter LANDLORD. Clerk tells him that he wishes for something to drink, and, taking the steak from his bag, desires him to cook it, by making a hissing noise, and going through the pantomimic process of frying.

The Landlord is delighted, and exit with steak.

Enter WAITERESS with a jug and a glass. Clerk is smitten with her charms, and invites her to drink. She indignantly refuses, motioning him back with her hand. He pleads, but in vain.

Exit Waiteress, haughtily.

Enter LANDLORD with tray. He places it before Clerk, who devours the steak, raising his eyes to the ceiling, and pressing his bosom to tell of its tenderness.

The Landlord is affected to tears, and, by shaking his head, expresses his fears that poor Clerk does not often have a steak for dinner.

When he has eaten enough, Clerk places the remainder of the steak in an old newspaper. He tells Landlord by gestures that it is for his wife and children, who are very dear to him.

He pays Landlord, who weeps.

Exeunt Clerk and Landlord.

Act III.

SWEEPSTAKES.

Dramatis Personæ.

> VILLAGERS.
> MERCHANTS.
> VILLAGE CRIER.
> BOYS.
> DONKEYS.
> POOR MOTHER.

SCENE.—*A country fair. Booths and tables laden with merchandi e in all directions.*

Enter MERCHANTS, who shake hands with each other, and proceed to their tables and arrange their wares. Other Merchants stand with trays of cakes and boxes of cigars, awaiting their visitors.

Enter VILLAGERS dressed in their best clothes, laughing and smiling. They advance to the different tables and purchase goods. Some buy silks and others necklaces. The Gentlemen deal largely with the Cigar Merchants, obtaining a cheroot and a light for the counter penny they hand him.

The Merchant with cakes is next visited, and his whole tray soon emptied. The pickle jar full of marbles for brandy balls is soon discussed.

Exeunt the different Dealers with empty trays, highly satisfied.

Enter VILLAGE CRIER. He informs the Villagers, by riding an imaginary horse, that there is to be a race for a Sweepstakes, and he beseeches them to give him money. They are delighted with the idea, and hand him some.

He bids them arrange themselves into a line, so as to form a racecourse, and then exit CRIER, ringing a bell violently.

Enter TWO BOYS, adorned with ribbons, and mounted on DONKEYS,* which they urge on with sticks. The Villagers are delighted, and laugh and stamp on the floor. The Village Crier stands at the end of the room, holding in his hand the sweepstakes. The excitement of the race grows immense; the spectators waving their handkerchiefs and cheering on the boys, who cannot make their Donkeys move.

Enter POOR MOTHER with a long pole, having a bunch of cabbages tied to the end of it. She hands it to her Son, and prays. The Boy holds it before his Donkey, who immediately gallops after it. The People cheer, and the CRIER hands the purse to the fortunate winner.

The Boy advances to his Poor Mother, and kneeling, presents the money to her with it.

CRIER and Villagers weep.

---

* Gentlemen may object to appear in this character, but they must not be listened to. Any one who has been newly married will perform the part to the life.

PIGTAIL.

A CHARADE IN THREE ACTS.

Act I.

PIG—

Dramatis Personæ.

Show-Keeper.
His Wife.
The Learned Pig Toby.
Spectators.

SCENE—*The interior of as how, with chairs placed round for* Spectaters.
Against the door a bookcase or desk for an organ.

Enter Show-Keeper and His Wife dressed in a man's greatcoat.
She seats herself at the organ, and commences playing.

[*Music on the piano.*

The Showman, bending forward, puts his hand to one side of his
mouth, as if shouting. He beckons the people outside to walk up,
holding forth a placard, written "Only a Penny." At last he takes up
a trumpet of roll of music, and blows through it.

Enter Spectators, who pay their money at the organ, and take their
places. The organ still continues playing, and the Showman blows
his trumpet louder and louder, until the Spectators grow impatient,
and advance to His Wife, holding out their hands to receive their
money back. Showman pacifies them, and having shut the door, leads
from the window-curtains the Pig Toby. It has a blue ribbon round
its neck, and its skin of white mackintosh is beautifully clean. The
Showman points to the Spectators, who are clapping their hands, and
the Pig grunts three times. His Wife, taking from her greatcoat
pocket a pack of cards, hands them to the audience, who choose a
card. The pack is then spread in a circle upon the ground, and the

Showman, pointing to it, stamps his foot to command the Pig to point out the chosen card.

The Pig, grunting, advances to the circle. [*Soft music on the organ.*

At last Toby stands before a card and grunts. The Spectators shake their heads to intimate that Toby has made a mistake.

The Showman beats Toby with a stick. [*Great squeaking.*

The animal begins again, and at last stands before the right card. The Spectators clap their hands for joy.

The Showman then dances, and invites Toby to do so also. The Pig stands on its hind feet, and endeavors to perform a jig. The Audience is delighted, and laughs merrily.

At last the Pig, taking a plate in its mouth, goes round to the Audience to collect halfpence, when

Exit the Audience rapidly, followed by Toby, and the Showman and His Wife sneering.

Act II.

—TAIL.

Dramatis Personæ.

BOLD PERFORMER.
OTHER ACTORS.
AUDIENCE.
RAGING LION.

SCENE—*Interior of a Theatre. Candles are placed for lamps before the stage, and seats are arranged for the* AUDIENCE *and Orchestra.*

Enter THE AUDIENCE running over the seats, and scrambling and pushing for the best places. Several screams are heard, and a fight takes place at the door. At last all are seated, when

Enter MUSICIANS, who gaze for some time upon the Audience, until whistling and clapping of hands begin, when they commence tuning their instruments. A bell is heard, and the music strikes up, the Audience all seating themselves. (*Music.*)

The curtain rises.

The scene is supposed to represent a desert in Arabia. Against the wall the window-curtains are drawn close, and the roaring of a lion is heard behind them.

The Audience all point to the curtains, to tell that they know where
the Lion is.

Enter Actors, dressed as a Prince and his followers, as richly as
possible.

Enter Bold Performer in bonds of jack-chain. He wears a large
cloak, and walks proudly, sneering at the Prince. He is ordered to
bow the knee, but haughtily refuses. The Prince points to the curtains.   [*Terrific roarings again heard.*

Bold Performer starts, but recovering himself, sneers at Prince. The
Prince stamps his foot and the curtains are drawn open, and discover
the Lion roaring. He has a fine mane of drawing-room mat, and a
long tail of Bell-rope, the tassel dragging on the ground.

The Audience applaud the Lion, who is confined in his cell by the
rails of a folding clothes-screen.

The Prince gives the signal, and the Lion is let loose. It rushes to
the Bold Performer and crouches before him. The Audience applaud.
He puts his foot on the beast, and opens his hands to the Spectators,
who cheer. Then holding out one arm, he makes the Lion jump over
it. Next he makes the brute lie down, and he uses him in a graceful
attitude for his pillow.

Renewed applause.

Last of all, having closely examined the Lion's tail, he opens its jaws,
and puts his head into its mouth. Pointing to the tail, he draws a
placard, written " Does it Wag?" and shows it to the Prince.

[*The Lion lashes its tail.*

The Prince with a look of horror nods his head, but in an instant
the Bold Performer's head is bitten off.* Bold Performer falls down.
The Audience scream, faint, rush to the door, when *exeunt.*

The Lion is secured and led off by Actors, and the Bold Performer,
supported by the Prince, staggers off.   [*Exeunt omnes.*

* It is for this point that the Bold Performer wears a s oak. He must cleverly slip it
over his head, on which is placed a piece of red silk.

Act III.

PIGTAIL.

Dramatis Personae.

Jolly Tars.
Their Sweethearts.
Captain.
Barbers.
Marines.

SCENE—*The front drawing-room quarterdeck of one of U. S. ships
The bolster on the Canterbury for a cannon.*

Enter Jolly Tars, with long pigtails of boas and twisted handkerchiefs. They are all putting quids of tobacco in their mouths. They
shake hands, and dance hornpipes.

Enter Captain, wearing a paper cocked-hat, and hair-brush epaulets.
His sword hangs by his side. Drawing it, he orders silence by stamp-
ing. Taking from his pocket a placard, he holds it up before the audience, and on it is written, "Pigtails must be cut off directly!"

The men fall back in horror; they then advance with clasped hands
imploringly to the Captain, who refuses, until at last he is overcome by
the touching spectacle, and weeps, dashing away the tear with manly
action. He stamps, when

Enter Marines, with brooms for muskets. They stand in a file, and
having gone through their exercises, drive back the Sailors.

Enter Barbers with their coats off, and aprons on. They carry
combs and scissors. The men collect in a group and grumble. The
Captain orders a Sailor to advance, and he refuses, folding his arms.
Captain waves his sword. The Marines present brooms, and are about
to charge, when

Enter Sweethearts, hurriedly. They stand with open arms before
the Jolly Tars, determined to protect their lovers with their lives.

Captain and Marines weep. Sweethearts, by their loving actions,
persuade the Jolly Tars to submit, imploring them with clasped hands
to go to the chair. Two advance unwillingly. The Barbers cut off
their pigtails. Their weeping Sweethearts pick them up, and kissing
them fondly place them in their bosoms. The whole of the men undergo the operation, each one on leaving the chair shaking his fist at

the trembling Barber. But the Marines protect the Haircutters, and with their brooms drive back the Sailors.

Exeunt Sailors, leaning on their Sweethearts' arms. The Marines once more go through their gun-exercises, when *exeunt*, led off by Captain, and followed by Barbers.

NEIGHBOR.

A CHARADE IN THREE ACTS.

Act I.

NEIGH—

Dramatis Personae.

DARIUS.
SIX CONSPIRATORS.
THEIR CHARGERS.
GROOM TO DARIUS.
HIS HORSE.
PERSIAN GENERALS AND SOLDIERS.
PERSIAN CITIZENS.

SCENE—*An imaginary plain of vast extent. Lamps are lowered, to denote that the sun has not yet risen.*

Enter DARIUS on foot, accompanied by his GROOM leading his HORSE. Darius is magnificently dressed in robes of scarlet drugget, and wears a turban of Indian shawl. He, by his actions, informs his Groom, who kneels before him, that he must, together with the Horse he leads, conceal himself behind the drawing-room curtains. The Groom salaams in answer, and taking the purse offered him by Darius, hides himself with his Horse.

Exit Darius.

Re-enter Darius on his Charger, surrounded by SIX CONSPIRATORS, all magnificently dressed and mounted. They shake hands, and then drawing themselves up in a line, await the rising of the sun.

The lamps are turned on, to intimate that the sun has just risen. Immediately the Groom, drawing aside the curtains, discovers himself and his Horse. The Charger of Darius, on perceiving his companion, neighs to it in recognition.

The Six Conspirators descend from THEIR CHARGERS, and stand in a row before Darius, who remains mounted. They bend the knee as a sign of their obedience. Darius courteously begs of them to rise, and they remount their Chargers.

Enter PERSIAN GENERALS in full armor of dish-cover breastplates, and turbans of rich shawls and scarfs. They lead on their Troops, carrying spears of brooms, and banners of fire-screens. The Generals bend the knee to Darius, who, by his affable pantomime, wins their love. The Generals, drawing their swords of walking-sticks, deliver them to the king, who immediately returns them. A crown of jelly mould is placed on the head of Darius. The Troops pretend to shout with loyalty, and wave their spears and banners high in the air.

Enter CITIZENS, appearing to shout, and dancing for joy. Darius addresses them in a few energetic gestures, frequently striking his breast. The citizens are melted to tears. They all kneel. The king distributes among them pieces of card counter money.

Exeunt procession to grand march on the piano.

Act II.

—BOR (Boar).

Dramatis Personae.

A COUNT (*in love with a Lady*).	GERMAN HUNTSMEN.
A LADY (*in love with a Count*).	SERVANTS.
HORSES. DOGS.	BOAR.

SCENE *represents, if possible, a wood in Germany. Huge trees are supposed to be visible on all sides. Hunting chorus on the pianoforte, at first at a great distance, and gradually increasing, when*

Enter a COUNT on horseback, and surrounded by GERMAN HUNTSMEN also mounted, and SERVANTS holding back the impatient DOGS. **The**

Count has his trouser stucked up, to show his boots, and wears a belt round his frock coat, and a feather in his hat. He is armed with a long spear of broom or curtain-rod, and has several knives in belt. The Huntsmen also wear imitation romantic German costumes, and carry long spears. A flask is passed round, from which they all drink. A horn is heard without.

Enter a LADY on foot, escorted by two servants, who hold her horse. She wears a long riding-habit of table-cover, and is armed with a short spear of bright poker. The Count, on seeing her, is startled, and expresses, by pressing his bosom, his love for her. She informs him in impassioned pantomime—*à la Celeste*—that she will join in the chase. The Count is alarmed, and turns aside in sorrow. He implores her, on his knees, to go back. She refuses. The Huntsmen mount their steeds.

Exeunt omnes, the Count escorts the Lady.

Enter a wild BOAR,* growling, he squats on the ground, and looks around.

The sounds of trumpets and the barking of dogs heard without.

Exit Boar rapidly.

Re-enter Boar, pursued by Dogs and Huntsmen, who cast their spears of brooms at the animal. The Dogs gain upon the Boar, who makes for the jungle of window-curtains. He is instantly surrounded by the Dogs. Several of them he is supposed to gore with his shoe-horn tusks.

The Huntsmen urge the Dogs on.

Enter the Lady, attended by the Count. Making a signal to the Count, she rushes to the Boar with pointed bright poker, and attacks it fiercely. The Boar springs upon her, and the Huntsmen drop their spears with alarm, as they perceive her overthrow by the savage animal.

The Count for a moment wrings his hands, then drawing his hunting-knife of walking-stick, he rushes boldly on the Boar, which immediately leaves the Lady, to engage the Count. [*Terrific combat.*

The Count is wounded, and fights on one knee, when he slays the Boar.

The Count has his wounds dressed by the Lady, who binds her handkerchief round his arm. Then falling on one knee, he declares his passion for her in amatory pantomime. She, turning her head on one side from modesty, accepts him.

---

* It will require great ingenuity in the making-up of the Boar. A brown mackintosh closely buttoned, might do for the skin, and on an emergency, shoe-horns could be used for tusks.

Huntsmen group around the lovers, holding their hats high in the air, as if cheering, whilst the dead Boar is placed in clothes-basket, and hoisted upon the shoulders of the Servants.   [*Grand tableau.*

Exeunt in procession, the piano performing Huntsman's March, dying away in the distance.

Act III.

NEIGHBOR.

Dramatis Personae.

SICK GENTLEMAN.
HIS WIFE.
NEIGHBORS.

SCENE—*The stage is divided by a screen into two rooms; one of them represents the bedchamber of* SICK GENTLEMAN, *with the curtains arranged as a bed. Chairs, &c.*

Enter SICK GENTLEMAN with nightcap and dressing-gown on. He is very weak, and bends his knees whilst walking. His WIFE follows, bearing the night-shade and the warming-pan. The Sick Gentleman seats himself, whilst his Wife warms the bed behind the curtains, and having given her Husband his physic, puts him to bed. She remains by his side until the invalid snores, then exit on tiptoe.

Enter into the other room the NEIGHBORS. One of them carries a large band-box drum, and the others trumpets of rolls of music. They place upon the table a black bottle and glasses, and commence drinking. Then, preparing their instruments, they begin playing.   [*Music.*

The Sick Gentleman is roused from his sleep, and starts up in his bed. He gazes wildly around, and shakes his fist at the screen. He in vain tries to go to sleep.

Enter his Wife wringing her hands. She rushes to the wall of screen, and knocks against it loudly, but the musicians do not hear her, and continue their concert.

Sick Gentleman puts on his dressing-gown, and jumping out of bed, paces the room with indignant strides. At last, taking a book, he seats himself, and leaning over the rushlight shade, tries to read.

The Neighbors at last lay aside their instruments to replenish their glasses.

The Sick Man throws away the book, and is helped by his Wife once more into his bed, and again he snores

The Neighbors now begin dancing to a drum accompaniment, opening their mouths as if singing, whilst hand in hand they are jumping round the table.

The Sick Gentleman is once more aroused. Nearly driven mad, he rages and jumps about the room in an agony of desperation. He throws the book against the screen, and dashes his nightcap on the floor.

His Wife is alarmed, and putting on her bonnet and shawl, stamps on the floor, and pointing to the screen, rushes out indignantly.

Enter the Wife into Neighbors' room. She goes through the pantomime process of informing them that her husband is sick in the next house. She thumps the table, and shakes her fist at them. They all laugh, and the drum strikes up again. Full of indignation, she rushes from the room, followed by Neighbors.

Sick Gentleman, surprised at this renewal of the noise, draws his dressing-gown round him, and pulling his night-cap tightly on his head, hurries from the room, shaking his fist at the ceiling to tell that he will be revenged.

PASTIL.

A CHARADE IN THREE ACTS.

Act I.

PAS—

Dramatis Personæ.

MESDEMOISELLES (*premières danseuses at the Academie*).

> SIGNOR.
> MUSICIANS.
> BOXKEEPER.
> SPECTATORS.

SCENE—*Interior of a Theatre. At the back is seen the stage, with candles ranged in front for lamps, and the sofa for orchestra. Chairs placed round for* SPECTATORS.

Enter SPECTATORS, in full dress. They are shown into their chairs by the BOXKEEPER, who hands to each a sheet of music for playbill.

Enter MUSICIANS into orchestral sofa, and the tuning of imaginary instruments commences. Some tune their bellows for violins, some sound a few notes on their trumpets of pokers, and others ascend the scale on their flutes of walking-sticks. The Spectators grow impatient, stamp upon the floor, and clap their hands, when a bell is heard to ring, and

Enter (on the stage) SIGNOR and MESDEMOISELLES. The Spectators raise their *lorgnettes* to examine them. They are greatly applauded, and bow gracefully in acknowledgment. The Signor is dressed as a Highland chief, with tartan scarf over his shoulder, and an ermine cuff hanging from his waist for philibeg. The Demoiselles wear the book muslin skirts, and if possible, the black velvet bodices of the Scottish lassies.

The orchestra performs the celebrated Highland Fling, and the *pas* commences. During the performance the applause increases. At each fresh round the Signor jumps higher and higher, and the Mesdemoiselles stamp harder and harder, according to the popular notion of the Scottish poetry of motion.

At the conclusion, the Dancers are called forward, and bouquets are showered down from all quarters. The Signor picks them up, and in the fifth position presents them to the Demoiselles. Renewed applause. The Dancers bow again and again, with their hands on their hearts to express their gratitude.

Act II.

—TIL.

Dramatis Personae.

CROCKERY MERCHANT.
LADY AND GENTLEMAN.
YOUNG THIEF.
HIS FRIENDS.

SCENE—*Interior of the warehouse of Crockery Merchant. In the centre a table covered with plates, dishes, and cups. In the front pans arranged near the door of the warehouse.*

Enter CROCKERY MERCHANT, with an apron on, and his ledger under

his arm.   Behind his ear is seen his pen.   He seats himself at the table
and awaits his customers.

Enter LADY and GENTLEMAN, who desire the Merchant to show them
his goods.   They are extremely delighted with the breakfast cups, and
the Gentleman drawing his pocket-book gives two notes for them.   The
grateful Merchant bows his Customers to the door, and then folding
up the notes, he pulls out the drawer and places them in the till of his
table.   Feeling exhausted, he throws his handkerchief over his eyes,
and falls asleep.

Enter YOUNG THIEF on tiptoe.   He points to the sleeping Merchant,
and to his own pocket, to show that he intends taking the notes.   He
advances cautiously to the table, and opening the till, takes out the
notes, and kisses them enthusiastically.   Thrusting them into his breast,
he hurries out of the shop, but at the door he stumbles over one of the
pans, and falls to the ground with a crash.   He, however, is quickly
rescued by his FRIENDS, and exit.

The Merchant is aroused.   Seeing the till open, he is surprised at the
absence of his notes.   He feels in his pocket, but without success, until
the truth bursts upon him, and he vows vengeance upon his despoilers.
Seizing his hat and umbrella, he prepares to sally forth.   But no sooner
has he reached the door than he is surrounded by the Friends of Young
Thief, who knock his hat down over his eyes and decamp, leaving the
poor Merchant groping about in the dark, and hitting right and left with
his umbrella.   *Exit* Merchant.

Act III.

PASTIL.

Dramatis Personae.

SICK GENTLEMAN.
HIS WIFE.
HIS DAUGHTERS.
DOCTOR.

SCENE—*Sleeping apartment in the house of* SICK GENTLEMAN.   *At the
end of the room the window curtains are arranged as a bed.*

Enter SICK GENTLEMAN, as pale as flour can make him, with his
dressing-gown and night-cap on.   He is supported by his wife and one
of his DAUGHTERS, the other one holding the rushlight shade, which

she places near the bed. The Sick Gentleman is placed on his couch, when he is "taken very bad indeed." By showing the whites of his eyes, and panting heavily, he greatly alarms his anxious wife, who hands to him his physic, whilst one of the Daughters holds a piece of sugar ready for him. He blesses them.

Enter DOCTOR with a gold-headed walking-stick to his mouth, and huge watch-seals hanging to his fob. He complains of the closeness of the room by holding his nose, and orders one of the Daughters to light some pastils, which is immediately done.

The Sick Gentleman is much refreshed by the delicious perfume, and expresses his delight by constant sniffing. The Doctor feels his pulse, and intimates by his actions, that "we must not worry ourselves, but keep ourselves in bed." After he has looked at the Sick Man's tongue, he, in action, informs the weeping Wife and Daughters, "that we must have pastils continually burning." Then placing his hand behind his back, receives his card-counter guinea, and leaves the room, followed by Sick Gentleman, his Wife, and Daughters.

BACKGAMMON.

A CHARADE IN THREE ACTS.

Act I.

BACK—

Dramatis Personæ.

TWO LITTLE BOYS.
SUSAN, *a Servant Girl.*
JOHN, *a Footman.*
POLICEMAN.
OLD MOTHER.
RECRUITING SERJEANT.

SCENE*—*A Street.*

Enter TWO LITTLE BOYS, who take cents from their pockets, and

* This Scene may be made by pinning several newspapers, or large pieces of paper.

show them as if for odd and even. The one who loses then makes a back, over which the other jumps. The other Boy then stands with his head down as if to make a back. "Higher!" cries his playfellow; the Boy makes a higher back, and the Boy is just about to jump over it, when

In rushes a POLICEMAN, and drives the Boys out. The Policeman shakes his cane after the Boys and *exit*.

Re-enter Boys, who point to where the Policeman has gone, laugh, and recommence their game at leap-frog.   [*Exeunt boys.*

Enter OLD WOMAN, SERVANT GIRL, and FOOTMAN. They stand and talk to each other, and make signs, as if the young people were going to be married. Show wedding-ring, kiss each other, and so on.

Enter RECRUITING SERJEANT.* Goes up to Footman, places a shilling in his hand, and marches him off. The Old Mother and Girl express sorrow violently, wringing their hands, and pretending to weep; Old Woman imitates the act of firing a gun to express the office of a soldier; young girl puts out her finger, as if to show that her chance of marrying is lost. Both weep and wail in comic pantomime.

Enter FOOTMAN running. Old woman and girl express great astonishment at his return; and he exhibits a large placard, on which is written—"Sent BACK, not short enough."   [*Scene closes.*

Act II.

—GAMMON.

Dramatis Personæ.

RICH OLD LADY.
SHABBY-LOOKING LOVER.

SCENE—*A Parlor.*

Enter RICH OLD LADY with a long purse in her hand. She begins to count her money, sighs deeply, takes a letter from her pocket, and reads.

against the window curtains, showing part of the window at back, and placing cheese, butter, etc., on dishes on a table behind. A lamp-post may be shown by introducing a straight prop with a candle alight on top, etc.

* The dress of this character may be easily made by fastening a red sash round his waist, putting a ribbon in his hat, etc.

Enter SHABBY LOVER, who advances to the Rich Old Lady, makes great protestations of affection, and tries to take the purse from her hand. She resists, when he drops on one knee, places his hand on his heart, and pretends to be violently in love. Old Lady seems subdued, and gives him her purse. He kisses her hand, rises, cuts a caper, and *exit*. Old Lady raises her hands in astonishment, and cries out—"He wants to gammon me, he does." [*Scene closes.*

————

Act III.

BACKGAMMON.

Dramatis Personae.

YOUNG LADY.
YOUNG GENTLEMAN.
VISITORS.

SCENE—*A Drawing-room.* VISITORS *arrange themselves in groups; one Young Lady plays the piano, another looks over a book of prints, a third amuses herself with the flowers on the table, etc.*

Enter YOUNG LADY and GENTLEMAN from opposite sides of the room. They advance, shake hands, and go to back of room. Young Gentleman comes forward with little table, which he places in centre. He then brings two chairs, which he places on either side of the table. One of the Visitors brings a draughtboard, which he opens. The Young Lady and Gentleman sit down to the table and commence rattling dice-boxes and moving the draughtmen. Visitors group themselves round the players. [*Scene closes*

A LITTLE MISUNDERSTANDING.

A CHARADE IN FOUR ACTS.

------•◄------

Act I.

A LITTLE MISS—

Dramatis Personae.

A YOUNG LADY OF FIVE.
HER MAMMA *and* SISTERS.
LADY VISITORS.
SERVANTS.

------•◄------

SCENE—*Parlor in the house of the Mamma.*

Enter MAID SERVANT, who dusts and arranges the furniture, and *exit.*

Enter THREE SISTERS, bringing with them a quantity of silk, lace, and other articles of dress. They sit down and begin working busily, one cutting out, another sewing, etc.

Enter MAMMA with CHILD OF FIVE in night-cap and morning dress. The Sisters clap their hands, laugh, and express surprise. They take the child's cap off, and exhibit its rough uncombed hair. One rings the bell, and makes signs to the servant, who enters. Servant goes out and presently returns with basin and water, combs, brushes, and various articles of toilette, which she sets down and exit. The Sisters then brush the child's hair, wash its face, and so on, the Mamma assist-ing. They then dress the Child in very fine clothes, a small bonnet, and parasol, white lace handkerchief in her hand, etc. The Child looks pleased, kisses her Sisters and Mamma, and struts about the room. Double knock heard at the door. Enter Servant introducing visitors. Sisters try to hide the litter, and Mamma brings forward the little Miss in her finery. Visitors express delight. Little Miss takes her seat in centre of room, the rest grouping round her with various signs of homage and admiration.   Mamma exclaims, "Pretty little Miss."

[*Scene closes.*

Act II.

UNDER—

Dramatis Personae.

> MAID SERVANT.
> POLICEMAN.
> MISTRESS.
> MASTER.

SCENE—*Kitchen in the house of the Lady, with table in centre, discovers maid-servant nicely dressed.*

Clock strikes nine, and three gentle taps are heard on the wall outside.   MAID goes out, and returns cautiously with a POLICEMAN on her
arm; they look lovingly on each other.   Maid prepares supper; spreads
a large cloth on the table so as nearly to touch the ground, and places
dishes and plates, knives and forks, etc.   They sit down and eat, the
maid-servant daintily, the policeman ravenously.   Just in the middle
of the feast a loud double knock is heard at the front door.   They rise
in confusion, the maid calling out "Master!"   Policeman hides under
the table, from which the maid hastens to clear the things.   Knocking
continues impatiently.   Policeman puts his head out from under the
cloth, the maid kisses him, and runs up stairs to open the door.   Noise
heard in the passage as if the MASTER and MISTRESS were remonstrat-
ing at being kept so long at the door.   Policeman is creeping cautiously
from under the table, when steps are heard outside, which cause him
instantly to hide again.

Enter Master, Mistress, and Servant, all disputing with many gestures.   Mistress looks about the room, goes to the cupboard, and at
last approaches the table, and is about to lift the cloth.   At this moment
the maid-servant rushes up to her master and falls fainting in his arms.
Mistress lifts up side of table cloth and discovers policeman under the
table.   The policeman then looks up from his knees, brandishes his staff,
and inquires in a loud voice, "Does MR. UNDERDOWN live here?"

Scene closes.

Act III.

STANDING.

Dramatis Personae.

TRAVELLER, *with Carpet Bag. etc.*
HACKMAN.
PUBLICAN.
CUSTOMERS.

SCENE*—*Bar of a Public House—Publican discovered behind, and Customers in front.*

Enter TRAVELLER and HACKMAN. They go up to counter and drink. Various persons close up to the Traveller, and request him to treat them. He nods, and publican serves out glasses and mugs to all. They all drink, and appear very merry. Publican holds out his hand for the money, after counting up the sum. Traveller pulls out a very long purse and pays. Hackman and Company dance for joy. [*Scene closes.*

Act IV.

A LITTLE MISUNDERSTANDING.

Dramatis Personae.

THE LITTLE MISS.
HER THREE SISTERS.
THE MAMMA.
A LOVER.
POLICEMAN.
MAID SERVANT.

SCENE—*A drawing-room. Curtain rises, and discovers a lady sitting with her two daughters, and the LITTLE MISS, finely dressed, as before. The young ladies are engaged in crochet work, and the LITTLE MISS admires her figure in the glass. A double knock is heard at the outer door.*

Enter SERVANT, bringing bouquet, which she takes to the Little Miss. The Sisters and Mamma express great surprise.

---

* This scene may be made by laying a shutter across a couple of chairs, and placing another shutter in front. Place pewter pots, glasses, etc., on the counter.

Enter LOVER, gaily dressed, with a crush hat under his arm. He advances to the Mamma, who bows and shakes hands with him. He then goes up to the Young Ladies, and begins to make himself agreeable. They turn away from him and pout their lips, at the same time pointing to the Little Miss, who is admiring the bouquet. The Lover starts, and rushes from the room.

The Mamma and Sisters look angrily at the Little Miss, and endeavor to obtain the bouquet. She resists and begins to cry; stamps on the floor, and turns over the chairs, and pulls about the curtains. Servant rings the bell, and calls " Police ! "

Enter LOVER with POLICEMAN, who brandishes his staff, and looks very important. Lover produces three large bouquets, one of which he gives to each of the young ladies. Policeman takes a great doll out of his pocket, and presents it to the Little Miss. Maid-Servant goes up to Policeman and boxes his ears; but the Policeman immediately shows her a wedding-ring, when she kisses him, and appears much pleased. Little Miss comes forward, nursing the doll. Lover takes bouquet from her hand, and gives it to the elder young lady. Young Ladies and Mother smile graciously upon him. The whole party then form a group about the lover and the young lady, and the Little Miss runs up to her mother and kisses her. Policeman and Maid-servant in the back-ground, whispering, and admiring the wedding-ring. Lover and Lady oin hands, and all bow to the audience.

CURTAIN.

ORPHEUS AND EURYDICE:

OR,

𝔗𝔥𝔢 𝔚𝔞𝔫𝔡𝔢𝔯𝔦𝔫𝔤 𝔐𝔦𝔫𝔰𝔱𝔯𝔢𝔩.

A CLASSIC DRAMA.

FEELING himself on Classic ground, the author has considered it his duty, in the present instance, to adhere strictly to the principles of Dramatic composition as enforced by Aristotle, but neglected by Fitzball and Shakspeare. The Unities of Time, Place, and Action, he has observed scrupulously (that is to say, as far as lay in his power, for he confesses himself in doubt as to what the Unity of Time really is, unless the circumstance of a Drama "going like one o'clock" may be considered an illustration of it). He has also preserved the Chorus—at the end of several of his parodies. With regard to the presence or absence of classic erudition displayed in his work, he can only say that whatever objections may be raised to the pathetic passages, the most invidious caviller will not deny that an intimate acquaintance with the ancients—even to the remotest period of antiquity—is evident in the jocular portions of it.

Dramatis Personæ.

PLUTO, *Monarch of* ——

PROSERPINE, *the Partner of his Fireside.*

CHARON, *an Ancient Mariner—the original Whitehall Boatman.*

CERBERUS, *a Watchman—the Dogberry of Heathen Mythology—a policeman.*

ORPHEUS, *the wandering minstrel.*

EURYDICE, *the young woman who led him astray.*

[*The curtain rises on a fireside group, in a locality which will soon be obvious, but which there is no occasion to mention by name.* PROSERPINE, *setting the tea things.* PLUTO, *toasting a muffin on the prongs of his fork.* CERBERUS *asleep on the hearth-rug.**

PLU. My dear, just ring for coal, it's dreadful weather,
    Make up the fire, and let's be snug together.

    [*He proceeds to butter the muffin, which* CERBERUS *smells.* PLUTO *raps him smartly on one of his noses.*

    Lie down! his hunger doesn't seem to stop;
    Hasn't the dog's-meat man brought round his sop?
    A precious night—upon the Stygian dyke
    For Charon's boat; 'twill founder—wherry like!
    The roads in such a state, too—all want paving,
    Remind me, dear (we musn't be too saving,
    And cures are more expensive than preventions)—
    To order in a load of Good Intentions.

                    [*A knock.* CERBERUS *growls.*
    Lie down, you whelp. My dear, he's such a snarler,
    I wonder you allow him in the parlor.
    See who it is.

PROS. (*going to door*). It's CHARON!

PLU.   Ask him in.

           [*Enter* CHARON *in a pilot coat and glazed hat.*

PROS. Why, I declare he's dripping to the skin.

CHA. A fare, sir.

PLU.   Male or female?

* The necessary "make-up" of this gentleman may at first dishearten amateur managers, let them be never so enterprising, by its apparent impracticability. It can, however, be easily accomplished. *Papier maché* casts of countenance, of a decidedly canine aspect, may be purchased at any toy shop; and as even two heads are better than one, the effect of a head-dress composed of three may be imagined. With a little attention to the appropriate action, this character, in the hands of any very young gentleman of active habits, may be made a very funny dog indeed.

CHA.   Gal!
PLU.   Admit her.
CHA. (*calling outside.*)   Now then, ma'am.

Enter EURYDICE, *carrying a bandbox, umbrella, and pattens.*

PLU.   Brother Jove! a splendid critter.
CHA. Hanythink more, sir?
PLU.   No, you may retire.
      Mix him a glass, my love, of liquid fire.   [*Exit* CHARON
EUR   This is the place, then! Well, upon my word——
PLU   Don't mention it—it's name is never heard.
      But may I ask the name of the divinity
      Who with her presence honors this vicinity?
EUR. Why, though I hate impertinent inquisitors,
      It's only right that folks should know their visitors.

SONG (EURYDICE).

AIR—"*Jenny Jones.*"

My name's Eury-dī-ce, excuse the penultimate,
    Made long, as the music and metre entails.
My father and mother pronounce it Eur-y̆-dice,
    Good truth, that's the way, but the prosody fails.
And indeed o'er all rules, both of grammar and poetry,
    Those of sweet music I prize far above,
For, indeed, in my heart, I do love that accomplishment,
    And Orpheus, my husband and master, I love.

I started from earth and the vale of my fathers,
    As fate had decreed o'er the Styx I should pass;
But I don't care two pins for my present predicament,
    And I shan't even say "Woe is me," or "Alas!"
For my husband has vowed to release and restore me
    To my home, and what's more, to my music, above!
For, indeed, in my heart I do love that accomplishment,
    And Orpheus, my husband and master, I love.

PLU. Take you away from here! to earth? Get out!
EUR. I mean to——
PLU.   Bother!
EUR.   *You*—beyond a doubt;
      And that ere long—
PLU.   Stuff! Once within our wickets,
      You come to stop. We don't give pass-out tickets.

SONG (Pluto).

Air—" It's no use knockin' at de door."

You have just come from town, and it's very plain to me,
You're wholly unacquainted with the sort of thing you'll see,
You may read above our gate, inscribed in letters clear,
" Of getting out all hope abandon, ye who enter here."
　　And it's no use knocking at the door any more,
　　It's no use knocking at the door.

CHORUS.

And it's no use knockin', etc.

EUR.　We'll see.

PLU.　　　　Oh yes, we'll see—but as you're come,
I think you'd better make yourself at home.
So, ere our spouse our bell and knocker wrings off,
Step up with Mrs. P., and take your things off.

CONCERTED.

Air—" Goin' ober de mountain."

EUR.　I'll be off, you'll very soon see;
PLU.　Make haste down and have some tea.
EUR.　Soon to hear him say, in accents bold—
PLU.　Well, if you prefer your muffins cold—
EUR.　" Re raw ! my true love,
　　　　Oh come along, my darling !"
　　　　(*To Pluto.*) Much distressed to leave you,
　　　　But don't let my parting grieve you.
PLU.　(*derisively.*) Yah ! yah ! yah ! yah ! yah !
　　　　Yah ! yah ! yah ! yah ! you !
EUR.　" Oh, come along from this low place,
　　　　I'm going over the mountains."

CHORUS.

Yah ! yah ! etc.

　　[*Exit* EURYDICE, *escorted by* PROSERPINE, *carrying a Led-
　　room candlestick.*

PLU.　What an idea ! unheard of, I must say !
　　　Get out of here, indeed ; I wish she may.

Yet I must take precautions with the slut,
She seems so sharp; who knows but she might cut.
With bolts and bars I'll make her fast—but steady.
Hang it! the jade seems fast enough already;
And with her tongue's incipient noise and chatter,
To shut her up, appears no easy matter.
Yet I must try; with heavy chains and thick locks,
That shall defy e'en Hobbs, the prince of picklocks.

> [*A street organ* is heard outside, playing "Jeannette and Jeannot."* PLUTO *starts, with an agonized expression of countenance.* CERBERUS *growls.*

What's that? Good heavens!

> [*The tune is continued with increased violence*

                    Help! Be quiet! Mercy!
(*Holding his ears.*)   He doesn't seem inclined to— *Vice versy.*
Oh dear! (*Runs to window.*)   Be off!

ORF.   (*Outside.*)   I shan't.
PLU.   Leave off!
ORP.   I won't.

> [*The tune increases in loudness; the agony of* PLUTO *in intensity.*

PLU.   What's to be done? it's getting louder.
(*With a yell of anguish.*)   Don't!
Our peace of mind for ever 'twill destroy.
Hie Cerberus! Good doggy! At him, boy.

> [*He opens the door, urging* CERBERUS *to the attack in the usual manner.* ORPHEUS *enters, partly dressed as an Italian boy, playing an organ.* CERBERUS *rushes at him growling, but is met boldly by* ORPHEUS, *who plays the organ full in his face. Unable to stand the infliction,* CERBERUS *runs away, yelping.*

PLU.   I say, move on—or I shall make you.
ORP.   Shall you?
Of peace and quietness I know the value.
PLU.   (*offering him a shilling.*)   Take this and go about your business.
ORP.   Stuff!
PLU.   Well, here's another—

---

* For the further assurance of despondent amateurs, these instruments of torture
may be hired for the night at very moderate charge.

ORP.   Pshaw! not half enough.

PLU   I offer'd you two shillings.

ORP.   Yes—you *did* I see;

But I, Sir, don't move on—under Eurydice.

PLU.   Who art thou, slave, whose noise our aching sconce hurts?

ORP.   Professor Orpheus—from the Ancient Concerts.

SONG.

ORPHEUS, *accompanying himself on the organ.*

AIR.—*Marble Halls.**

The minstrel boy, to Old Scratch has gone
    For his wife in hopes to find her,
The monster organ he has girded on,
    Of a wild Italian grinder.
Sound of woe! said the wand'ring bard,
    As all the world so fears thee,
E'en Pluto's self—clean off his guard
    Will be thrown, whene'er he hears thee.

[*He follows* PLUTO *round the stage, playing and singing* **to the**
    symphony; PLUTO *holding his ears.*

PLU.   I say, let's come to terms.

ORP.   My wife!

PLU.   I can't——

You ask too much; but pray desist——

ORP.   I shan't.

SECOND VERSE.

The minstrel swell—and in language plain,
    Declares, if kept asunder
From the spouse he loves, he won't refrain;
    For he cannot move on under
The terms just named, which you must allow—
    To sink all lies and knavery—
Are cheap as dirt—to suppress this row,
    To submit to which is slavery.

* The author has taken care to select two airs, which may be found arranged on almost any organ.

ORP.   Give me my wife, or else your life you'll find
       Like Mantalini's—" One demnrtion grind."
PLU.   Never!
ORP.   Then I resume my dulcet strain,
       For I can turn—and turn—and turn again.
                                        [*Turning the handle.*
       I'll play a waltz—
PLU.   Oh, heavens! mind your stops;
       I hate all dances, though the son of Ops.   [ORPHEUS *plays.*
       Monstrum horrendum—cease thy painful twingings—
       Direst machine of all *informe ingens!*
       Behold me kneeling by your side—who wouldn't
       Kneel e'en by Jupiter's. By Jove! I couldn't.
       See, I turn suppliant—I—Ammon's brother!
ORP.   For that good turn—I'll treat you with another.   [*Grinds.*
PLU.   Hold! I give in—'tis useless to rebel.
ORP.   It must be so. Pluto, thou reason'st well.
PLU.   I'll give you up your wife—mine too—if wanted,
       Rather than be by such a nuisance haunted.
       Though of concession it's a fearful stretcher.
ORP.   Look sharp, or else——   [*Threatens to play.*
PLU.   " That strain again!"   I'll fetch her.
                                        [*Exit precipitately*
ORP.   Come! for subduing wrong, oppression, crimes,
       My organ equals Herald, Tribune, Times;
       "Music hath charms to soothe the savage breast,
       And soften"—everybody knows the rest.
       I question, if the rudest Goth or Vandal,
       Could well resist my overtures by Handel.
       Pluto (*calling*), I can't stand here all night, you know,
       Settle my little claim, and let me go,
       Or you shall hear from me without delay——
PLU.   (*running in.*) None of your airs, old fellow—drop it, pray.
ORP.   My wife, then——
PLU.   Here she comes.

                       Enter EURYDICE.

ORP.   My life!
EUR.   My joy!
ORP.   My lost Eurydice!

Eur.   My minstrel boy!

Orp. Pack up your things!

Plu.   Oh, yes—·by all means pack!

Eur. And have you really come to take me back?

Orp. (*to* Pluto.) She needn't stop?

Plu.   Not e'en to tea or sup:
She's quite a riddle—so I give her up.
Be off about your business—I entreat,
And pray remove it to some other street.

Orp. But we must have safe conduct—

Plu.   Baneful stranger!
It's conduct such as yours in which there's danger.

Orp. (*threatening the organ.*) At once decide—

Plu.   For forms I'm no great stickler—
I hate all rows, and *that* sort in partic'lar.
Charon!

Enter Charon.

Cha.   Your honor!

Plu. (*pointing out* Orp. *and* Eur.) Fares for earth—the trouble
I'll pay you for—

Cha.   Back fares is always double.

Plu. All right—

Orp.   Come, dearest, since it seems we're free—

Plu. Stop, won't you say good night to Mrs. P.?
N'importe—You've got your wife back, and I'm glad on't.
(*Aside*) Some day I hope and trust he'll wish he hadn't.

Orp. (*to audience.*) The power of Music—as I think we've shown
All I require—is, for its length—you'll own
That never was a story of more glee
Than this of Orpheus and Eurydice.

"IRRESISTIBLY IMPUDENT."

BY FRANK CAHILL.

A FARCE IN ONE ACT.

In the following dramatic trifle, the most extraordinary liberties have purposely been taken with the usual mode of conducting stage-business. This kind of burlesque is always productive of great merriment to the audience, who, when they discover that the blunders are a part of the play, never fail to acknowledge the harmless deception by peals of laughter and applause.

In the first scene, the names that are left blank are to be filled up with the real names of the actors who personate the characters.

Characters.

DICK CALMLEIGH.
MR. WIGLEY.
CHARLES, *his Son.*
JENNIE HAYNE, *Mr. Wigley's Ward.*
PROMPTER.

SCENE I.—*A Parlor.*

Enter WIGLEY *and* CHARLES.

WIGLEY. You are now twenty-one, Charles, and it is time you thought of some profession. You cannot expect to be dependent upon me for ever.

CHARLES. My dear father, it has long been my wish to do something for myself—so the sooner the better.

WIGLEY. What profession would you like?

CHARLES. A lawyer's. How delightful it must be, to be the champion of the innocent, and to vindicate those who have been traduced. To be enabled to liberate the falsely-accused husband, the injured wife, and the crushed son, to the bosom of their anxious and loving families! Oh, I should glory in being a lawyer!

WIGLEY. Unsophisticated youth! I am afraid that you will find vice pay better than virtue. However, we will call upon Judge Futvoye to-morrow, and talk to him about it. [*A pause.*

WIGLEY (*aside, in a stage whisper*). Why don't you go on?

CHARLES (*aside*). Mr. —— ought to come on; you gave the cue.

PROMPTER (*talking off*). Mr. ——, Mr. ——, the stage is waiting.

DICK (*talking off*). Why didn't you tell me before? It's your fault.

PROMPTER (*talking off*). No it ain't.

Enter DICK CALMLEIGH.

DICK (*looking off towards* PROMPTER). Yes it is. (*To* WIGLEY.) So Charles is going to study the law.

PROMPTER (*talking off*). That's not your line.

DICK. Eh?

PROMPTER (*talking off*). Ah, Mr. Wigley. Hullo, Charles——

DICK. Oh, yes. Ah, Mr. Wigley! Hullo, Charles, how are you? Nice weather.

MR. WIGLEY. Splendid. You're a late riser, Mr. Calmleigh.

DICK. Yes; I was up late last night, reading.

CHARLES. My father and I were just talking about the profession I am to follow.

DICK (*aside to* PROMPTER). What's my word?

PROMPTER (*giving cue*). Indeed, and what pro——

DICK (*aside*). Oh, yes. (*Aloud.*) Indeed! and what profession have you decided upon?

MR. WIGLEY. Charles has decided upon the law.

Enter JENNIE HAYNE. DICK *goes to back of stage and sits down.*

JENNIE. Oh, Mr. Wigley, I have had such a delightful walk this morning. I have been as far as Chinioquack Lake.

PROMPTER (*talking off*). That's your cue, Mr. ——.

DICK (*starting up*). Eh?—what?—so it is. (*Aside to* PROMPTER.) What have I to say?

PROMPTER (*talking off*). Your walk appears to——

DICK (*aside.*) That's it. (*Aloud.*) Your walk appears to have done you good, for your cheeks rival the roses that you must have met.

JENNY. Oh, Mr. Calmleigh! [*A pause.*

PROMPTER (*talking off*). Why don't you go on, Mr. ——

DICK. Why don't you prompt me?

Enter PROMPTER, *with a book in his hand.*

PROMPTER. Oh, this will never do.

DICK. You mustn't come on the stage, you'll spoil the whole piece.

PROMPTER. Spoil the piece! why you don't know a word of your part.

DICK. Now, I like that, because you don't understand how to prompt, you say I don't know my part. (*Addressing* WIGLEY.) Mr. —— don't I know my part?

WIGLEY. I won't say that, but when I gave you the cue you certainly didn't go on with your lines.

DICK. No, of course not; it was Mr. ——'s (*the* PROMPTER) fault.

PROMPTER. I think it very unfair to lay it at my door, Mr. ——.

DICK. Now, I appeal to you, Miss ——, is it my fault?

JENNIE. Really, Mr. ——, it seems so.

DICK. You're mistaken, Miss ——, I know every word, if I am only prompted. (*To* CHARLES.) You're going to be a lawyer,—is it my fault?

CHARLES. As a lawyer, certainly it was.

DICK. That's too bad, Mr. ——, I am sure I have been studying my part for the last three weeks.

WIGLEY. Oh, never mind, let us try it over again.

PROMPTER. Let us drop the curtain, and commence on the next scene, that will be best. Perhaps Mr. —— is better up in the next scene.

DICK. Well, I'll agree to that. (*To audience.*) Isn't it absurd of them to say that I don't know my part? Now I'll just show them, in the next scene, that I can pay as much attention to my cues, as any of them. Mr. —— (*the* PROMPTER) is not very——

PROMPTER. There, that will do.

DICK. Is that my cue?

PROMPTER. No, no, we want to drop the curtain.

DICK. Why didn't you say so before? All right.

[DICK *and* PROMPTER *centre.* JENNIE *and* CHARLES *left.* WIGLEY *right.*
[*Scene closes.*

SCENE II.—*The same.*

Enter DICK *and* JENNIE.

DICK. It's no use telling me there must be something the matter with you,—what is it?

JENNIE. Really, Mr. Calmleigh, you take a great interest in my affairs.

DICK. Of course I do, I like you.

JENNIE. Sir!

DICK. I mean, like you as though you were my daughter, but I am hardly old enough to be your father, am I?

JENNIE. Do not be ridiculous.

DICK. Of course I won't, but I know there's something on your mind, so confide in me like a father.

JENNIE. I think it very impolite of you, to worry me in this way.

DICK. Now, I like that. ·Worry you? why I want to help you to bear your sorrow. You're in love, that's what it is.

JENNIE. Have you discovered it, then?

DICK. Certainly I have, and so is Charles, do you think I haven't eyes? Ah, I'm a sharp fellow, I tell you.

JENNIE. Has Charles told you?

DICK. Oh, no, he hasn't told me anything, but I've noticed it for some time, he's desperately in love with Miss Finniken. Who you are in love with, I——. (JENNIE *gives a scream, and faints.* DICK *catches her in his arms, places her in a chair, and beats the palms of her hands.*) What extraordinary creatures these women are? What in the name of fortune could make her go off in this way! (JENNIE *slightly recovers.*) That's right! do you feel better now?

JENNIE (*faintly*). Where am I? Frank—— Frank——

DICK (*aside*). Hullo! she's in love with a Frank!

JENNIE (*rising from chair*). I feel better now,—thank you—I'll go to my own room.

DICK. Can I assist you?

JENNIE. Thank you, no.

[DICK *leads* JENNIE *to door, who exits.*

DICK. A decided case of love in its most malignant form; symptoms aggravated.

Enter CHARLES. *He does not perceive* DICK.

CHARLES (*agitated*). I don't care. I never will. I love——

DICK. Love! You're in for it too, are you?

CHARLES. You here! I do not understand you.

DICK. Of course you don't. You're in love, old fellow. Can I help you? Make a confidant of me.

CHARLES. I do not know why you should thrust yourself into my affairs.

7

DICK. Bless you, I don't want to know anything about your affairs. You're in love; love always wants a confidant; make one of me. Here I am; so go ahead and pour your griefs into my ear.

CHARLES. Will you oblige me by minding your own business?

DICK. That is my business. I want to alleviate the sufferings of my fellow-creatures as much as I can; so tell me all about it; you'll feel better for it afterwards.

CHARLES (*aside*). Confound this fellow! (*Aloud.*) Will you leave off troubling me?

DICK. I never heard such a fellow! Only fancy! tells me I'm troubling him! You're as bad as Miss Hayne, for she, poor girl, is desperately in love.

CHARLES. Did she tell you so?

DICK. No, not exactly. I say, do you know anybody of the name of Frank?

CHARLES. Yes, I know Frank Coleman.

DICK. Well, she's in love with him.

CHARLES. What!

DICK. Oh, yes; she fainted just now; and as she was coming to, she called upon Frank.

CHARLES. Ah! this perfidy, this perfidy!

[Walks up and down stage rapidly.

DICK. I say, old fellow, have some regard for the carpet.

CHARLES (*stopping suddenly before* DICK). Now, answer me.

DICK. Certainly, I'll answer you; only keep cool.

CHARLES. You say she called upon Frank?

DICK. Yes, she called upon Frank, but he didn't come.

CHARLES. That is sufficient, sir. Oh, Jennie, Jennie! I didn't think you capable of this.   [*Exit hurriedly.*

DICK. What extraordinary people they are in this house! I've only been here two days, yet everything seems topsy-turvy. I wonder what my uncle could have been thinking of, when he gave me that letter of introduction to old Wigley. I feel that it must be near lunch time, so I'll go and see.   [*Exit* DICK.

Enter JENNIE.

JENNIE. I won't stay here any longer. I'll pack up my things and run away; then, under an assumed name, and with spectacles, I'll seek a situation as governess. This is a cruel, heartless world, and Charley is false to me.   [*Cries.*

Enter CHARLES.

CHARLES. Oh! you are there, are you?

JENNIE (*drying her eyes*). Yes, sir, I am here; and how dare you speak to me?

CHARLES. I suppose you want to blind my eyes by being indignant; but it won't do, Miss.

JENNIE. What do you mean, sir? You had better go and marry Miss Finniken.

CHARLES. I marry Miss Finniken! No, indeed. You had better go and marry Frank.

JENNIE. What do you mean by requesting me to marry Frank?

CHARLES. What do you mean by requesting me to marry Miss Finniken?

JENNIE. What I say. I suppose you don't mean to deny that you intend marrying Miss Finniken?

CHARLES. Yes, I do. Who told you I was?

JENNIE. Mr. Calmleigh.

CHARLES. Bother Mr. Calmleigh! he had no right to say any such thing.

JENNIE. And you're not going to marry Miss Finniken?

CHARLES. No, certainly not.

JENNIE. Oh, I'm so glad.   [*Attempts to take his hand.*

CHARLES. Stay! who is this Frank that you called upon when you fainted?

JENNIE (*laughing*). Ha! ha! ha! and is that what made you jealous?

CHARLES. Really, Miss Hayne, I see nothing to laugh at.

JENNIE. Don't you know who Frank is? Why, Frances, my maid, to be sure.

CHARLES. Is that so? Oh! forgive me, Jennie.

[*He takes both her hands in his, and shakes them joyously.*

Enter DICK.

DICK. That's right—that's as it should be. What's the use of being dull?

CHARLES. I have a word to say to you, Mr. Calmleigh.

DICK. Don't be particular, you can say half-a-dozen, if you like.

CHARLES. What did you mean, sir, by telling me that Miss Hayne was in love with Frank Coleman?

JENNIE. And what did you mean, sir, by telling me that Charles was engaged to be married to Miss Finniken?

DICK. One at a time, if you please. It is impossible to answer two different questions at once.

CHARLES. Well, sir, answer me.

DICK. Don't get excited. Look at me, I'm not excited. I merely told Miss Hayne what your father told me. He said you were——

CHARLES. Yes, yes; you needn't go on any further, I understand it now.

JENNIE. How understand it, Charles?

CHARLES. My father wishes me to marry Miss Finniken, and threatens to disinherit me, if I do not.

JENNIE. And are you going to, Charles?

CHARLES. Never, dearest! rather would I perish.

[*Takes her hands again, and gazes upon her fondly.*

DICK. What an interesting picture!

CHARLES. Mr. Calmleigh, I have to apologize for getting angry with you. I see it is not your fault.

DICK. Don't mention it, I beg; I like people to get angry with me, it amuses me. But you are two——you understand.

CHARLES. No, I do not understand.

DICK. What charming innocence! You two want to be made one.

CHARLES. I do not allow comparative strangers to pry into my affairs.

DICK. That's singular; upon my word you're a most extraordinary young man.

CHARLES. Upon my word, you're a most impudent young man.

DICK (*laughing*). That's good; now that's exceedingly funny,—why I'm known as the most bashful young man in New York.

JENNIE (*aside to Charles*). He must have altered wonderfully during the last two days.

CHARLES. There is no getting angry with you—we will let you into our secret; Jennie and I love one another most passionately.

DICK. I thought so. But that will never do,—oh! it will never do.

JENNIE. Oh, Mr. Calmleigh, why not?

DICK. Old Wigley,—I beg your pardon—your guardian, will never consent. He has made up his mind that Charley is to marry Miss Finniken.

CHARLES. Cannot you help us to get his consent?

DICK. Now, that's delicious!

JENNIE. Oh, do help us, Mr. Calmleigh.

DICK. You know you don't allow strangers to pry into your affairs.

CHARLES *and* JENNIE (*one on each side of* DICK, *they each take an arm, and look into his face coaxingly*). We didn't mean it. Won't you help us?

DICK (*looking at* CHARLES). I don't think I can.

JENNIE (*squeezing his arm*). Yes, you will.

DICK (*looking at* JENNIE). Lovely woman has gained the day. I'll try it. (*Putting himself into an attitude of defiance.*) Old Wigley, come on; I'm ready for you.

JENNIE *and* CHARLES. How can we thank you?

DICK. Look here,—you'd better see the old boy, and tell him that you must marry Jennie; and if he won't let you, why——

CHARLES. What?

DICK. No, that won't do; you can't whip your own father; and,—don't be angry with me,—I can't do it, because I'm his guest, you see.

CHARLES. I'll go to my father, and tell him you wish to see him here.

DICK. Very well.

CHARLES. Come, Jennie, let us go.   [*Going.*

DICK. I say, old fellow, seeing that it's for you, I don't mind giving him a whipping for your sake.

CHARLES. Not for the world.

DICK. Well, as you like.

JENNIE. Pray, Mr. Calmleigh, do not get excited.

DICK. No, I won't. I'll keep as cool as a refrigerator. Go along. and send the governor here.

CHARLES. Do your best for us. Come, Jennie.

[*As they are going out,* JENNIE *returns, shakes hands with* DICK, *and exits.*

DICK. There,—go along with you. This is splendid. Something I never expected. Got to have an interview with an obdurate father on behalf of injured innocence in distress. If the worst comes to the worst, shall I drop him out of the window?—that will be no good,—this confounded room is on the ground floor,—pity it is not on the fourth story. Just my luck! No matter; stony-hearted parent, come on!   [*Fights desperately with an imaginary being.*

Enter MR. WIGLEY.

MR. WIGLEY. Why, what's,—what's the matter, Mr. Calmleigh?

DICK. Nothing, nothing. I was merely punching a cruel and ty-rannical father's head. (WIGLEY *looks round room.*) An imaginary father.

MR. WIGLEY. Oh! You wish to see me, Mr. Calmleigh, I believe?

DICK. You are right in your belief. That's a nice shirt. Where do you buy your shirts?

MR. WIGLEY (*aside*). Confounded impudence! (*Aloud.*) Is that all you wished to see me about?

DICK. Dear me, no. Let us sit down. (*They get chairs, bring them to centre of stage, and sit down.*) You have a son.

MR. WIGLEY. Really——

DICK. Now, don't deny it. You know you have a son.

MR. WIGLEY (*testily*). Of course I do.

DICK. A son who is good, wise, witty, amiable, clever, charitable, and,—and,—and so forth. (*Aside.*) I think that's a pretty good character for a son.

MR. WIGLEY. I am happy to find you have such a good opinion of my son.

DICK. Your son is in love.

MR. WIGLEY. Don't know that? Of course he is in love with Miss Finniken.

DICK. Yes, but he wants to marry somebody else.

MR. WIGLEY (*starting up*). What?

DICK. Now, don't get excited. What an excitable family yours is!
[*Rises from chair.*

MR. WIGLEY. If my son marries anybody else but Miss Finniken, I'll disinherit him. Why, she has a hundred and twenty thousand dollars in her own right.

DICK. But your son don't love her.

MR. WIGLEY. He must, he shall love her. Whom does he want to marry instead?

DICK. That fascinating and charming young lady, Miss Hayne.

MR. WIGLEY. My ward! why she has only twenty thousand dollars; a mere trifle.

DICK. You are a peculiarly funny old boy, to call twenty thousand dollars—a trifle.

MR. WIGLEY. No matter, sir. Why do fathers have sons? I wish there were no such things as sons. They're enough to drive one mad.
[*Walks up and down stage in a great passion.*

DICK. That's capital, capital. (*Sits astride of a chair, rests his arms upon the back of it, and contemplates* MR. WIGLEY.) If you were to go into training, you'd make a first-rate pedestrian. How's your wind?

MR. WIGLEY. Pshaw! You're every bit as bad as my son.

DICK. Don't say that, don't say that, you hurt my feelings. (*Rises from chair.*) For I'm sure I'd marry Miss Finniken, and her hundred and twenty thousand dollars, if you'll only say the word.

MR. WIGLEY. I suppose you are commissioned by my son, to tell me of his wish to marry Miss Hayne.

DICK. You hit the nail on the head that time.

MR. WIGLEY. Then tell him, if he does not do as I wish, I never want to see him again.

DICK. Very well. Who's your tailor?

MR. WIGLEY. What has that to do with you, sir?

DICK. Oh, nothing, only you'd better order a suit of mourning.

MR. WIGLEY. What for, sir?

DICK. Simply that you won't see your son any more. He told me with tears in his eyes, that, if he couldn't get your consent, he'd kill himself.

MR. WIGLEY (*eagerly*). Did he say so?

DICK. You haven't been in his room lately. Bless you, he has there poisons of every kind, from the slow brandy to the sudden strychnine.

MR. WIGLEY. Do you really think he will poison himself?

DICK. Haven't the slightest doubt of it. Shall I ring the bell for twelve men, and a Coroner, or does that flinty heart of yours soften?

MR. WIGLEY (*affected*). My poor boy!

DICK. A propitious moment! The stern parent relents, so call in the children to be forgiven. (*Goes to the door, and calls off.*) Charles, Miss Hayne, come here,—receive your father's blessing, and be happy.

Enter CHARLES *and* JENNIE, *who kneel at* WIGLEY'S *feet.*

CHARLES. Will you consent?

WIGLEY (*turning away from them*). I cannot. I won't.

DICK (*running to door, and calling off*). Mary—John—somebody, bring some strychnine for Mr. Charles.   [CHARLES *and* JENNIE *rise.*

JENNIE. Pray, pray, forgive us.

WIGLEY (*goes to chair, and sits down*). No, I shan't.

DICK. Oh! but you must; we want to finish the play, and it will never do to end it without the parent's blessing.

WIGLEY. I don't care. I won't do it.

DICK. You must. You know it is usual in such cases.

WIGLEY. Oh! if it is usual. Children, come here! (*He joins* CHARLES *and* JENNIE'S *hands together, they kneel down, and he blesses them in a melo-dramatic manner.*) There, will that do?

[CHARLES *and* JENNIE *rise.*

DICK. Now everything is finished as it should be. (*To audience.*) You knew it would end that way—didn't you? A farce always does. The parent relents—the lovers are made happy—and as a matter of course, down comes the curtain.

CHARLES (*to* DICK). Before the curtain falls let us thank you——

JENNIE. For you are——

DICK. So "Irresistibly Impudent."

DICK, *centre.*   CHARLES *and* JENNIE, *left.*   MR. WIGLEY, *right.*

CURTAIN.

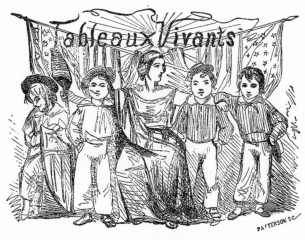

OR,

Living Pictures.

THIS style of amusement is already tolerably well known, and quite popular in many places, but owing to a want of *savoir faire* on the part of those who arrange the " living pictures," they are rarely produced with much effect, except at our best theatres, at the close of melo-dramas, pantomimes, or extravaganzas.

Of course, the performance of the home-circle troupe will hardly expect to rival these, yet by following our directions carefully, some very brilliant and pleasing scenes may be arranged, with but little trouble, and at an almost nominal expense.

The things to be observed in getting up a tableau, are just the same as in painting a picture. Light and shade, color and tone, are the means by which all pictorial effects are produced on the stage or on the canvas, and he who best understands their employment, is the best artist. Without doubt, the best place for the arrangement of tableaux, is a parlor, separated from the audience by folding-doors. The stage, heretofore described, however, may be made to answer very well, if there is sufficient room on each side of the curtain to conceal one or

7*

two persons, to superintend the burning of colored lights, the shifting of screens, etc.

It is impossible to give any fixed rules which will apply to all tableaux, as the effects required for different subjects are totally different. But a few general directions may not be amiss, as they will be found of frequent service, and will suggest many more. The costuming of the performers will be one of the most important features, and will depend entirely upon their taste and resources. Hints have already been given on this subject, as also on the "making up," by painting, etc. The colors of the garments used in tableaux are much more to be considered than in dramatic representations, as much of the beauty of the picture depends upon a harmonious and pleasing distribution of tints. As a general rule, the lightest colored figures should be kept in the back-ground, to relieve the darker ones. A strong "bit of color," such as a scarlet shawl, or a military coat, gracefully disposed in the middle ground, between the nearest and farthest figures, will have a good effect in many scenes, whether worn by some character, or thrown over a piece of furniture. At the same time, great care should be taken to avoid the common and vulgar error of combining too many gay colors. Indeed, the two great reasons of the want of artistic effect in tableaux, as commonly arranged, are first, too much light, and second, too much color. In almost every tableau where more than three figures appear, one at least should be in shadow, relieved by something light behind. The following diagram will show how the shadow may be gained:

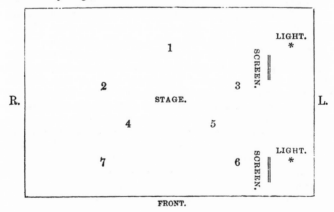

FRONT.

Suppose the figures 1, 2, 3, 4, 5, 6, 7, to represent the performers. The two lights, indicated thus *, illuminate the back of the stage, forming a light background. Figure 1 will then be in range of both lights; figure 2 will be partially shaded by figure 5; figure 3 will be partially shaded by the screens; figures 4 and 5 will be in full light; figure 6 in deep shadow from both screens, and figure 7 dimly illuminated by the rear light only. Here we have a different degree of light for almos. every character, and the effect will be found a charming one. Foot lights should hardly ever be used in arranging tableaux, as they givᵉ shadows exactly the opposite of picturesque. The lights should be bril liant, placed high up, and few in number. A good effect may some- times be got by cross-lights, but, generally, it is best to have them aᴸ on one side of the stage.

Colored lights are capable of being used with very happy results, and it is by no means a difficult matter to produce them, either by colored fires, such as are used at the theatres, or by filling globes with colored liquids, and placing them in front of the lamps, like those we see in the windows of chemists' shops. Red fire, which is beautiful for lighting up the finale of a scene, especially where the subject is heroic, national, or martial, may be made from the following receipt (care must be taken to preserve the proportions):

Five ounces nitrate of strontia (dry); one-and-a-half ounces finely-powdered sulphur; take five drams chlorate of potash, and four drams sulphuret of antimony, and powder them separately in a mortar; then mix them on paper, and having mixed the other ingredients (previously powdered), add these last, and rub the whole together on paper. For use, mix a little spirits of wine with the powder, and burn in a flat iron pan or plate.

A beautiful green fire, forming a fine contrast to the former, may be made by powdering finely and mixing well thirteen parts flour of sulphur, five parts oxymuriate of potassa, two parts metallic arsenic, and three parts pulverized charcoal. Then take seventy-seven parts nitrate of baryta, dry it carefully, powder it, and mix the whole thoroughly. A polished reflector, fitted on one side of the pan in which this is burned, will concentrate the light, and cast a brilliant green lustre on the figures.

A bluish-green fire may be produced by burning muriate of copper, finely powdered and mixed with spirits of wine, and several other colors can be obtained by a little study of chemistry; but the smoke and smell of these preparations render them less pleasant for the drawing-room than the globes filled with colored liquids. Where a window opens from the side of the stage, the fire might be burned outside, or even in a hall, where a door could be opened. Generally, however, the other plan will be found the neatest and simplest. Sulphate of copper, dissolved in water (after having been heated and pulverized), will give a beautiful blue liquid. The common red cabbage, or litmus, so well known in chemistry, will give three different colors, thus:

Slice the litmus thin, and pour boiling water on it. Decant the infusion, when cold, and add a small quantity of alum dissolved in water, which will give a clear rich purple. If potash dissolved in water be used instead of alum, the water will assume a brilliant green tint. A fine crimson may be got by a few drops of muriatic acid, instead of alum or potash.

For ghostly scenes, where a sepulchral unearthly effect is desired, the following may be tried, and if properly managed, will astonish even the performers themselves:

Mix some common salt with spirits of wine, in a metal cup, and set it upon a wire frame, over a spirit-lamp. When the cup becomes heated, and the spirits of wine ignite, the other lights in the room should be extinguished, and that of the spirit-lamp shaded in some way. The result will be that the whole group—faces, dresses, and all —will be of one dingy yellow tint, no matter how bright their costumes or how rosy their cheeks may be.

Another great accessory to the tableau, but one which cannot always be had, is thin gauze, or common mosquito netting—in fact, any stuff which can be seen through—to interpose between the audience and the scene. Several curtains of this, made to let down from rollers, one after another, will give a beautiful, misty, vanishing appearance; and if enough be unrolled, the tableau appears to vanish entirely, allowing room for a change of scene, if desired. This gauze should be carefully managed, as the disclosure of a ragged edge would dispel all the illusion. Many scenes should have one thickness before them at first, to prevent a too startling distinctness; and some may be concealed entirely by the gauze, which is gradually rolled up, until the tableau becomes visible. These varieties of effect, however, depend on the subjects, and the talent of those who arrange them.

A number of almost supernatural effects may be procured by the aid of a magic lantern; and that instrument will be found quite invaluable to the amateur theatrical company. Its use, in getting up tableaux or scenes containing ghosts, dreams, or fancies of any kind, is very great.

These, with a few screens for shading certain figures, are about all the appurtenances required for arranging excellent tableaux which are at all difficult to procure. The materials for all else may be found in almost any house, either in the city or country. The tableaux which follow are intended more to suggest how such things are to be done, than as models. After two or three of them have been got up, careful attention having been paid to the directions, it will be an easy matter to invent new ones. The great requirement on the part of the performers is, of course, merely to remain perfectly still—a feat which may be acquired to a wonderful degree by practising before a mirror. Where a large group is to be *posed*, there is often a tendency to laugh —why, it is hard to say ; but this may be overcome by frequent rehearsals. In fact, none but the very simplest tableaux should be produced without three rehearsals at least, and many require half-a- dozen.

We need scarcely add, that appropriate music on the piano-forte, harp, or other instrument, will add much to the effect of any tableaux.

————o————

THE ARMY AND NAVY.

In the centre of stage the Goddess of Liberty is sitting, resting upon her shield, and holding in her hand a pole, on the top of which is the Phrygian cap. On left centre of stage, a sailor is standing with the American flag in his hand. On the right centre a soldier is standing, also with a banner in his hand. The flags are crossed, and their faces are turned towards audience.

POSITION OF CHARACTERS IN TABLEAU.

STAGE.

FRONT OF STAGE.

1. Goddess of Liberty. 2. The Sailor. 3. The Soldier.

In this tableau as much light should be thrown upon the stage as possible. The Goddess of Liberty should have bare arms, and be arrayed in a loose, flowing, white garment. The shield of liberty can easily be made out of cardboard, with the assistance of some blue and red paint. The liberty cap can also be made in the same way. With regard to the soldier and sailor, we presume that all our readers will be enabled to costume them without our assistance. Just before the curtain descends, a good effect can be produced by igniting some red fire on each side of stage.

———o———

THE GAMBLER'S WARNING.

At right centre of stage is a table covered with green baize, around which six or seven men are sitting, playing at cards. At the back of stage is a sideboard with decanter and glasses. A negro in a white jacket is standing at sideboard, pouring some liquor into a tumbler; near him, and leaning against the sideboard in an easy attitude, is one of the gamblers. On the left of stage some gauze should be stretched across diagonally, behind which is the figure of a woman, with one arm laid across her breast, and the other pointing upward. All the figures at the table are intently watching the cards, with one exception; he is standing erect, with an expression of wonderment and terror upon his face, and is looking at figure behind gauze. His left hand is resting upon the table; the right is outstretched, holding a card; two cards are upon the floor, as though they had just fallen from his hand.

POSITION OF CHARACTERS IN TABLEAU.

STAGE.

FRONT OF STAGE.

1 The table at which the gamblers are sitting
2. The sideboard.
3. Gauze stretched across stage.
4. Figure behind gauze.

5. The figure standing erect.
6. The negro.
7. Man leaning against sideboard.

In this tableau the right of stage should be in full light; the left in shadow. A strong soft light should be thrown upon the figure behind gauze, which can be made by letting the light shine through a globe of clear water. After a few moments, a good effect could he obtained by letting a blue light fall upon character on left, and a red one upon the gamblers. It can easily be done by using colored water in the globes.

The figure behind gauze should be attired in a white robe, looking very pale, with a sorrowful expression upon her face. The gamblers should be well, but showily dressed, with heavy moustaches, otherwise cleanly shaved. The figure standing at table should be neatly dressed, and wearing no beard or moustache.

———o———

MISCHIEF IN SCHOOL.

For this tableau the stage should be furnished with desks, benches, etc., to resemble a school as nearly as possible. A black board is hung at the back of the stage, in centre, and a boy stands on a stool before it, sketching a ridiculous caricature of the master. Three or four others stand around him, in school-boy position, watching the progress of the drawing. A desk is placed at right of stage, at which a boy sits, pretending to study, but with his eyes fixed on the door, left, where the master is seen entering with a long rod in his hand, and a grim smile on his face. Two boys are in the act of scuffling at the left of stage, concealed from the master by the door. Another stands on a table, near the desk, right, with the dunce's cap on his head. Three others are playing marbles near the group, centre.

The diagram on page 160 will explain the positions:

Some of the boys may be eating apples, cakes, etc., and a variety of books, maps, inkstands, rulers, and other school-furniture should be scattered about here and there. As the interest of the scene depends entirely upon the surprise, but little attention need be paid to the effects of light and shade, etc., the main object being to have all the groups in plain sight, and naturally arranged.

———o———

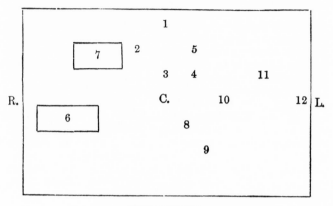

FRONT OF STAGE.

1. Boy at black board.
2, 3, 4, 5. Boys looking on.
6. Boy at desk, pretending to study.
7. Table, with boy in dunce's cap.
8, 9, 10. Boys playing marbles.
11. Boys scuffling.
12. Door, with master entering.

————o————

THE BURGLARY.

Unlike the above, this scene owes its charm chiefly to the pictu-
resqueness of its effects. The scene is a chamber, with a bed, right,
in which a man is sleeping. Another, roughly dressed and closely
muffled up, with a hat slouched over his eyes, stands over the sleeper,
with a knife raised above him. The robber should be "made up" in
the most repulsive manner possible—his face slightly smutted with
burnt cork, a black patch over one eye, a red handkerchief loosely
knotted about his neck, and his whole appearance that of a scoundrel of
the lowest class. (*See Introduction.*)

In the centre, another burglar is kneeling on one knee in front of a
trunk, taking from it a variety of articles, some of which are scattered

about him. Among these, some pieces of plate, jewelry, and ornaments of porcelain or metal, with some blue, green, crimson, or other gay stuffs, will give brilliancy to the scene, and should be illuminated by a dark lantern in the hand of the burglar who is examining them. A centre-bit, chisel, and pistols, should lie near him, and he should be made up similarly to the first. The chamber should contain a bureau, dressing-case, etc. ; and a looking-glass may be so placed at back of stage as to reflect one of the burglars with good effect.

The light on the stage should be very dim, and unless the stage be very large, that of the lantern will be sufficient. The burglar at the bed should shade the sleeper, and be only in a half-light himself. The one at the chest should have his face in full light, and great care should be taken in making him up. For low or villanous characters, an additional ghastliness may be produced by showing no white of shirt or collar, having simply a black or colored handkerchief around the throat. A black cloth tied around the head, and under the chin, gives a pecu liarly horrible effect.

FRONT OF STAGE.

1. Bed, with man asleep.
2. Burglar with knife.
3. Trunk, with articles scattered about.
4. Burglar with lantern.

Of course, the sleeper's clothing should be hung upon a chair near the bed, and other appointments arranged about the stage to give an air of naturalness.

A single thickness of gauze in front of the scene will add to its gloomy air.

————o————

CAGLIOSTRO'S MAGIC MIRROR.

This tableau illustrates the tradition of the Magic Mirror possessed by Count Cagliostro, a so-called magician, who lived some time during the seventeenth century. In the present scene, he is supposed to be showing a young courtier the image of his lady-love, who is deceased.

A large frame should be set up in the rear of the stage, centre, with a large volume open before it. A lamp, one of curious form, if such can be got, stands just behind the volume, and across the open pages of the latter a naked sword is laid. If a human skull can be had, that also may be placed on the book.

On the left of the frame, in shadow, stands Count Cagliostro, pointing towards the vision. On the right, the young nobleman stands in an attitude of fear and wonder. The vision is in the centre of the frame, standing just back from it, and is represented by a young girl, extremely pale, in a long, sweeping, white robe, with her hands crossed upon her bosom, and her eyes turned upwards. One or two thicknesses of gauze should be stretched over the frame, and the vision illuminated by two lights, placed one on each side, behind, and concealed by the frame. If curtains can be attached to the latter, so as to prevent the light of these lamps from falling on anything but the girl, the effect will be beautiful.

The costume of the Count should be a small black cap, with a single drooping black feather, a long black cloak or robe, with a lace collar turned over it, and ruffles about his wrists; black stockings and knee-breeches, pumps with large buckles, and a small sword, complete the dress. His face should be rather pale, with a black moustache and heavy black eyebrows. His expression should be solemn, and a little scornful.

The young courtier should have a somewhat rich dress. A dark coat, with gold lace on the cuffs, collar, and lappels; light-colored knee-breeches, white stockings, pumps with rosettes, a dress sword, lace collar and wristbands, and (if possible) a powdered court wig. He may have a slight moustache and imperial, but should appear much younger than Cagliostro, and should stand more in the light. Directions for producing these occasional lights and shades will be found in the introduction.

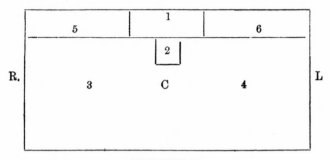

FRONT OF STAGE.

1. A large table, upon which the girl who represents the vision, is to stand. Upon its front edge the frame is to be rested.

2. Small stand, covered with dark cloth, supporting book, lamp, sword, etc.

3. Cagliostro.

4. Courtier.

5, 6. Curtains stretched from the side of the frame, to conceal the lamps which light up the vision.

The frame may easily be made of narrow boards, roughly nailed together, and covered with black velvet, neatly tacked on.

----------O----------

THE DRUNKARD'S HOME.

A dilapidated room, with an empty grate, and an empty saucepan lying on its side, so that the audience can see the interior. In one corner of the room (L.) a bed of straw, upon which two children are lying. The elder, a girl, is supporting the younger, a boy, and is leaning over him, as though she were trying to soothe him and keep him quiet. A mother is sitting upon a stool (R. C.), holding a baby closely to her breast, with an old worn-out shawl wrapped around it. On the right, the drunkard is stretched upon the ground, insensible from drink. His clothes are torn and muddy; by his side is an old and battered hat; in his hand is an empty bottle, which he still clutches firmly. The wife is gazing upon the husband, with a look of mingled love and sorrow.

Everything is to denote, as much as possible, misery and want. The woman to have hollow eyes and sunken cheeks. The children upon the straw are to have bare arms, and to be "made up," so as to appear wretchedly thin and emaciated. (*See instructions for making up.*)

POSITION OF CHARACTERS IN TABLEAU.

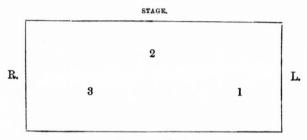

1. The bed of straw, upon which the children are lying.
2. The wife.
8. The drunkard.

To heighten the effect of this tableau, some fine gauze might be stretched across the stage, so as to give everything a dim and cheerless appearance. In using gauze, care should be taken that the whole front of the stage be carefully covered, so as not to mar the effect by having a stronger light at the bottom, sides, or top, than in the centre. Instructions are given in the introduction to tableaux, how the gauze can be fixed.

————o————

SIGNING THE PLEDGE.

The same room as in the Drunkard's Home. In the centre of the stage is a stool. The drunkard is kneeling upon one knee, with his face towards the audience. He has a pen in his hand, and is signing his name to a paper that is upon the stool. His eldest daughter is looking timidly over his right shoulder, with her left hand resting upon him. On the right of the drunkard is the temperance advocate; he has an ink-horn in his hand, and is looking down, smiling benignantly.

upon the signer. At the left centre the wife is kneeling down; on one arm she holds her babe, while the other is uplifted towards heaven. Her face is upturned also, with an expression of gratitude and happiness upon it. The boy has hold of his mother's skirt, and is looking at her with wondering eyes.

POSITION OF CHARACTERS IN TABLEAU.

STAGE.

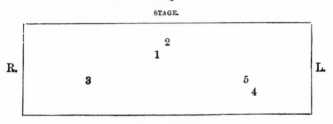

FRONT OF STAGE.

1. The drunkard signing pledge.
2. The daughter.
3. The temperance advocate.
4. The mother, with her babe.
5. The little boy.

Instead of dropping the curtain, for the last tableau, "The Drunkard's Home," some gauze might be let down, gradually increasing in thickness, till it completely shuts out the tableau from audience. "Signing the Pledge," might then be arranged, which must be done quickly, but noiselessly; then clear away *all* the gauze, and have a subdued light fall upon the whole group. A good soft light can be obtained by letting the gas, or lamp, shine through glass globes, containing water. The globes, such as are seen in chemists' shop-windows, can easily be obtained at any druggist's fixture store, at a small cost. The above tableaux, if arranged and conducted properly, will have a very pleasing and telling result.

————o————

THE TEMPERANCE HOME.

A room comfortably, but meanly furnished, with a square piece of drugget in centre of stage. A deal table is placed on the middle of carpet, upon which are laid some tea-things, as though supper was about to be served. At left of stage, the husband is standing, with his hat on, and a basket of tools at his back, as though he had just come in from work. The boy is clutching him round the leg, and looking up into his face. The girl is sitting on a chair (R.), nursing the baby, and is looking towards her father with a smile of welcome. The wife is standing by a chair, as though she had just risen from it, with her body inclined toward her husband, one hand is extended, and in the other she holds some needle-work.

POSITION OF CHARACTERS IN TABLEAU.

STAGE.

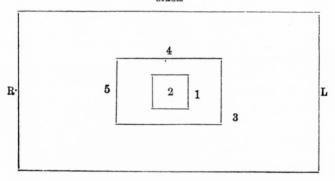

FRONT OF STAGE.

1. A piece of drugget.
2. A deal table.
3. The husband, with boy clinging to his leg.
4. The wife.
5. The daughter, with baby.

In this Tableau, as much light should be thrown upon the stage as possible, so as to give the whole chamber a comfortable and pleasant appearance.

We presume, we need not tell the performers in this tableau, that all the figures should be economically, but neatly dressed; so as to make the illusion greater to the audience, with regard to its being the home of a mechanic.

THE DUEL.

At the back of stage five or six chairs are piled one on top of another. Also at back of stage (L.), a table, upon which are some bottles and glasses; under table a pack of cards is scattered. On the left of stage, one of the duellists stands, in his shirt sleeves, looking towards left at his opponent, with a grim smile upon his countenance. He is wiping his sword with a handkerchief, that he holds in his left hand. His second has his right hand resting upon the duellist's left arm, looking at him with an anxious face, and is pointing off with his left hand, as if advising him to fly. On the right of stage, a wounded man is lying, in his shirt sleves, with his head and shoulders supported by his second, who is in a kneeling position, and looking at the injured man with a terrified expression. By the side of the fallen man is a doctor, examining the wound with professional calmness. On the backs of some of the chairs, the coats, vests, neckties, etc., are carelessly thrown. In the centre of stage is a sword lying upon the floor.

POSITION OF CHARACTERS IN TABLEAU.

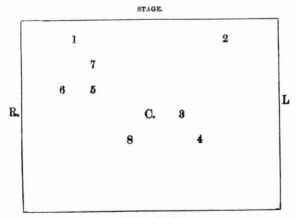

1. Chairs.
2. Table.
3. The duellist wiping his sword.
4. His second.
5. The wounded man.
6. His second.
7. The doctor.
8. A sword.

In this tableau the lights should be softened as much as possible.

A fine gauze stretched across stage would add much to the appearance of this tableau. The wounded man is to be "made up" so as to appear extremely pale and ghastly. To heighten the effect, a few drops of blood can be seen upon his shirt, which can be easily represented by a little crimson lake being smeared upon a piece of rag, and pinned upon it.

--------o--------

LOVE AND JEALOUSY.

To the right centre of stage, a cavalier, dressed in a slashed doublet and jacket, trunk hose, low shoes, with large pink rosettes, and a velvet cap and feather. At his side hangs a rapier. A guitar, upon which he is playing, is suspended from his neck with a blue ribbon. The cavalier wears a small moustache, and carries himself jauntily. To the left centre of stage, a man, enveloped in a dark cloak, lined with red, creeping stealthily towards the cavalier. In his right hand is a poniard. A slouched hat, with feather, is to be pulled down over his brow, and a heavy beard and moustache is to be worn; also black stockings and low shoes. With his left arm he is holding the cloak to his face, as though trying to disguise his features.

POSITION OF CHARACTERS IN TABLEAU.

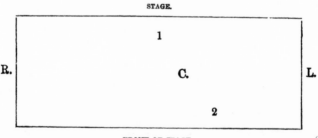

STAGE.

R.   1   **C.**   2   **L.**

FRONT OF STAGE.

1. The cavalier.
2. The man with poniard.

Stage to be rather dark. The cavalier to be in full light, with his back turned toward assassin, who is to be in deep shadow.

THE MUSIC LESSON.

The stage for this tableau is arranged like a lady's boudoir, with the usual complement of birds, cages, flower-pots, toilet appurtenances, drawing and embroidery materials, etc. A sofa is set in the centre, a little back, and a folding screen placed zigzag just behind it. On the sofa a young lady is seated, holding a guitar listlessly in her left hand, while a gentleman, kneeling gracefully before her, is kissing her right. He should be so placed, however, as to show his profile to the audience, as it is in bad taste ever to turn the back directly towards the front of the stage. Over the top of the screen, immediately behind the young couple, is seen the head of another man—the father or guardian of the lady—intently regarding her with an expression of comical horror and surprise.

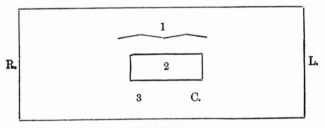

FRONT OF STAGE.

1. The guardian, behind the screen.
2. The sofa, with the young lady.
3. The gentleman, kneeling.

Some sheet music should be carelessly scattered about the floor and sofa, with the hat and gloves of the gallant teacher of music. The young lady should be in an easy, elegant position, with her face a little averted, but her eyes turned towards her suitor. A little rouge may be effectively used upon her cheeks, for producing the blush which is supposed to be natural to such occasions. The face of the guardian should be carefully "made up" with reference to age and expression, with eyebrows strongly arched, wrinkles, a ferocious moustache, curled up at the ends, etc.

If conveniences can be had for getting up picturesque and elegant costumes, the suitor may be dressed as a cavalier, with doublet, belt,

8

lace collar and cuffs, knee-breeches and stockings, and a rapier. His
hat should then be a wide-brimmed black felt, caught up on the left side
with a buckle and feather, and his gloves should be riding gauntlets.
The lady should also have a dress in accordance with the styles of the
middle ages, which may be learned by consulting the French prints
representing similar scenes, and her hair should be drawn straight
back from her forehead, and powdered. A large white ruffle around
the guardian's neck, will be in keeping, and add to the ludicrousness
of his appearance. If, however, the resources of the parlor theatrical
troupe are limited, the costume of the day may be used.

In arranging the light, care should be taken to have the guardian's
face in half-shade, and the strongest light upon the lady. Some heavy,
dark curtains may be hung at the sides of the stage, to bring out the
colors of the sofa, the lady's dress, etc., and the ornaments and toilet-
articles should be strewn about with an easy graceful negligence.

--------o--------

THE FOUR SEASONS.

The four seasons of the year, Spring, Summer, Autumn and Winter,
represented by female figures, make a very beautiful tableau, if artisti-
cally arranged. The stage should have three platforms placed upon
it, each a little higher than the one in front of it, something like the
steps of a staircase, receding from the audience. Spring, represented by
a little girl, dressed in pure white, with a basket of flowers, which she is
apparently strewing before her, stands upon the stage, in front, nearest
the audience. A single thickness of gauze is run across in front of the
first platform, upon which stands Summer—a young girl just growing
into womanhood, crowned with a wreath of summer flowers, and
holding an apron full of summer fruits, mingled with flowers. Her
dress is also to be white, but trimmed with chaplets of green leaves.
Another thickness of gauze is stretched behind her, in front of the
platform which supports Autumn—a smiling matron, in a dress of
richer material, with a garland of autumnal leaves about her head. In
her arms she holds a sheaf of grain, and a sickle in one hand, while a
piece of vine, laden with grapes, is carelessly thrown over her shoulder.
Winter stands on the furthest platform, with a third screen of gauze in
front of her. She is an old crone with a sallow and wrinkled face, and

her bent form is heavily draped in a long robe of dull brown or grey woollen. Upon one shoulder she bears a fagot of dry sticks, and in her hand an axe. If an additional wintry effect is desired, pieces of small glass tubing (which can be procured at almost any chemist's shop), may be attached to the edge of her robe, in imitation of icicles, and flour may be scattered upon her head and shoulders, to represent snow.

5	1	5
6	2	6
7	3	7
	4	

R. ... L.

FRONT OF STAGE.

1. The first and highest platform, with Winter.
2. The second, supporting Autumn.
3. The third, for Summer.
4. The figure of Spring.
5, 5. The first gauze.
6, 6. The second gauze.
7, 7. The third gauze.

The gauze screens will shade the figures sufficiently, without any different degrees of light being thrown upon them.

PARLOR GAMES

A Repertory of Social Amusements,

CONTAINING AN EXPLANATION OF

THE MOST ENTERTAINING GAMES,

SUITED TO THE FAMILY CIRCLE FOR A RECREATION, SUCH AS

GAMES OF ACTION.—GAMES WHICH REQUIRE ATTENTION MERELY.—
GAMES WHICH REQUIRE MEMORY.—CATCH GAMES, WHICH HAVE
FOR THEIR OBJECT TRICK OR MYSTIFICATION.—GAMES
IN WHICH AN OPPORTUNITY IS AFFORDED TO DIS-
PLAY GALLANTRY, WIT, OR SOME SLIGHT
KNOWLEDGE OF CERTAIN SCIENCES.—
FORFEITS, ETC.

AT merry Christmas-time, or on a wet day in the country, or in the city too, for that matter, or on a winter's evening, when the fire is burning cheerily, pussy purring on the hearth, and the lamps lighted, young folks are often at a loss, and their elders too, sometimes, to know how to amuse themselves. Some people will say, "There are books, let them read." We would whisper in their ears an adage as old as the hills, but none the less true or pithy; it is this: "All work and no play makes Jack a dull boy." And again, let us remember that we also were once young, and laughed as heartily over "Blind Man's Buff" as the youngest of our acquaintance.

All the apparatus required in "Parlor Games" is good temper, good spirits, and gentleness, so that at any moment amusement for an evening can be obtained by anybody who wills it.

We do not wish to read our young friends a homily upon politeness, as this is not a book of etiquette, but we would impress upon them that good temper is indispensable in games of any kind. We have known the pleasure of a whole party marred simply by the unreasonableness and ill-humor of one of the players, who, because he could not guess the answer of some game, declared that we had cheated him, and refused to play any longer, thus casting a gloom upon all who were playing.

Roughness, too, we would particularly caution our boy friends to avoid. Very often, when carried away by the buoyancy of their spirits, they are apt to forget that young ladies are present, and participating in the pleasures of the game. There is no occasion for an exhibition of strength; if you are caught, submit to it; if you are forfeited, pay the fine without a murmur, or with a pleasant remark.

Very often your little brothers or sisters will spoil a game by revealing who it is that is caught, or telling the answer to "Twenty Questions," before the person whose turn it is to guess it, has given it up. Do not be angry with them, but take another question, and begin again, for in all probability letting the secret out was merely childish importance, in knowing the answer as well as his elder brothers and sisters. Explain to him that he must not do so for the future, as he spoils the game; and, take our word for it, he will try to avoid doing so again.

We have heard many people say, "Oh, he's too young, he can't play." We say not so; no child is too young to join in healthy and innocent pastime. There is no occasion to give a child a prominent part to perform, or to let him perform any part at all; but you can lead him to believe that his presence is in every way as desirable as that of the oldest person present. Not that we advocate deception as a general thing, but we do countenance it where it is used for the purpose of making children happy. We ourselves have, in the game of "Fox and Goose," carried a child on our arm throughout the whole; he had nothing at all to do with it, but he laughed as loudly and as heartily as any of the party.

Many of these games are quite new, and have never appeared in print before. They have been selected and invented by a gentleman who is thoroughly conversant with the "Parlor Games" of Europe. In some cases the forfeit has to be paid by a kiss; of course that is only intended for a family party; in a mixed assembly some other mode of payment can be substituted.

With these remarks, we leave our readers to enjoy themselves over "Parlor Games."

Games of Action.

------◂------

THE LEG OF MUTTON.

Almost every one is acquainted with this game. The players place
their fists alternately one upon the other, then the fist which is lower-
most is withdrawn and placed on the top of the pile, each as he withdraws his fist counting one, two, and so on, to nine. As soon as the ninth
fist is placed on the top, the whole pile is overturned, each hand being
withdrawn as quickly as possible. The one who has pronounced the
word nine, must endeavor to catch one of his companions by the hand,
saying " *This is my leg of mutton.*" If he fails to do this, he has to pay
a forfeit. If he succeeds in catching a hand, he says to the player who
has allowed himself to be caught, " *Will you do one of three things?*"
If the player is polite, he simply answers, " *I will, if I can.*" Others
might reply, " *I will, if I like.*" Then the winner gives him three things
to do, and he performs either at his choice.

------o------

THE FAGOTS.

This game consists in forming a double circle, the players placing
themselves two by two, so that each gentleman, by holding a lady in
front of him, makes what is called a fagot. It is necessary that the
players should be of an even number. The circles being formed, two
persons are chosen, the one to catch the other. When the person who
is pursued does not wish to be overtaken (which would oblige him to
take the place of the pursuer), and at the same time desires to rest, he
places himself in front of any one of the fagots he chooses, but within
the circle, so that this fagot is then composed of three persons, which
is contrary to rule. Then the third one, who is on the outside of the
circle, must at once run to avoid being caught. If he *is caught*, he
takes the place of the pursuer, who, in his turn, starts off, or, if he pre-

fers it, enters into the circle, and places himself before one of the fagots, thus obliging a new player to run like the former one; this one himself can at once oblige another player to run, by placing himself, in his turn, before a fagot, and it is this which gives life to the game, provided the players have a fair share of spirit and agility.

————o————

THE WOLF AND THE HIND.

In this game all the ladies present can find employment, but only one gentleman is required, and the one who is considered the most agile should be chosen, for, in truth, he will find exercise enough for his dexterity and his patience.

This personage is called in this game the Wolf; the eldest lady present is the Hind; all the others place themselves in a line behind her, according to their ages, and are called the Hind's fawns.

It is the Wolf's part to catch the lady who is at the extremity of the line, and he manifests his hostile intentions by the following conversation:—"*I am a Wolf, and I will eat you.*"

The Hind answers—"*I am a Hind, and I will defend myself.*"

The Wolf replies—"*I must have the youngest and tenderest of your fawns.*"

After this dialogue, the Wolf endeavors to seize the desired prey, but the Hind, extending her arms, keeps him off; but if he succeeds in passing her, the young lady at the end of the line may abandon her place before he can catch her, and place herself in front of the Hind, where she no longer runs any risk, and so with the rest in succession, until the Hind becomes the last of the line.

Then the game ends; the unskilful Wolf must pay as many forfeits as he has allowed young ladies to escape, and the players select a successor if they wish to renew the game.

If, on the contrary, before the end of the game, he succeeds in seizing one of the young fawns, he does not eat her, but he has a right to claim a kiss from her, and to make her pay a forfeit, which promises new pleasure at the end of the game.

This game, requiring, as it does, much quickness of movement and agility, is not as well fitted for the house as for a lawn or a field, where it presents a picturesque view to the lookers-on, and at the same time enables the players to display to advantage the grace and rapidity of their movements.

BLIND-MAN'S BUFF SEATED.

In order to play Blind-Man's Buff seated, the company arrange themselves in a circle upon chairs which are placed very near together. The person chosen by lot, or who voluntarily offers to play the part of the blind man, allows a handkerchief to be bound over his eyes by a lady, if the player is a gentleman, and by a gentleman, if it is a lady who undertakes this part.

When all are satisfied that the blind man cannot discern the objects which surround him, the players hastily change their places in order to baffle his sagacity. Then he approaches the circle without groping, for this is expressly forbidden, and seats himself in the lap of the first person he comes across, and without employing the sense of touch, but simply by listening to the stifled laughter around him, to the rustling of the robes, the sound of which often discovers the wearer, or perhaps by a fortunate guess, he is enabled to tell the name of the player upon whose lap he is seated, and in case he is unacquainted with the name of the personage, describe her in such a manner that she can be recognised.

If the blind man guesses correctly, the person discovered takes his place, puts on the bandage, and performs the same part. If, on the contrary, he is mistaken, the company clap their hands to inform him of his error, and he renews the experiment in the same manner, and without employing any other means than those authorized by the game.

It is customary for the company, in order to prevent the blind man from recognising persons too readily, to resort to various little stratagems, as for instance, some spread over their laps the skirts of their neighbors' dresses, others cover theirs with the cushions of the chairs. The ladies who are dressed in silk, place their shawls over their laps; in fine, all try to disguise themselves in the best manner possible.

—————o—————

BLIND-MAN'S BUFF BY THE PROFILE.

When this game is played in a proper manner it is very entertaining. The following is the method of playing it.

In this game the blind man's eyes are not bandaged, but he is notwithstanding obliged to exercise all his penetration. A piece of white and rather fine linen is stretched upon a frame like a screen, in the same way as when exhibiting a magic lantern. The blind man is seated upon a stool, so low that his shadow is not represented upon the linen, which is spread over the screen. Some distance behind him a single lighted taper is placed upon a stand, and all the other lights in the room are extinguished.

When these arrangements are made, the rest of the company form a kind of procession, and pass in single file, between the blind man (who is expressly forbidden to turn his head) and the table upon which the light is placed. This produces the expected effect; the light of the candle, intercepted by each of the company in turn, as he passes before it, casts upon the piece of white linen a succession of shadows quite accurately defined.

As these shadows move before him, the blind man is obliged to name aloud the person who he supposes is passing at the moment, and the errors into which he falls cause shouts of laughter, more or less prolonged.

It is hardly necessary to say that each one, as he passes before the light, tries to disguise his air, his height, his gait, to prevent his being recognised.

It is not usual to give forfeits in this game, still it would seem proper to demand them of those who are discovered. In this way it would probably afford entertainment to a greater number of players

————o————

BLIND-MAN'S BUFF WITH THE WAND.

Blind-Man's Buff with the Wand is a game well adapted for the parlor.

The blind man with his eyes covered with a bandage, is placed in the middle of the room, and a long wand is put into his hands. The rest of the company join theirs, and, forming a circle, wheel around him, at the same time singing some lively air, in which they all join.

When the song is finished, they stop, and the blind man, extending his wand, directs it, by chance, towards one of the company, who is obliged to take hold of it by the end presented to him. Then the blind man utters three cries, which the other must repeat in the same tone. If the latter does not know how to disguise his voice, he is easily guessed, and takes the blind man's place; otherwise the circle wheels around him, stops again, and so on as before.

PORCO, OR ITALIAN BLIND-MAN'S BUFF.

This game is similar to "Buff with the Wand."

Several persons, male and female, join hands so as to form a circle, and one person, who is blindfolded, is placed in the centre, with a small stick in his or her hand. The players dance round the hoodwinked person, who tries to touch one of them with the wand, and if he succeeds, the ring of people stops. The player then grunts like a pig —hence the name of the game—crows, or imitates some animal, and the person touched must endeavor to imitate the noise as closely as possible, without discovering his or herself. If the party touched is discovered, then the hoodwinked player transfers the bandage and the stick to that player, and takes the vacant place in the ring of persons, who once more resume their dance, until another player is touched.

————o————

FRENCH BLIND MAN.

In this game, instead of blindfolding one of the players, his hands are tied behind him, and in that difficult way he must endeavor to catch one of his companions, who must, when caught, submit to the same restraint.

————●————

THE RIBBONS.

Each person in the company takes a ribbon, and holds it by one end. The other ends are all united in the hand of the one who leads the game, and who consequently is placed in the middle of the circle.

When he says—" *Pull* " they must let go, when he says " *Let go* " they must pull the ribbon which they hold. It is astonishing how many forfeits are won at this simple game.

————o————

THE COTTON FLIES.

One of the players takes a flake of cotton or a bit of down, which he casts into the air in the midst of a circle formed by those present who are seated close together. He at once puffs with his breath to keep it floating in the air, and the one towards whom the flake takes its course must puff in the same way to keep it from falling upon his lap, which would cost him a forfeit.

Nothing is more amusing than to see ten or twelve people, with up-turned faces, blowing and puffing, each in his own way, to send from one to the other, this flake of cotton. Sometimes it happens that as one cannot laugh and puff at the same moment, the tuft of cotton falls into the mouth of one of the company, who in vain tries to find breath enough to blow it away. This excites the laughter of the other players, who demand from him a forfeit for his gluttony.

———o———

THE HUNTSMAN.

This game is one of the liveliest winter evening's pastimes that can be imagined. It may be played by any number of persons above four. One of the players is styled the "Huntsman," and the others must be called after the different parts of the dress or accoutrements of a sports-man: thus, one is the coat, another the hat, whilst the shot, shot-belt, powder, powder-flask, dog, and gun, and every other appurtenance be-longing to a huntsman, has its representative. As many chairs as there are players, excluding the Huntsman, should next be ranged in two rows, back to back, and all the players must then seat themselves; and being thus prepared, the Huntsman walks round the sitters, and calls out the assumed name of one of them: for instance, "Gun!" when that player immediately gets up, and takes hold of the coat-skirts of the Huntsman who continues his walk, and calls out all the others, one by one; each must take hold of the skirts of the player before him, and when they are all summoned, the Huntsman sets off running round the chairs as fast as he can, the other players holding on and running after him. When he has run round two or three times, he shouts out "Bang!" and immediately sits down on one of the chairs, leaving his followers to scramble to the other seats as they best can. Of course, one must be left standing, there being one chair less than the number of players, and the player so left must pay a forfeit. The game is con-tinued until all have paid three forfeits, when they are cried, and the punishments or penances declared. The Huntsman is not changed throughout the game, unless he gets tired of his post.

COPENHAGEN.

First procure a long piece of tape or twine, sufficient to go round the whole company, who must stand in a circle, holding in each of their hands a part of the string—the last takes hold of the two ends of the tape. One remains standing in the centre of the circle who is called "the Dane," and who must endeavor to slap the hands of one of those who are holding the string, before they can be withdrawn. Whoever is not sufficiently alert, and allows the hands to be slapped, must take the place of the Dane, and in his turn, try to slap the hands of some one else.

THE CAT AND THE MOUSE.

Let all the company join hand in hand in a circle, except one who is placed inside, called the Mouse, and another outside, called the Cat. They begin by running round, raising the arms; the Cat springs in at one side and the Mouse jumps out at the other; they then suddenly lower the arms so that the Cat cannot escape. The Cat goes round mewing, trying to get out; and as the circle must keep dancing round all the time, she must try and find a weak place to break through. As soon as she gets out she chases the Mouse, who tries to save herself by getting within the circle again. For this purpose they raise their arms. If she gets in without being followed by the Cat, the Cat must pay a forfeit, and try again; but if the Mouse is caught she must pay a forfeit. Then they name who shall succeed them; they fall into the circle, and the game goes on as before.

HUNT THE HARE.

The company all form a circle, holding each other's hands. One, called the Hare, is left out, who runs several times round the ring, and at last stops, tapping one of the players on the shoulder. The one tapped quits the ring and runs after the Hare, the circle again joining hands. The Hare runs in and out in every direction, passing under the arms of those in the circle until caught by the pursuer, when he becomes Hare himself. Those in the circle must always be friends to the Hare, and assist its escape in every way possible.

THE KEY GAME.

This game may be played by any number of persons, who should all, except one, seat themselves on chairs placed in a circle, and he should stand in the centre of the ring. Each sitter must next take hold, with his left hand, of the right wrist of the person sitting on his left, being careful not to obstruct the grasp by holding the hands. When all have, in this manner, joined hands, they should begin moving them from left to right, making a circular motion, and touching each other's hands, as if for the purpose of taking something from them. The player in the centre then presents a *key* to one of the sitters, and turns his back, so as to allow it to be privately passed to another, who hands it to a third; and thus the key is quickly handed round the ring from one player to the other; which task is easily accomplished, on account of the continued motion of the hands of all the players. Meanwhile, the player in the centre, after the key has reached the third or fourth player, should watch its progress narrowly, and endeavor to seize it in its passage. If he succeed, the person in whose hand it is found, after paying a forfeit, must take his place in the centre, and give and hunt the key in his turn ; should the seeker fail in discovering the key in his first attempt, he must continue his search until he succeeds. When a player has paid three forfeits, he is out.

————o————

HUNT THE SLIPPER.

This is usually an in-door game, although there is no other objection to its being played on a dry piece of turf than that the slipper cannot be heard, when struck by its momentary possessor, when passing round the joyous ring. Several young persons sit on the floor in a circle, a slipper is given to them, and one, who generally volunteers to accept the office in order to begin the game, stands in the centre, whose business it is to " chase the slipper by its sound." The parties who are seated, pass it round so as to prevent, if possible, its being found in the possession of any individual. In order that the player in the centre may know where the slipper is, it is occasionally tapped on the ground, and then suddenly handed on to the right or left. When the slipper is found in the possession of any one in the circle, by the player who is hunting it, the party on whom it is so found takes the latter player's place.

CATCH THE RING.

In order to p.ay this capital game, the chairs are placed in a circle, just so far apart, that each person sitting can easily reach the hand of another person on either side of him.   One person stands in the middle of the circle.   A piece of string with a wedding, or a larger ring of brass, upon it, is then tied, of a sufficient length to reach all round the circle, so that each person may catch hold of it.   The players are then to slide the ring along the string, passing it from one to the other, and the game is, for the person who stands in the centre to try to catch the ring.   When he catches it, the person with whom he finds it is to go out into the centre.

[Forfeits may be added to this game, if preferred, each person caught with the ring paying forfeit.]

————o————

JACK'S ALIVE.

A small piece of stick is lighted at one end, and the blaze blown out, leaving the sparks.   It is then passed from one of the company to the next on his right hand, and so on round the circle, each one saying, as he hands it to his neighbor, "Jack's alive."   The player who holds the stick when the last spark dies out must consent to have a delicate moustache painted on his face with the charred end of the stick, which is then relighted, and the game goes on.   Should the wearer of the moustache have Jack die a second time on his hands, an imperial, whiskers, or exaggerated eyebrows may be added to his charms.   While Jack is in a lively condition, with his sparks in fine brilliant order, he is passed carelessly from one player to another; but when he shows symptoms of dying, it is amusing to see how rapidly he changes hands, for each player is bound to receive him as soon as his neighbor pronounces "Jack's alive."

In case the moustache decorations are objected to, a forfeit may be paid, instead, by those who hold Jack dead.

————o————

TWIRL THE TRENCHER.

A wooden platter or a plate, is brought in, and given to a person who is to be the leader. The leader then takes a name himself, and gives a name to each of the company. Numbers will do, or the Christian or familiar names by which they are usually known, or the names of animals or flowers may be adopted. Each person must be sharp enough to remember his or her name directly it is mentioned. Each person has a chair, and a large circle (the larger the better) is formed around the plate. The leader then gives the plate a spin, and calls out the name of the person who is to catch it. Leader then runs to his seat, leaving the plate spinning, and when the person named fails to catch the plate before it has done spinning, he or she must pay a forfeit, which must be held until all the players have forfeited.

[This game excites a great deal of merriment, and should be played in a spirited manner. The plate should be fairly spun, and the names distinctly but quickly called out. A little stratagem should be employed by looking towards one person, and then calling out the name of another quite unexpectedly. Nobody should demur to pay a forfeit if fairly fined, and each person should remember his own forfeits.]

Games requiring Memory and constant attention.

THE FIELD OF THE CLOTH OF DAMASK.

When you have cleared the table of everything it has upon it, ask Mary to bring you a small plate (a round piece of wood is better), and, after ranging yourselves round the table, choose partners previously to beginning.

CHOOSING PARTNERS.

At every party there are some good genial souls who lead all the fun and know most of the games. Fix upon two of these for Field-Marshals, and call them respectively Sir Loin and General Kettle. These officers will, upon being raised to such dignity, commence choosing (alternately) their soldiers from among the company; and, as they select these valiant recruits, will perform the short ceremony of conferring titles, commencing, if a gentleman, with a sharp blow of a walking stick across the shoulders, and, if a lady, with a kiss; concluding with the gift of a name, of which a suitable list is annexed :—

Dramatis Personae.

SIR LOIN.	GENERAL KETTLE.
GENERAL GOOSE.	GENERAL TONGS.
LIEUTENANT-GENERAL DUCK.	LIEUTENANT-GENERAL CARVER.
MAJOR-GENERAL MUFFIN.	MAJOR-GENERAL FORK.
COLONEL CRUMPET.	COLONEL COFFEEPOT.
COLONEL CARROT.	COLONEL CORKSCREW.
MAJOR O'MUTTON.	MAJOR CRACKER.
PRIVATE PARTRIDGE.	MAJOR SPIT.
" PINE.	CORPORAL STEEL.
" POTATO.	" TOASTRACK.
" PLUM.	PRIVATE PLATE.
" PEACH.	" PAIL.
" PIGEON.	" POTLID.
" PEAR.	" POKER.

With power to add to their number.

THE GAME.

GENERAL KETTLE *takes the Plate (which is called "the Plum-pudding")
between his fingers and thumb, ready for spinning on the table, and
begins :—*

"As I was sitting on the fire this morning, spluttering with rage at
having no enemy to boil, who should come along in his bag and string
but old Plum-pudding! The moment he caught a sight of me off he
ran, I after him; when, turning round a corner, I ran up against Major
O'Mutton." At this word General Kettle spins round the "Plum-
pudding," which Major O'Mutton has to keep up, continuing the story
in his assumed character until he has mentioned "Plum-pudding," and
introduced the name of an antagonist, who, in his turn, must continue
the game.

It will be seen that the two greatest difficulties of the game consist
in keeping up the "Pudding," and continuing the story. The first is,
however, very easy after a little practice, there being numerous devices
to keep it from falling, such as patting it on one side until it recovers
its perpendicular, or dexterously giving it a twist with finger and
thumb as it slackens in its speed. The second is more difficult; but
there is one safe rule which will help you on amazingly. Never think
of yourself *as* yourself—always remember that you are Muffin, Partridge, Goose, Tongs, Toastrack, or Steel, as the case may be; for if
you are not vigilant you will have to give

FORFEITS.

Firstly—For letting the " Plum-pudding" fall.

Secondly—For speaking of yourself as a human being.

Thirdly—For failing to continue the story.

Fourthly—For omitting to mention "Plum-pudding;" **and**

Fifthly—For calling an "enemy" by a wrong title.

TERMINATION OF THE GAME.

One hundred forfeits is a good limit to the game when the armies are numerous and light-hearted; but the number may be less, and the fun as furious, when the party is a small one.

At the finish of the game the army that has given the least number of forfeits is declared the victor, its forfeits are returned to it, and its commander-in-chief calls a court-martial, at which the penalties to be inflicted upon the defeated army are adjudged.

PENALTIES.

Sir Loin's Army.

Basted.—You are pursued and beaten with handkerchiefs round the room.

Seasoned.—You are to kiss every lady in the room, and have your face slapped in return.

Trussed.—You are to be skewered with two walking-sticks into a corner, until some lady is kind enough to release you with a kiss.

Roasted.—You must walk up to every lady in the room: if she does not wish to kiss you she catches hold of your arms and gives you a turn: when a lady is not kind enough to give you a chaste salute you are said to be "done," etc., etc.

General Kettle's Army.

Scrubbed.—You must ask every lady to kiss you; if any one refuse she must scrub your face with her handkerchief; as soon as you are kissed you are at liberty.

Scoured.—The same.

Sharpened.—Two gentlemen (the Grindstones) try their utmost to prevent you from catching and kissing the lady you have selected.

Blackleaded.—You must go round to each of the company and ask them what they think of you. They, in reply, are to say something disparaging.

Washed.—The exact reverse of Blackleading, for all the company must reply with fulsome praise etc., etc.

It will be noticed that, although these penalties are described above as for gentlemen, a moment's thought will suggest the means of adapting them for ladies.

HOW WE PLAYED THE GAME AT OUR HOUSE.

Example is far better than precept; therefore imagine us all around the table, a merry group. Our Generals have chosen each an army; the "Pudding" (we always use a round piece of wood in preference to a plate) has been found, and off goes the stately

General Kettle.—As I was sitting on the fire this morning, spluttering fiercely at having nobody to boil, who should come along but "Plum-pudding" in his bag and sling! "Hollo!" said I, "are you looking for me?" "No," he replies, "it's Major-General Muffin *I* want."

(General Kettle spins the "Pudding." Up springs Major-General Muffin, cautiously trying to keep up the "Pudding.")

Major-General Muffin.—May I be toasted this minute if I ever could find out what the old "Pudding" wanted with me! I hadn't long been baked; I was quite unknown to the officers, and had only one enemy, and that was Corporal Toastrack.

(Up comes Corporal Toastrack as quickly as he can; but, as he was talking in an undertone to the pretty Miss —— ("stay, that's a forfeit!") to General Tongs, down went the "Pudding," which was a forfeit for him, off leads Muffin again as at first, not spinning the Pudding till the last word.)

Major-General Muffin.—Still a muffin is a muffin, say what you will. I am independent; I don't care for "Plum-pudding;" and if I had him here, although he looked as fierce as he did in the butcher's shop, I would fight even Corporal Steel.

(And off goes the "Pudding," but Steel had noticed the allusion to the butcher's shop, and was on the alert.)

Corporal Steel.—The ridiculous idea! Corporal Steel can fight anybody, even Mr. Hodgson.

("Stop, stop!" we all cried; "that's a forfeit;" so Muffin had another turn.)

Major-General Muffin.—Fight or no fight, this has nothing to do with the "Plum-pudding;" the poor fellow wasted away with grief, and during dinner-time, did nothing but bewail his unhappy fate. "Ah!" said he, "I wish I had never known that Lieutenant-General Carver."

Lieutenant-General Carver.—He never *did* know me properly, for I had a very great respect for him, and wouldn't have touched a single currant if I had not been forced to it. You see I was invited to his birth-day party on Christmas-day. I went the more readily as I went to pay some delicate attentions to General Goose.

("Forfeit! forfeit!" they all cried; "you never mentioned 'Plum-pudding!'" So General Goose went on after the payment of the forfeit.)

General Goose.—Hm! hm! Ah! So says I—as I was walking to office—and—and—so—I *can't* get along.

("Two more forfeits if you please," said that sharp, hard Major Steel; "one for failing to continue the story, and the second for speaking of yourself as a human being.")

Major-General Muffin.—"I can't get along," says Plum-pudding. "Well," I replied, "I don't wonder at it. Look at your clumsy bag and long string. But if you will wait a little while I'll send an old friend of yours to you, one General Kettle."

(Off goes the "Pudding"—up comes General Kettle.

General Kettle.—A very old friend indeed, but not so welcome as he expected; for although I took hold of him by the neck, and jumped on to the fire with him——

("Forfeit!" they all cry; for General Kettle was so anxious· to construct a good story that he let the "Pudding" fall.)

In this way we continued, causing great fun, until we had surrendered our hundred forfeits; when General Kettle's army having given but forty, while Sir Loin's had been stripped of sixty, General Kettle claimed the victory, and immunity from punishment, for his side. The court-martial was then called, whereat the appropriate punishments were adjudged and inflicted; everybody admitting (as well as they could for laughing) that it was the best game they had ever played at. And what everybody says, you know, must be true.

————o————

THE FLOUR-MERCHANT.

The one who personates the Flour-Merchant will try every way to dispose of his stock of flour, by asking question after question of the others, who must, in their answers, be careful not to use these words: *flour, I, yes,* or *no,* as they are forbidden, and the one who is caught using them is considered out of the game.

The Flour-Merchant must persevere in his endeavors to make the players use one of the interdicted words. For instance :

"Do you wish any flour to-day?"

"There is none required."

"But you will soon want it; let me persuade you to take some."

"That is impossible."

"Why so? It is the very best of flour; just look at it; it is so very fine and white."

"The quality is a matter of indifference to me."

"But it will make such good sweet bread. Do take some."

"You have had my answer."

"Have I? I must have forgotten it. What was it?"

"My answer was, decidedly not any."

"But, madam, consider; it is a very reasonable price."

"I will not take any."

The Flour-Merchant having succeeded in making her say "*I,*" proceeds to the next one.

———o———

THE ELEMENTS.

In this game the party sit in a circle. One throws a handkerchief at another, and calls out AIR! The person whom the handkerchief hits must call Eagle, Vulture, Lark, Pigeon, Hawk, Goose, Partridge, Woodcock, Snipe, or some creatures that belong to the air, before the caller can count ten; which he does in a loud voice, and as fast as possible.

If a creature that does not live in the air is named, or if a person fails to speak quick enough, a forfeit must be paid.

The person who catches the handkerchief throws it to another, in turn, and cries out EARTH! The person who is hit must call out Elephant, Horse, Dog, Cat, Mouse, Guinea Pig, Ox, or any creature which lives upon the earth, in the same space of time allowed the other.

Then throw the handkerchief to another, and call out WATER! The one who catches the handkerchief observes the same rules as the preceding, and is liable to the same forfeits, unless he calls out immediately, Trout, Mackerel, Herring, Sole, or the name of some creature that lives in the water.

Any one who mentions a bird, beast, or fish twice is likewise liable to a forfeit.

If any player calls FIRE! every one must keep silence, because no creature lives in that element.

HOW DO YOU LIKE IT?

This is an excellent and very amusing game for winter-evening parties. It may be played by any number of persons. The company being seated, one of the party, called the Stock, is sent out of the room, and the company then agree upon some word which will bear more than one meaning. When the Stock comes back, he or she asks each of the company in succession, "How do you like it?" One answers, "I like it hot;" another, "I like it cold;" another, "I like it old;" another, "I like it new." He then asks the company in succession, again, "When do you like it?" One says, "At all times;" another, "Very seldom;" a third, "At dinner;" a fourth, "On the water;" a fifth, "On the land," etc. Lastly, the Stock goes round and asks, "Where would you put it?" One says, "I would put it up the chimney?" another, "I would throw it down a well;" a third, "I would hang it on a tree;" a fourth, "I would put it in a pudding." From these answers, a witty girl may guess the word chosen; but, should she be unable to do so, she has to pay a forfeit. Many words might be chosen for the game, such as—

Aunt and ant.   Rain and rein.
Plane and plain.   Vice, a tool; and vice, a crime.
         Key, of a door; and quay, a place for ships.

————o————

THE BUTTERFLY.

By the exercise of a true and delicate politeness, this game may be rendered extremely agreeable to the young ladies who have been invited to join in it; and the mischief of their answers adds in no slight degree to its charm.

Each of the gentlemen plays the part of an insect, such as the *Butterfly*, from which the game takes its name, and with which it commences; the *Humble Bee*, the *Ant*, the *Fly*, the *Caterpillar*, etc.

The young ladies take each the name of a flower, as the *Rose*, the *Pink*, the *Tuberose*, the *Violet*, the *Hawthorn*, etc.

When all these names are distributed and agreed upon, each player should be careful to remember them, so as not to pronounce any name that has not been chosen. Each player also must be prepared to answer as soon as the one who is speaking pronounces his assumed name. The speaker, however, when pronouncing the name, must have the address to look at some other person of the company. A wrong name pronounced, a wrong or tardy reply, are all faults which require a forfeit.

EXAMPLE.

THE BUTTERFLY.

"Here am I, suddenly transported into a garden of flowers; and such flowers!—all alike beautiful! Here I find the sweet perfume of the *Tuberose*——"

THE TUBEROSE.

"Away, ugly insect! Do not approach me! I have not forgotten that yesterday you embraced one of the most beautiful of my sisters, and now she is dead. Give me the *Ant* for my choice."

THE ANT.

"Since you permit me, sweet flower, I will climb to the top of your perfumed cup, before the *Sun** (1) has finished half his course. I will seek a shelter there until the *Gardener* (2) comes, with his *Watering Pot* (3), to give a new charm to your beauty. Until this moment, I have paid my homage to the *Violet*"——

THE VIOLET.

"At last I shall find a moment for repose! Vainly I kept myself concealed beneath the grass! this cruel insect has persecuted me worse than any *Humble Bee*"——

The *Humble Bee* then takes up the word, and the game continues; but it must be observed, that the *Insects* are not allowed to address themselves to anything but a *Flower*, and a *Flower* cannot address itself to anything but an *Insect*. Any mistake of this kind costs a forfeit, as well as the mention of any *Flower* or *Insect* which any of the players has named before.

* 1, 2, 3. The speaker must endeavor to introduce in a natural manner into his discourse the words *Sun*, *Gardener*, *Watering Pot*. These three words, for which the players are less prepared than they are for the names of the *Flowers* and *Insects*, commonly cause numerous forfeits, because many of the players forget, when the *Sun* is named, that they must rise from their seats; when the word *Gardener* is mentioned, the *Flowers* must extend their hands, as if to supplicate his care, while the *Insects*, alarmed, make a gesture as if about to fly, from dread of his presence; and finally, when the word *Watering Pot* is pronounced, all the *Flowers* must stand erect, as if reanimated by the freshness of the water; while the *Insects*, with one knee bent to the earth, seem overwhelmed from the same cause. These different postures, which form a pretty tableau, only cease when the speaker, whether gentleman or lady, names some *Flower* or *Insect*, which, in its turn, takes up the discourse.

CROSS PURPOSES.

This is another very entertaining game.

One player goes around among the circle and whispers in each one's ear an answer he is to make to the next player, who comes after him asking questions.   For instance, Charles goes round to Nos. 1, 2, 3, and 4.

To No. 1, he whispers: "Hot, sweet, and strong."

To No. 2, "With pepper and vinegar."

To No. 3, "With my best love."

To No. 4, "No, indeed."

And to the whole circle an answer of some kind.

Jane comes after Charles to ask any questions her own wit may suggest.

She asks No 1, "What kind of a week have you passed?"

No. 1, "Hot, sweet, and strong."

To No. 2, "Shall you ever marry?"

No. 2, "With pepper and vinegar."

To No. 3, "How will you keep house on these?"

No. 3, "With my best love."

To No. 4, "No, indeed!"

Much amusement is sometimes made by the total variance of the questions and answers, and sometimes a very hard blow is administered to some of the company; but, of course, no offence can be taken.

--------o--------

THE HORNED AMBASSADOR.

This is a game which, if played with spirit, creates much merriment.   It is played in this way:—

A number of papers, twisted like a lamplighter or a curl paper, are all the materials necessary.   The first player turns to the person on his left hand, and, with a bow, says: "Good morning, Royal Ambassador, always royal; I, the Royal Ambassador, always royal, come from his Royal Majesty (pointing to his neighbor on his right, who must bow), always royal, to tell you he has an eagle with a golden beak."

The second player must repeat this to his left-hand neighbor exactly word for word as he hears it, adding brazen claws.   If he leaves out a word, or makes any mistake, he must have one of the papers twisted into his hair. Then he becomes a one-horned ambassador, and must call himself so, instead of royal.

For instance, No. 1 says:—

"Good morning, Royal Ambassador, always royal; I, the Royal Ambassador, always royal, come from his Royal Majesty, always royal, to tell you that he has an eagle with a golden beak."

No. 2, "Good morning, Royal Ambassador, always royal; I, the Royal Ambassador, come from"——

Having left out *always royal* after his own name, No. 2 is horned, and says: "Good, etc.; I, a One-horned Ambassador, always one-horned, come from his Royal," etc.

When his neighbor has gone on, he must add diamond eyes to the eagle—each player must add something to the eagle—and he must say he comes from his One-horned Majesty, instead of his Royal Majesty.

By this time a good many of the party will be well horned; and, as every horn incurs a forfeit, the game may cease until they are redeemed. Sometimes the ambassador becomes seven or eight-horned before the game is over.

————o————

THE GAME OF THE RING.

This game is nothing else than an application of one of the methods employed to tell several numbers thought of, and should be played in a company not exceeding nine persons, in order that it may be less complicated. Request any one of the company to take a ring, and put it on any joint of whatever finger he may think proper. The feat then is, to tell what person has the ring, and on what hand, what finger, and on what joint.

For this purpose, term the first person 1, the second 2, and so on; also term the right hand 1, the second 2. The first finger of each hand, that is to say, the thumb, must be denoted as 1, the second 2, and so on to the little finger. The first joint of each finger, or that next the extremity, must be called 1, the second 2, and the third 3.

Let us now suppose that the fifth person has taken the ring, and put it on the first joint of the fourth finger of his left hand. Then, to solve the problem, nothing more is necessary than to discover these numbers; 5, equivalent to the person; 2, the hand; 4, the finger; and 1, the joint.

Commence by requesting any of the party to double the number of the person, which will give 10, and to subtract 1 from it; desire him then to multiply the remainder, 9, by 5, which will give 45; to this product bid him add the number of the hand, 2, which will make 47, and then add 5, which will make 52. Desire him then to double this last number—the result will be 104—and to subtract 1, leaving 103. Tell him then to multiply the remainder by 5, which will give 515, and to add to the product the number expressing the finger, which will make 519. Then bid him add 5, which will make 524; and from 1048, the double of this sum, let him subtract 1, which will leave 1047. Then desire him to multiply this remainder by 5, which will give 5235, and to add to this product 1, the fourth finger indicating the joint, which will make 5236. In the last place, bid him again add 5, and the sum will be 5241, the figures of which will clearly indicate the person who has the ring, and the hand, finger, and joint on which it was placed.

It is evident that all these complex operations merely amount, in reality, to multiplying by ten the number which expresses the person, then adding that which denotes the hand, multiplying again by ten, and so on. As this artifice may be detected, it would be better, when performing this feat, to employ the method previously described, when no one of the numbers exceeds nine—for, on account of the numbers which must be subtracted, the operation will be more difficult to be comprehended.

--------o--------

THE ALPHABET: OR, I LOVE MY LOVE WITH AN A.

Formerly this game was confined to the players saying in rotation, "I love my love with an A, because he is AMIABLE, ARDENT, ASPIRING, AMBITIOUS," and so on, through as many letters of the alphabet as might be approved of, each player having to invest his love with a quality beginning with the letter in question. Forfeits were exacted,—firstly, for the repetition of any quality mentioned by a previous player; secondly, for faults of spelling.

As, however (thanks to the progress of education), people are no longer in the habit of loving others because they are Andsome, Onorable, or Helegant, the latter opportunity may be said to be almost obsolete. It has therefore been decided to improve the former, by increasing the difficulty of finding words.

The game, as it is at present played, will be understood from the following specimens:—

"I love my love with an A, because he is AFFECTIONATE, because his name is AUGUSTUS, because he lives in ALBANY. I will give him an AMETHYST, I will feed him on APPLE-TARTS, and make him a bouquet of ANEMONES."

"I love my love with a B, because she is BEAUTIFUL, because her name is BEATRICE, because she lives in BOSTON. I will give her a BROOCH, I will feed her on BERRIES, and make her a bouquet of BLUE-BELLS."

This form need not be strictly adhered to, we merely offer it as a model. The leader of the game may vary it as he thinks fit; but whatever form he may choose to adopt, the others must imitate closely (allowing for the variation of the sexes). Failure in this must be punished by a forfeit; the old regulation as to repetition and mistakes in spelling (accidents which will happen, even now, in the best educated families) still holding good.

The whole alphabet may be gone through in this manner, if the interest of the game lasts long enough. It is advisable, however, to exclude the latters K, Q, X, and Z, which offer too many difficulties.

———o———

THE DEAF MAN.

The person on whom this temporary infirmity is imposed must stand out in the middle of the room, and to all that is said must answer, three times following, "I am deaf; I can't hear." The fourth time, however, the answer must be, "I can hear." The fun, to all but the unfortunate victim, is, for the first three times to make the deaf man some agreeable proposal, such as bringing a lady to him and asking him to salute her, to which he is obliged to turn a deaf ear; while the fourth time he is requested to perform some humiliating act, such as to take a lady to another gentleman to salute, sing a comic song, recite extempore verses in praise of the prettiest girl in the company, and to all these agreeable invitations his ears must be suddenly open In fact, he must illustrate exactly the inverse of the old proverb, "None so deaf as those who won't hear." He is not obliged to accede to the requests that are made to him in the intervals of his deaf fit. This would be too severe.

THE ANTS AND THE GRASSHOPPER.

Lots are drawn to decide which of the company shall first undertake the part of the Grasshopper. This important matter settled, the chosen individual stands up, the other players (who represent the Ants) seating themselves in a circle around them. The Grasshopper writes on a piece of paper the name of a particular grain—or other article of food suitable to his species—to which he has taken a fancy. The memorandum he conceals for the present. He then advances, with a profound salutation, to the Ants, whom he addresses something in the following manner:—

"My dear and hospitable friends, I am very hungry. Would any of you lend me a little provision of some kind to be going on with?" Then, addressing some particular Ant, "You, my dear friend, I know your goodness of heart; I am sure you will help me with a trifle?"

The Ant addressed, replies, "I have nothing but a grain of barley" (or any other grain according to fancy).

"Thank you, I don't care for it. And you, neighbor," addressing another Ant, "is there nothing better you can offer me?"

"A grub."

"Thank you, I would rather not."

He begs from all the players in turn, who propose a *fly, a grain of wheat, oats, hayseed,* etc.—always an article which a Grasshopper might be expected to eat, and which has not been mentioned before. When he has gone all round, without the article he has written being named by any one, the Grasshopper pays a forfeit, and proceeds with his second question. If, however, one of the Ants should hit upon the identical thing, "I will take it with pleasure, neighbor,"·cries the Grasshopper, "and may you be rewarded." He then produces his piece of paper, proving that the article proposed was the one he had thought of; the Ant pays a forfeit, and becomes Grasshopper in his turn. Instead, however, of recommencing the game, he continues it in the following manner:—"Neighbor," he says to an Ant, "I have eaten abundantly, thanks to the kindness of your companions. I should like a dance. What dance would you recommend?" (The name of a dance is written down, secretly, as in the case of the food.)

The question goes round as before—the Ants proposing various dances, such as *the polka, the fandango, the schottische, the minuet, the quadrille,* etc. The Grasshopper treats these suggestions (his own not being among them) with the greatest contempt. Any player proposing a dance previously named, pays a forfeit. The Grasshopper of course, does the same, should the round terminate without the dance of his memorandum being mentioned, and proceeds to write the third question. If, on the contrary, an Ant should hit upon the right dance, they change places, as in the first instance; and the new Grasshopper (having paid a forfeit) continues:—

"Well, I will dance, my friends. But I see no fun in dancing without music. What instrument would you recommend?"

The Ants recommend various instruments, such as *the violin, the piano, the cornet, the harp*, etc.—subject to the same conditions as the previous rounds.

The fourth Grasshopper (supposing an unlucky insect to have hit on the identical instrument) takes up the thread:—

"I have had enough dancing; I feel rather tired; I should like a nap. I always consult you, my friends; what sort of couch would you advise me to sleep on?"

The Ants reply, each in his turn—*moss, stubble, sand, clover, a rose-leaf*, etc., etc.

At length the fifth and last Grasshopper puts the question.

"My good friends, I should sleep very comfortably, but for a slight misgiving. I am afraid of being pounced upon by some hungry bird. What bird do you think I have most reason to fear?"

ANSWERS :—*The rook, the partridge, the pigeon, the lark*, etc., etc.

Should the bird whose name has been written down be mentioned, the too-prophetic Ant pays a forfeit, and the game is finished. If not, the Grasshopper not only pays a forfeit, but has to put the question round a second time, then a third, and more still if necessary. Nor is that all—from the commencement of the second round, he has to pay a forfeit *for every answer* till the identical bird is named. The result is, generally, that the Grasshopper, despairing of being able to redeem the number of forfeits exacted from him, cries for mercy; the pitch of mental anguish to which he is wrought, keeping up the excitement of the game to the very end.

————o————

CLAPPERTON: OR, THE GOOSE'S HISTORY.

This game was suggested by the ancient one of Coach, but is much altered to avoid both the necessity of young and old making themselves giddy by twirling round when their names are mentioned, and to effect a compromise in the redemption of the forfeits; the ordinary mode being often singularly tiresome. In the History of the Goose, a commencement of which is appended, to show the sort of story which should be invented for the occasion, *no* notice is to be taken when *her* name occurs, but whenever the word Drake or Doctor is mentioned, every one is to clap his hands once, unless the two are joined, when two merry claps must sound. Any one omitting to clap at the right place, or clapping when the Goose is named, pays a forfeit, and *all* the forfeits may be redeemed by quoting *two* lines of verse, varied by kissing the mantelpiece, etc., if the little ones present prefer it to the former mode. " A Goose feeling out of spirits one morning, consulted her favorite Doctor Drake (two claps), who advised her to go a long journey to foreign countries, which she resolved to do. So making, by the Doctor's (one clap) advice, a good meal of cabbage-stalks and apple-parings, she set out from Dingle Farm, escorted by Doctor Drake (two claps). A shrill scream soon announced some disaster, and the Doctor (one clap) was obliged to extract two thorns from one of the Goose's wings, and to bathe her foot, stung by nettles, in a ditch, before they could proceed. After this they got on pretty well, though Goose was so fat that she could not have forced her way through one of the styles, had not the Doctor (one clap) given her a good push behind. Part of the journey lay through a meadow, in which two Miss Chickens, admiring the Goose and the Drake (one clap), joined them; but they talked so fast, the Doctor (one clap) soon gave them to understand their company was unacceptable. A Cock in the neighborhood seemed disposed to fight Doctor Drake (two claps) for his rudeness to his daughters, but the Doctor (one clap), not thinking it becoming to his professional dignity to engage in battle, only quacked a haughty reply, and went on with his patient."

---o---

STORY-PLAY.

You are to whisper a *word*, which must be a substantive, to the person who begins the play, and who is to tell a short story or anecdote, into which the word is to be frequently introduced. It requires some ingenuity to relate the story in so natural a manner, that the word shall not be too evident, and yet it may be sufficiently marked. When the story is finished, each of the party endeavors to guess the word; and the person who discovers it tells the next story. The following is a specimen:—

"Three young children were coming down the Mississippi with their father in a sort of boat, which they call there a pirogue. They landed on a desert island in that wide river on a bitter snowy evening, in the month of December; their father left them on the island, promising to return after he had procured some brandy at a house on the opposite bank. He pushed off in his little boat, to cross the river; but the wind was high, and the water rough. The children watched him with tears in their eyes, struggling in his pirogue against the stream, till about half way across, when they saw the boat sink, and never more saw their father. Poor children! they were left alone, exposed to the storm, without fire, shelter, or even food, except a little corn.

"As the night came on, the snow fell faster; and the eldest, who was a girl only six years old, but very sensible and steady for her age made her little sister and her infant brother creep close to her, and she drew their bare feet under her clothes. She had collected a few withered leaves and branches to cover them, and in this manner they passed the long winter's night. Next morning, she tried to support her poor weeping companions by giving them corn to chew; and sometimes she made them run about with her, to keep themselves warm.

"In this melancholy state, you may imagine what was her joy when, in the course of the day, she discovered a boat approaching the island. It happily contained some good-natured Indians, who took compassion on the children, shared their food with them, and safely conveyed them to New Madrid in their own *boat*."

---o---

THE DUTCH CONCERT.

In this game all the parties sit down. Each person makes a selection of an instrument—say one takes a flute, another a drum, a third the trombone, and a fourth the piano, and each person must imitate in the best way he can the sound of the instrument, and the motions of the player. The leader of the band, commencing with his instrument, all the others follow, tuning some popular air, such as "Yankee Doodle," "Pop goes the Weasel," "Bobbing Around," "In the Days when we went Gipseying," or any other air. The fun consists in this, that the leader may take any instrument from either of the players, who must watch the leader, and take the instrument which he was previously playing. *If he fails to do so, he pays a forfeit.* Or if he makes a mistake, and takes the wrong instrument, he pays forfeit. Suppose A be the leader, playing the violin, and B to be one of the band, playing the trombone. Directly A ceases to play the violin and imitates the trombone, B must cease the trombone, and imitate the violin, and immediately A returns to the violin, B must take the trombone, or whatever other instrument A was playing the moment before he took the violin. If he makes a mistake, he pays forfeit.

[This is a very laughable, though rather noisy game. It should not be continued too long. A good leader will soon be able to impose forfeits upon all the players.]

————o————

MY LADY'S TOILET.

Each having taken the name of some article of dress, chairs are placed for all the party but one, so as to leave one chair too few. They all sit down but one, who is called the Lady's Maid, and stands in the centre; she then calls out " My Lady's up and wants her shoes," when the one who has taken that name jumps up and calls " Shoes!" sitting down directly. If any one does not rise as soon as called, she must forfeit. Sometimes she says " My Lady wants her whole toilet," then every one must jump up and change chairs, and as there is a chair too few, of course it occasions a scramble, and whoever is left standing must be Lady's Maid, and call to the others as before.

————o————

SIMON SAYS.

This, if well managed, is a very comical game. The players are arranged in a line, the player who enacts Simon standing in front. He and all the other players clench their fists, keeping the thumb pointed upwards. No player is to obey his commands unless prefaced with the words, " Simon says." Simon is himself subjected to the same rules. The game commences by Simon commanding,—" Simon says, *turn down :*" on which he turns his thumbs downwards, followed by the other players. He then says, " Simon says, *turn up*," and brings his hands back again. When he has done so several times, and thinks that the players are off their guard, he merely gives the word, " Turn up," or "Turn down," without moving his hands. Some one, if not all, is sure to obey the command, and is subject to a forfeit. Simon is also subject to a forfeit, if he tells his companions to turn down while the thumbs are already down, or *vice versâ*. With a sharp player enacting Simon, the game is very spirited.

––––––o––––––

THE PHILHARMONIC CONCERT.

If music is the food of love, noise in this game is the food of fun. It proceeds in the manner and form following :—The players seat themselves and form a circle, each adopting an instrument of which he is the imaginary performer. One chooses the violin, and draws his right hand backward and forward over his left arm; another the horn, and puffs out his cheeks, imitating the acting of a horn blower; another the piano, and strums with his hands upon his knees; another the harp, taking a chair or any other suitable piece of furniture to play on; and so on through as many instruments as there are performers. Each player must imitate the action, and, as well as he is able, the sound of the instrument upon which he is supposed to be performing. The spectacle which is then presented by this orchestra of imaginary musicians, all playing *con furore*, is irresistibly ludicrous, and renders the gravity which is prescribed on pain of forfeit a sheer impossibility. In the middle of the circle the conductor takes his post, a-straddle on a chair with the back before him, in such a manner as to figure a desk. on which he beats time. He may get himself up after the similitude of the great Monsieur Jullien, whose attitudes and gestures, at the most excited pitch of his last "Universal Smash" polka, may be adopted as a model, but will need no exaggeration to be made as amusing as those of the orchestra he directs. In the midst of the indescribable confusion of sounds over which he presides, the conductor suddenly singles out one of the performers, and asks him why he is at fault. The individual so addressed must at once, and without a moment's hesitation, give some answer corresponding to the nature of the instrument; for instance, the fiddler may say his bow wanted rosin, the harp player that one of his strings had broken, the clarionet player that his instrument was broken-winded. Any failure to do this, or any repetition of an excuse previously given, will necessitate a forfeit. This game in some respect is similar to the *Dutch Concert*, and should not be played in a *very quiet* family.

SCHEHERAZADE'S RANSOM.

Three of the company agree to sustain the parts of the Sultan, the Vizier, and the Princess Scheherazade. The Sultan takes his seat at the end of the room, and the Vizier then leads the Princess before him, with her hands bound behind her. The Vizier then makes a burlesque proclamation, that the Princess having exhausted all her stories, is about to be punished, unless a sufficient ransom be offered. The rest of the company then advance in turn, and propose enigmas (which must be solved by the Sultan or Vizier), sing the first verse of a song (to which the Vizier must answer with the second verse), or recite any well known piece of poetry in alternate lines with the Vizier. Forfeits must be paid either by the company when successfully encountered by the Sultan and Vizier, or by the Vizier when unable to respond to his opponent, and the game goes on till the forfeits amount to any specified number on either side. Should the company be victorious, and obtain the greatest number of forfeits, the Princess is released, and the Vizier has to execute all the penalties that may be imposed upon him; if otherwise, the Princess is led to execution. For this purpose she is blindfolded and seated on a low stool; the penalties for the forfeits, which should be previously prepared, are written on slips of paper and put into a basket, which she holds in her hands, which are still tied behind her. The owners of the forfeits advance in turn, and each draws one of the slips of paper. As each person comes forward, the Princess guesses who it is, and if right, the person must pay an additional forfeit, the penalty for which is to be exacted by the Princess herself. When all the penalties have been distributed, the hands and eyes of the Princess are released, and she then superintends the execution of the various punishments that have been allotted to the company.

————o————

THE LAWYER.

The company must form in two rows, opposite to and facing each other, leaving room for the Lawyer to pass up and down between them.

When all are seated, the one who personates the Lawyer will ask a question or address a remark to one of the persons present, either standing before the person addressed, or calling his name. The one spoken to is not to answer, but the one sitting opposite to him must reply to

9*

the question. The object of the Lawyer is to make either the one he speaks to answer him, or the one that should answer to keep silent; therefore he should be quick in hurrying from one to another with his questions, taking them by surprise, and noticing those who are the most inattentive. No one must be allowed to remind another of his turn to speak. When the Lawyer has succeeded in either making one speak that should not, or finding any that did not answer when they should, they must exchange places with each other, and the one caught becomes Lawyer.

This game will be found quite amusing if conducted with spirit.

———o———

THE PAINTER AND THE COLORS.

One of the party assumes the character of a Painter, the other players adopt the names of the various colors. The Painter pretends that he is employed to paint a picture, and when he mentions the word *palette*, all the rest of the players cry "*colors*." If he mentions the word *colors*, they all cry "*Here we are*." If he says *pencil*, they answer "*brush*." If he asks for his *brush*, they cry "*easel*." If the painter mentions any color by name, the person who represents that color cries out the name of another color, and then the player representing the last named color says, "*There you are, Mr. Painter*."

Any deviation from these rules incurs a forfeit, and the principal fun of the game is in the color cited by the Painter, naming a color ridiculously unfit for the purpose required. For example:

PAINTER. At last my talents have been recognised, and I may now consider my fortune made, when a nobleman of great taste has commissioned me to paint him a picture representing Anthony and the beauteous Cleopatra. I now proceed to charge my *palette*.

ALL THE COLORS. Colors! colors!

PAINTER. The most beautiful *colors*.

ALL. Here we are!

PAINTER. I can't use you all at once; my *pencil*.

ALL. Brush! brush!

PAINTER. True, I will give you the *brush*.

ALL. Easel!

PAINTER. Silence, or I will not employ any of you. Now I commence the hair of my Cleopatra, which must be *black*.

BLACK. Red! red!

RED. There you are, Mr. Painter!

PAINTER. The eyes must be *blue*.

BLUE. Yellow! yellow!

YELLOW. There you are, Mr. Painter!

PAINTER. For the cheeks I will have a superb *vermilion.*

VERMILION. Green! green!

GREEN. There you are, Mr. Painter!

PAINTER. All the colors——

ALL. Here we are! here we are!

PAINTER. Will find their place, thanks to the delicacy of my *pencil.*

ALL. Brush! brush! (*Great confusion.*)

————o————

POKER AND TONGS: OR, HOT BOILED BEANS.

This is decidedly about as noisy a game as can well be imagined, but it also has the merit of being equally simple. Some small article is to be hidden, the party, whose business it is to discover it, being sent out of the room while that is being done. Another of the players now takes a pair of tongs in one hand, and a poker in the other. The seeker of the hidden treasure is then called in, and begins to hunt for the concealed article. While he is at a distance from the spot where it has been placed, the poker, which is held between the legs of the tongs, is made to strike them alternately with a slow motion, so as to produce a kind of melancholy music. But as he approaches the concealed treasure, the music becomes more lively, and as he recedes from it more slow and solemn; but when his hand is placed on the spot where the article is to be found, the musician plays a loud and noisy tune on his uncouth instrument. In cases where the rough music produced by the poker and tongs is offensive to the ears of invalids or others, the progress of the player in his search may be announced by assuring him that he is "very cold," "rather warmer," "very hot," or "burning his fingers," as he approaches or recedes from the hidden object. This game is sometimes called *Magic Music.*

————o————

THUS SAYS THE GRAND MUFTI.

In this game one of the company sits in a chair, and is called the Mufti, or the Grand Mufti. He makes whatever grimace or motion he pleases, such as putting his hand on his heart, winking, sneezing, coughing, stretching out his arm, smiting his forehead, etc. At each movement he says, "Thus says the Grand Mufti," or "So says the Grand Mufti." When he says, "Thus says the Grand Mufti," every one must make just such a motion as he does; but when he says, "So says the Grand Mufti," every one must keep still. A forfeit for a mistake is exacted.

————o————

CHARACTERS: OR, WHO AM I?

One of the party is sent out of the room; some well known hero, or equally well known character from a book, like Dickens's novels, or Shakspeare's plays, is selected, and when the absentee returns to the assembly, he or she is greeted as the person fixed upon, and he must reply in such a manner as to elicit more information as to the character he has unconsciously assumed.

Suppose the game has commenced, and when the player enters the room, he is thus accosted:

"Your military ardor must have been very great, and you had a very adventurous spirit, when you left your home in England, and set out with a determination to fight the Turks."

"Yes, I was always very fond of adventure."

"Well, you had plenty of them; and when you were taken prisoner and sold to the Bashaw, your mistress to whom he presented you, felt so much sympathy and affection for you, that you were sent to her brother, but he not being so well pleased with you, treated you cruelly."

"He did, and although I suffered much from his treatment, I suffered more in the idea of being a slave."

"The thought must have been terrible to you," remarks another of the players, "or you would not have killed your master, hid his body, clothed yourself in his attire, mounted his horse, and galloped to the desert, where you wandered about for many days, until at last you reached the Russian garrison, where you were safe."

"And well pleased was I to reach there in safety, but was I then content with my travels?"

"For awhile, but the spirit of enterprise, so great within you, caused you to set sail for the English colony of Virginia; when you were taken a prisoner again by the Indians, and your head placed upon a large stone, in order to have your brains beaten out with clubs."

" What a dreadful situation I was in, with only enemies around me."

" But there was one who proved a friend; the young and beautiful princess, finding that her entreaties for your life were useless, rushed forward, laid her head upon yours, and thus resolved to share your fate, or save your life."

" I am deeply grateful to Pocahontas for her noble act, and I am also glad to find myself so renowned a person as Captain John Smith."

Or suppose a lady has left the room, and on re-entering she is thus addressed:—

" Your Majesty's many remarkable adventures savor more of romance than reality. Accomplished, beautiful, spirited, and very courageous, you command our respect, especially for the vigorous and energetic action you displayed in trying to aid your royal husband, who was preparing to maintain his just rights to the crown of England. After purchasing aid and military stores in Holland you set sail for England, when there arose a great storm which increased in violence, until at length the danger became so imminent, that all the self-possession of the passengers was entirely gone, and you alone were quiet and composed, rebuking their panic, and telling them not to fear, for 'Queens of England were never drowned.'"

" That was a terrible storm, and we were all thankful when we reached land in safety."

"But you had to put back to the port from which you sailed, which caused some delay, but the second voyage was more prosperous, although you were closely pursued by an English squadron, which came into port the night after you landed, and the next morning the village was bombarded by your enemies' ships. You and your attendants escaped into the open fields, stopped at a trench, and were obliged to remain there for two hours, the balls passing over your heads and covering you with dirt; but there soon came an army to your relief, at the head of which you marched triumphantly on, stopping on your way to take a town held by your husband's enemies. Thus was added the glory of a conquest to your other triumphs."

" Well, was I enabled to reach my husband after so many adventures ?"

" Yes, but in a short time you were obliged to separate again, as you were accused of treason, for introducing munitions of war from foreign countries, for the purpose of disturbing the public peace. After passing through many privations and dangers in order to escape, you embarked and set sail for France; but while yet at sea some ships were seen pursuing and firing upon you; then your courage and

resolution was displayed, while all the others were in despair and terror; you took the command of the ship—gave instructions to the pilot
how to steer—ordered every sail to be set that the ship might be driven
through the waters as rapidly as possible—forbade the captain to fire
back upon the pursuers, fearing that it would occasion delay—and gave
him positive orders, that so soon as all hope of escape was gone, he
must set fire to the magazine of gunpowder, that by the explosion you
might all be destroyed. In the meantime the ships were all rapidly
nearing the French coast, when some French vessels hove in sight,
who hastened to your aid and put the pursuers to flight."

"What pleasure we all felt when we were safely landed in France,
feeling at last secure."

"You were secure then, but well-nigh exhausted, and were glad to
find some straw in the corner of a wretched cabin, where the Queen
of England lay down to rest and sleep. You were soon, however,
escorted in state to Paris, and there lived in great splendor."

"And what became of my royal husband?"

"His fate was a sad one. After remaining a prisoner for some time,
the members of Parliament brought him to a mock trial, treating him
with every indignity, and condemned him to death on the ground of
treason. He fell beneath the executioner's hand, and this blow completely prostrated your heroic nature."

"And well it might, for was not he, for whom I exerted my strength
and energies, dead; there was no more for Henrietta, Queen to
Charles I. of England, to do."

--------o--------

THE AVIARY.

A keeper is first chosen, and then all the company assume the
names of different birds, which they communicate to the keeper, but
do not make known to each other. The keeper then sets down the
names of the players, with that of the birds they severally represent,
lest he should make any mistake, and opens the game in a bombastic
strain, somewhat similar to the following:—

"Beautiful ladies and brave gentlemen. Regardless of toil, trouble,
or expense, I have collected together the most magnificent aviary ever
seen in this or any other part of the habitable globe. My birds are
distinguished by the beauty of their plumage, form, and color; the
melody of their voices, and their general intelligence." He then

repeats the names of the birds thought upon, and expresses his desire to know which of his birds are objects of affection or antipathy to the company. Turning to the nearest lady, he says—

" To which of my birds will you give your heart?"

"To which will you reveal your secret?"

" From which would you pluck a feather?"

The lady may probably reply—

" I will give my heart to the eagle."

" I will tell my secret to the nightingale."

" I will pluck a feather from the owl."

The keeper makes a note of these dispositions, and then addresses the same questions to a gentleman, who may reply—

" I will give my heart to the dove."

" I will tell my secret to the lark."

'I will pluck a feather from the bird of paradise."

When any player says he will give his heart to a bird named by another for the same gift, or which is not in the keeper's list, he must pay a forfeit, and make a new choice; and, if he makes a similar mistake a second time, he must pay another forfeit. The game being one solely depending on memory, the players must pay great attention to the list of birds, when read by the keeper, and to the choice of those who speak first.

When all have answered, the keeper announces the names of the persons represented by the birds, and commands each to salute the bird to which his or her heart was given,—to whisper a secret to the one thought worthy of such confidence, and receive a forfeit from the one whose feather was to be plucked.

The players are forbidden to give their hearts or secrets to themselves, under penalty of a forfeit, or desire to pluck their own feathers under a penalty of two.

————o————

THE SPORTSMAN.

One person of the company assumes the character of the Sportsman, and each of the rest takes the name of some animal of the chase. The play consists in all or each of the persons who represent the animals, replying to the Sportsman in certain conventional words, relative to the particular description of field-sports he may mention. Thus when the Sportsman speaks of a " *gun*,"

All the animals exclaim—" *Take care, take care*."

A *setter*,

The Rabbit cries—" *To your burrow, to your burrow.*"

A *greyhound*,

The Hare says—" *Run, friends, run.*"

A *staghound*,

The Stag says—" *I have good legs.*"

A *trap*,

The Fox says—" *Not such a flat.*"

A *hunting-horn*,

The Stag and Fox exclaim—" *Hark away.*"

The *powder flask*,

All the birds cry—" *Fly away, fly away*," and move their arms, as if in the act of flying.

The *game-bag*,

All the animals drop their heads upon their breasts as if dead, except the Fox, who says—" *I don't care.*"

Those who fail in giving the proper reply, at the proper time, must deposit a forfeit.

EXAMPLE.

SPORTSMAN. What a beautiful September morning! I think I shall go out and try my new *gun*.

ALL THE ANIMALS. *Take care, take care.*

SPORTSMAN. My *setters*, too, require exercise.

RABBIT. *To the burrow, to the burrow.*

SPORTSMAN. I will not require the *greyhounds* to-day.

HARE. *Run, friends, run.*

SPORTSMAN. Where is my *powder-flask?*

BIRDS (moving their arms). *Fly away, fly away.*

SPORTSMAN. Put away that *hunting-horn*, I do not want it.

STAG *and* Fox. *Hark away.*

SPORTSMAN. Unkennel the *stag-hound.*

STAG. *I have good legs.*

SPORTSMAN. Well, gamekeeper, anything in the *trap* this morning ?

Fox. *Not such a flat.*

SPORTSMAN. Take the *game-bag* and follow me. (All but the fox drop their heads.)

Fox. *I don't care.*

It will be obvious that this simple, though amusing game, may be prolonged for a considerable time, the Sportsman being careful to *mark down* any of the *game*, who may not, either by word or gesture, make the proper reply.

THE ACROSTIC SALE.

This is an excellent game for young persons, stimulating their inventive talents, and is a good exercise in spelling. The person who opens the game announces that he has just returned from the city, where he purchased an article, which he names, the name containing just as many letters as the number of the company assembled to play the game. He further states, that he is willing to barter the article for as many other articles as the company, excluding himself, number; but the initial letter of each article offered must be in regular succession the letters composing the article bartered. Furnished with a pencil and paper, the seller notes down the offers of the buyers, and, when correctly completed, he reads them aloud; and, in an affected, pompous manner, though quite *impromptu*, declares what he intends to do with the articles thus acquired. For example, in a company composed of eleven persons, the seller says:—

" I have just returned from the city, where I purchased a pianoforte, but I wish to barter it—speaking to the first person—what will you give me for the first letter, P ?" The first person and the other nine, make consecutively their offers, and the seller carefully records them, after which he says:—

" You propose to barter for my

P a Pen.	F a Fan.
I an Inkbottle.	O an Oar.
A an Anchor.	R a Ruby.
N a Newspaper.	T a Teacup.
O an Orchard.	E an Evergreen.

" I accept the offer, and this is the way I intend to use the articles so acquired.

" The *Ruby* I will have mounted in a ring, and will ever treasure it in remembrance of the donor. The *Fan* I will present to a certain lady, who, at present, shall be nameless. Then I will ride into the country, where, sitting in my *Orchard*, I will read my *Newspaper*, and with my *Pen* and *Inkbottle*, write letters to you, my dear friends, from whose agreeable society I shall then be absent. When tired of writing, I will proceed to the river, where, with my *Oar*, I will row on the water till evening, then *Anchor* the boat; and, after taking tea from my *Teacup*, will go into the garden, and superintend the planting of my *Evergreen*."

This relation being terminated, the ten other players become the sellers of various articles in the same manner. Forfeits are levied when articles are offered for sale containing more or less letters than the number of purchasers, or for any error in the spelling of the articles offered in exchange.

————o————

THE TRADES.

A GAME OF PANTOMIME.

Each one of the company chooses a trade, which he exercises in the following manner:

The shoemaker mends shoes.

The washerwoman washes clothes.

The painter paints a portrait.

The cook kneads the bread.

The locksmith hammers upon an anvil.

The spinner turns her wheel, etc., etc., etc.

One of the players acts as king or queen, and commences the game by working at his own trade. In the meanwhile all the others must make the movements appropriate to theirs. If the king suddenly changes his trade, and takes up that of one of the company, all the rest must remain inactive except the player whom the king is imitating, and he must at once take up the king's trade, until the latter is pleased to adopt another; then that player in his turn takes the king's trade, and all the rest remain idle until the king returns to his original trade, which is the signal for all present to recommence their own.

If any one of the company makes a mistake he pays a forfeit.

————o————

THE FICKLE MUSICIAN.

This game is but a variation of the preceding one, and is thought to be more entertaining.

All the company form a circle in the apartment. The person who leads the game takes his place in that part of the circle where he is most easily visible to all. When the other players have each chosen their trades, they must perform the gestures suited to them to the best of their ability—for example, the writer by writing and folding a letter, the painter by sketching upon the wall, and so on.

Then he who leads the game moves his fingers as if playing upon the flageolet, and may if he chooses at the same time sing some well known song.

As soon as he ceases and takes up the trade of one of the players, the latter must play the flageolet in his turn, moving his fingers as if he had the instrument in his hand, without however being obliged to sing, but when the leader of the game resumes the flageolet, or takes up the trade of another of the players, he who is playing the flageolet must at once return to his own trade; if he fails to do so he pays a forfeit to the leader of the game.

It is evident that this game requires much attention, for when the leader of the game possesses address and quickness, it is in his power to obtain a great many forfeits.

---o---

THE ECHO.

This game is played by reciting some little story, which Echo is supposed to interrupt, whenever the narrator pronounces certain words which recur frequently in his narrative. These words relate to the profession or trade of him who is the subject of the story. If, for example, the story is about a soldier, the words which would recur the oftenest would be those which relate to military apparel—such as the *uniform*, the *gaiters*, the *musket*, the *sabre*, the *scabbard*, the *bayonet*, the *knapsack*, the *cap*, the *plume*, the *pouch*, the *powder flask*, and *accoutrements*.

Each one of the company, with the exception of the person who tells the story, takes the name of *soldier*, *uniform*, *gaiters*, etc., etc., except *accoutrements*, which word comprises all these objects in general. When the speaker pronounces one of these words, he who has taken it for his name, ought, if the word has been said only once, to pronounce it twice; if it has been said twice to pronounce it once; when the word *accoutrements* is uttered, all the players, except the *soldier*, ought to repeat together the word *accoutrements*, either once or twice, as directed above.

EXAMPLE.

A brave soldier, soldier (*soldier*) received one morning orders to march. Too regardful of his duty to subject himself to blame, he at once opened his knapsack (*knapsack, knapsack*), from which he drew out a pair of bran new gaiters (*gaiters, gaiters*), he put on his uniform, uniform (*uniform*), took his sabre (*sabre, sabre*), his pouch, pouch (*pouch*), his musket (*musket, musket*), armed himself with his bayonet, bayonet (*bayonet*), and placing his cap (*cap, cap*) upon his head, after having well dusted the plume, plume (*plume*), he gaily descended the stairs to bid adieu to his hostess, and set out for the army without forgetting any of his accoutrements (all, except the soldier, *accoutrements, accoutrements*).

When he had gone about three miles, he was so tired that he was obliged to stop for a moment, in a wood through which he had to pass; at the foot of an oak he found a seat of moss, very convenient for him to repose upon, and leaning his musket (*musket, musket*) against the trunk of a tree, he sat down and soon fell asleep. He had not slumbered long when piercing cries awaked him. He at once seized his musket, musket (*musket*), and ran with all speed towards the place whence the cries seemed to come. What a spectacle! Four ruffians were dragging off a young woman, to whom they addressed insulting epithets, as she struggled in their grasp. At first the soldier, soldier (*soldier*), takes aim with his musket (*musket, musket*), but the young woman struggled so violently that he was fearful of wounding her in his attempt to render her assistance. Nothing remained for him to do but to resort to another weapon, his sabre, sabre (*sabre*), and his bayonet (*bayonet, bayonet*). "Stop, ruffians!" he cried. The bandits seeing that they had to deal with only one man, divide into two parties; two of them secure the woman, while the other two advance to attack the soldier, soldier (*soldier*). The latter takes advantage of this moment, when, without danger to the lady, he can use his other weapon, and brings to the ground one of his assailants, by a shot from his musket (*musket, musket*). The other, to avenge his comrade, discharges a pistol, which pierces the cap (*cap, cap*) of the soldier, soldier, (*soldier*), without wounding him. The latter attacks him with the bayonet (*bayonet, bayonet*), and stretches him upon the ground beside his comrade. At sight of this, the two others set the woman at liberty and take to flight. The brave soldier (*soldier, soldier*) casts upon the ground his knapsack, uniform, gun, pouch and cap (repeat each of these words twice) in less than a second. "Take care of my accoutrements" (all: *accoutrements, accoutrements*), he says to the woman, and with his drawn sabre (*sabre, sabre*) in his hand, he flies in pursuit of the bandits. One of them stumbles over the root of a tree and falls; the soldier, soldier (*soldier*), without stopping for a moment, strikes him with his sabre (*sabre, sabre*), upon the head, and then hastens after the fourth brigand, whom he overtakes and fells to the ground.   He then returns to the spot where he had thrown down his accoutrements (*accoutrements, accoutrements*) that he might run the faster; woman, knapsack, musket, pouch, cap, (repeat twice each word) all had disappeared, as well as the two ruffians whom he had first wounded; nothing was left to him but his gaiters (*gaiters, gaiters*), and sabre, sabre (*sabre*), without the scabbard (*scabbard, scabbard*), and he was obliged to repair to the nearest magistrate to make a deposition of the facts, and complete his accoutrements (all: *accoutrements, accoutrements*).

This story may serve as a model for an infinite number of others. The narrator must be careful to require forfeits from those who, carried away by the interest of the tale, forget to perform the part of ECHO, or who fail to do so the requisite number of times.

————o————

THE BOARDING SCHOOL MISTRESS:

OR,

THE TELL-TALE LITTLE FINGER.

This game is particularly intended for young ladies; if, however, a few young gentlemen are of the company, their presence may contribute to render it the more amusing.

All the company place themselves in a semicircle, within which is a seat more elevated than the rest, for the schoolmistress, whom they at once proceed to choose.   The latter selects another of the company, who takes her place upon a stool in front of her companions, and must be prepared to answer all the accusations which the mistress may bring against her.

MISTRESS.   You ventured to go out yesterday without my permission--where did you go?

ACCUSED.   To my Aunt's (here she points to one of her companions, who must at once answer, "Yes, mistress," or pay a forfeit.

MISTRESS.   That is not all; you have been somewhere else, my *thumb* tells me so.   At the word *thumb* the ACCUSED answers—"It knows nothing about it," which she repeats until the MISTRESS names another finger.

MISTRESS.   And what is worse you did not go alone.

ACCUSED.   It knows nothing about it.

MISTRESS.   Still it says that you were in a grove.

ACCUSED.   It knows nothing about it.

MISTRESS.   And that a handsome young man was there at the same time.

ACCUSED.   It knows nothing about it.

MISTRESS.   You have even dined in company with him. It is my *middle finger* tells me this.

ACCUSED.   Do not believe it. (This is the phrase where the middle finger is spoken of.)

MISTRESS.   And in a private room.

ACCUSED.   Do not believe it. My neighbor knows to the contrary. (She points to another young lady, who must answer— *Yes, mistress.*)

MISTRESS.   After the dinner, which lasted for a long time.

ACCUSED.   Do not believe it.

MISTRESS.   The young man brought you back in a carriage.

ACCUSED.   Do not believe it.

MISTRESS.   And the carriage was overturned in crossing a brook.

ACCUSED.   Do not believe it.

MISTRESS.   And when you returned, your dress was wet and torn.

ACCUSED.   Do not believe it. I can bring the testimony of one, two, or three of my companions. (She points towards those who are inattentive to the game in preference to the others. They must answer— *Yes, mistress,* or pay a forfeit.)

MISTRESS.   It is my *little finger* that has told me so.

ACCUSED.   Pardon me, mistress, it has told a falsehood. (All the young ladies say at the same time—"Ah! the wicked little finger!")

MISTRESS.   It insists upon it, however.

ACCUSED.   It has told a falsehood. Ask all my companions.

All, without uttering a word, lift up the right hand as if to attest the falsehood of the accusation. The slightest hesitation is punished by a forfeit.

MISTRESS.   It says that all these young ladies tell a falsehood.

All rise. Those who keep their seats pay a forfeit. The Accused returns among her companions ; a new Mistress is chosen, who designates a new culprit, and the game continues.

If, on the contrary, the first Mistress, content with the testimony which the young ladies have given without rising, announces that the little finger declares that it was mistaken, she can bring forward new charges, to which the culprit must answer in the same manner as before described.

MY AUNT'S GARDEN.

The company form a circle, and the one who understands the game best, turns to his next neighbor and speaks as follows:

"I come from my aunt's garden! In my aunt's garden are four corners."

Each of the players repeats in succession the same phrases without adding or leaving out a syllable, under penalty of a forfeit, and at the same time losing his turn to complete the sentence, when the one who is next to him takes it up without giving him time to correct himself.

When the turn comes again to the first speaker, he repeats what he nas just said, and adds, "In the first corner there is a geranium."

The others then in their turn repeat, not only this phrase, but that which they have already repeated, paying a forfeit for the least mistake.

This round finished, the leader of the game repeats the whole, and adds—"In the second corner there is a rose, I would like to kiss you, but I dare not."

After the third round he adds—"In the third corner there is a lily of the valley, tell me your secret."

Then each player after having repeated the whole of these phrases in his turn, whispers a secret into the ear of his next neighbor.

At the end of the fourth repetition, the chief player adds—"In the fourth corner there is a poppy—that which you told me in a whisper repeat aloud."

In proportion as the discourse, which has now arrived at its climax, passes round the circle, each player finds himself obliged to divulge the secret which he has confided to his companion, causing often considerable embarrassment to those who had not expected the game to take this turn, and to find themselves laid under this obligation.

————o————

THE KEY OF THE KING'S GARDEN.

This game, like "My Aunt's Garden," consists of short sentences which each player is obliged to repeat without mistake, but to which new sentences are affixed, which must be repeated by each one in his turn, and without error, under penalty of a forfeiture.

The following are some of the phrases, which may be multiplied tc infinity:

"I sell you the Key of the King's Garden."

"I sell you the Cord that held the Key of the King's Garden."

"I sell you the Rat that gnawed the Cord," etc.

"I sell you the Cat that ate the Rat," etc.

"I sell you the Dog that killed the Cat," etc.

"I sell you the Stick that beat the Dog," etc.

"I sell you the Fire that burnt the Stick," etc.

"I sell you the Water that quenched the Fire," etc.

"I sell you the Pail that carried the Water," etc., etc.

———o———

THE LITTLE MAN'S HOUSE.

All the company place themselves in a circle, and the one who understands the game conducts it.

The leader of the game begins thus,—presenting a key or some other article to his neighbor, he says to him—"I sell you my Little Man." All having repeated this, the leader says—"I sell you the House of my Little Man."

The third time the leader says—"I sell you the Door of the House of my Little Man."

The fourth time—"I sell you the Lock of the Door," etc.

The fifth time—"I sell you the Key of the Lock," etc.

It is evident that this game may be prolonged to any extent. It resembles the game of "The Key of the King's Garden."

For every mistake the player pays a forfeit.

———o———

RUN FOR YOUR LIVES.

This game is a very pretty variation of that of "The House of the Little Man," "The Key of the King's Garden," and others of the same kind. It differs from them, however, in this, that some sort of a story must be invented, and this story must have a particular ending, which will lead to the penalty of forfeits; the mistakes also committed in the repetition of the phrases, of which the story is composed, lead likewise to the paying of forfeits.

EXAMPLE.

The leader of the game says to his right hand neighbor—"Here is an engraving"——

The right hand neighbor repeats these words to *his* right hand neighbor, and so on to the last player.

When the last player has repeated these words to the leader of the game, the latter continues—

"Here is an engraving which represents a young lady " (repeated throughout the circle as before). "Here is an engraving," etc.,——"stopped by three robbers " (as before).——"Here is," etc.,——"the firs: seizes her " (as before).——"Here is," etc.,——"the second puts a poniard to her heart" (as before).——"Here is," etc.,——"the third now perceiving the police officers coming up, cries out—'*Run for your lives!*'"

At this cry all the company start up and run away, except those who, unacquainted with the game, remain in their seats, during this alarm, and are therefore obliged to pay a forfeit for their ill-timed sense of security.

———o———

CONFESSION BY A DIE.

The company, which may consist of both sexes, and of any number, first agree upon the choice of a Confessor, and when he is chosen the game commences.

He takes some blank cards, equal in number to that of the persons who compose the company, keeps another for himself, upon which he secretly writes that which (for this occasion) he intends to call a sin or forbidden act. Then addressing himself to the one who is nearest to him on the right, he commands him to rise, places in his hand a die, which the other rolls upon the table, and the number of spots upon its upper surface indicates the number of faults of which he must accuse himself.

The penitent takes his seat, writes out his confession, hands it respectfully to the confessor, who compares it with the sin which he has written down in advance. If this sin is found in his confession the penitent pays a forfeit; if not, he is pronounced absolved; but in either case his confession is read aloud, because the other players, when summoned in their turn, are not allowed to accuse themselves of a sin which any of those who precede them may have acknowledged themselves guilty of. The result of this is, that some one of the number at last names the fault inscribed upon the card of the Confessor.

The following is an example of this game, in which the sin written down as a heinous offence, is *Idleness*.

The confessor, addressing one of the ladies of the company, says—"**My daughter,** is there not something that weighs upon your conscience?"

"Alas! yes, my father."

"Rise, take this die, and cast it upon this table. You have thrown a four: confess your four sins."

The penitent writes out her confession, and hands it to him. The Confessor, after having read the confession to himself, says, "Go, my daughter; you are innocent, for these are the faults of which you have confessed yourself guilty :—

"'I have frequented balls.

"'I have slandered my neighbor.

"'I have gone every evening to the theatre.

"'I have eaten meat in Lent.'

"These sins are forgiven. Go in peace, and be more careful for the future."

"And you, my son, is there nothing with which you have to reproach yourself?"

"Alas! too much, my father!"

"Rise," etc., as above. "You are guilty, pay a forfeit, for you accuse yourself—

"'Of having spent yesterday at the gaming-table.

"'Of being addicted to all kinds of intoxicating drinks.

"'Of carefully avoiding all kinds of labor,'" etc., etc., etc.

The Confessor does not declare the name of the sin inscribed upon his card until all the company have confessed.

The round finished, another Confessor is named, who also chooses a sin which he considers heinous, and the game recommences; and in this second round, or in as many as may follow, it is forbidden to select a fault already written down by any of the Confessors who have previously officiated, or any acknowledged by the penitents; any error of this kind is easily ascertained, as all the confessions are preserved until the game terminates. This rule greatly multiplies the forfeits.

————o————

THE CURATE.

In this game one of the company must act the part of the Curate, and the remainder must, each one, select a trade or profession. Then the Curate must address one of the company with the words, "I have just come from your house, Mr. Optician, or Madam Dressmaker," (or he may name any one of the trades chosen,) "but I did not find you in; where were you?"

I. Then the person questioned replies: "I was at the tailor's, the hairdresser's, the jeweller's," etc., naming any one of the trades selected.

II. The person who has chosen the trade named, instead of replying, "It is not true," inquires, "For what purpose?" and the other must frame an answer suitable to the trade which he has named.

For example: if he says he has been to the bookseller's, he must answer, "It was to obtain books; but where were you?" The bookseller will then excuse his absence by saying, "I was at the bookbinder's," who in his turn must ask him, "For what purpose?" when he will reply, "To have some books bound; but where were you?" Then the bookbinder must excuse himself by referring to some other of the trades selected. A forfeit is due from every player who fails to make an answer suitable to the trades named, or who gives, as a motive for a visit, any reason previously given.

The players also may say that they have been to the Curate's, and at his question, "For what purpose?" they must answer, "To be married," or make some reply suitable to a Curate's profession; "but where were you?" and the curate is also obliged to make an answer that suits the trade of that one of the company whom he says he was visiting.

This game is very useful in giving young persons correct general ideas concerning the various trades and professions.

————o————

THE PAGE OF LOVE.

He who proposes this game (and no one ought to propose a game that does not know how to lead it, unless for the purpose of designating another player to conduct it who understands it well), he, I say, who proposes this game, distributes a pack of cards, by twos or threes, equally among the company, according to their number, until he has dealt out all but a few, which he reserves as his own stock—this he alone is at liberty to inspect, which he does when he pleases, since he takes no other part in the game than the supervision necessary to conduct it. Those who have received their cards must keep them carefully concealed, so as not to give any advantage to their companions.

After the cards are all distributed, the leader of the game says to the person nearest to him, "Have you read the Page of Love?"

He answers, "I have read the Page of Love."

"What have you seen upon the Page of Love?"

" I have seen" (here the person who replies names any card which he fancies, provided it is not among those which he holds in his own hand).

The leader of the game inspects his stock, and if the card named is among them, the person who has named the card pays a forfeit; if it is not in the stock, then each player examines his cards, and the one who has it places it in the hands of the leader.

If the person who names the card and the one who finds it are of different sexes, the result is a kiss between them; if of the same sex, both pay a forfeit. In either case the game continues; that is to say, the one who has responded questions in his turn his right-hand neighbor, employing the phrase already given—" Have you read ?" and so on, until all the cards are returned to the dealer.

In naming card after card, it is natural that some of them should be named a second time. The player who is guilty of this mistake is obliged to pay a forfeit. To discover this, and avoid useless trouble, the leader should keep the named cards carefully together, let none of the company see them, and inspect them whenever a player names a card.

It is an absolute rule that every named card which is found among those collected in his hand, should cost a forfeit to the one who through carelessness or forgetfulness has committed this fault. In proportion as the cards are gradually withdrawn from the hands of the players, those who are left without any retire from the game. They are not allowed to give advice to the others, who are still playing, under the penalty of paying a forfeit.

————o————

CUPID'S BOX.

This game, invented to compel forfeits, is played in the following manner:

The one who commences offers a box to his right-hand neighbor, and says: "I sell you my Cupid's Box, which contains three phrases— *To Love, to Kiss,* and *to Dismiss.*" The neighbor answers: " Whom do you love ? whom do you kiss ? whom do you dismiss ?"

At each of these questions, which are put separately, the person who has given the box names some individual present whom he *Loves, Kisses,* or *Dismisses.* The person whom he kisses must in reality kiss him, and the one that he dismisses pays a forfeit. A player may *Love,*

Kiss, or *Dismiss* several, or even all of those present; but this is permitted only once during the game—a regulation which brings it to a termination.

---o---

THE INTERRUPTED REPLY.

The company place themselves in a circle. The one who commences says in a whisper to his right-hand neighbor, "Of what use is a book?" (or any other article he may select.)

His neighbor must answer, correctly, "It is of use to read," and then ask another question of *his* right-hand neighbor—for instance, "Of what use is a goblet?"

The art in this game consists in so framing one's questions, that they will produce answers altogether unsuited to the preceding question. If the answer is, "It is of use to drink from," a laughable consequence ensues; for, when the round is finished, or in other words, when the person who has commenced the game has been questioned in his turn, the questions and answers are repeated aloud, by taking the answer of the person on the player's right as a reply to the question of the person on his left, it follows, that to the question, "Of what use is a book?" one of the company has answered, "It is of use to drink from;" and so on with the rest of the questions and answers.

𝔎uses and ℭatch ℭames,

HAVING FOR THEIR OBJECT

TRICK AND MYSTIFICATION.

SCISSORS CROSSED OR NOT CROSSED.

Each player in his turn passes to his neighbor a pair of scissors, or any other object, saying—"I give you my scissors crossed (or not crossed").

If the former, the player, as he utters the words, must cross his arms or his feet in a natural manner. If the latter, he must be careful to keep them separate. The person who receives the scissors must be careful to imitate this action. Many persons, from mere want of attention, render themselves liable to forfeits in this game, and without knowing why—their surprise produces the chief part of the amusement.

———o———

THE MOLE.

This simple game consists merely in saying to one of the players—
" Have you seen my mole?"

The latter answers, " Yes, I have seen your mole."

" Do you know what my mole is doing?"

" Yes, I do know what your mole is doing."

" Can you do as it does?"

The person who replies must shut his eyes at each answer; if he fails to do so he pays a forfeit.

———o———

I HAVE JUST COME FROM SHOPPING.

The company form a circle, and one of the party who composes it says to her right hand neighbor—"I have just come from shopping."

" What have you bought?" rejoins the latter. " A robe, a vest, stockings, flowers;" in fine, anything that comes into the purchaser's head, provided that in uttering the words she can touch an object similar to the one she names. Those who neglect to do this must pay a forfeit; a forfeit can be required also from any one who names an object which has been named by any player previously.

———o———

THE COOK WHO LIKES NO PEAS.

The leader of the game must put the following question to his right hand neighbor, and also to all the players in succession.

" My cook likes no peas—what shall I give her to eat?"

If any player replies—" Potatoes, parsnips," the other answers, " She does not like them; pay a forfeit."

But if another says, "Onions, carrots, veal, chickens.' She likes them, and consequently no forfeit is required of the player.

The trick of this game is evident. It is the letter *P* that must be avoided. Thus, to escape the penalty of a forfeit, it is necessary that the players should propose some kind of vegetable or food in which the letter *P* does not occur, such as beans, radishes, venison, etc., etc.

--------o--------

THE DIVINER.

The point of this game consists in divining a word which is named, together with several others. Two of the players commonly agree between themselves to place it after an object that has four legs, for instance, a quadruped, a table, etc., etc.

EXAMPLE.

If Emily wishes to have Henry guess the word which Susan has secretly told her, she says to him, "Susan has been shopping; she has bought a rose, a dress, some jewelry, a table, a bonnet, a shawl"——

Henry of course will easily guess that the object in question is a *bonnet*, for the word "*table*," which precedes it, has four legs.

--------o--------

THE CHERRIES.

Each of the company takes the name of a fruit, as a Pear, Apricot, Peach, Plum, etc.

A basket of cherries, with their long stems, is placed on the table.

Then the person who conducts the game says, "Who will have some cherries?" Each one replies, "I will," and takes one from the basket.

The company then take their seats, except the questioner, who stands in the middle of the circle, and says, "I should like to exchange my cherry for a pear," or any other fruit he chooses to name, which may have been selected by the players. The one who has taken the name of "Pear," must answer immediately, "I have got a pear." "Well, then," says the questioner, "give me your pear and I will give you my cherry." "How will you have it?" replies the person thus addressed, "by the fruit or by the stem?" Let us suppose the questioner says, "By the fruit." In that case the other has several ways of obeying. He may place the stem in his mouth, and let the cherry be taken from it, or put it in his hair, or in his slipper, or under a candlestick.

There is still another way of replying to the words—" By the fruit," that is, to throw the cherry in his face. Then confused and mortified, he replies—" This pear is not ripe." He then pays a forfeit, and renews his questions, naming another fruit which he chooses, and with the same results.

Sometimes, instead of wishing to have it by the fruit, the questioner asks to have it by the stem. Then the other, holding the cherry between his fingers, offers the stem of the fruit, and lets him take it.

Instead of holding it between his fingers, he puts the cherry in his mouth, the questioner seizes it by the stem, but to no purpose, the cherry becomes detached, the other swallows it, leaving him the stem, disappointing him, and claiming a forfeit into the bargain. His only resource then is, to offer to exchange his cherry for some other fruit, when the person who has taken this fruit for his name, tries to entrap him in the same way.

————o————

THE SLAVE DESPOILED.

This game was formerly a favorite game with our grandmothers and grandfathers, and for this reason we cannot omit describing it to our readers.

The game is played by choosing a King or a Queen, who takes his or her seat upon a high chair or throne at one end of the parlor; then a Slave is chosen, who seats himself upon a stool at the foot of the throne.

The King calls upon one of the company by name, and says to him —" Come up near my slave."

If the person thus summoned is unacquainted with the game, he is apt to come suddenly forward, when, after paying a forfeit for his trouble, he is obliged to take the place of the Slave, without having the reason explained to him, in order not to put the others on their guard. If the person is familiar with the game, he says—" Sire, may I dare ?" The King replies—" Dare ! " Then he comes forward, and says— " Sire, I have obeyed. What shall I do now ?"

The King then commands him to despoil the Slave of some article of his clothing, naming any that he pleases, for instance, a comb, a breast-pin, a bracelet, handkerchief, etc.

But the other, under the same penalty (that is of a forfeit) must be careful not to obey, without pronouncing beforehand the formula—'Sire, may I dare?' To which the King replies as before—"Dare!"

After obeying the order, the player says again—"I have obeyed. Sire, what shall I do next?" The King then either commands him to do something else, or says—"Return to your place." This command, however, the player must be careful not to obey at once, if he wishes to avoid paying a forfeit, and taking the place of the Slave. He must answer—"Sire, may I dare?" and he must not return until he has received the answer—"Dare!"

It very rarely happens that the Slave finds himself despoiled of many articles of his apparel, since the person commanded to perform this office is pretty sure, sooner or later, to neglect the formula, thereby becoming a Slave in his turn, and in his turn liable to be despoiled.

————o————

THE PIGEON FLIES.

This is a very simple game. Each one of the company places a finger upon a table, or upon the lap of the leader of the game, and each must raise his finger as soon as the leader says—"*Pigeon* (or he may name any other bird) *flies.*"

If, out of mischief, he names any object that is not a bird, and any one of the players raises his finger by mistake, the latter pays a forfeit, for he ought not to raise it except after the name of some bird or winged insect.

————o————

THE SORCERER BEHIND THE SCREEN.

The players conceal behind a screen, or behind the door of an adjacent chamber, the one of their number from whom they wish to obtain forfeits. The rest of the company place themselves out of his sight, and the one who leads the game calls out to him—

"Are you there? Are you ready?" "Yes, begin!"—"Do you know Miss —— ?" (naming one of the ladies of the company.) "Yes." —"Do you know her dress?" "Yes."—"Her shawl?" "Yes."—"Do you know her slippers?" "Yes."—"Her collar?" "Yes."—"Her gloves?" "Yes."—"And her ring?" "Yes."—"You know

10*

then everything that she wears?" "Yes."—"Her belt?" "Yes.
—"Her fan?" "Yes."

The questioner adds as many articles of dress as he pleases, or
changes them at his pleasure. The other always answers, "Yes."
"Since you know her so well, tell me what article of her dress I touch?"

If the sorcerer has not been let into the secret before the commencement of the game, he, of course, names a number of articles
before he hits upon the right one, and he pays a forfeit for every mistake he commits; he pays a forfeit also when he names an article
which the questioner has not mentioned.

If acquainted with the game he would say, "You touch Miss ——'s
ring," because this is the only article before which the questioner has
placed the conjunction "*and,*"which is the word of recognition to the
sorcerer instructed in the game.

When any of the players acquainted with the game wish to impose
upon one of their number, previous to selecting him they choose two
or three sorcerers, who know the game. The latter feign to mistake
once or twice to excite no suspicion, and as soon as the last one of
them has guessed rightly (which he could have done at first if he had
chosen), he names as his successor the poor dupe at whose expense
they have previously agreed to amuse themselves.

———o———

THE KNIGHT OF THE WHISTLE.

This, though a very simple game, is one of the most amusing we
have ever seen. The person who is to be made the Knight of the
Whistle, must not have seen the game before. He should be asked if
he has ever been made a Knight of the Whistle? If he answers "No!"
his consent must be asked, and he must then be told to kneel down to
receive the knighthood. Some one must then sit down, and the
knight kneeling, rests his head in the lap of the person who is sitting,
and all the persons gather round and pat gently on his back, while they
repeat these words :—

> Here we unite
> With fond delight,
> The Tulip, Lily, and the Thistle,
> And with due state,
> We now create—
> The one who kneels Knight of the Whistle!

A whistle and a piece of string, some twelve or fourteen inches long should have been previously prepared, and while the person has been kneeling down, it should be fastened to his back, by the button on his coat, or by the aid of a pin. This done, he should be told to listen to the sound of the whistle, that he may know it again. Some one should then sound the whistle, and when the knight has confessed that he should know the sound again, he is told to stand up, and the company form a circle all around him. Then the fun consists of some one behind his back catching the whistle (without *pulling* at the string), and sounding it—dropping the whistle the instant it has sounded. The knight (having been previously told that he is to catch the whistle) will jump round, and will probably seize hold of the hands of the person who sounded it, but at the same moment he will unconsciously have conveyed the whistle to those on the opposite side. And thus, the more anxious the knight gets, the more he embarrasses himself, because, at every turn, he conveys the whistle to some one behind him. This creates very good laughter.

[Care should be taken not to have the string too long, or when the knight turns, the whistle will fly to the front of him, and he will discover the trick. A very small toy whistle, and one that is easily sounded, will be the best. But a small key will do, when no better can be had. Those who form the ring, should occasionally pretend to be passing the whistle from hand to hand. This game cannot be played more than once of an evening, unless a visitor may happen to enter, and who has not seen it. Ladies, as well as gentlemen, may be made knights.]

---o---

THE WITCH.

A trick to discover a given word by the assistance of a confederate, who enacts the *witch.* Having entered the room, and taken your seat, you are addressed by his witch (who makes mystic passes, etc., over you with a wand) in different sentences, each commencing with a consonant in the word, in rotation. These sentences she divides by waving her wand over your head. The vowels are expressed by thumps on the floor with her wand—thus: a single thump for A; two for E; three for I; four for O; and five for U.

EXAMPLE.

The word chosen is *Boatman.* The witch commences; *B*-e prepared, my trusty spirit, to answer my questions. (*Thump, thump, thump !—*

a wave of the wand—thump!   *T*-o answer my questions, O spirit, so mind—(*a wave of the wand*) *M*-ind what you are about (*thump*).   *N*-ow explain the oracle."

The mystification of the audience may be increased by fixing on the second and third letter instead of the first.

————o————

TOMBOLA.

This novel game is productive of much fun.

The mistress of the house who desires to set up a lottery, should have provided beforehand a number of fancy articles, toys, and elegant nicknackeries; and among these should be prepared one in particular, destined to the discomfiture of some luckless expectant. This lot should be carefully enveloped in several wrappers of tissue paper, and well laid up in cotton, and may consist of any absurd and childish or worthless article. It should be placed the last according to the law of gradation observed with respect to the remaining lots, set out on the table and left uncovered. When the time of drawing has arrived, the master of the house takes a pack of cards, which he distributes among the drawers, according to their several wishes—an agreed price being set upon each card. When this is done he takes another pack, from which a number of cards are drawn without being looked at, equal to the number of lots, and one is placed under each. He then turns up the remainder of the pack, laying down each card in succession and calling it out. The drawer who has a similar card to the one called out, places his beside it. When the whole are thus gone through, those who remain holders of cards corresponding to those under the lots are declared the winners; but of what, remains to be seen. The card under each lot is called out, beginning with the first; and the drawer who holds a similar one carries off the lot. Thus in succession through all the lots, until the last, or the great "sell" lot.

So much for the technical arrangement of the game; now let us sketch its dramatic effect—the movement and excitement to which it gives rise. As one by one the cards in the drawers' hands are proclaimed worthless, the laugh at their disappointment stimulates them to make another venture, and a general bidding takes place for those that remain, and as their number diminishes, and the consequent probability of any one of them becoming a prize increases, they fetch higher and still higher prices. The anxiety—the mingled hope and fear with which all eyes are fixed on the card about to be turned up, are emotions which not the coolest and soberest of the company can guard against; and when, at last, the lots are distributed to the winners, each is in more or less trepidation, lest his prize entitle him to the honor of contributing to the general mirth by being presented with the "sell," and having deliberately to unfold layer after layer of the paper and wool until he reaches the kernel of the mortifying joke which is cracked against him.

The mistress of the house retains from the proceeds of the lottery the cost of the various articles drawn for, and the remainder is devoted to some charitable purpose.

Games

IN WHICH OCCASION IS FOUND TO DISPLAY GAL LANTRY, WIT, OR SOME FAMILIARITY WITH NATURAL HISTORY, MYTHOLOGY, &c.

THE BOUQUET.

Each player in his turn supposes himself a bouquet, composed of three different flowers. Each one must name aloud to the leader of the game the three flowers of which he considers himself composed.

The leader of the game writes down the names of the three flowers, and adds to what he has written, without informing the other, the names of any three persons of the company he may choose.

He then asks the player to what use he intends to put the three flowers he has chosen. The player tells him to what use he means to put them, and the leader of the game applies it to the three persons that he has written down.

EXAMPLE.

THE LEADER OF THE GAME. Miss Julia, choose your three flowers.

JULIA. The Marigold, the Bachelor's Button, and the Rose.

THE LEADER. I have written them down. Now what will you do with your Marigold?

JULIA. I will throw it over my shoulder.

THE LEADER. And the Bachelor's Button?

JULIA. I will put it at my window.

THE LEADER. And the Rose?

JULIA. I will put it on the mantel-piece.

THE LEADER. Very well, you have thrown Adolphus over your shoulder, you have put Miss Maria at your window, and adorned your mantel-piece with Charles. And now, Mr. Adolphus, it is your turn to speak. Choose your three flowers.

————o————

FLORA'S BOUQUET.

Each player chooses three flowers, having a well known signification, either complimentary or uncomplimentary, to suit the person for whom he secretly designs them; he binds them together, deposits the bouquet in a vase, writes upon the vase a motto, and sends it to the person whom he intends it for.

EXAMPLE.

A young lady, who is annoyed by the importunities of a disagreeable admirer, expresses herself thus:

"I choose a *Poppy*, a *Pink*, and a *Thistle*.

" The *Poppy* is a symbol of the wearisomeness which leads to sleep, the *Pink* is that of self-conceit, and the *Thistle* is that of the wreath which self-conceit merits.

" To tie this bouquet, I take a piece of ribbon-grass.

" I place it in a vase of the commonest earth.

" I write upon the vase: 'Praise be according to merit.'

" I address the whole to Mr. ———, and spare him the trouble of thanking me."

A young man composes his bouquet in the following manner:

"I choose a *Rose*, a *Pansy*, and a *Lily of the Valley*.

"The *Rose* is the symbol of beauty, the *Pansy* that of wit, and the *Lily of the Valley* that of virgin simplicity.

" I tie this bouquet with a piece of ivy, symbolical of my constancy.

" I place it in a vase of gold, upon which I write: 'To Beauty, adorned by Virtue.'

' And I present it to Miss———."

————o————

THE FOOL'S DISCOURSE.

This game has a great resemblance to that of *Cross Questions*, inasmuch as each one of the company gives a sentence to his neighbor, while the one whose office it is to ask the questions stands a little apart, so as not to hear it.

When all the sentences are given, the leader of the game approaches, and addresses to each player a particular question, to which the latter answers by pronouncing quickly the sentence which he has received. Many amusing singularities and inconsistencies are the result.

This game presents no other difficulty than that of knowing how to put the questions skilfully, and to vary them in such a manner that they may suit all sorts of answers.

Let us suppose that the persons who compose the company have each received a question, and that EDWARD, the questioner, asks the question—" Do you ride out often ?"

EMILY.   Upon a chair.

EDWARD.   Do you love reading?

EMMA.   With a little sauce.

EDWARD.   Have you good friends ?

ADOLPHUS.   One at a time.

EDWARD.   Do you like dancing ?

VIRGINIA.   In a church.

Etc., etc.

————o————

THE DESCRIPTION.

Before commencing the game, the gentlemen and ladies, in equal number, proceed, separately, to choose an umpire; the ladies one of their sex, the gentlemen one of theirs.

The players then range themselves in a single line, the ladies occupying the right wing, and the gentlemen the left. A table, furnished with writing materials, is placed at each extremity of the line, before which the umpires take their seats, provided with everything necessary to the progress of the game. Then they draw up, separately, a series of questions, disposed in triplets, of a number equal to the number of couples that compose the company. These questions are arranged as follows :

FOR THE LADIES.

If I should decide to have a lover, I should wish him to have his—

FIRST LADY.   { Hair,
              { Eyebrows,
              { Complexion.

SECOND LADY.	{ Forehead, Nose, Mouth.
THIRD LADY.	{ Eyes, Cheeks, Ears.
FOURTH LADY.	{ Mouth, Teeth, Neck.
FIFTH LADY.	{ Chest, Shoulders, Height.
SIXTH LADY.	{ Arms, Hands, Nails.
SEVENTH LADY.	{ Knees, Legs, Feet.

FOR THE GENTLEMEN.

If I should decide to make love to a lady, to please me she must have her—

FIRST GENTLEMAN.	{ Waist, Countenance, Voice.
SECOND GENTLEMAN.	{ Birth. Fortune, Talents.
THIRD GENTLEMAN.	{ Character, Heart, Mind.
FOURTH GENTLEMAN.	{ Sight, Hearing, Smelling.
FIFTH GENTLEMAN.	{ Touch, Taste, Carriage.
SIXTH GENTLEMAN.	{ Sleep, Appetite, Memory.
SEVENTH GENTLEMAN.	{ Health, Fashion, Disposition.

These series of questions are more or less numerous, according to the number of the players.

When they are all written down on either side, the female umpire addresses the lady nearest to her, and requests her to fill up the blanks opposite the three parts of the first series. We will suppose that she writes—

> After Hair—*Brown.*
> After Eyebrows—*Grey.**
> After Complexion—*Olive.*

The second lady replies by filling up the blanks to the second series of questions, and so on with the rest.

In the mean while the male umpire addresses the gentleman nearest to him, and requests him in the same manner to write his preferences opposite the series of questions which he has drawn up for him. We will suppose that the latter writes—

> After Waist—*Moderate.*
> After Countenance—*Open.*
> After Voice—*Harsh.*

The rest write in the same way, according to their tastes, opposite the questions proposed to them.

When all are filled up, the female umpire proposes to the first gentleman the question put to the first lady, by saying,

"If you intended to select a sweetheart, of what color would you choose to have

> Her Hair ?—*Blonde.*
> Her Eyebrows ?—*Red.*
> Her Complexion ?—*Olive.*†

The umpire writes down these answers; then returning to the first lady, she asks her for the reason of her preference, article by article, and makes a note of these also; she then returns to the gentleman, and inquires for his reasons, which must be different from those of the lady.

The umpire on the gentlemen's side follows the same course towards the ladies, questioning them, one after the other, as to their preference regarding the question proposed to the gentleman whose place in the line corresponds with theirs; then he demands the reasons for this preference from each; and so on until all the questions have been discussed.

---

* The players must be careful not to repeat the same word in the same series of questions; for instance, *brown* hair, *brown* eyebrows; in this case a forfeit must be paid

† The unfortunate gentleman who by chance prefers the same color or other quality which one of the ladies may have written in her answer, can only redeem his faults by paying a forfeit.

THE CULPRIT'S SEAT.

A good memory and a ready wit are highly essential in this game—memory to the president, appointed to receive in secret the accusations which the other players (who are so many judges) bring before him, and to interrogate upon each article the person to whom chance or his own choice has assigned the part of the criminal, and placed upon the Culprit's Seat—wit to the judges, in order that they may so frame their accusations as not to wound the sensibility of the accused.

The following is the course of the game :

The company form a semicircle, in the midst of which the president is seated; the criminal places himself opposite to him upon a stool, and the president opens the court.

"Honorable judges," he says, " do you know wherefore the accused is upon the stool of penitence ?"

" We know."

The judges then advance successively to the president, and whisper in his ear the reasons that they choose to give him.

This done, each resumes his place, and the president, addressing the pretended culprit, says—

"You are accused of such or such a crime (he names in detail the accusations): Do you know who has complained against you for each of these offences ?"

The accused repeats one after the other, and at each accusation names one of the judges; if he mistakes in every case, he pays a forfeit, and keeping his place upon the Culprit's Seat, he must answer to a new round of accusations: if he guesses a single one of his accusers, the latter takes his place, pays a forfeit, and waits to be accused in his turn.

This game requires great attention on the part of the accusers; they must consider the age, the sex, the personal, as well as mental qualities of the person who occupies the Culprit's Seat. When one wishes to pay the culprit a compliment, one must be careful not to accuse him of a quality that he or she does not possess; neither should this quality be exaggerated, as it would then seem ironical; if the accusation relates to a fault or a foible, it is better to make a false accusation, than to aim at a real failing, as this would wear the appearance of rudeness. In general, it is necessary to avoid all excesses, strictly to observe the rules of politeness, the neglect of which often gives rise to quarrels, both in the game itself, as well as in other social relations.

————o————

THE SECRETARY.

This game can be played in two ways; in both it is necessary for the company to range themselves around a table, furnished with the requisite number of pens, and other materials for writing.   The Secretary (the person who conducts the game) distributes to each of the players a blank card or a square piece of paper.

When it is decided to follow the older method of playing the game, all write their names legibly at the top of the card, which has been given to them, and place it in the hands of the Secretary, who shuffles the cards or squares of paper thoroughly together, and lets each person draw one at random, without allowing the others to see the name which is written upon it.   Then each one, separately, and without the slightest reserve, writes below this name his opinion of the person who bears it, folds the paper, and gives it a second time to the Secretary, who, after he has collected them all, shuffles them anew, and then reads them off aloud, without permitting any one to inspect the handwriting.   The reading finished, all the papers are cast into the fire, to avoid the ill-feeling which might arise if the authors of the contents were known.

As this game is liable to give rise to personalities, which occasion unpleasant results, the following is a new method of playing it, from which no such consequences are to be apprehended.

When the Secretary has distributed his blank cards, each player adopts a name that suits his fancy, or is in harmony with the qualities which he flatters himself that he possesses, and writes it at the top of the paper below his real name, without allowing his neighbors to see the name which he has chosen.   This done, the Secretary collects the cards, transcribes upon as many similar ones the adopted name of each person, shuffles them, and distributes them to the players, each of whom, racking his brain to guess the person to whom the name written on the card dealt to him belongs, writes out a random description of him which he signs with his own adopted name.

In this way a player often gives a flattering description of a person, whom he would not have treated so tenderly if he had known whom he really was describing, and treats very severely another of whom he would wish to say nothing but what was complimentary.   The Secretary, after reading the papers, supplies the real to the feigned names, and no one has a right to be offended at raillery, or to plume himself upon praises, which have been bestowed upon him by mere chance.

————o————

THE NARRATIVE.

In this game, as in that of "The Secretary," all present must range themselves around a table, but instead of the square pieces of paper distributed to each person, as is necessary when a continued narrative is required, a single sheet of paper is sufficient for all the company.

The players agree aloud as to the title of the narrative; then the leader of the game commences the story by writing two or three lines, as well as the first word of the following line. He then folds down the paper above his first word, which he shows to the player who is to follow him. This word serves as a hint to the continuation of the narrative, with which the second player is to proceed, and so on, until the story is thought to be sufficiently complicated.

EXAMPLE.

In a company composed of nine persons, four ladies (Edith, Julia, Leonora, and Caroline) and five young gentlemen (Augustus, Henry, Frank, Charles, and Edward), all seated around a table, Edward proposes the game of "The Narrative," and gives aloud for its title, "*The fortunate and unfortunate adventures of Miss Palmer*.

This is all that is requisite for the company to know. Then he writes secretly his two lines, and places at the beginning of the third line the word which is to serve as a cue for his right-hand neighbor; he then folds the paper so that only the last word can be seen, and passes it to Caroline, who pursues the same course.

The following is an example of the incoherent sentences thus strung together; at the head of each we place the name of the person who is supposed to have written them, while we write in italics the only words of the narrative which the next player is allowed to see.

THE FORTUNATE AND UNFORTUNATE ADVENTURES OF MISS PALMER.

EDWARD. In a country which the geographers have neglected to inscribe upon the map, lived young Miss Palmer, and I will now write her *history*.

CAROLINE. It can be nothing but a tissue of falsehoods; but we shall judge of that when we come to the *reading*.

FRANK. It was her favorite amusement, and her choice, ill-directed, soon gave her a turn for the *romantic*.

JULIA. Miss Palmer dreamed of nothing but elopements, spectres, subterranean dungeons, turrets, and *mysterious brigands*.

AUGUSTUS. Carried off by this band of ruffians, she lived confined in a gloomy dungeon, with bread and water for her only *nourishment*.

LEONORA. What care she took to furnish it abundantly to the poor! Her charity was to her an unbounded source of innocent *pleasures*.

HENRY. After immoderate indulgence in them, on leaving the ball, the wheel of the carriage became entangled in that of a *swill-cart*.

CHARLES. Reduced to the necessity of emptying her own swill! What a sad lot for a person of her *condition!*

EDITH. The one imposed upon her seemed very hard, and she would have preferred death to the necessity of taking such a *husband*.

SECOND ROUND.

EDWARD. At last she is married. May she live happily in the bosom of her *family!*

CAROLINE. Her own was a singular mixture; not one of them but had a hump back or a *wry neck*.

FRANK. The pain she suffered from it was excruciating. To get rid of it she was obliged to tie around her neck one of her *woollen stockings*.

JULIA. Add to that a pair of wooden shoes, which produced corns, and when she walked almost put her ankle *out of joint*.

AUGUSTUS. But she made a stout resistance, giving her rival a box with a *five-leaved clover*.

LEONORA. Already it commenced to wither and droop, and the mourning of Nature accorded with the sadness of her *heart*.

HENRY. Yes, it was her favorite dish; every day Miss Palmer had a plate of it served up before her, until the day that saw her descend into the *tomb*.

CHARLES. All is over, then; she has succumbed to her fate. I see, in imagination, the finest *procession*.

EDITH. All the city was crowded into the square, to hear the music and the *musketry*.

The whole is then read, and the mixture of so many ideas, ridiculously put together, almost always produces recitals that are extremely comical.

--------o--------

THE WRITTEN CONFESSIONS.

In this game there should be an equal number of either sex, besides a gentleman or lady who is chosen to act the part of a confessor.

This grave personage distributes to each of his penitents a square piece of paper, upon which they are to inscribe three sins or faults which they may remember to have committed. He then addresses them in a short discourse, enforcing the duty of frankness in this act of humility. The penitents listen to the injunction, and receive the paper with an air of great respect; each writes his name on the top, and beneath it the required confession; they then replace them in the hands of the confessor, who divides them into two piles, one for the ladies, and the other for the gentlemen; he next shuffles the two piles separately, and taking from each one the confession that chance has brought to the top, he calls up the lady and gentleman to whom they belong, and reads aloud their contents, and if the two papers indicate faults that have a similarity with each other, he declares the penitents absolved, and sends them back into the circle to sit side by side. If, on the contrary, the sins which they have confessed are of a different nature, he informs them that they must prepare to undergo the penance which the company shall think suitable to impose upon them, and directs them to take their places in opposite corners of the room, until all the confessions are inspected.

After the inspection of the confessions is completed, the confessor and the absolved penitents (if there are none, the confessor alone) decide upon the penalties, and as fast as these are performed, the culprits, returning into the pale of the society, unite with it in pronouncing upon the fate of those yet remaining to be punished.

The following are examples of confessions:

HARRIET. I confess that I spend a little too much time at my toilet; that I love to be surrounded by admirers; that I always strive to depreciate the merit of my rivals.

HENRY. I confess that I prefer the pleasures of the table to more important duties, the gaming-table to the desk, and the love of the fair sex to everything else.

THE CONFESSOR. Although these faults are quite natural, yet I cannot excuse them, because those confessed by the one and the other do not sympathize together. Go *you* into that corner, *you* into that, to await the penance which we, in our wisdom, may see fit to impose upon you.

JULIA. I confess that I am given to slandering my neighbors, and that I am inclined to anger and jealousy.

ADOLPHUS. I confess that I have a natural proneness to find rivals in all those who approach the individual whom I love; that I am subject to fits of passion, which, in my cooler moments, I myself condemn;

and that I sometimes make remarks not always justifiable respecting those who displease me.

THE CONFESSOR.   You are both very culpable; but the similarity that exists between your faults renders you worthy of excuse; return together into the circle, and try to improve yourselves the one by the other, etc., etc., etc.

————o————

MARRIAGES FROM SIMILARITY OF CHARACTER, AND DIVORCES FROM INCOMPATIBILITY OF TASTES AND TEMPER.

These two games form in fact but one, such is the resemblance between the course to be pursued by both.

The company commence by seating themselves before a table; the ladies are seated on one side, the gentlemen on the other.   The gentleman and lady opposite each other are the future spouses in the game of Marriages, or the discontented spouses in the game of Divorces.

If there are one or more gentlemen or ladies left after the couples have been formed, they compose the tribunal; if there are none left, one of the couples is chosen to represent it.   Then each person takes a sheet of paper, and without any concert with the others, traces upon it a sketch of his character.

When all have finished, and it should be done as quickly as possible, the tribunal, which is seated at the upper end of the table, calls up the pair of future spouses most distant from it, and commands them to give up the several sheets of paper upon which they have written their characters—the tribunal then reads aloud the qualities or defects which the couple have attributed to themselves.   If there is a great similarity of character between the pair, they are declared man and wife, and invited to form part of the tribunal; if, on the contrary, their tastes are opposite, the tribunal decides that there is no reason why the marriage should take place, and requires a forfeit from each.

In the game of Divorces the only difference is that the marriage is confirmed, where there is a similarity of tempers, and both are required to give a forfeit for having demanded a separation, without just cause; while, on the contrary, the marriage is dissolved where incompatibility really exists, and the pair is divorced, and invited to augment the number of the judges.

It is evident that this game has much analogy with that of "The Confessions." and some others.

COMPLIMENTS.

A circle is formed ; a gentleman and lady sitting alternately. Polite ness demands that the game should be commenced by a lady.

"I should like," she says, " to be *such or such an animal.*" (The more abject or disgusting this animal is, the more difficult is it to invent the compliment which the lady has the right to expect.)

Suppose, for example, she has chosen the *hornet.* She inquires of her left hand neighbor if he knows why she has made so strange a choice.

The latter, who is not expected to pay her a compliment, replies simply, from the well known nature of the animal, "Because you wish that all living beings should avoid the place where you have chosen your abode."

The lady inquires of her right hand neighbor, "What advantage would I find in this transformation?"

Answer. That of escaping from a crowd of admirers whom your modesty makes you look upon as importunate.

If the gentleman first addressed pays the lady a compliment, or if the second fails to do so, both pay a forfeit.

Then it becomes the turn of him who pays the compliment to form a wish.

He expresses, for example, a desire to be a goose. Then he asks the lady whom he has just complimented if she can divine what can be his motive? "It is," she replies, " that you may inhabit indifferently either the land or the water." Then addressing himself to the lady on his right hand, he says—"What advantage would I find in such a metamorphosis?" "The hope so dear to your heart of one day saving your country, as the geese of the capitol once saved Rome."

One round is enough at this game, because nothing is more tiresome than compliments, when prolonged, however much they may be merited. It is necessary, however, to complete the entire round, in order to deprive no one of his or her turn, as the little part each plays is always flattering to the vanity, even of those among the company the least susceptible of it.

————o————

THE THREE KINGDOMS.

The player who has proposed the game withdraws into an adjoining chamber, while the rest of the company agree upon an object that he must guess.

When the word is agreed upon they recall him; he has the right to ask twelve questions, which refer at first to the kingdom* to which the object belongs that is expressed by the word selected, upon the present condition of this object, the country where it is most frequently found, and finally, upon the metamorphosis which it has undergone, its use, and its qualities.

The players should answer in a manner calculated to describe the object, yet not too plainly. But, on the other hand, those who give false notions of the object are liable to the penalty of a forfeit. The questioner who, after twelve answers which are recognised as satisfactory by the company, fails to guess the object, pays a forfeit in his turn, and withdraws a second time, while the rest of the players agree upon another word, which he must try to guess in the same manner.

EXAMPLE.

The questioner, having heard the signal, re-enters, and directs his questions somewhat in this manner:—

1. "To what kingdom does the object† thought of belong?"

One of the players answers: "To the *Vegetable Kingdom*, and no other."

2. "Is it growing at present, or put to use?"

"Put to use."

3. "Is it an article of furniture?"

"No."

4. "What use is it commonly put to?"

"It is commonly covered, at regular intervals, with a fluid of a color completely opposite to its own."

5. "In what places is it most commonly produced?"

---

* There are three kingdoms in nature, to wit, *The Animal Kingdom*—which comprehends everything that has life and movement, and everything that has formed part of an animated being, such as horn, ivory, skin, hair, wool, silk, etc., etc.

The Vegetable Kingdom, which includes trees, plants, flowers, leaves, fruits, bark, in a word, all that the earth produces which has life without movement.

The Mineral Kingdom, which includes everything that has neither life nor movement, as stones, diamonds, etc.

† An object may belong to two or even the three kingdoms at once. A shoe, for instance, belongs to the *animal* kingdom by the leather and the skin of which it is composed, to the *vegetable* kingdom by the thread with which it is sewed, and to the *mineral* kingdom, if it is furnished with nails.

It is necessary, therefore, before selecting a word, to enumerate its different parts, which may connect it with one or more of the three kingdoms.

"In New England, New York, and New Jersey."

6. "Ah, I know that it is not linen, for neither of these **states is** celebrated for that article."

"No, but linen has something to do with it."

7. "What metamorphosis has it undergone?"

"A very great one. It has been cast into the water, beaten, crushed, reduced to pulp, then reunited into a solid body, such as we see it every day."

8. "It is *Paper* then?"

"You have guessed it."

The player whose answer leads the questioner to guess the riddle, then pays a forfeit, and becomes the questioner in his turn.

Let us suppose that he is endeavoring to divine the object next thought of, he begins with the same question as his predecessor.

1. "To what kingdom does it belong?"

"To the three kingdoms."

2. "Is it put to use then?"

"Yes."

3. "Is it an article of furniture?"

"Portable furniture."

4. "What is its ordinary use?"

"To guard against dampness."

One of the players here makes the observation that this reply is not exact, and that the respondent owes a forfeit.

The latter replies—"Why, if I said that it shielded from the rain, he would guess it without difficulty."

The questioner replies hastily, "It is an *umbrella*."

"There! I could not save my forfeit; it is very annoying."

"Go, go into the next room; it is your turn to guess."

The *umbrella*, in truth, belongs to the *animal* kingdom by its silk covering and its whalebone frame, to the *mineral* kingdom by its fastenings of copper and of steel wire, and to the *vegetable* kingdom by its handle, of what wood soever it may be made.

Paper made of old rags is of the *vegetable* kingdom purely, since the linen is made of hemp or flax, and muslin and calico are made of cotton, which belong to the vegetable kingdom.

THE TRAVELLER'S TOUR.

This game may be played by any number of persons.

One of the party announces himself the Traveller, and about to take a little tour. He calls upon any of the party for information respecting the objects of the greatest interest to be noticed in the different towns and villages through which he intends passing.

He is given an empty bag, and to each of the persons joining in the game are distributed sets of counters with numbers on. Thus, if twelve persons were playing, the counters required would be up to number twelve, and a set of ones would be given to the first person, twos to the second, threes to the third, and so on.

When the traveller announces the name of the place he intends stopping at, the first person is at liberty to give any information, or make any remark respecting it; if he cannot do so, the second person has the chance, or the third, or it passes on until some one is able to speak concerning it. If the traveller considers it correct information, or worthy of notice, he takes from the person one of his counters, as a pledge of the obligation he is under to him. The next person in order to the one who spoke last is to proceed, so as not each time to begin with number one. If no one of the party speaks, the traveller may consider there is nothing worthy of notice at the place he has announced, and he then passes on to another.

After he has reached his destination, he turns out his bag to see which of the party has given him the greatest amount of information, and that person is considered to have won the game, and is entitled to be the Traveller in the next game.

If it should happen that two or more persons should have given the same number of counters, those persons are to be allowed in succession to continue to assist the Traveller and deposit their pledges, until one *alone* remains.

EXAMPLE OF THE GAME.

TRAVELLER. I intend to take a little excursion this summer, and shall soon start from New York for Niagara; but as I wish to stop at several places, I shall travel slowly. My route will be by steamboat up the Hudson to Albany, thence through the centre of the state to the Falls.

NUMBER ONE. Soon after leaving New York city you come to the Palisades, which form one of the first objects of interest in your route.

The noble river is then walled in for thirty miles by high precipitous rocks, upon whose summits imagination has but to place some ruined castles to suggest olden memories, and the inferiority of the scenery of the vaunted Rhine to that of the Hudson must be confessed.

TRAVELLER. Thank you for this information; pray deposit a counter in my bag, that I may remember to whom I owe it. I propose to stop at Tarrytown.

NUMBER Two and THREE not answering,

NUMBER FOUR. Pray visit the spot of André's arrest. After the final arrangements with Arnold in regard to the betrayal of West Point were made, André proceeded on horseback to New York, and when he reached this spot supposed himself to be within the British lines, and thus secure from danger. Here he was stopped by three soldiers, whose names will ever be held in remembrance—Paulding, Williams, and Van Wart. Instead of showing his passport, he inquired whence they came, and receiving for answer "from below," he responded "So do I," showing at the same time his uniform as a British officer. "We arrest you as an enemy to our country," replied these soldiers; and resisting all his attempts at bribery, they led him captive to the head-quarters of the American general. His sad fate is well known. Hung as a spy near this place, his remains were left here a few years, but are deposited among England's illustrious dead in Westminster Abbey. Number Four deposits a counter.

NUMBER SEVEN. The Hudson is rich in revolutionary reminiscences. A short distance from Tarrytown, on the opposite shore, you will reach Stony Point, the scene of Mad Anthony Wayne's daring exploit in 1779, when, without firing a single gun, the fort here situated was surprised and taken by assault, forming one of the most brilliant exploits achieved during the war. A counter of Number Seven is put into the bag.

TRAVELLER. I cannot stop long here, but must proceed with my journey. Where shall I stop next?

NUMBER NINE. You pass then at once into the Highlands. Here the Hudson has burst its way at some distant period through the mountains, leaving on each side a rampart of almost perpendicular hills of from six hundred to seventeen hundred feet above the level of the river. Most prominent among them are the Dunderberg, Anthony's Nose, and Butter Hill. Number Nine deposits a counter.

NUMBER TWELVE. In the bosom of the Highlands you will find West Point, which is unquestionably the most romantic spot on the river. The village is placed upon the top of a promontory one hundred and eighty-eight feet above the river, where there is spread out a level plateau or terrace more than one mile in circumference. Number Twelve puts a counter into the bag.

TRAVELLER. Can you give me any other information?

NUMBER TWO. West Point is the seat of the United States Military Academy, established in 1812; the land was ceded to the United States by New York in 1826. Number Two deposits a counter.

NUMBER SIX. It is famous as the scene of Arnold's treason. During the Revolution this post was considered the key of the Hudson, and a heavy chain was here stretched from shore to shore. The British were very anxious to obtain possession of this place, which they would have done had Arnold's treason succeeded. Number Six hands the traveller a counter.

TRAVELLER. Are there more objects of interest on the river?

NUMBER EIGHT. Notice the Catskill Mountains, which present a very abrupt front to the river and run nearly parallel to it for twenty miles. The views from the Mountain House are grand and majestic— up and down the Hudson one can see for seventy miles either way— and the Fall of the Katers Kill, three miles from the House, is exceedingly beautiful. Number Eight deposits a counter.

TRAVELLER. My time will not permit me to visit all objects and places of interest; the principal ones must content me; my next resting-place will be Albany.

NUMBER THREE. You will find Albany pleasantly situated. From the top of the capitol, which is built on a hill, the view is very fine. You will find all the public State buildings worthy a visit, as well as those for educational and literary purposes, Albany being distinguished for these last. Number Three deposits a counter.

TRAVELLER. I shall no doubt find pleasure in visiting them, but after leaving Albany I shall be obliged to hasten, taking the cars from there as the most expeditious way. Shall I stop at Schenectady?

No one replies, so the Traveller considers there is nothing peculiarly interesting there, and proceeds to another place, asking—"Where would you advise me to stop?"

NUMBER FIVE. The beauty of Trenton Falls is well and widely celebrated. Stopping at Utica, you will have a slight detour of sixteen miles to make in order to reach them, but you will be fully compensated for the trouble. Number Five deposits a counter.

NUMBER NINE. When again on your route, do not fail to stop at Syracuse, at which place, in connexion with the village of Salina, a few miles distant, you will find the most extensive salt manufactories in the United States. Salt is obtained from the various salt-springs here abundant, in several ways, by boiling, evaporation, etc.,—and the processes are exceedingly interesting. Number Nine hands a counter.

TRAVELLER.   Shall I find more objects of interest here?

NUMBER ELEVEN.   Syracuse is situated on Onondaga Lake. In the southern part of this State lie a cluster of lakes of which this is one, all remarkable for beautiful scenery. The tourist for pleasure will not regret the time spent among them. Number Eleven deposits a counter.

TRAVELLER.   I am much indebted to my friends for the information I have received; *which* one will give me an account of my place of destination?

NUMBER NINE.   On the western border of the State, in a river or strait of thirty-four miles in length, running from Lake Erie to Lake Ontario, and pouring the waters of the Great Lakes over a precipice of one hundred and sixty-five feet in perpendicular height, thunders the far-famed and unrivalled cataract of Niagara, in whose presence all stand dumb with no power to describe, but only to wonder and adore. About three miles below its commencement the river divides into two arms, which embrace an island called Grand Island, twelve miles long and from two to seven wide. Nearly three miles below Grand Island the Rapids commence, and after a course of rather more than half a mile, terminate in the Great Cataract. Goat Island, a quarter of a mile wide and half a mile long, extends to the very brow of the precipice, and divides the Falls into two portions, the higher of which is on the American side, but the greatest body of water is on the Canadian. The American Fall is again subdivided very unequally by Iris Island, with the greater of these subdivisions nearest the New York shore. Of the grandeur and sublimity of this scene, and of the emotions with which it fills the soul, I am utterly unable to speak.

The Traveller having reached his place of destination, examines his bag, and finding that Number Nine has deposited the most counters, he is considered to have won the game and is entitled to be the Traveller in the next game.

———o———

THE RHYMING GAME.

One person thinks of a word, and gives a word that will rhyme with it; the players, while endeavoring to guess the word, think of those that will rhyme with the one given, and instead of speaking, define them; then the first person must be quick in guessing what is meant by the description and answers, if it is right or no, giving the definition to the question. Here are two examples:

" I have a word that rhymes with bun."

" Is it what many people call great sport or merriment?"

" No, it is not fun."

" Is it a troublesome creditor?"

" No, it is not a dun."

" Is it a kind of fire-arm?"

" No, it is not a gun."

" Is it a religious woman who lives in retirement?"

" No, it is not a nun."

" Is it the act of moving very swiftly, or what one does when in great haste?"

" No, it's not to run."

" Is it a quibble, or play upon words?"

" No, it is not a pun."

" Is it a word that we often use to denote that a thing is finished?'

" No, it is not done."

" Is it a weight?"

" No, it is not a ton."

" Well, is it that luminary that shines by day, and brightens everything it shines upon?"

" Yes, it is the sun."

The one who guessed the word will then, perhaps, say:

" I've thought of a word that rhymes with sane."

" Is it a native of Denmark?"

" No, it is not a Dane."

" Is it used by old gentlemen?"

" No, it is not cane."

" Is it what is meant when we say we would be glad to do so and so?"

" No, it is not fain."

" Is it what we all suffer when in great distress?"

" No, it is not pain."

" Is it a Christian name?"

" No, it is not Jane."

" Is it to obtain by success, to win?"

" No, it is not to gain."

" Is it the hair that grows on the neck of animals?"

" No, it is not the mane."

" Is it a very narrow way or passage?"

" No, it is not a lane."

" Is it that which causes so many disappointments to the young?"

" No, it is not rain."

" Is it a square of glass?"

" No, it is not a pane."

" Is it to be proud of one's own accomplishments?"

" No, it is not vain."

" Is it the first in importance; or the ocean?"

" No, it is not the main."

" Is it another name for poison?"

" No, it is not bane."

" Is it that object which is placed on the top of spires and is moved by the wind?"

" Yes, it is a vane."

———o———

CRAMBO.

This game is played as follows:—Each player has to write a *noun* on a small piece of paper, and a *question* on a larger one. All are then thrown together and shuffled, and a question and noun being drawn out, a reply must be given in poetry, in which the noun is introduced. The following may suffice for examples:

Q. Are you fond of poetry?
Noun. Fire.

" Had I the soul of him who once,
    In olden time, ' Father of History' was named,
    I'd prove my love, not by mere affirmation,
    But by glowing thoughts and words of FIRE
    Writ down on the spotless page,
    And thus convey my feelings to posterity."

Q. Define the term Imagination.
Noun. Bridge.

" 'Tis like a castle built on high,
    A thing without foundation;
    A BRIDGE by which we reach the sky;
    Is this Imagination?"

The shorter the reply is, the better; it may be an original impromptu, or a quotation. Those who are clever and quick-witted can make this game a very amusing and lively one, by introducing into the answers sly allusions to various parties in the room, as the papers are collected and read aloud by one person, so that no one is presumed to know by whom they were severally written.

————o————

BOUT RHYMES..

These are attributed to the French; being invented, it is said, by Dulot, a poor poet, who employed himself in finding rhymes for others to fill up with words, in the days when sonnets were fashionable. Make, for instance, a sonnet of the following rhymes:

> love, prove, home, roam, fears, tears, rose,
> those, green, seen, cause, laws, hours, flowers.

It is not necessary that good poetry should be made. The following, for example, will show what fun may sometimes arise from the use of these rhyming words:

> Mary, you say I do not love,
>   And that from thee I wish to roam;
> Dearest, my words and actions prove
>   That thy neat dwelling is my home.
> Then dim not those sweet eyes with tears—
>   For which I fain would find a cause;
> Pale not thy cheeks with needless fears,
>   Breathe not a word against love's laws!
> O class me not, my love, with those
>   Who waste away their precious hours,
> For though I rather like the rose,
>   I'm not so very fond of flowers;
> By thy *dear* side I'm seldom seen
>   Where flowers are sold, *I'm not so green!*

————o————

THE LITTLE FORTUNE TELLER.

This game is played by any number of persons, and is productive of much amusement. Make a board after the following pattern,—a square of eleven with the figure one for the centre. The person who wishes to try his fortune must place the finger on the board without

11*

looking at it; then refer to the list for the number marked on the square touched, and you will obtain an answer, which, like those given by professed fortune-tellers, will often prove false or ridiculous; as, for instance, when a married lady is told that she longs to be married (84), or a child of seven is informed that he will be married this year (89); but it is a very amusing game notwithstanding.

117	118	119	120	121	82	83	84	85	86	87
116	78	79	80	81	50	51	52	53	54	88
115	77	47	48	49	26	27	28	29	55	89
114	76	46	24	25	10	11	12	30	56	90
113	75	45	23	9	2	3	13	31	57	91
112	74	44	22	8	1	4	14	32	58	92
111	73	43	21	7	6	5	15	33	59	93
110	72	42	20	19	18	17	16	34	60	94
109	71	41	40	39	38	37	36	35	61	95
108	70	69	68	67	66	65	64	63	62	96
107	106	105	104	103	102	101	100	99	98	97

ANSWERS TO FORTUNE-TELLER.

1. A life full of changes—die rich.
2. Early marriage and prosperous.
3. Many lovers, but die single.
4. A speedy journey of great importance.
5. Become rich through a legacy.
6. Hours of pleasure, years of care.
7. Your present lover is false.
8. You will marry your present choice.
9. Wed thrice, and die in widowhood.
10. You will travel over land and sea.
11. If not already wed, you never will be.
12. Gaming will be your ruin.
13. You will be very happy in marriage.
14. You will change your love soon

15. A long life and prosperous.
16. A rival will cause you tears.
17. Beware of a false friend.
18. Fate decrees you two partners.
19. A large family of prosperous children
20. You will not wed your present lover.
21. You will soon fall desperately in love.
22. You will soon be in mourning.
23. You will gain an estate by industry.
24. You will better yourself by marriage.
25. You will soon lose by fraud.
26. You will marry an ill-tempered person
27. A sudden rise attends you.
28. You will see an absent lover.
29. Many enemies, but finally triumph.
30. A bad partner, but happy reformation
31. A speedy proposal of marriage.
32. A present, and a new lover.
33. Invitation to a gay party.
34. A serious quarrel.
35. A disgraceful intrigue.
36. A run of ill luck.
37. Gifts of money.
38. A good partner in marriage.
39. You will become rich.
40. Money through love.
41. Cash by trade.
42. A long journey.
43. Important news soon.
44. Mind what you say to a lover
45. A present from a distance.
46. A dispute with one you love
47. Visit from a distant friend.
48. A lawsuit.
49. Advancement in life.
50. Love at first sight.
51. A prize worth having.
52. Wealth, dignity, honor
53. Visit to a foreign land.
54. Profit by industry.
55. A multitude of cards

56. Preferment through a friend.
57. Second partner better than first.
58. Surmount many difficulties.
59. A false friend.
60. A pleasing surprise.
61. A change in your affairs.
62. A ramble by moonlight.
63. Injured by scandal.
64. Unpleasant tidings.
65. Great loss and disappointment.
66. About to attend a christening.
67. Change of situation.
68. A handsome present soon.
69. An invitation to a marriage.
70. News from sea.
71. Happiness or marriage.
72. Pleasant intelligence from abroad.
73. An agreeable partner.
74. You are in love, though you won't allow it.
75. A quarrel with your intended.
76. Disappointment in love.
77. You will fall in love with one who is already engaged.
78. You will inherit an estate shortly.
79. An unexpected death.
80. You meditate an elopement.
81. A dangerous illness.
82. Crosses and disappointments await you.
83. You have three strings to your bow.
84. You long to be married.
85. Your intended is in the sere and yellow leaf.
86. A lapful of money and a lapful of children.
87. You will marry a widow or widower.
88. You will have few friends.
89. You will be married this year.
90. You will be apt to break your promise.
91. Marry in haste and repent at leisure.
92. You are in danger of losing your sweetheart.
93. Beware of changing for the worse.
94. You shall have many offers.
95. You will be happy if contented.
96. You will shortly obtain your wishes.

97. An advantageous bargain.
98. You will see your intended next Sunday for the first time.
99. Others will covet your good luck.
100. Travel in a foreign land.
101. Venture freely and you will certainly gain.
102. Your present speculations will succeed.
103 You love one who does not love you.
104. Wealth from a quarter you little suspect.
105. You will obtain your wishes through a friend.
106. A fortune is in store for you—persevere.
107. Alter your intention; you cannot succeed.
108. Remain at home for the present.
109. Ill luck awaits you.
110. Prepare for a journey.
111. You will succeed according to your wishes.
112. Beware of enemies who seek to do you harm.
113. Misfortune at first, but comfort and happiness after.
114. Prosperity in all your undertakings.
115. Rely not on one who pretends to be your friend.
116. Change your situation and you will do better.
117. It will be difficult for you to get a partner.
118. Your love is whimsical and changeable.
119. You will meet with sorrow and trouble.
120. Your love wishes to be yours this moment.
121. You will gain nothing by marriage.

————o————

THE TORN LETTER.

A lady presents to a gentleman a paper containing certain injurious phrases which he is accused of having written about her, and asks if he can justify his infamous conduct. In order to do so, he proves that the letter has been torn in half, by adding to the end of each line certain other expressions, which he declares were to be found in the original manuscript, and which quite alter the meaning of the letter to one highly favorable to the lady.

EXAMPLE.

" I confess to a great contempt for
  Miss ———, whom I consider

the most ridiculous person
in the world.   She is entirely
without sense, heart, or beauty,
The man whom she may
love is much to be pitied: the
man who could love her
if any such exist, is
entitled to our execration."

To make this somewhat scurrilous production palatable, the penitent
has only to add to each line (in their place) the following words:—

—the idiots who cannot admire
—charming.   Otherwise I should be
—breathing.   She is without equal
—faultless.   Only those who, being
—feel envious, could detract from her.
—prefer, and who cannot appreciate her
—crime of separating her from the
—sincerely, few would be responsible for;
—not so much selfish thoughtlessness
— ? —

By placing which in proper connexion with the lines given, the letter will be found to read as follows:—

" I confess to a great contempt for *the idiots who cannot admire* Miss
————, whom I consider *charming.   Otherwise I should be* the most
ridiculous person *breathing.   She is without equal* in the world.   She is
entirely *faultless.   Only those who, being* without sense, heart, or beauty,
feel envious, could detract from her.   The man whom she may *prefer, and
who cannot appreciate her* love, is much to be pitied: the *crime of separating her from the* man who could love her *sincerely, few would be
responsible for;* if any such exist, is *not so much selfish thoughtlessness*
entitled to our execration?"

————o————

ENTREE: OR, "HOW DO YOU LIKE IT?" "WHERE DO YOU LIKE IT?" "WHEN DO YOU LIKE IT?"

This is a pleasing amusement for the Christmas fireside, and may be
played by any n᷉mber.   One of the players (who volunteers or is se-

lected by chance) leaves the room, or goes out of hearing of the others who join in the game. When he has left them, the players fix upon a subject,—for instance, an eatable, a piece of furniture, an article of clothing, or anything to which the above questions will apply, and by the answers to which questions, the player who has left the room must endeavor to guess the subject fixed upon, the other players striving to mislead him by their answers, which, however, must be applicable. For example, after the subject is decided upon, the player outside is called in. After making his *entrée*, he proceeds to the nearest player, and asks him the first question, " How do you like it?" who, supposing the subject to be a bed, might answer, "I like it warm;" he then passes to the next player, who might like it cold; the third might like it high; the fourth low, and so on. After he has been once round, he begins again, asking the second question, "Where do you like it?" to which the replies might be "in a house," "in a stable," "in a kitchen," "in a parlor." He then asks the third question, "When do you like it?" to which one might reply, "in the morning;" another, "at night;" a third, "when he is ill;" a fourth, "when he is well," etc. During the time of his asking these questions he is at liberty to guess the subject, and should he do so, the player last questioned must go out; but should he perform his three rounds without discovering it, he must take another turn outside; and in either case a new subject is chosen.

Another mode is, for one player to leave the room, while those who remain fix upon a subject; the outside player is then called in, and asked the questions in succession, when much amusement is created by the apparent absurdity of his answers. The players take it by turns to go outside.

--------o--------

PROVERBS.

This game, like that of " *Entrée*," is a trial of skill between one player and all the rest; on his side to discover a secret—on theirs, to prevent or render difficult its discovery.

One of the company having left the room, the rest select some proverb in his absence. On his re-admittance, he must ask random questions of all the party in turn, who, in their replies, must bring in the words of the proverb in succession. The first person who is addressed will introduce the first word of the proverb in the answer, the second person, the second word; and so on until the proverb is exhausted

For instance, "Honesty is the best policy," is the one selected, and suppose the first question to be,

"Have you been out to-day?" the party questioned might say,

"Yes, I have, and very nearly lost my purse; but it was picked up by a boy who ran after me with it, and whose 'honesty' I was very glad to reward."

He then passes on to the next and says, "Were you in the country last summer?"

"Yes, in a most lovely place, where it 'is' very mountainous."

To the next one he asks, "Are you fond of reading?"

"Oh, yes, it is one of 'the' sweetest pleasures."

To another, "Which do you prefer, summer or winter?"

"Both are so delightful, that I do not know which I like 'best.'"

To the last, "Can you tell me if there are any more words in this proverb?"

"I will give you the last word, but I would show greater 'policy' if I refused to answer you."

The person must then guess it or forfeit, and the one whose answer first gave him the idea must take his turn of being guesser. If any are unable to bring in their word, they must likewise pay a forfeit. It is an extremely amusing game, from the laughable way in which some of the words are necessarily introduced.

The proverb should be a familiar one, and care should be taken to speak the word of the proverb as distinctly as the others, but not to emphasize it.

---o---

WHAT IS MY THOUGHT LIKE?

The leader of the game, having thought of some object, asks his companions, "What is my thought like?"

As all are ignorant of what he is thinking about, their answers can of course be but random ones. When he has questioned them all, they must give a reason why the answers given resemble the thought. Suppose he had thought of a rose, and one of the party had said, "His thought was like a little child," the reason given might be because both are tender and fragile, and must not be treated roughly. Another might have said "Like a piano;" here the reason might be given because sweetness comes from both. If any one is unable to find any similarity in his answer to the thought, he must pay a forfeit.

"What's my thought like?" is not suited to very young children; those of a much larger growth need not scorn this trial of their wit and intellect, while there is fun enough about it to prevent its being dull to any. As an example of the manner in which it is played, we will describe a round of it which took place by our own fireside this season. One of the party thought of a newspaper, and the successive answers to the question, "What's my thought like?" were, a chair, a pincushion, a spoon, a watch, a comb. When the thought was declared, the *chair* was in great dismay, protesting that she could not possibly find a resemblance, till it was suggested that each might *conduce to repose.* This, for want of a better reason, was admitted; and the next person was asked, " Why is a newspaper like a pincushion?" The answer given was, "Because if it do not contain something pointed and hard-headed it is of no value." Then the resemblance between a newspaper and a spoon was said to consist in each of them giving the *result of a division ;* and a newspaper and a watch were each said to give *note of the time.* Why a newspaper was like a comb, was not quite so evident; and many answers were suggested, till at last it was agreed that the best reason was, "Because it is the province of each to smooth roughness, to disentangle difficulties, and to connect parties together, without showing its teeth." Children like conundrums, and this game bears so great a resemblance to them, that it engages the attention even of those who are too young to join in it.

————o————

READY RHYME.

This game should not be attempted by very young players, as it would most likely prove tedious to many of them ; but to those who are fond of exercising their ingenuity, it will prove very amusing. Two, four, or more words, are written on paper, and given to each player: the words must be such as would rhyme together; thus, suppose the party have chosen "near, clear, dell, bell," all endeavor to make a complete verse, of which the words given shall compose the rhyme.

When all are ready, the papers must be thrown in a heap, and read aloud, and those who have not succeeded must be fined, the fine being the recital of a piece of poetry, or any of the numerous forfeits we give in another place. One of the papers might read thus:

> A gentle brook was murmuring *near*,
> Afar was heard the tinkling *bell*,
> And peaceful zephyrs, pure and *clear*,
> Refreshed us in that shady *dell*.

Another would be quite different:

> Fairies in the distant *dell*,
> As they drink the waters *clear*,
> From the yellow cowslip *bell*,
> What have they to heed or *fear ?*

————o————

THE GAME OF CONSEQUENCES.

This game requires paper and pencils, and each one is to write according to the directions which are given by the leader. The first one is told to write one or more terms descriptive of a gentleman, who does so, and then folds down the paper so as to conceal what is written, and hands it to the next one, who, after receiving the order, writes, folds the paper down as before, and passes it on to the next one, and so on, until the directions are exhausted. The leader then reads the contents of the sheet aloud, which from its inconsistencies and absurdities will cause much amusement.

Let us suppose these to be the directions of the one acting as leader :

" Begin by writing a term descriptive of a gentleman."

" A gentleman's name ; some one you know or some distinguished person."

" An adjective descriptive of a lady."

" A lady's name."

" Mention a place and describe it."

" Write down some date or period of time when a thing might happen."

" Put a speech into the gentleman's mouth."

" Make the lady reply."

" Tell what the consequences were ?"

" And what the world said of it ?"

The paper being opened, we will suppose it to read as follows:

"The modest and benevolent Nena Sahib, met the beautiful and fascinating Lola Montez, at Barnum's Museum, on the 4th of July, 1776. He said, 'Dearest, I adore you,' and she replied, 'I'm very fond of it." The consequences were, that they were married, and the world said, 'All's well that ends well.'"

———o———

CAPPING VERSES.

There are many games in which the reader of poetry finds his memory agreeably taxed. We will give you two or three. One is called

LAST LETTERS.

One person gives a line or a verse of poetry; the next one must give another, beginning with the last letter of the first line; and the third takes the last letter of the second line to commence his. For instance Number One gives—

"Dear to this heart are the scenes of my childhood."

Number Two takes D, the last letter of the first line, to begin his verse—

"Dear creature! you'd swear,
   When her delicate feet in the dance twinkle round,
That her steps are of light, that her home is the air,
   And she only, *par complaisance*, touches the ground."

Another D for Number Three, who gives—

"Devoted, anxious, generous, void of guile,
   And with her whole heart's welcome in her smile."

Number Four, with E for his letter, hesitates; this costs him a forfeit, for the least hesitation in this game must pay that penalty. So, as Number Four is outlawed by hesitating over a difficult letter, Number Five gives—

"Edward will always bear himself a king."

Still another game of this kind is for the last *word* instead of *letter* of the first line taken to begin the second, as Number One (poor fellow he has the heartache) gives—

"Ah, shouldst thou live but once love's sweets to prove,
   Thou wilt not love to live, unless thou live to love."

Number Two—at whom Number One has been casting unutterahly tender glances—says, rather sharply,

> 'Love is a sickness full of woes,
> All remedies refusing;
> A plant that with most cutting grows."

And the others carry on the game.

————o————

THREAD PAPER POETRY.

This is another interesting game, and one which requires more play of intellect.

A piece of paper and a lead pencil are all the preparations necessary. The first player takes the paper and writes upon it a line of poetry, a quotation; the name of the author may be added, though it is not necessary. When the line is written, he folds the paper so as to hide what is written, and passes it to the second player, telling him the last word of the line. The second must then write a line to rhyme with the first, and also add a line of his own, and pass the paper on.

For instance No. 1 writes—

> " This Nymph to the destruction of mankind."—*Pope.*

doubles the paper, and passes it to No. 2, who adds—

> " Had three small mice, and all were blind ;
> The least ran after the butcher's wife."—*Nursery Rhymes.*

No. 3, a sentimental maiden, writes—

> " And then she cried, 'I'm weary of my life,
> My dream of love is over—he is gone.' "—*Original.*

No. 4, also a maiden, who has lately studied Byron—

> " The spell is broke, the charm is flown !
> Thus is it with life's fitful fever."—*Byron.*

No. 5, a grave, sedate man, writes—

> " I look upon thee, now, as lost for ever;
> To me, at least, it is as if thou wert dead."—*Authority forgotten*

No. 6, thinking dead a solemn word, gives—

> " I care not, so my spirit last long after life has fled."—*L. E. L*

And so on. This specimen is enough to show how the game goes. Sometimes the cross readings are very amusing. The paper is to be read aloud after it is filled up, and some very curious combinations are often found.

————o————

GEOGRAPHICAL PLAY.

Let each person of a party write on a piece of paper the name of some town, country, or province; shuffle these tickets together in a little basket, and whoever draws out one is obliged to give an account of some production, either natural or manufactured, for which that place is remarkable. This game brings out a number of curious bits of information which the party may have gleaned in reading or in travelling, and which they might never have mentioned to each other, but from some such motive.

Let us suppose there to be drawn Nuremberg, Turkey, and Iceland, of which the drawers narrate thus:—

Nuremberg has given to the world many useful inventions. Here were first made the pocket-watch, the air-gun, gun-lock, and various mathematical and musical instruments; and at present half the children of Europe are indebted to Nuremberg for toys; and the industry of the inhabitants is extended to teaching birds to pipe.

Turkey is celebrated for its costly carpets, which all the efforts of European art and capital have failed in closely imitating; yet these carpets are woven by the women among the wandering tribes of Asiatic Turkey. The " Turkey Bird" is, however, very absurdly named, since it conveys the false idea that the turkey originated in Asia, whereas it is a native of America. Neither is " Turkey Coffee" grown in Turkey, but is so named from the great consumption of coffee in that country.

Iceland produces in abundance a certain lichen called Iceland Moss, which is brought to America as a medicine, but is in its native country used in immense quantities as an article of common food. When the bitter quality has been extracted by steeping in water, the moss is dried and reduced to powder, and then made into a cake with mea! or boiled and eaten with milk.

————o————

Forfeits.

Young people are often at a loss for good forfeits in their games. In the schemes of advice upon the subject, the penalties they impose are sometimes vulgar, or highly absurd, creating confusion where innocent pleasure is designed. The following are suggested to help our young friends out of the difficulty.

These forfeits, it will be seen, have each a separate name and number. Now, a good plan would be for a person who is to take an active part in the evening party to read them over during the day, and to become acquainted with them. Then, in allotting the forfeits, *when* they are called, thus:

"HERE'S A PRETTY THING, AND A VERY PRETTY THING, AND WHAT SHALL THE OWNER OF THIS THING DO?"

The person awarding the forfeits may call out "No. 1," "No. 10," "No. 15," or any other number; or may say (which would be more amusing), "*Hush a bye, baby!*" "*Hobson's Choice!*" "*Dot and Carry One!*" etc. This work may be laid on the table, to afford further explanation of the forfeits, or be held in the hand of the person who is holding up the forfeits while they are being cried; and this person can at once explain what is to be done. In this way the redemption of the forfeits will go on freely, without stoppage or hesitation, and a capital evening's amusement be derived.

1. THE KNIGHT OF THE RUEFUL COUNTENANCE.

The player whose forfeit is cried is so called. He must take a lighted candle in his hand, and select some othe: player to be his squire, who takes hold of his arm, and they then both go round to all the ladies in the company. It is the squire's office to kiss the hand of each lady, and after each kiss to wipe the knight's mouth with a handkerchief. The knight must carry the candle through the penance, and preserve a grave countenance.

2. JOURNEY TO ROME.

The person whose forfeit is called must go round to all in the company, to tell them that he is going on a journey to Rome, and that he will feel great pleasure in taking anything for his Holiness the Pope. Every one must give something to the traveller. (The more cumbersome or awkward to carry, the more fun it occasions.) When he has gathered all, he is to carry the things to one corner of the room, and deposit them, and thus end his penance.

3. LAUGHING GAMUT.

Sing the laughing gamut without pause or mistake, thus:

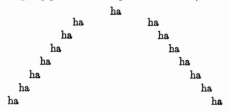

4. THE MEDLEY.

Sing one line of four different songs without pausing between them. It would be well to find four lines that afford humor, taken consecutively, such as—

> "All round my hat."
> "A rare old plant is the ivy green."
> "Sweet Kitty Clover, she bothers me so."
> "In the Bay of Biscay, O."

5. HOBSON'S CHOICE.

Burn a cork one end, and keep it clean the other. You are then to be blindfolded, and the cork to be held horizontally to you. You are then to be asked three times which end you will have? If you say "Right," then that end of the cork must be passed along your forehead; the cork must then be turned several times, and whichever end you say must next be passed down your nose; and the third time, across your cheeks or chin. You are then to be allowed to see the success of your choice.

[This will afford capital fun, and should be played fairly, to give the person who owns the forfeit a chance of escape. The end of the cork should be thoroughly well burnt. As a joke for Christmas time, this is perfectly allowable; and the damp corner of a towel or handkerchief will set all right. It should be allotted to a gentleman, and one who has a good broad and bare face.]

6. POETIC NUMBERS.

Repeat a passage of poetry, counting the words aloud as you proceed, thus:

Full (one) many (two) a (three) flower (four) is (five) born (six) to (seven) blush (eight) unseen (nine) and (ten) waste (eleven) its (twelve) sweetness (thirteen) in (fourteen) the (fifteen) desert (sixteen) air (seventeen)! This will prove a great puzzle to many, and afford considerable amusement.

7. HUSH-A-BYE, BABY.

Yawn until you make several others in the room yawn.

[This can be done well by one person who can imitate yawning well, and it will afford indescribable mirth. It should be allotted to one of the male sex, with a large mouth, and a sombre or heavy appearance, if such a one can be found in the party.]

8. THE BEGGAR.

A penitence to be inflicted on gentlemen only. The penitent takes a staff, and approaches a lady. He falls on his knees before her, and, thumping his staff on the ground, implores "Charity." The lady, touched by the poor man's distress, asks him—"Do you want bread?" "Do you want water?" "Do you want a half-cent?" etc., etc. To all questions such as these the Beggar replies by thumping his staff on the ground impatiently. At length the lady says, "Do you want a kiss?" At these words the Beggar jumps up and kisses the lady.

9. THE PILGRIM.

The Pilgrim is very like the Beggar. A gentleman conducts a lady round the circle, saying to each member of it, if a gentleman, "A kiss for my sister, and a morsel of bread for me." If a lady, "A morsel of bread for my sister, and a kiss for me." The bread is of no particular importance, but the kiss is indispensable.

10. THE EGOTIST.

Propose your own health in a complimentary speech, and sing the musical honors.

11. DOT AND CARRY ONE.

Hold one ancle in one hand, and walk round the room.
[This is suited only to gentlemen.]

12. THE IMITATION.

If a gentleman, he must put on a lady's bonnet, and imitate the voice of the lady to whom it belongs; if a lady, then a gentleman's hat, etc. Sometimes these imitations are very humorous. A sentence often used by the person imitated should be chosen.

13. GOING TO SERVICE.

Go to service; apply to the person who holds the forfeits for a place —say, "as maid of all work." The questions then to be asked are: "How do you wash?" "How do you iron?" "How do you make a bed?" "How do you scrub the floor?" "How do you clean knives and forks?" etc., etc. The whole of these processes must be imitated by motions, and if the replies be satisfactory, the forfeit must be given up.

14. KISSING THE CANDLESTICK.

When ordered to kiss the candlestick, you politely request a lady to hold the candle for you. As soon as she has it in her hand, she is supposed to be the candlestick, and you, of course, kiss *her*.

15. THE DISAPPOINTMENT

A lady advances towards the penitent, as if to kiss him, and when close to him, turns quietly round and allows the expected kiss to be taken by her nearest neighbor.

16. THE FLORIST'S CHOICE.

Choose three flowers. Example: Pink, Fuchsia, and Lily. Two of the party must then privately agree to the three persons of the forfeiter's acquaintance to be severally represented by the flowers. Then proceed: What will you do with the Pink? Dip it in the water! What with the Fuchsia? Dry it, and keep it as a curiosity! With the Lily? Keep it until it is dead, then throw it away! The three names identified with the flowers are now to be told, and their fates will excite much merriment.

17. THE FOOL'S LEAP.

Put two chairs back to back, take off your shoes, and jump over them. (The fun consists in a mistaken idea that the *chairs* are to be jumped over, whereas it is only the *shoes !*)

18. THE RIDDLE.

Guess the answer to this Riddle.

It is said there's a person you've loved since a boy,
Whose hand you must kiss ere I give you this toy;
It is not your father, or mother, or sister,
Nor cousin, or friend—take care not to miss, sir.

[Himself.]

19. THE SECRET.

This consists in whispering a secret to each member of the company.

20. THE SCHOLAR'S "SPELL."

Spell Constantinople, a syllable at a time. After spelling Con-stan-ti, all the others are to cry out "no, no," meaning the next syllable. If the trick is not known, the speller will stop to show no mistake has been made, which is another forfeit; on the contrary, if no stop is made, the forfeit is restored.

21. THE BLIND MAN'S CHOICE.

The one who is to pay a forfeit stands with the face to the wall; one behind makes signs suitable to a kiss, a pinch, and a box on the ear, and then demands whether the first, second, or third be preferred; whichever it chances to be, is given.

22. THE CLOCK.

A player is condemned to transformation to a clock. He stands before the mantelpiece, and calls a player (of the opposite sex) to him. The person thus called upon, asks the "clock" what time it is. The clock replies, whatever hour he likes,—claiming the same number of kisses as he names hours of the day.

If approved of, the player who has asked the time takes the place of the clock, and calls upon another; the original ceremony being repeated in turn by all the players of the company.

23. ARIADNE'S LEOPARD: OR, THE HOBBY HORSE.

The penitent, on his hands and knees, is obliged to carry round the room a lady who is seated on his back, and whom all the gentlemen (himself excepted) are privileged to kiss in turns.

24. HIT OR MISS.

You are to be blindfolded, and turned around two or three times. Then you are to walk towards one of the company, and the handkerchief is to be taken off, that you may see the person you have touched. Then you are to kiss her hand.

25. THE QUIET LODGER.

The person who owns the forfeit may be called upon to choose one or two musical instruments. Having done so, he may be requested to imitate them.

26. STOOPS TO CONQUER.

Crawl around the room on all fours forwards. Your forfeit shall then be laid upon the floor, and you must crawl backwards to it, without seeing where it is placed.

27. THE SOFA.

The penitent places himself in the same position as for "Ariadne's Leopard," that is to say, on all fours. He, however, remains stationary, receiving on his back a lady and a gentleman, who sit comfortably down and exchange a kiss.

28. THE GALLANT GARDENER.

Compare your lady-love to a flower, and explain the resemblance. Thus—

> My love is like the blooming rose,
> Because her cheek its beauty shows.

Or (facetiously)—

> My love is like a creeping tree—
> She's always creeping after me.

29. THE STATESMAN.

Ask the penitent what district he would like to represent in Congress; when the selection is made, he is to spell its name backwards, without a mistake; if he fail, he knows not the requirements of his constituents, and must lose his election.

30. TO BE AT THE MERCY OF THE COMPANY.

This consists in executing whatever task each member of the company may like to impose upon you.

31. KISSING UNDER THE CANDLESTICK.

This consists in kissing a person over whose head you hold a candlestick.

32. TO KISS YOUR OWN SHADOW.

Place yourself between the light and the person you intend kissing, on whose face your shadow will be thrown.

33. TO KISS THE ONE YOU LOVE BEST WITHOUT ITS BEING NOTICED.

Kissing all the ladies in the company one after another without any distinction.

34. THE TWO GUESSES.

Place your hands behind you, and guess who touches them. You are not to be released until you guess right.

The person who owns the forfeit is to be blindfolded; a glass of water and a teaspoon are then to be got, and a spoonful given alternately by the members of the company, until the person blindfolded guesses aright.

35. THE EXILE.

The penitent sent into exile takes up his position in the part of the room the most distant from the rest of the company—with whom he is forbidden to communicate. From there he is compelled to fix the penance to be performed by the owner of the next forfeit, till the accomplishment of which he may on no account leave his place. This may be prolonged for several turns. The last penitent, as soon as he has acquitted himself satisfactorily, takes the place of the exile, and passes sentence on the next.

36. THE "B" HIVE.

Repeat, without stopping, "Bandy-Legg'd Borachio Mustachio Whiskenfusticus the bold and brave Bombardino of Bagdad helped Abomilique Blue Beard Bashaw of Babelmandeb to beat down a Bumble Bee at Balsora."

37. THE TRIO.

Kneel to the wittiest, bow to the prettiest, and kiss the one you love the best.

38. ROB ROWLEY.

Repeat the following —

"Robert Rowley rolled a round roll round,
A round roll Robert Rowley rolled round,
Where is the round roll Robert Rowley rolled round?"

39. THE STATUE OF LOVE.

The player who owns the forfeit cried, takes a candle in his hand, and is led by another to one end of the room, where he must stand

and represent the Statue of Love; one of the players now walks up, and requests him to fetch some lady, whose name he whispers in Love's ear; the Statue, still holding the candle, proceeds to execute his commission, and brings the lady with him; she in turn desires him to fetch some gentleman, and so it continues till all have been summoned. The players brought up by Love must not return to their seats, but stand in a group round Love's standing-place, until he has brought the last person in the company, when they hiss him most vigorously, and the forfeit terminates.

40. THE CHANCE KISS.

The penitent takes from a pack of cards the four kings and the four queens, shuffles them, and, without looking at them, distributes them to a proportionate number of ladies and gentlemen. The gentleman finding himself possessed of the king of hearts kisses the lady holding the queen, and so on with the rest.

41. THE BLIND QUADRILLE.

This is performed when a great number of forfeits are to be disposed of. A quadrille is danced by eight of the company with their eyes blindfolded, and as they are certain to become completely bewildered during the figures, it always affords infinite amusement to the spectators.

42. THE TURNED HEAD.

This penalty should be imposed upon a lady. The fair one, whose head is to be turned, is invested with as many wrappings as possible, but every cloak, shawl, victorine, etc., is to be put on hind side before, so as to present the appearance of "a turned head." She should be furnished with a muff, which she must hold behind her as much as possible in the usual manner, but her bonnet must be put on in the proper way. Thus equipped, she must enter the room walking backwards, and until her punishment is at an end, must continue to move in the same way.

43. THE KING OF MOROCCO IS DEAD.

The culprit takes a candle in his hand, and stepping forward, places another in the hands of a person of a different sex; then both march to opposite sides of the apartment. They then assume a mournful air, and advance towards each other with a slow and measured step. When they meet they raise their eyes to the ceiling, utter some words in a sepulchral tone, then, with downcast eyes, they march on, each to take the place occupied by the other.

This procedure is repeated as often as there are phrases in the following dialogue :—

THE GENTLEMAN.   Have you heard the frightful news?

THE LADY.   Alas!

THE GENTLEMAN.   The King of Morocco is dead.

THE LADY.   Alas! alas!

THE GENTLEMAN.   The King of Morocco is buried.

THE LADY.   Alas! alas! alas!

THE GENTLEMAN.   Alas! alas! alas! and four times alas!

       He has cut off his head with his steel cutlass!

Both then march to their places with an air of melancholy. Having reached their places, they run gaily to resume their seats among the company.

44. THE YARD OF LOVE RIBBON.

One or more yards of Love Ribbon may be inflicted as a penalty.

He (or she) who suffers this infliction, must choose out a lady (or a gentleman), lead her (or him) into the middle of the circle, take her hands in his, extend them as far as the length of his arms will permit, and give (or receive) a kiss to (or from) the other. This is repeated with the same person as often as the number of yards of Love Ribbon are inflicted.

45. THF JOURNEY TO CYTHÈRE.

The person upon whom this penalty is inflicted leads another, of the opposite sex, behind a screen or a door. Here the gentleman kisses the lady, and touches any part of her dress which he may choose.

On their return from the journey, they present themselves before all the company in turn, and the gentleman asks each of them what part of the lady's attire he has touched. At each mistake on their part, he kisses that portion of the lady's dress which has been named by them. If, at last, some one of the company guesses correctly, he kisses the lady, or if it is a lady, she receives a kiss from the gentleman.

If, on the contrary, no one guesses rightly, the gentleman names aloud the part of the lady's dress which he has touched, and kisses the lady once more before conducting her to her seat.

46. LOVE'S ARCH.

The gentleman (or the lady) upon whom this penalty is inflicted, proceeds to take a lady (or a gentleman) whom he leads into the middle of the apartment, where both hold their hands entwined, and their arms raised in the form of an arch. Then the lady names a gentleman, and the gentleman a lady; the couple named are to pass together beneath Love's Arch, but when they have half passed it, the arms fall, encircling them, and hold them prisoners until the gentleman has snatched a kiss. This done, the arms are raised, the imprisoned pair proceed onward, then pause to form a second arch; the latter summon a third couple, who are forced to pay the same tribute in passing beneath the arch; and who then advance to form a third, and so on as long as there are a gentleman and lady remaining.

After each pair of the company has formed an arch, all return to their places.

47. THE CONVENT PORTER.

The person paying forfeit places himself at the door of a chamber, which he must open and shut at the proper moment. A gentleman withdraws into this chamber, supposed to be the parlor of a convent. When he has entered and the door is closed, he knocks softly. The porter opens the door, and the gentleman whispers in his ear the name of the lady with whom he desires an interview.

The porter then says aloud, "The brother N—— desires to see sister N—— in the convent parlor." The lady enters, and the door is closed behind her. Some one knocks again, the porter opens the door, the gentleman comes out, and the lady names another gentleman, whom the porter introduces in the same manner. This proceeding is repeated so long as there remains to be called upon a person of a different sex from the one last admitted, unless to abridge the ceremony some one takes it into his head to summon the whole convent at once. Then the porter, who under no pretext has the right to enter, nor even to open the door until some one knocks, can take his revenge by turning the key, and keeping the whole company for a short time prisoners.

48. THE FACE OF WOOD.

The personage condemned to this penalty places himself erect, with his back against a door. In this position he calls up a person of a different sex, who takes her place, face to face in front of him. The latter calls up a third, who takes his position with his back towards her, and so on with all the company, care being taken that the last couple in the file shall be placed back to back.

Then the leader of the game gives a signal, at which all the company must turn and kiss the person in front of whom this movement places him.

The result is, that the person paying forfeit finds himself in front of the *Face of Wood*, upon which he is bound to bestow a kiss as tender as those, the echoes of which he hears repeated behind him.

49. THE DECLARATION OF LOVE.

The gentleman condemned to this penalty must place himself upon his knees before the lady, who is pointed out to him, or whom he loves the best, and declare his passion for her in impromptu verses.

Example.

In spite of your coldness,
I love you, my dear;
If love is a crime,
See the guilty one here.

50. THE COMPARISON.

As a penalty a person is directed to compare any of the company to some object or other, and then to explain in what he resembles this object, and in what he differs from it.

A lady compares a gentleman to a sheet of white paper.

He resembles it in the facility with which he receives first impressions; he differs from it in the readiness with which he receives a crowd of impressions, in succession, which efface each other in their turn.

A gentleman compares a lady to a clock; like this piece of furniture, she adorns the place which she occupies; she differs from it in rendering us forgetful of the hours which it recalls.

51. THE EMBLEM.

It differs from the comparison in this, that it offers an intellectual resemblance only between the person and the object.

A young gentleman names the Salamander as the emblem for a lady. "Why?" asks the latter. "Because you live tranquilly amid the flames which devour all who approach you."

A lady gives a Well as the emblem of a learned man who is somewhat uncommunicative. "It is deep," she says, "but it is necessary to draw from it that which it contains."

52. THE SPIRIT OF CONTRADICTION.

To perform this penalty it is necessary to execute the reverse of the orders received from the company. Happy the man to whom the ladies say, that they do not wish a kiss from him.

53. THE TRIP TO CORINTH.

A gentleman holding a white handkerchief in his hand is led around the circle by the person paying the forfeit, who holds in his hand a lighted candle.

The gentleman holding the handkerchief kisses all the ladies in turn, and with an air of great politeness, wipes the lips of his guide, who remains an idle spectator of a scene not a little vexatious to him.

54. KISSES AT SECOND HAND.

This penalty should be inflicted upon a lady. She who is directed to perform it chooses a female friend ; she then presents herself to a gentleman who kisses her, and she then carries the kiss to her companion. This may be repeated as many times as there are gentlemen in the company.

55. SHOOT THE ROBIN.

This is done by blindfolding the owner of the forfeit, and leading him to a part of the room where a sheet of paper or a handkerchief has been pinned to the wall. He is directed then to shoot the robin, which he must do by starting forwards, extending his right arm, and pointing his finger so as to touch the sheet of paper. Whenever he succeeds in doing so, his forfeit is restored. His finger had better be blackened with a coal, or burnt cork, or something that will leave a mark on the paper.

56. THE STUPID KISS.

Kiss both the inside and the outside of a reticule, without opening it. This can only be done when the drawing-string of the reticule is some distance from the top, and when the lining appears above it. When you kiss the lining of the flaps or scollops at the top of the reticule, then you may be said to kiss the inside ; or hang the reticule against the wall, and kiss the side that is out and the side that is in, or next the wall

FOR

Winter Evening Amusement.

AGON: OR, THE QUEEN'S GUARDS.

The estimation in which the games of Chess and Draughts have been held for years by thousands renders it unnecessary to offer any remarks upon the advantages arising from games of skill, as affording a healthful and amusing intellectual relaxation.

Every one experienced in the game of Draughts is aware that after a few moves it is almost always possible to say which player will eventually win the game; hence, first-rate players, to have the necessary excitement to play, give the first move, which to two good players is, in this game, of importance, besides one or two pieces to less experienced players; in truth, a readiness in determining which player has the move, as it is called, over any particular piece, furnishes a key to almost every variety which can be made in the game.

With respect to Chess—"pensive Chess" as a poet has designated it —the heavy, forward step of its Rook, the sprightly skipping step of its Knight, the solemn diagonal step of its Bishop, the unlimited step of its Queen, the slow stately step of its King, and the short restrained step of its Pawns, with the amazing variety of combinations thence arising, must for ever render the game the favorite study and delight of the thoughtful philosophic mind that can calmly contemplate the mysterious field, and see order reign amidst seeming confusion; but to the ordinary mind the game must be as a sealed book. A game that may occupy a medium state between these two celebrated games, may therefore be considered a desideratum; such a one, it is presumed, will be found in the game of AGON.

In this game no advantage will be obtained or lost by having the first move, and it will be impossible for any player to determine which has the advantage until the game may be fairly considered to be won.

In variety of situations, the game will be found almost equal to Chess, and from the mathematical figure of the board (being a combination of hexagons), many symmetrical figures and situations may be devised, and the game played from these particular positions, thus affording an endless variety of amusement.

DIRECTIONS FOR PLAYING.

Each player has seven pieces, viz. one Queen and six Guards. To commence the game the pieces are to be arranged as follows:—

Put the two Queens on two opposite corners, and the Guards on each side of the Queens, each color alternate, with one hexagon left vacant between each piece (two hexagons will be vacant on each side farthest from the Queens). (*See Fig.* 1.)

If the players so agree, the game may be commenced by each alternately placing a piece anywhere on the board, and then, when all the pieces are laid down, each alternately moving forward to obtain the middle. Having decided which shall move first, the players alternately move a

Fig. 1.

READY TO COMMENCE THE GAME.

piece towards the centre, one hexagon at a time, or to the next hexagon of the same color, so that the piece shall remain at the same distance from the centre, it not being allowed to move a piece backward.

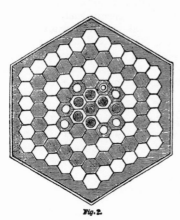

Fig. 2.

THE DARK PIECE BETWEEN THE TWO LIGHT ONES STANDING IN A RIGHT LINE MUST BE PUT BACK.

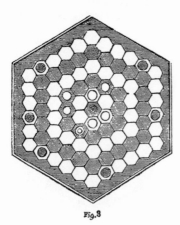

Fig. 3

THE DARK QUEEN, BEING IN A RIGHT LINE BETWEEN TWO LIGHT PIECES, MUST RETIRE.

Any piece, except the Queen, being in a position between two of the adversary's, so that the three pieces form a straight line, must be taken off the board for the next move, and put down anywhere in the outer row. (*See Fig.* 2.)

If the Queen should be placed in the position between the adversary's, so that the three pieces form a straight line, the Queen must be removed for the next move, but may be put in *any place*, being vacant, the player pleases. (*See Fig.* 3.)

That player who can first put all the pieces in the middle, that is, the Queen in the centre and the six guards around her, wins the game. (*See Fig.* 4.)

The players, being supposed to be sitting opposite each other, have the board placed with two corners right and left of each, and if the pieces have been placed as in *Fig.* 1, the color of those pieces the Queen of which is on the right hand, is to be taken by each player.

Two experienced players may put the pieces in a particular position, symmetrically or otherwise, and, each taking the colors alternately, endeavor to win the game.

LAWS OF THE GAME.

I. None but the Queens are to occupy the centre.

II. No piece must be put between two of the adversary's, standing in a right line.

III. No piece must be moved backwards.

IV. Of two or more pieces liable to be put back at one time, the Queen must be first moved off; any others at the player's option.

V. Any piece touched must be moved, or the move lost.

VI. Should the player put the six Guards in the middle, leaving out the Queen, such player loses the game by forfeit, as both are prevented from accomplishing the ultimatum of the game.

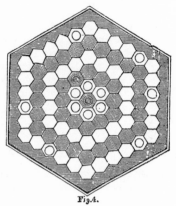

Fig.4.

HINTS TO PLAYERS.

No advantage will be gained, but, on the contrary, frequently a loss, by throwing back one only of the adversary's pieces, as the piece thrown back may be placed so as more readily to obtain a much better position than that thrown back from.

As no piece is allowed to move backward, the Queens must not be moved into the centre too hastily, as when there (having no move unless thrown out) their usefulness is impaired.

The player should endeavor to obtain such a position as to be able to throw back several pieces by following moves, and then move on to the middle before the adversary can overtake or get between the pieces.

The surest mode to win the game, is to crowd the adversary's pieces as quickly as possible towards the middle, at the same time taking up a position to be able to throw back all his pieces in succession, as soon as an opportunity offers.

When a player has the Queen in the middle, if not able to win the game, he may often re-open it by bringing a piece against the adversary's, so that if his Queen should be thrown back, he may throw back another piece in return; hence, in throwing back the Queens, the greatest caution is always necessary.

The player will generally find it advantageous to have one piece at a greater distance from the centre than any of the adversary's; it must, however, be in a position to get to the middle when the game is drawing to a conclusion.

The position shown in *Fig.* 2 is certain loss of the game to the dark pieces; the light pieces having forced the dark Queen to move into the centre, will be able to throw back a dark piece every move, and thus win the game; but should the light pieces be moved too early into the middle, it will be impossible to throw back the dark Queen without hazarding the re-opening of the game.

————o————

AMERICAN BAGATELLE.

Although this game bears the name of Bagatelle, it has scarcely any resemblance to that game, either in the form of the board, or the skill

requisite for playing. A strong and a quick hand are the most necessary qualifications of the player. The board, which is of the following form, has raised sides like the bagatelle board, and contains within its circumference nine flat pieces of ivory let into the wood, on which the numbers one to nine are marked, in the same order as in the holes of the bagatelle board; on each of these spots a small wooden pin, resembling a skittle pin, is placed, that on the central spot being white. The object of the player is to knock down as many of these pins as possible, that he may count the numbers on which they stood: this he effects by means of the spinner, *a*. Fig. 2, which consists of a piece of wood with a round flat top, from which a peg or

foot projects: a piece of string is wound tightly round this peg, and passed through the slit in the raised side at one end of the board, *a*, Fig. 1. The spinner is then pressed closely against the side with the left hand, while the player, grasping the handle *b*, attached to the string in his right, pulls the string forcibly, and with a sudden jerk; the consequence is, the string is unwound from the spinner, and the latter, falling on the board, has acquired the spinning motion a humming-top would have acquired under nearly similar circumstances. Away goes the spinner into the midst of the pins, knocking down some and passing safely between others: in the course of its evolutions it soon reaches the side of the board, and, if it is spinning with tolerable force, the instant it touches the wood it flies off suddenly at a tangent, and again dashes among the pins. The principal amusement consists in watching the progress of the spinner, as it bounces from one side of the board to the other, and when it appears about to expire, it suddenly perhaps starts forward, and wins the player the game. The game, as in bagatelle, is counted by adding together the numbers marked on the spots on which the fallen pins stood, and may be decided by one, two, or three spins from each player, to be previously agreed upon.

————o————

MERELLES: OR, NINE MEN'S MORRIS.

This is an ancient English game, and ought not to be laid aside; so we resuscitate it for the benefit of Young America. It used to be

played in England on the ground with stones, but may be played best on a table in-doors. The form of the Merelle table, and the lines upon it, as it appeared in the fourteenth century, are here represented. These lines are still the same. The black spots at every angle and intersection of the lines are the places for the men to be laid upon. The men are different in form and color, for distinction' sake. The manner of playing is briefly thus:

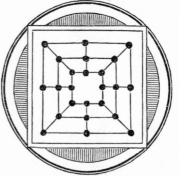

There are two players; each has nine men (either draughts or counters), one set black and the other white. The pieces are to be laid down by the players alternately, the first object of each being to place his pieces, so that there may be three in one line (as on 6, 14, 21—4, 5, 6—10, 11, 12, etc.), and also to prevent his adversary doing so. (The angles, as 18, 21, 24, are not counted as one line.) When one player succeeds in this, he takes that one of his adversary's pieces from the board which he considers most advantageous to himself. All the pieces being laid down the game proceeds, by moving the pieces along the lines to other spots, each player's object still being to place his men, and to take the forfeit as before described ; he must not, however, take either of his adversary's which are already in their desired position, unless the line become broken. The game is decided by the men becoming blockaded, or being removed from the board, as in draughts.

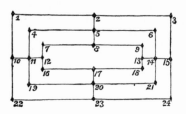

The following game will elucidate the above rules. The figures are placed on the diagram only for convenience of notation.

PLACING THE PIECES.

White.	Black.
7	16
18	9
11	10
4	19
5	6
2	8
14	23
20	22
1	24 × 1

THE MOVES.

	White.		Black.	
1.	14 to 15		10 to	1
2.	11	10	19	11
3.	2	3	9	13
4.	3	2	13	9
5.	18	13	16	17
6.	7	12	6	14
7.	5	6	8	5
8.	12	7	9	8
9.	7	12	8	7
10.	12	16	11	12
11.	10	11	7	8
12.	20	19 × 14	8	9
13.	19	20	12	7
14.	6	14 × 5	1	10
15.	2	5	7	8
16.	14	6 × 9	*Black resigns*	

The diagram for the game may be drawn upon a slate, or upon a piece of stiff paper; and wafers or colored papers may be used where no better materials can be found.

———o———

FOX AND GEESE.

This is a game somewhat resembling that of "Merelles," in the manner in which the pieces are moved, but in other respects, as well as in the form of the table, it differs materially; the intersections and angles are more numerous, and the dots of course increased, which adds to the number of the moves.

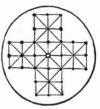

To play this game, there are seventeen pieces called Geese, which are placed as we see them in the engraving, and the Fox stands in the middle, distinguished either by his size or difference of color. The business of the game is to shut the Fox up so that he cannot move. All the pieces have the power to move from one spot to another, in the direction of the right lines, but cannot pass over two spots at one step. The Fox tries to take the Geese, which he does by hopping over them, just as if he were a king at draughts.

There is another method of playing Fox and Geese on a chessboard, namely, with four white men, representing the Geese, and one black one, representing the Fox.

The Geese are ranged on the four white squares nearest one player, and the Fox may be placed where his owner pleases.

The best place for him is that marked in the diagram, as he can manœuvre in a very puzzling way.

The Geese can only move forward, and the Fox moves either way. The object of the Geese is to pen up the Fox so that he cannot move, and the Fox has to break through.

If the game is properly played, the Geese must win, the secret being to keep them all in a line as much as possible. The Fox tries to prevent this plan from being followed up; and if he can succeed in doubling the Geese, or getting one to stand before another, he is nearly sure to pass through them.

―――――O―――――

THE GAME OF SOLITAIRE.

This game is named "*Solitaire,*" because it is played by one person only. It is supposed to have been invented in America, by a Frenchman, to beguile the wearisomeness attendant upon forest life, and for the amusement of the Indians, who pass much of their time alone at the chase, often lying in wait for their prey for hours together. From the children of the forest this game has become popular among the fashionable circles in our own country, and has also passed into Europe where, at the present day, it is sufficiently in vogue to be known and played by all classes of society.

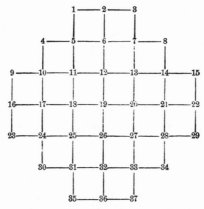

This game is played with a board pierced with thirty-seven holes, in each of which is placed a small peg, with the exception of one, which is left empty; thus there are thirty-seven holes and thirty-six pegs.

The above diagram points out the place which each hole occupies on the board.

One peg takes another when it can leap over it into an empty hole beyond, as the men are taken in the game of draughts.

It is necessary, therefore, for the player so to calculate his progress that, at the close of the game, but a single peg should be left upon the board. To accomplish this requires much more attention and calculation than one would at first sight believe.

We proceed to give some examples of the method by which this may be effected, which will facilitate the discovery of others that may be equally successful.

THE METHOD OF PLAYING THE GAME BY REMOVING PEG NO. 1, AND TERMINATING BY PEG NO. 37.

Remove Peg No. 1			From	33	to	20	From	5	to	18
From	3	to	1	20	to	7		18	to	20
	12	to	2	9	to	11		20	to	33
	13	to	3	16	to	18		33	to	31
	15	to	13	23	to	25		2	to	12
	4	to	6	22	to	20		8	to	6
	18	to	5	29	to	27		6	to	19
	1	to	11	18	to	31		19	to	32
	31	to	18	31	to	33		36	to	26
	18	to	5	34	to	32		30	to	32
	20	to	7	20	to	33		26	to	36
	3	to	13	37	to	27		35	to	37

THE METHOD OF PLAYING THE GAME BY REMOVING PEG NO. 37 AND FINISHING BY PEG NO. 1.

Remove Peg No. 37			From	5	to	18	From	33	to	20
From	35	to	37	18	to	31		20	to	18
	26	to	36	29	to	27		18	to	5
	25	to	35	22	to	20		5	to	7
	23	to	25	15	to	13		36	to	26
	34	to	32	16	to	18		30	to	32
	20	to	33	9	to	11		32	to	19
	37	to	27	20	to	7		19	to	6
	7	to	20	7	to	5		2	to	12
	20	to	33	4	to	6		8	to	6
	18	to	31	18	to	5		12	to	2
	35	to	25	1	to	11		3	to	1

THE METHOD OF PLAYING THE GAME CALLED THE CURATE IN THE MIDST OF HIS FLOCK.

Remove Peg No. 19			From	11	to	9	From	29	to	27
From	6	to	19	26	to	24		14	to	28
	4	to	6	35	to	25		27	to	29
	18	to	5	24	to	26		19	to	21
	6	to	4	27	to	25		7	to	20
	9	to	11	33	to	31		21	to	19
	24	to	10	25	to	35				

THE METHOD OF PLAYING THE GAME CALLED THE CORSAIR.

Remove Peg No. 3	From 3 to 13	From 4 to 17
Form 13 to 3	10 to 12	16 to 18
15 to 13	24 to 10	25 to 11
28 to 14	26 to 24	23 to 25
8 to 21	36 to 26	26 to 24
29 to 15	1 to 11	30 to 17
12 to 14	11 to 25	35 to 25
15 to 13	9 to 11	34 to 32
20 to 7	12 to 10	

Take nine Pegs of the eleven which remain with the "*Corsair*" (which is Peg No. 2, and which is taken afterwards by Peg No. 37), these are Pegs Nos. 6, 11, 17, 25, 19, 13, 21, 27, 32, Peg 37 to 35.

THE METHOD OF PLAYING THE GAME CALLED THE TRIPLET.

Remove Peg No. 19	From 31 to 18	From 22 to 20
From 6 to 19	19 to 17	8 to 21
10 to 12	16 to 18	32 to 19
19 to 6	30 to 17	28 to 26
2 to 12	21 to 19	19 to 32
4 to 6	7 to 20	36 to 26
17 to 19	19 to 21	34 to 32

When two persons play together with two separate boards, or alternately with one, the player who leaves upon the board the fewest isolated pegs is the winner.

———•◆•———

And Curious Paradoxes.

EVER since the days of the Egyptian Sphynx, Puzzles, Paradoxes, Riddles, and other mystifications have been popular sources of amusement. From the simplest Riddle to the most abstruse Paradox, they are all productive of a peculiar and lively pleasure. The youthful mind is by nature analytical and inquiring, and takes delight in searching to the bottom of anything that appears difficult to understand. Puzzles, therefore, are excellent means for the development of these natural tendencies, combining, as they do, the elements of work and play. They strengthen the memory by exercising it, teach us application and perseverance, enable us to improve the faculty of holding several ideas in the mind at once, and, in short, are highly beneficial to all the more intellectual qualities.

The pleasure of arriving at the correct solution of a difficult problem, after a long and patient study over it, is as great as that arising from any other mental victory, and even the study itself has no small amount of pleasure in it.

The Puzzles in the following pages, have been selected from many sources, and a considerable number of them have never before been in print. The explanations of them have been prepared with much care, so as to render them explicit and easy of comprehension; but our young friends should remember that the pleasure lies in working out the answers themselves, instead of jumping at once to the printed solutions.

———o———

1. THE CARD CHAIN PUZZLE.

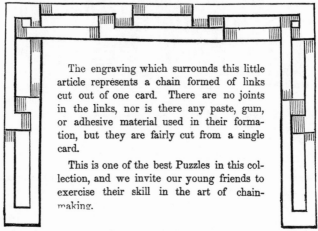

The engraving which surrounds this little article represents a chain formed of links cut out of one card. There are no joints in the links, nor is there any paste, gum, or adhesive material used in their formation, but they are fairly cut from a single card.

This is one of the best Puzzles in this collection, and we invite our young friends to exercise their skill in the art of chain-making.

2. THE MAGIC SQUARE.

With seventeen pieces of wood (lucifer matches will answer the purpose, but be careful to remove the combustible ends, and see that they are all of the same length) make the following figure:

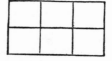

The Puzzle you propose is—to remove only five matches, and yet leave no more than three perfect squares of the same size remaining.

3. THE PRACTICABLE ORCHARD.

Plant sixteen trees in ten rows, with four trees in each row.

4. THE OCTAGON PUZZLE.

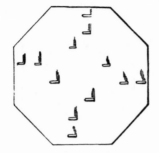

I have a piece of ground, which is neither square nor round,
  But an octagon; and this I have laid out
In a novel way, though plain in appearance, and retain
  Three posts in each compartment; but I doubt
Whether you discover how I apportioned it, e'en tho'
  I inform you 'tis divided into four.
But, if you solve it right, 'twill afford you much delight,
  And repay you for the trouble, I am sure.

5. THE METAMORPHOSIS PUZZLE.

Procure a piece of thin wood, cardboard, or writing paper; let the same be formed into a perfect square (3 in. or more), after which divide it into fifteen parts, and with them form the accompanying diagrams:

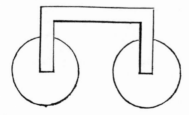

6. THE DIVIDED SQUARE.

Divide this square into four equal parts, so as to obtain two dots in each division, and eight in the centre.

7. PUZZLE PLEASURE GARDEN.

By aid of hoe, and rake, and spade,
And perseverance too,—I've made
A pleasure garden,—and a view
Of the self-same I give to you.
Within this piece of fancy ground,
Which by a wall's encompassed round,
Are zig-zag walks both plain and neat
That lead into a calm retreat,
And all who would an entrance find
Should this observe, and bear in mind,

They *once* and *only once* must tread
O'er *every* path, 'round every bed
Of plants and flowers that deck this maze,
In which a fountain freely plays.
Now, those who may, with firm resolve,
This little puzzle truly solve,
And to the fount admittance gain,
May at their pleasure there remain,
And then retrace their footsteps o'er
Till they regain the garden door.

8. THE FLORIST'S PUZZLE.

A florist planted thirty-one varieties of flowers (only one of each kind), so that he had one circle containing eighteen varieties; seven circles with six varieties in each; six straight rows with six varieties in each; and three straight rows with six varieties in each.

9. THE FARMER'S PUZZLE.

A farmer planted eleven trees in eleven rows, with three trees in each row. How were they planted?

10. THE PROTEAN PUZZLE.

Take a piece of stiff cardboard, let the same be formed thus—

say five inches long, by one inch broad; cut it into eleven pieces, and with them represent a cross. Again, by reversing, form the various figures given below.

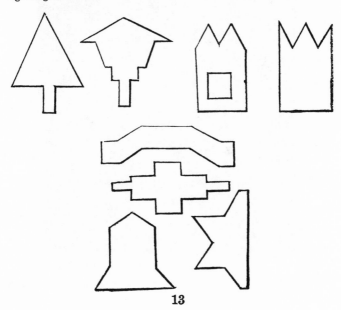

13

11. THE TRAVELLER'S MAZE.

Instructions to the Traveller through the Maze.

The instructions for this fireside amusement are as follow: The Traveller must enter at the opening at the foot, and must pass between the lines forming the road to the Castle in the middle. There are no bars in the route: one road crosses another by means of a bridge, so that care must be taken that, in following the route, the Traveller does not stray from one road to another, and thus lose the track. For instance, on entering, he will have to pass *under* a bridge of another

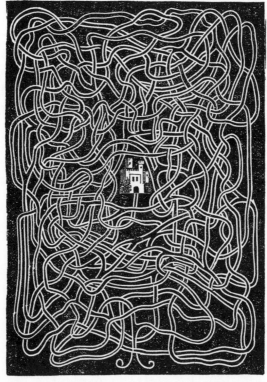

road crossing over his path: in continuing the route he will next pass *over* a bridge crossing another road, and thus continue his course. A little practice will accustom the Traveller to the method of the Maze. It is not a fair test of the merits of the Maze to commence from the centre; but the Traveller will be at full liberty, *when* he has entered the Castle, to get out again if he can.

12. THE GEOMETRICAL ORCHARD.

In laying out an orchard of peach trees, a farmer planted twenty-seven trees so as to have nine rows, and six trees in each row. How did he do this?

13. THE HEXAGON PUZZLE.

To arrange the following five pieces into a perfect *hexagon*—that is, a figure having six equal sides.

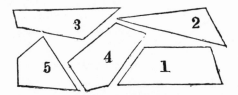

14. THE CARPENTER'S PUZZLE.

A plank was to be cut in two; the carpenter cut it half through on each side, and found he had two feet still to cut How was it?

15. PUZZLE PURSE.

With a piece of morocco, or any other suitable material, let a purse be constructed similar to the one given here. The puzzle is to open the same without removing any of the rings.

16. PROBLEM OF MONEY.

Place ten half-dimes in a row upon a table. Then taking up any

one of the series, place it upon some other, with this proviso, that you
pass over just one dime. Repeat this till there is no single half-dime
left.

17. THE APPLE-TREE PUZZLE.

How can ten apple trees be planted, so that there shall be five rows,
and four trees in each row?

18. THE ANGULAR PUZZLE.

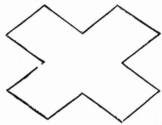

Cut a piece of cardboard into
the form of, and of equal proportions to, the figure given here, after
which, produce, with the same,
three successive pyramidal or angular boxes, alternately bearing the
respective numbers of 7, 6, and 5
corners, still keeping the cardboard
in one piece.

19. THE PERPLEXED CARPENTER.

There is a hole in the barn floor just two feet in width and twelve
in length. How can it be entirely covered with a board three feet
wide and eight feet long, by *cutting the board only once in two?*

20. THE MAGIC OCTAGON.

Upon a piece of cardboard draw
   The three designs below;
I should have said of each shape four,
   Which when cut out will show,
If joined correctly, that which you
   Are striving to unfold,—
An octagon, familiar to
   My friends both young and old.

21. THE BLIND ABBOT AND THE MONKS.

To arrange counters in the eight external cells of a square, so that there may always be nine in each row, though the whole number may vary from eighteen to thirty-six.

To give an air of interest to this problem, the old writers state it in the following manner :—A convent, in which there were nine cells, was occupied by a blind abbot and twenty-four monks, the abbot lodging in the centre cell, and the monks in the side cells, three in each, forming a row of nine persons on each side of the building, as in the accompanying figure.

3	3	3
3		3
3	3	3

Fig. 1.

4	1	4
1		1
4	1	4

Fig. 2.

The abbot, suspecting the fidelity of the monks, frequently went round at night and counted them, when, if he found nine in each row, he retired to rest quite satisfied. The monks, however, taking advantage of his blindness, conspired to deceive him, and arranged themselves in the cells as in Fig. 2, so that four could go out, and still the abbot would find nine in each row.

2	5	2
5		5
2	5	2

Fig. 3.

1	7	1
7		7
1	7	1

Fig. 4.

The monks that went out returned with four visitors, and they were arranged with the monks as in Fig. 3, so as to count nine each way, and consequently the abbot was again deceived.

Emboldened by success, the monks next night brought in four more visitors, and succeeded in deceiving the abbot by arranging themselves as in Fig. 4.

Again four more visitors were introduced, and arranged with the monks as in Fig. 5.

Finally, even when the twelve clandestine visitors had departed, carrying off six of the monks with them, the abbot, still finding nine in

0	9	0
9		9
0	9	0

Fig. 5.

5	0	4
0		0
4	0	5

Fig. 6.

each row, as in Fig. 6, retired to rest with full persuasion that no one had either gone out or come in.

22. THE PEACH ORCHARD PUZZLE.

A New Jersey farmer planted twenty-seven peach trees in ten rows, with six trees in each row. How did he plant them?

23. THE GRASPING LANDLORD.

Suppose a certain landlord had eight apple trees around his mansion, around these eight houses of his tenants, around these ten pear trees,—he wants to have the whole of the pear trees to himself, and allot to each of his tenants one of his apple trees in their place. How must he construct a fence or hedge to accomplish it?

24. LOVE'S PUZZLE.

Cut a piece of thin wood about four inches long and three-quarters broad. Perforate it with three holes. Cut pieces of bone, cork, or wood, into the shape of two hearts, and then arrange the whole upon strings, as in the diagram. The puzzle is, to get the two hearts upon the same loop. It is a good puzzle for lovers, and suggests the idea of the "union of hearts," of which, when solved, it may be considered a prognostic.

25. THE DISHONEST JEWELLER.

A lady sent a diamond cross to a jeweller to be repaired. To provide against any of her diamonds being stolen, she had the precaution to count the number of diamonds, which she did in the following manner:—She found the cross contained in length from A to B, nine diamonds; reckoning from B to C, or from B to D, she also counted nine. When the cross was returned, she found the number of diamonds thus counted precisely the same, yet two diamonds had been purloined. How was this managed?

```
                    A
                    o
                    o
                    o
C o  o  o  o  o  •  o D
                    o
                    o
                    o
                    o
                    o
                    B
```

26. THE GARDENER'S PUZZLE.

A gardener having twenty-four rose-bushes, planted them in two beds, twelve bushes in each, and each bed containing six rows, with four bushes in each row. Anxious to appear singular, the gardener planned each bed entirely different from the other in design. How was this done?

27. THE CIRCLE PUZZLE.

Twenty lines upon paper place,
On every line five circles trace;
These circles should just in amount,
Or number, thirty-seven count;
And every circle, orb, or round,
Upon an angle should be found—
At an equal distance, too, should be
Upon each line—solve this for me?

28. THE SQUARE PUZZLE.

Arrange the pieces in the following figure, so that when set close together they shall form a perfect square.

29. THE TREE PUZZLE.

Arrange fifteen trees in sixteen rows, with three in each row; also two rows of four trees, and one row of seven trees.

30. THE GEOMETRICAL PUZZLE.

Given, a square, to divide it into seventeen smaller but equal squares.

31. THE PUZZLE OF THE CHRISTIANS AND TURKS.

Fifteen Christians and fifteen Turks being at sea in the same vessel, dreadful storm came on which obliged them to throw all their merchandise overboard; this, however, not being sufficient to lighten the ship, the captain informed them that there was no possibility of its being saved, unless half the passengers were thrown overboard also. Having therefore caused them all to arrange themselves in a row, by counting from nine to nine, and throwing every ninth person into the sea, beginning again at the first of the row when it had been counted to the end, it was found that after fifteen persons had been thrown overboard, the fifteen Christians remained. How did the captain arrange those thirty persons so as to save the Christians?

32. THE TULIP PUZZLE.

A gentleman having nineteen tulips, planted them in nine rows, with five in each row. How did he plant them?

33. THE THREE GENTLEMEN AND THEIR SERVANTS.

Three gentlemen and their servants having to cross a river, find a boat without its owner, which can only carry two persons at a time. In what manner can these six persons transport themselves over by pairs, so that none of the gentlemen shall be left in company with any of the servants, except when his own servant is present?

34. THE DROVER'S PROBLEM.

One morning I chanced with a drover to meet,
    Who was driving some sheep up to town,
Which seemed very near ready to drop from the heat,
    Whereupon I exclaimed with a frown:—

" Don't you think it is wrong to treat animals so ?
    Why not take better care of your flock ?"
' I would do so," said he, " but I've some miles to go
    Between this and eleven o'clock."

" Well, supposing you have," I replied, " you should let
    Them have rest now and then by the way."
" So I will, if you believe I can get
    There in time for the market to-day.

" Now as you seem to know such a lot about sheep,
    Perhaps you'll tell us how many I've got ?"
" No, a casual glance as they stand in a heap,
    Won't permit of it, so I cannot."

" Well, supposing as how I'd as many again,
    Half as many, and seven, as true
 As you're there, it would pay me to ride up by train;
    Because I should have thirty-two."

35. THE MARKET WOMAN'S PUZZLE.

A market woman bought 120 apples at two for a cent, and 120 more of another sort, at three for a cent, but not liking her bargain, she mixed them together, and sold them out again at five for two cents, thinking she should get the same sum; but on counting her money, she found, to her surprise, that she had lost four cents. How did this happen ?

36. THE PLUM TREE PUZZLE.

A farmer planted nine plum trees in ten rows, with three trees in each row. How were they planted ?

37. THE LAND PUZZLE.

There is a square piece of land containing twenty-five acres, designed for the reception of twenty-four poor men and their governor, who are each to have a house situated in its own ground, the governor's in the centre. How many persons' land must the governor pass through before he gets to the outside of the whole ?

38. THE NINE DIGITS.

Place the nine digits (that is, the several figures or numbers under ten) in three rows, in such a way that, adding them together either up or down, across, or from corner to corner, they shall always make fifteen

39. THE LANDLORD TRICKED.

Twenty-one persons sat down to dinner at an inn, with the landlord at the head of the table. When dinner was finished, it was resolved that one of the number should pay the whole score; to be decided as follows. A person should commence counting the company, and every seventh man was to rise from his seat, until all were counted out but one, who was to be the individual who should pay the whole bill. One of the waiters was fixed upon to count the company out, who, owing his master a grudge, resolved to make him the person who should have to pay. How must he proceed to accomplish this?

40. THE SCISSORS ENTANGLED.

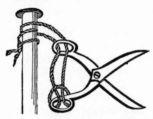

This is an old but a capital puzzle. A piece of double twine is fastened to a pair of scissors (as shown in the cut), and both the ends are held with the hand, whilst some person extricates the scissors from the twine.

41. THE CARPENTER PUZZLED.

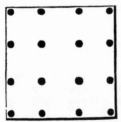

A ship having sprung a leak at sea, and being in great danger, the carpenter could find nothing to mend it with, except a piece of wood, of which the annexed is a correct representation; supposing the black dots in it to represent holes in the wood, thus apparently preventing him from cutting out of it the sized piece he wanted, which was exactly one quarter of the board. Required, the way in which he must cut this piece of wood, to obtain out of it a piece exactly one-fourth its own size having no holes in it.

42. THE MECHANIC'S PUZZLE.

A piece of wood or cardboard, 10 inches long, by 2 inches wide. is to be cut in such a manner as to form a perfect square, without waste.

43. THE GRECIAN PARADOX.

Protagoras, a Greek philosopher, agreed to instruct a young man in oratory for a sum of money, one half of which was paid down, and the remainder to be liquidated *when the pupil made his first successful pleading in the courts.* Long after the instructions were concluded, the pupil neither paid *nor pleaded,* and Protagoras brought an action for the recovery of the unpaid money. The question is, could Protagoras recover the same?

44. THE FIVE ARAB MAXIMS.

Explain the five Arab maxims following:

Never	All	For he who	Every thing	Often	More than
Tell	You may know	Tells	He knows	Tells	He knows
Attempt	You can do	Attempts	He can do	Attempts	He can do
Believe	You may hear	Believes	He hears	Believes	He hears
Lay out	You can afford	Lays out	He can afford	Lays out	He can afford
Decide upon	You may see	Decides upon	He sees	Decides upon	He sees

45. THE JESUIT'S PLACARD.

On Sunday the 8th of October, 1850, when the Pope went to celebrate the Nativity of the Virgin, at Rome, the following Placard was posted in various parts of the city. We give a translation, in which the double meaning will be better seen.

MORTE A
MAZZINI
LA REPUBLICA E
IL PIU INFAME GOVERNO
ABASSO
IL DOMINO DEL POPOLI

PIO NONO
VIVA LUNGAMENTE
IL PIU DOLICE GOVERNO
E QUELLO DEI PRETI
IL POTERE DEI PRETI
REGNI IN ETERNO.

46. A DOZEN QUIBBLES.

1. How must I draw a circle round a person placed in the centre of a room, so that he will not be able to jump out of it, though his legs should be free?

2. I can stretch my arms apart, having a coin in each hand, and yet, without bringing my hands together, I can cause both coins to come into the same hand. How is this to be done?

3. Place a candle in such a manner, that every person shall see it except one, although he shall not be blindfolded, or prevented from examining every part of the room, neither shall the candle be hidden.

4. A person may, without stirring from the room, seat himself in a place where it will be impossible for another person to do so. Explain this?

5. A person tells another that he can put something into his right hand, which the other cannot put into his left.

6. How can I get the wine out of a bottle if I have no corkscrew, and must not break the glass, or make any hole in it or in the cork?

7. If five times 4 are thirty-three, what will the fourth of twenty be?

8. What two numbers multiplied together will produce seven?

9. If you cut thirty yards of cloth into one yard pieces, and cut one yard every day, how long will it take?

10. Divide the number 50 into two such parts that, if the greater part be divided by 7, and the less multiplied by 3, the sum of the quotient and the product will make 50.

11. What is the difference between twice twenty-five and twice five and twenty?

12. Place four fives so as to make six and a half.

Answers to Practical Puzzles.

1. ANSWER TO CARD CHAIN PUZZLE,

Take a card, say four inches long and two and a half inches wide, or of any other size thought fit; but the larger the card the better it is for practice. Draw a light pencil line from A to B, and another line from C to D, at about a quarter of an inch from the edge of your card. Now lay the card in water for a short time; after which split it down from the edge, with a pen-knife, as far as the pencil line, and then put the card aside

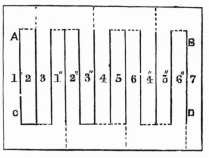

until it is perfectly dry, when you will resume your task as follows:—
With a sharp pen-knife cut right through the *straight* lines indicated in the engraving, but only half way through the *dotted* lines, as that is the *split* portion of the card. The figures show the bar of each link of the chain. Thus 1 and 1″ belong to the same link, and are connected at the top and bottom, the latter by the upper half of the split, and the former by the under half of the split; the links 2 and 2″ are also connected in the same way, and so on to the end of the chain until every link is released, thus forming a cable, which, if not useful for any mechanical purpose, will at least serve to amuse.

2. ANSWER TO THE MAGIC SQUARE.

This seeming impossibility is rendered easy by removing the two upper corners on each side and the centre line below, when the three squares will appear thus:—

This ingenious device is the best problem for parlor magicians we are acquainted with.

3. ANSWER TO THE PRACTICABLE ORCHARD.

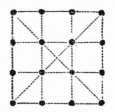

4. ANSWER TO OCTAGON PUZZLE.

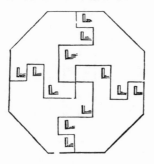

5. ANSWER TO THE METAMORPHOSIS PUZZLE.

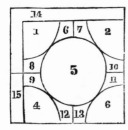
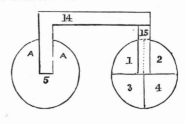

6. ANSWER TO THE DIVIDED SQUARE.

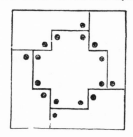

7. ANSWER TO PUZZLE PLEASURE GARDEN.

Enter at door, No. 1; then pass on to the following numbers—15, 20, 8, 40, 19, 36, 12, 3, 32, 43, 10, 50, 33, 41, 28, 37, 25, 11, 22, 39, 30, 7, 35, 26, 34, 46, 38, 2, 45, 14, 42, 31, 5, 24, 21, 29, 6, 18, 49, 4, 27, 48, 9, 17, 23, 16, 44, 52, 58, 55, 57, 60, 56, 53, 54, 61, 59, 62. You then return in the same order from 62 to 59, 61, 54, etc., etc.

8. ANSWER TO FLORIST'S PUZZLE.

To plant 31 kinds of flowers, one of each kind, so as to have 18 varieties in one circle; 7 circles with 6 varieties in each; 6 straight rows with 6 varieties in each and 3 straight rows with 5 varieties in each.

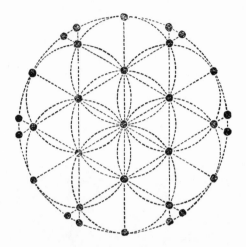

This will make a pretty flower-bed if smaller plants are put where they come nearest together.

9. ANSWER TO FARMER'S PUZZLE

They were planted as represented in the following illustration:—

⁷0. ANSWER TO THE PROTEAN PUZZLE.

Cut the cardboard as in figure A, and with the pieces the bifferent diagrams may be formed.

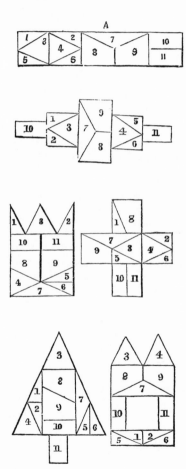

A

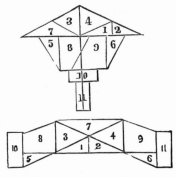

11. KEY TO THE TRAVELLER'S MAZE.

On entering the Maze, pass to the left, leaving the road to the right (which is a feint). In following up the course, after some windings, we fall into a cross road, a little below on the left of the Castle. Turning to the right we come to a fork, close to the entrance of the Castle. Take the *lower* road, *leading to the left*, which passes close over the flagstaff of the Castle. We then fall into a branch road up and down, close under a bridge; take the road down, and this will lead to a point, or meeting of four roads. Take the road leading to the right of the Castle, and by following it up, we pass close to the right corner of the Castle. A little further on the road again separates into two, under a bridge; come down, and avoiding the road leading to the left of the Castle, we come to a fork a little to the left of the entrance. By taking the lower road, and avoiding the road to the right, the Castle will at once be reached.

12. ANSWER TO THE GEOMETRICAL ORCHARD.

The trees could be planted in a great many ways so as to answer the conditions of the problem. Below we give two of the prettiest:—

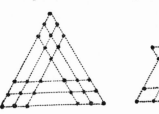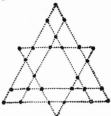

13. ANSWER TO HEXAGON PUZZLE.

Arrange the pieces in this manner :—

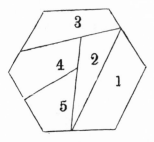

14. ANSWER TO THE CARPENTER'S PUZZLE.

The plank was to be cut in this way :—

15. ANSWER TO PURSE PUZZLE.

Pass loop *a* up through ring No. 2 and over No. 1, then pass loop *b* over rings 1 and 2 up through No. 2, and over No. 1, as before; when the same may be easily drawn through rings 3, 4, 5. Again pass loop *c* through ring No. 7 over 8, draw it up through ring 6, and the purse is complete

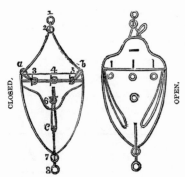

16. ANSWER TO MONEY PROBLEM.

1 2 3 4 5 6 7 8 9 10 half-dimes.

Place 4 upon 1, 7 upon 3, 5 upon 9, 2 upon 6, and 8 upon 10.

17. ANSWER TO APPLE TREE PUZZLE.

Either of these three diagrams will answer the conditions of the problem.

18. ANSWER TO ANGULAR PUZZLE.

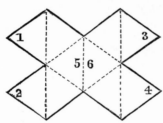

Cut the cardboard half through at the dotted lines, to enable it to bend the more readily; close the spaces between 1—2 and 3—4 by bringing the ends together; bend the whole between 5 and 6, and the seven-cornered box will be produced; then fold the parts 1—2, and 3—4, underneath each other,

and the six-cornered box will be formed; and by again placing the angular sections inwards, the remaining box will present itself.

19. ANSWER TO THE PERPLEXED CARPENTER.

The board was cut after the manner of the annexed diagram:

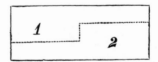

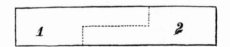

20. ANSWER TO THE MAGIC OCTAGON.

The pieces are put together in the following manner:

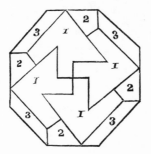

21. ANSWER TO THE PROBLEM OF THE BLIND ABBOT AND THE MONKS.

It is almost needless to explain in what manner the illusion of the good abbot arose. It is because the numbers in the angular cells of the square were counted twice; these cells being common to two rows, the more therefore the angular cells are filled, by emptying those in the middle of each band, these double enumerations become greater; on which account the number, though diminished, appears always to be the same; and the contrary is the case in proportion as the middle cells are filled by emptying the angular ones, which renders it necessary to add some units to have nine in each band.

22. ANSWER TO THE PEACH ORCHARD PUZZLE.

He planted them as in the following diagram:

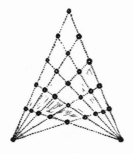

23. ANSWER TO THE GRASPING LANDLORD.

24. ANSWER TO LOVE'S PUZZLE.

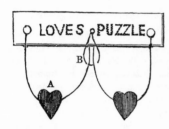

First draw the heart A along the string through the loop B, until it reaches the back of the centre hole, then pull the loop through the hole, and pass the heart through the *two* loops that will then be formed; then draw the string back through the hole as before, and the heart may easily be passed to its companion.

25. ANSWER TO THE DISHONEST JEWELLER.

The jeweller arranged the diamonds thus:

$$
\begin{array}{ccccccc}
 & & & \mathbf{A} & & & \\
 & & & \circ & & & \\
 & & & \circ & & & \\
\mathbf{C} & \circ & \circ & \circ & \circ & \circ & \mathbf{D} \\
 & & & \circ & & & \\
 & & & \circ & & & \\
 & & & \circ & & & \\
 & & & \circ & & & \\
 & & & \circ & & & \\
 & & & \circ & & & \\
 & & & \mathbf{B} & & &
\end{array}
$$

26. ANSWER TO THE GARDENER'S PUZZLE.

They were planted in the following manner:

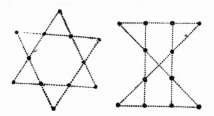

27. ANSWER TO THE CIRCLE PUZZLE.

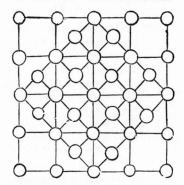

28. ANSWER TO THE SQUARE PUZZLE.

Arrange the pieces as in the following diagram:

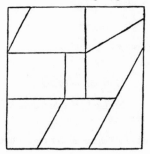

29. ANSWER TO THE TREE PUZZLE.

Arrange the trees in the following manner:

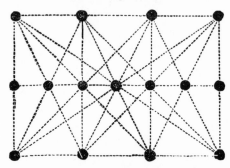

30. ANSWER TO THE GEOMETRICAL PUZZLE.

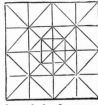

Divide each side of the square into four portions. By drawing lines across each way to these points you produce sixteen of the squares. Unite the points by which the diamond is formed; within which you will find a square one quarter the size of the first. Next draw a diamond within this quarter-sized square, and by drawing lines—like a Saint Andrew's Cross—through the whole figure, you have the points for the seventeenth square, as in the figure.

31. ANSWER TO THE PUZZLE OF THE FIFTEEN CHRISTIANS AND FIFTEEN TURKS.

The method of arranging the thirty persons may be deduced from these two lines in English:

$$\overset{4}{\text{From}} \overset{5}{\text{numbers}} \overset{2}{\text{aid}} \overset{13}{\text{and}} \overset{1}{\text{art}}$$

$$\overset{2}{\text{Never}} \overset{2}{\text{will}} \overset{3}{\text{fame}} \overset{1}{\text{depart.}}$$

Or these two French verses—

$$\overset{4}{\text{Mort,}} \overset{5}{\text{tu}} \overset{2}{\text{ne}} \overset{13}{\text{faillras}} \overset{1}{\text{pas}}$$

$$\overset{2}{\text{En}} \overset{2}{\text{me}} \overset{3}{\text{livrant}} \overset{1}{\text{le}} \overset{2}{\text{trepas.}}$$

Or the following Latin one—

$$\overset{4}{\text{Populeam}} \overset{5}{\text{Virgam}} \overset{3}{\text{Mater}} \overset{1}{\text{regina}} \overset{2}{\text{ferebat.}}$$

Attention must be paid to the vowels a, e, i, o, u, contained in the syllables of these verses; observing that, a is equal to 1, e to 2, i to 3, o to 4, and u to 5. You must begin then by arranging 4 Christians together, because the vowel in the first syllable is o, then 5 Turks, because the vowel in the second syllable is u, and so on to the end. By proceeding in this manner, it will be found, taking every ninth person circularly, that is to say beginning at the first of the row, after it is ended, that the lot will fall entirely on the Turks.

FOR EXAMPLE.

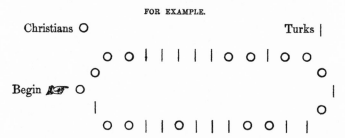

Christians O   Turks |

Begin ☞ O

The solution of this problem may be easily extended still farther. Let it be required, for example, to make the lot fall upon 10 persons in 40, counting from 12 to 12. Arrange 40 ciphers in a circular form, as below:—

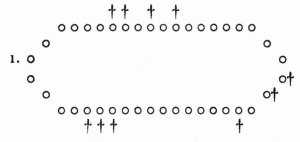

Then beginning at the first, make every twelfth one with a cross, continue in this manner, taking care to pass over those already crossed, still proceeding circularly till the required number of places has been marked. If you then count the places of the marked ciphers, those on which the lot falls will be easily known; in the present case they are the 7th, 8th, 10th, 12th, 21st, 22nd, 24th, 34th, 35th and 36th.

14

A captain obliged to decimate his company might employ this expedient, to make it fall on the most culpable.

It is related that Josephus, the historian, saved his life by means of this expedient. Having fled for shelter to a cavern with forty other Jews after Jotapat had been taken by the Romans, his companions resolved to kill each other rather than surrender. Josephus tried to dissuade them from their horrid purpose, but not being able to succeed, he pretended to coincide with their wishes, and retaining the authority he had over them as their chief, to avoid the disorder which would necessarily be the consequence of this cruel execution if they should kill each other at random, he prevailed on them to arrange themselves in order, and beginning to count from one end to a certain number, to put to death the person on whom that number should fall, until there remained only one, who should kill himself. Having all agreed to this proposal, Josephus arranged them in such a manner, and placed himself in such a position, that when the slaughter had been continued to the end, he remained with only one more person, whom he persuaded to live.

Such is the story related of Josephus by Hegesippus; but we are far from warranting the truth of it. However, by applying to this case the method above indicated, and supposing every third person was to be killed, it will be found that the two last places on which the lot fell were the 16th and 31st, so that Josephus must have placed himself in one of these, and the person whom he was desirous of saving in the other.

32. ANSWER TO THE TULIP PUZZLE.

Either of the annexed diagrams will answer the conditions of the problem :

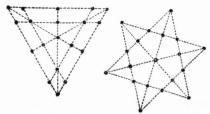

33. ANSWER TO PUZZLE OF THE THREE GENTLEMEN AND THEIR SERVANTS.

First, two servants must pass over; then one of them must bring back the boat, and repass with the third servant; then one of the three servants must bring back the boat, and stay with his master whilst the other two gentlemen pass over to their servants; then one of these gentlemen with his servant must bring back the boat, and, the servant remaining, his master must take over the remaining gentlemen. Lastly, the servant who is found with the three gentlemen must return with the boat, and at twice take over the other two servants.

34. ANSWER TO THE DROVER'S PROBLEM.

Ten in the flock; ten, as many again; five, half as many; seven besides; total, thirty-two.

35. ANSWER TO THE MARKET-WOMAN'S PUZZLE.

On the first view of the question, there does not appear to be any loss; for if it be supposed that in selling five apples for two cents, she gave three of the latter sort (viz. those at three for a cent) and two of the former (viz. those at two for a cent), she would receive just the same money as she bought them for; but this will not hold throughout the whole, for, admitting that she sells them as above, it must be evident that the latter stock would be exhausted first, and consequently she must sell as many of the former as remained overplus at five for two cents, which she bought at the rate of two for a cent, or four for two cents, and would therefore lose. It will be readily found, that when she had sold all the latter sort in the above manner, she would have sold only eighty of the former, for there are as many threes in one hundred and twenty, as twos in eighty; then the remaining forty must be sold at five for two cents, which were bought at the rate of four for two cents, viz:

```
     A.   C.      A.      C.
If 4 :  2  :: 40  :  20, prime cost of 40 of the first sort.
   5 :  2  :: 40  :  16, selling price of ditto.
                        ——
```

4 cents loss.

36. ANSWER TO THE PLUM TREE PUZZLE.

The annexed diagram will show how they were planted.

37. ANSWER TO THE LAND PUZZLE.

Two; for the ground being a square, it will consist of twenty-five plots, each containing five acres, as seen in the diagram.

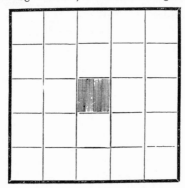

38. ANSWER TO THE NINE DIGITS.

15	6	7	2
15	1	5	9
15	8	3	4

15 15 15 15

39. ANSWER TO THE LANDLORD TRICKED.

Commence with the sixth from the Landlord.

40. ANSWER TO THE SCISSORS PUZZLE.

The scissors may be released by drawing the noose upwards through the eye of the scissors, and passing it completely over them.

41. ANSWER TO THE CARPENTER PUZZLED.

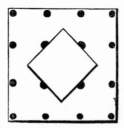

An examination of this diagram will show how the square piece was cut from the board.

42. ANSWER TO THE MECHANIC'S PUZZLE.

Cut the wood or pasteboard, as in this diagram,

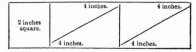

and with the pieces form a square thus:—

43. GRECIAN PARADOX.

History informs us, both parties argued in person; Protagoras contended that whichever way the cause was decided he must recover, for if the pupil lost, the money must be paid according to decree of court; but if the pupil gained, the *successful pleading* would make the money due according to agreement.

On the contrary, the pupil contended that the money ought *not* to be paid; for if he (the pupil) gained, the decree of court would excuse him from payment; but if he lost, the *unsuccessful pleading* would equally excuse him from payment according to agreement.

The perplexed judges came to no determination, and dismissed the case, which operated as an extinguishment of Protagoras's claim; but is it *reasonable* that Protagoras should lose his money in consequence of the caprice of the pupil not following his profession?

44. ANSWER TO THE ARAB'S MAXIMS.

Read the first and second alternately. "Never tell all you may know, for he who tells everything he knows, often tells more than he knows." Then the first and third, first and fourth, first and fifth.

45. ANSWER TO THE JESUIT'S PLACARD.

Let the lines in the two placards be read right across.

DEATH TO	PIUS THE NINTH
MAZZINI	FOR EVER
THE REPUBLIC IS	THE MILDEST OF GOVERNMENTS
THE MOST INFAMOUS OF GOVERNMENTS	IS THAT OF THE PRIESTS.
DOWN WITH	THE POWER OF THE PRIESTS
THE DOMINION OF THE PEOPLE.	FOR EVER.

46. ANSWER TO A DOZEN QUIBBLES.

1. Draw it round his body.

2. Place the coin on a table, then, turning round, take it up with the other hand.

3. Place the candle on his head, taking care that no mirror is in the room.

4. The first person seats himself in the other's lap.

5. The last person's left elbow.

6. Push the cork into the bottle.

7. $8\frac{1}{4}$.

8. 7 and 1.

9. Twenty-nine days.

10. 35 and 15.

11. Twice twenty-five is fifty; twice five, and twenty, is thirty.

12 $5\frac{3}{8}$ ·5.

LOVE PUZZLES ALL.

AND

Parlor Magic.

A MISCELLANEOUS COLLECTION OF INTERESTING AND
AMUSING EXPERIMENTS FOR HOME ENTERTAIN-
MENT.

In this nineteenth century, when education is a universal thing,
and the development of the intellect is considered a paramount object,
we are not content to know facts merely, as our ancestors were, but we
must inquire into the whys and wherefores.   In former times, if a child
studied mathematics, all that was required was that the "rules" should
be committed to memory, to be used when wanted.   Now, however,
learning rules by rote does not suffice, except, perhaps, in the crudest
of the backwoods' educational institutions.   The pupil is now expected
not only to know the fact that the two acute angles of a right-angled
triangle are equal to one right-angle, but also to know, and to be able
to explain *why* they are so.

This tendency of the age, to base everything upon a solid intellectual foundation, and to reason from cause to effect, and *vice versâ*, has opened a wide field in the domain of amusement, unknown to the generations of bye-gone centuries. What was formerly attributed to the interposition and direct agency of supernatural powers, is now understood to be the natural result of natural causes. A man who had seen a ten-cylindered lightning press throwing off its editions of a daily paper, could hardly attribute Faust and Gutenberg's clumsily-printed bible to *diablerie*. Yet, at the time that volume appeared, its printers were universally condemned as sorcerers, and were accused everywhere of having sold their souls to his Satanic majesty.

Now-a-days, there is nothing to which science has not been applied to a greater or less degree, and with the happiest, as well as the most wonderful results. Steamboats plough the waters—rail-cars rattle across plains and through mountains—and the new and old worlds are joined by the magic and friendly grasp of the Atlantic telegraph. Science rules the world, and her sway extends from the joining of two mighty nations, to the perforation of a postage stamp, or the pointing of a pin !

Of course, when the scientific application of natural forces is the actual foundation of commerce, art, and industry, it must also extend to amusement, and here, its effects are quite as striking as elsewhere. Chemistry, electricity, magnetism, galvanism, mechanics, and mathematics, all contribute their share towards furnishing recreation and sport for the social gathering or the family fireside. The magical combinations and effects of chemistry have furnished at almost infinite variety of pleasant experiments, which may be performed by our youthful friends with great success if a little care be taken, and the other branches of natural science are nearly as replete with interest.

The following *repertoire* of such tricks and illusions will be found exceedingly complete, although pains have been taken to select only the best and most startling of them. A large number are entirely new, but are described with sufficient clearness to enable any person of ordinary intelligence to become expert in them, with a little practice. The tricks of legerdemain (Fr. *leger-de-main ;* sleight of hand) will require the most attention and frequent repetition to insure success, although science has less to do with most of them than manual dexterity.

In regard to tricks with cards, the writer would say that it was at first contemplated to introduce a number of them, but that a consideration of the conscientious scruples entertained by many persons against even the sight of a pack of cards, has decided him in leaving this department out of the present volume. Those who have no prejudices against such amusements, may find a large and interesting collection in the MAGICIAN'S OWN BOOK,* published by Dick and Fitzgerald, of this city.

In closing, we have only to state that the experiments which follow, have been chosen with the greatest care from an immense number, and that every one is known to be practicable and satisfactory, when properly understood. If any difficulty is experienced in performing them, the operator may rest assured that study and practice will ultimately overcome it, and bring him out victorious.

THE BALANCED TURK.

A decanter or bottle is first obtained, and in its cork is placed a needle; on this is balanced a ball of wood, having a cork or wooden

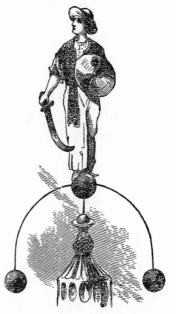

figure cut out, standing on the top, such as that seen in the picture. From the ball project two wires bent semicircularly, having at their extremities two bullets. If the little apparatus be made as we have shown, you can give the bullets a twist, and the whole will turn round on the needle, the figure standing upright all the while, and twist it about from side to side as much as you like, it will always regain its erect position. The two bullets, in this case, cause the centre of gravity to fall below the ball on which the figure is placed, and, in consequence, as the centre of gravity always assumes the lowest position, it cannot do so without making the figure stand erect, or, in other words, until the bullets themselves are equally balanced. Any boy may whittle one of these little toys out with a jack-knife, and cut any figure that may suit his fancy. To make a

* The Magician's Own Book, containing over one thousand tricks, and illustrated with five hundred engravings. Dick and Fitzgerald, New York.

curious little variation of this experiment, drive a needle, head first, into the end of a cork; into each side of the cork stick a common fork; then invert a tumbler, and place the point of the needle on it, and give the cork a twirl with the fingers, when it will revolve for half an hour or more.

THE MECHANICAL BUCEPHALUS.

The illustration of the horse furnishes a very good solution of a popular paradox in mechanics: Given, a body having a tendency to

fall by its own weight; required, how to prevent it from falling by adding to it a weight on the same side on which it tends to fall. The engraving shows a horse, the centre of gravity of which is somewhere about the middle of its body. It is evident, therefore, that were it placed on its hinder legs on a table, *a*, the line of its *direction* or centre would fall considerably beyond its base, and the horse would fall on the ground; but to prevent this, there is a stiff wire attached to a weight or bullet connected with the body of the horse, and by this means the horse prances on a table without falling off; so that the figure which was incapable of supporting itself is actually prevented from falling by adding a weight to its unsupported end. This seems almost impossible; but when we consider that, in order to have the desired effect, the wire must be bent, and the weight be further under the table than the horse's feet are on it, the mystery is solved, as it brings the total weight of bullet and horse in such a position that the tendency is rather to make it stand up than to let it fall down.

THE BALANCED COIN.

This engraving represents what seems to be an astounding statement, namely, that a quarter or other piece of money can be made to spin on the point of a needle. To perform this experiment procure a bottle, cork it, and in the cork place a needle. Now take another cork and cut a slit in it so that the edge of the coin will fit into the slit; next place two forks in the cork, as seen in the engraving, and placing the edge of the coin on the needle, it will spin round without falling off. The reason is this, that the weight of the forks, projecting as they do so much below the coin, brings the centre of gravity of the arrangement much below the point of suspension or

the point of the needle, and therefore the coin remains perfectly safe and upright.

THE COMPLACENT VIZIER.

Among the novelties which scientific investigation has added to our toys are several figures which will raise themselves upright when thrown down, and regain the erect position, notwithstanding their equilibrium is disturbed. The figures themselves are made of the pith of elder trees, or any other very light substance. Each is placed on half a bullet, as at *A*, or may be made to stand on its head, as at *B*, by making its cap of lead. Their appearance

is very droll when they are moved about, as they seem every moment to be falling over and yet continually right themselves. The philosophy of this is that the centre of gravity being in the base and always trying to assume the lowest position, it keeps the figures upright. However much the equilibrium is disturbed, it will always try to regain its original position.

THE REVOLVING IMAGE.

This little figure may be made to balance itself amusingly. Get

a piece of wood about two inches long; cut one end of it into the form of a man's head and shoulders, and let the other end taper off to a fine point. Next, furnish the little gentleman with a pair of wafters, shaped like oars, instead of arms; but they must be more than double the length of his body; stick them in his shoulders, and he is complete. When you place him on the tip of your finger, if you have taken care to make the point exactly in the centre, he will stand upright, as seen in the engraving. By blowing on the wafters he may be made to turn round very quickly. It is explained by the reasons that were given in the experiment of the "Balanced Coin."

THE SPANISH DANCER.

The laws which govern the motion of bodies are capable of many pleasing illustrations, and the example which we now give of causing rotary motion is very interesting and easily performed.

Take a piece of card, and cut out a little figure like that in the engraving, and paste or gum it in an erect position on the inside of a watch-glass, A. Then procure a black japanned waiter, B, or a clean plate will do, and holding it in an inclined position, place the figure and watch-glass on it, and they will, of course, slide down.

Next, let fall a drop of water on the waiter, place the watch-glass on it, and again incline the waiter, and instead of the watch-glass sliding down, it will begin to revolve. It will continue to revolve with increasing velocity, obeying the inclination and position of the plane, as directed by the hand of the experimentalist. The reason of this is, in the first place, in consequence of the cohesion of the water to the two surfaces, a new force is introduced by which an unequal degree of resistance is imparted to different parts of the watch-glass in contact with the waiter, and consequently, in its effort to slide down, it revolves. Again, if the drop of water be observed, it will be seen that it undergoes a change of figure; a film of water, by capillary action, is drawn to the foremost portion of the glass, while by the centrifugal force a body of water is thrown under the hinder part of it. The effect of both these actions is to accelerate the motion, or in other words, to gradually increase the speed.

THE MAGIC BLOW.

If a stick is taken and tapered off to the ends equally from the centre, and the stick itself be not too thick, and if it is then placed with its tapered ends resting on two wine-glasses, a good smart blow being struck on its centre, it will break in two without damaging the wine-glasses. The cause of this  involves a curious principle of the laws of force, of which there are many illustrations well known to every one. The blow being given very quickly and evenly, and the substance which strikes having a rapid motion, it is suddenly arrested in its downward course by the stick across the wine-glasses, and it passes through it, or breaks it, because there is not time enough for the momentum of the blow to spread along the stick and break the glasses. Another illustration is firing a candle through an inch board. If a gun be loaded with powder, and a candle just fitting the barrel is inserted in place of a bullet, and the gun fired against a door or other piece of wood, the candle will pass through, leaving a clean, smooth hole, because when the candle comes to the door, it is evident something must give way, and as the candle is moving so fast, it actually has not time to break, and the wood is perforated. In many countries of Europe, where liberty has no existence, except in name, letters are opened by the Post-office, an impression of the seal being first taken by striking a piece of lead sharply on it, when the lead receives the impression without breaking the seal. The letter is then opened and read, and re-sealed with the lead reverse, so that the recipient little suspects that his letter has been unfairly opened.

THE MAGIC VESSEL

On the bottom of a vessel lay three pieces of money; the first at A, the second at B, and the third at C. Then place a person at D, where

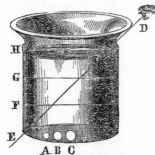

he can see no further into the vessel than E. You tell him, that by pouring water in the vessel you will make him see three different pieces of money; and bid him observe, that you do not convey any money in with the water. But be careful that you pour the water in very gently, or the pieces will move out of their places, and thereby destroy the experiment.

When the water rises up to F, the piece at A will be visible; when it reaches G, both A and B will be visible; and when it comes up to H, all three pieces will be visible.

TO PRODUCE FIRE FROM CANE.

The Chinese rattans, which are used, when split, for making cane chairs, will, when dry, if struck against each other, give fire, and are used accordingly, in some places, in lieu of flint and steel.

HAT MEASUREMENT.

Very few people are aware of the height of the crown of a stovepipe hat. A good deal of fun may be created by testing it in this way : Ask a person to point out on a wall, with a cane, about what

he supposes to be the height of an ordinary hat, and he will place the cane usually at about a foot from the ground. You then place a hat under it, and to his surprise he finds that the space indicated is more than double the height of the hat.

CURIOUS EXPERIMENT WITH A TULIP.

The bulb of a tulip in every respect resembles buds, except in its being produced under ground, and includes the leaves and flower in miniature, which are to be expanded in the ensuing spring. By cautiously cutting, in the early spring, through the concentric coats of a tulip root, longitudinally from the top to the base, and taking them off successively, the whole flower of the next summer's tulip is beautifully seen by the naked eye, with its petals, pistil, and stamens.

THE IMMOVABLE CARD.

Take an ordinary visiting card and bend down the ends as represented in the annexed figure, then ask any person to blow it over.

This seems easy enough, but it may be tried for hours without succeeding. It is, however, to be done by blowing sharply on the table at some distance from the card.

TO BALANCE A STICK ON THE EDGE OF A GLASS OF WINE.

Take a stick a foot long (a little more or less), and two penknives of *equal weight;* stick them by the point on a level on each side of the stick, parallel, at the distance of about three inches from the end you place on the glass, and be careful that the curves in the handles are turned towards the glass, as represented in the accompanying engraving. You may then drink off the wine, and the stick will still continue its extended position, and not fall off. Great care should

be taken to have the knives equally balanced, or the experiment will not be successful.

THE MAGIC TUMBLER.

The air which for about forty miles surrounds our earth has a defi nite weight; and although we can neither see nor feel it; we are con.

scious of its presence by the momentary operation of breathing. The weight of a column of air one inch square, and forty miles high, is about fifteen pounds. The reason why we are not crushed down by this enormous weight is, because we are surrounded on all sides by it, and as the pressure or weight is equal all around, it becomes, as far as we are personally concerned, insensible.

That the air *does* exert a definite pressure, in consequence of its weight, may be easily proved by any one with the above simple apparatus—only a tumbler and a sheet of paper. Fill a tumbler quite full of water, and carefully draw over its top a sheet of clean letter paper, and be careful to see that there are no bubbles of air in the water ; place your hand over the paper while inverting it, and when the glass is mouth downwards the water will be kept in, until the paper becomes wet through. The air pressing against the mouth of the tumbler is of greater weight than the contained water, and so until some air can get in, to supply the place of the water, it cannot fall out.

THE BOOMERANG.

The Boomerang is a weapon used by the savages of Australia. By them it is made of a flat piece of hard wood. The peculiarity of this instrument is, that in whatever direction it is thrown, it will return to the place from whence it started. The Australian aborigines use it with great dexterity, making it travel round a house and return to their feet, or they can throw it on the ground so that it will fly into the air, form a perfect arc over their heads, and strike them on the back. This curious instrument can be made in miniature, and is a very amusing toy for the parlor.

How to Make a Parlor Boomerang.

Get a piece of tolerably stiff cardboard, and cut from it a figure resembling No. 1, and you will have a Boomerang.

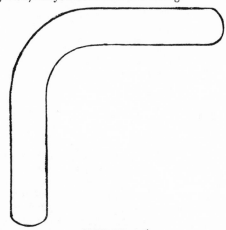

BOOMERANG. NO. 1.

The next thing is to propel it through the air so that it will return

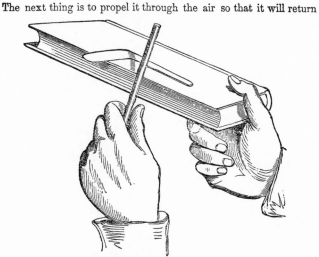

BOOMERANG. NO. 2.

to your feet; to do this lay the Boomerang on a flat book allowing one end to project about an inch, then holding the book at a slight angle to strike the projecting end of the boomerang with a piece of stick or heavy penholder, as represented in No. 2, when it will fly across the room and return to your feet.

To change the subject entirely to a seeming wonder, we will tell you how to support a pail of water by a stick, only half of which, or less, rests

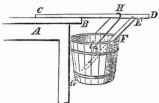

upon the table. Let A B be the top of the table, and C D the stick which is to support the bucket. Place the handle of the bucket on the stick in such a manner that it may rest on it in an inclined position, as H i, and let the middle of the bucket be a little within the edge of the table; to keep this apparatus properly in its situation, place another stick, E F G with the end resting against the bucket at the bottom, its middle, F, resting on the opposite top edge of the bucket, and its other extremity, E, against the first stick, C D, in which a notch must be cut to retain it. The bucket will thus be kept in its situation without inclining to either side, and if not already filled with water, it may be filled with safety.

The science of optics is full of interesting and extraordinary facts, which admit of many amusing demonstrations. We need only mention the magic lantern, an instrument that should be possessed by every school; the kaleidoscope, whose changes are not to be counted, and by

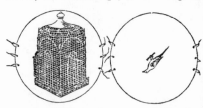

whose means a few bits of broken glass and pearl buttons, in fact, any small things having color, may be made to assume the prettiest of shapes, always changing, and never twice the same. These and some others are beyond the reach of many, and therefore we illustrate the Thaumatrope or Wonder-turner, because every child can make one for himself.

Cut out a piece of cardboard of circular form, and affix to it six pieces of string, three on each side. Paint on one side of the card a bird and on the other a cage, taking care to paint the bird upside down, or the desired effect will not be produced. When showing the toy, take hold of the centre strings between the fore-finger and thumb and twirl the card rapidly round, and the bird will appear snugly ensconced in its cage. The principle on which this effect is produced is, that the image of any object received on the retina or optic nerve is retained on the mind about eight seconds after the object causing the impression is withdrawn, being the memory of the object; consequently the impression of the painting on one side of the card is not obliterated ere the painting on the other side is brought before the eye. It is easy to understand from this fact how both are seen at once. Many objects will suit the Thaumatrope, such as a juggler throwing up two balls on one side, and two balls on the other; and according to the pairs of strings employed, he will appear to throw up two, three, or four balls; the body and legs of a man on one side, and the arms and head on another; a horse and his rider; a mouse and trap. But we leave it to the ingenuity of our readers to devise for themselves.

THE DIOPTRICAL PARADOX.

Construct a machine similar to that represented in the annexed cut. Its effect will be, that a print, or an ornamented drawing, with any object, such as an ace of diamonds, etc., in the centre, F, will be seen as an ace of clubs when placed in the machine, and viewed through a single plain glass only, contained in the tube E. The glass in the tube which produces this surprising change, is somewhat on the principle of the common multiplying glass, as represented at G, which, by the number

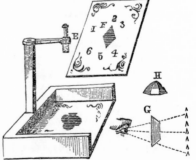

of its inclined surfaces, and from the refractive power of the rays proceeding from the objects placed before it, shows it in a multiplied state. The only difference is, that the sides of this glass are flat, and diverge upwards from the base to a point in the axis of the glass like a cone; it has six sides, and each side, from its angular position to the eye, has the property of refracting from the border of the print F, such a portion of it (designedly placed there) as will make a part in the composition of the figure to be represented; for the hexagonal and conical figure of this glass prevents any part of the ace of diamonds being seen; consequently, the ace of clubs being previously and mechanically drawn in the circle of refraction in six different parts of the border, at 1, 2, 3, 4, 5, 6, and artfully disguised in the ornamental border, by being blended with it, the glass in the tube at E will change the appearance of the ace of diamonds, F, into the ace of clubs, G. In the same manner many other prints undergo similar changes, according to the will of an ingenious draughtsman who may design them. The figure of the glass is shown at H.

DECEPTIVE VISION.

Stick a fork in the wall, about four or five feet from the floor, and on the end of it place a cork; then tell some person to place his forefinger by the side of the cork; when he has measured the height carefully, tell him to walk backwards about five yards, then shut one eye, and walk forward and try to knock the cork off the fork with one blow of the forefinger. The probabilities are, that he will make the attempt a dozen times before he is successful.

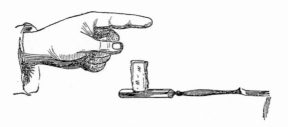

THE MAGIC INCENDIARY.

A vessel containing a certain white powder is placed upon the table by the wizard—the man who is held in great awe by the juveniles, on account of his seeming supernatural powers, and yet beloved by them because he affords them much pleasure by the exhibition of his talents, to say nothing of the bon-bons, apples, oranges, almonds, and sugar-plums which he causes to issue from an apparently empty drawer, or handkerchief, and upon which they are allowed to feast. This said wizard having placed the above-mentioned powder on the table, now advances, waving his wand and uttering the magic words, *cassafelto, presto, aldiborontiphoskiphorniosticos,* when lo! of a sudden the room is lighted up with a brilliant light, so effulgent that it dims the eyes of the spectators! The secret is this:—The powder is composed of equal weights of loaf-sugar and chlorate of potash, separately reduced to fine powder, and then well mixed together. This is placed in some vessel, such as a cup, or in fact anything that will prevent the fire from injuring the table. When this powder is touched with the least drop of sulphuric acid it will instantly burst into a flame; if therefore the end of the glass rod be dipped in the acid immediately before use, it will on being brought into contact with the deflagrating powder cause it to ignite.

MAGICAL COLOR CHANGES.

When a man perceives the nature and reason of a thing, it ceases to be magical to that particular individual; for which reason none of the experiments presently to be detailed will appear in the slightest degree magical to the chemist. Quite otherwise to such persons as are not chemists. To them the color-changes about to be mentioned will appear very extraordinary.

Experiment 1.

Dissolve about ten grains, a good pinch, of iodide of potassium, sometimes called hydriodate of potash, in pure water—*i. e.* distilled water; put the solution aside in a wine glass or phial. Get a chemist to dissolve for you (the operation is not easy), two grains of corrosive sublimate in an ounce of distilled water. He will label it "Poison," of course. When this solution is prepared and given into your possession, do not let it out of sight for a single instant, and any portion which may not have been used in your experiment throw away.

By adding a solution of iodide of potassium and solution of corrosive sublimate to each other in various proportions, you will get some of the strangest changes of color imaginable. The tints rapidly vary from all shades, beginning with canary yellow, up to the most lovely carnation; and the formation of each separate color takes place not irregularly, but in festooned garlands, as if some invisible fairy amused herself by throwing flower garlands into the liquid. Presently, if either of the solutions be added beyond the limit of certain proportions, the mixture suddenly becomes colorless. This beautiful experiment is of more value than that of furnishing a means of chemical amusement. It illustrates to those who are unacquainted with chemistry the method followed by chemists in speaking so confidently as they do about the presence of this or that thing. The beautiful play of colors just supposed to have been produced by mixture of the two agents, iodide of potassium and corrosive sublimate (bichloride of mercury), is yielded by no other agents; consequently, if a certain unknown liquid yields the above tints, as particularized, when tested with iodide of potassium, it is an unknown liquid no longer: it contains corrosive sublimate, or bichloride of mercury. The latter substance is a frightful poison, far more violent than arsenic, but less to be dreaded, notwithstanding—1. For the reason that arsenic is devoid of taste, whereas sublimate has a powerful taste (dip the end of a straw in your solution and taste it), and therefore can hardly be administered by a murderer to his victim; 2. Because there is an antidote for sublimate in the shape of white of egg, mingled with water, which curdles it, and renders it innocuous, whereas there is practically no antidote to arsenic.

Experiment 2.

Take a piece of copper—say a cent, or any copper coin—drop a little vinegar upon it, allow the vinegar to remain for a few moments, then finally immerse the coin in some water contained in a wine glass. However pure the water might have been previously to this operation, it will now be charged more or less with copper. Perhaps the non-chemical experimentalist, unaccustomed to testing, had better make a tolerably strong solution of copper, by taking out the copper coin, smearing it with vinegar, and reimmersing it several times following. Instead of vinegar, aquafortis may be used, and with quicker effect, though vinegar will answer every purpose.

Pour in a little solution of prussiate of potash into a portion of the copper solution, and a mahogany-red color will be evolved.

Into a second portion of the copper solution pour in a little hartshorn, and mark the lovely blue color which is generated. No metal in creation, other than copper, when dissolved and the solution treated by prussiate of potash and hartshorn, successively can yield by the first a mahogany-red or brown color, by the second a blue color. Which facts being duly committed to mind, the reader will perceive the method of determining the presence of copper. Usually hartshorn is quite sufficient to the end in question, without the use of prussiate of potash, or any other testing.

Experiment 3.

To change Iron apparently into Copper.—If a piece of iron or steel—

the blade of a knife, for example—be immersed in a solution of copper the copper is deposited in the metallic condition upon the iron or steel, and creates the notion in the mind of the observer unacquainted with chemical science, that the result is a case of transmutation. It has no pretensions to be regarded in that light; it is merely the deposition of one metal upon the surface of another.

Should you desire to surprise a friend by this sort of transmutation, and surprise him effectually, it will be necessary to operate on a somewhat stronger solution of copper than the one just mentioned. You had better dissolve a drachm of blue vitriol (which is a salt of copper) in a pint of water, which will be enough to furnish a good bath, capacious enough to dip a knife blade into. Depositions of copper will speedily take place, and in a few minutes the iron knife will apparently be transmuted into copper.

Copper is a very poisonous metal: it frequently gets into articles of both food and drink, where its presence is highly undesirable. Wherever present in the soluble form, it admits of being discovered by one of the methods indicated above. If the solution be at all strong, the mere immersion of an iron knife blade, well freed from grease, into the liquid, will sufficiently indicate the presence of copper, without having recourse to any further test.

Experiment 4.

Dissolve a piece of sulphate of iron,* about the size of a filbert, in about a pint of water, and divide the solution into three portions.

To the first portion add a little infusion or tincture of gall nuts (either will do), and remark the black tint developed; it is merely writing ink, which, as ordinarily made, is composed of this sort of black iron liquid, thickened, more or less, with gum water.

To the second portion add a little of prussiate of potash solution, or even a small crystal of the same; and remark the lovely blue tint developed. It is Prussian blue, or rather, one of the many varieties of Prussian blue which are known to chemists.

To a third portion add a little of solution of the salt termed red prussiate of potash. By contact with this, the iron solution will yield a color so exactly like the tint of blood, that former chemists imagined the real color of blood to be due to the active principle of this very agent.

Experiments involving change of color by the mixture of different

---

* Otherwise known as green vitriol and " copperas," though it contains not one particle of copper.

tests, should not be looked upon only as mere matters of amusement. They display the principles upon which chemical analysis is conducted, and, duly pondered, are very instructive.

THE MIMIC VESUVIUS.

This experiment is a demonstration of the heat and light which are evolved during chemical combination. The substance, phosphorus, has

a great affinity for oxygen gas, and wherever it can get it from, it will, especially when aided by the application of heat. To perform this experiment, put half a drachm of solid phosphorus into a Florence-oil flask, holding the flask slantingly, that the phosphorus may not take fire and break the glass; pour upon it a gill and a half of water, and place the whole over a tea-kettle lamp, or any common lamp, filled with spirits of wine: light the wick, which should be about half an inch from the flask; and as soon as the water is boiling hot, streams of fire, resembling sky-rockets, will burst at intervals from the water; some particles will also adhere to the sides of the glass, immediately display brilliant rays, and thus continue until the water begins to simmer, when a beautiful imitation of the aurora borealis will commence, and gradually ascend until this collects into a pointed cone at the mouth of the flask; when this has continued for half a minute, blow out the flame of the lamp, and the apex of fire that was formed at the mouth of the flask, will rush down, forming beautiful illumined clouds of fire, rolling over each other for some time, and when these disappear, a splendid hemisphere of stars will present itself. After waiting a minute or two, light the lamp again, and nearly the same phenomena will be displayed as at the beginning. Let a repetition of lighting and blowing out the lamp be made for three or four times, so that the number of stars may be increased; and after the third or fourth act of blowing out the lamp, the internal surface of the flask will be dry. Many of the stars will shoot with great splendor from side to side, whilst others will appear and burst at the mouth of the flask. What liquid remains in the flask will serve for the same experiment three or four times, without adding any water. Care should be taken, after the operation is over, to put the flask in a cool and secure place.

THE MIMIC GAS HOUSE.

The next illustration shows a simple way of making illuminating gas by means of a tobacco pipe. Bituminous coal contains a number of chemical compounds, nearly all of which can, by distillation, be converted into an illuminating gas; and with this gas nearly all our cities are now lighted in the dark hours of night. To make it as represented in our engraving, obtain some coal dust (or walnut or butternut meats will answer), and fill the bowl of a pipe with it; then cement the top over with some clay, place the bowl in the fire, and soon smoke will

be seen issuing from the end of the stem; when that has ceased coming, apply a light, and it will burn brilliantly for several minutes; after it has ceased, take the pipe from the fire and let it cool, then remove the clay, and a piece of coke will be found inside; this is the excess of carbon over the hydrogen contained in the coal, for all the hydrogen will combine with carbon at a high temperature, and make what are called hydro-carbons—a series of substances containing both these elemental forms of matter.

TO PLACE A TEA-KETTLEFUL OF BOILING WATER UPON THE NAKED HAND WITHOUT INJURY.

Whilst a tea-kettle is boiling upon the fire, and for a few seconds after its removal, a layer of steam exists between the bottom of the

15

tea-kettle and the water which it contains. Now the layer of steam in question is a bad conductor of heat; wherefore the tea-kettle may be taken direct from the fire and laid flat upon the hand without giving rise to any disagreeable perception of heat. I have heard the success of this experiment attributed to a deposition of soot upon the outside of the tea-kettle. This is an error : a perfectly clean tea-kettle, heated over a charcoal fire, which deposits no soot, may be handled as described above.

TO FILL WITH SMOKE TWO APPARENTLY EMPTY BOTTLES.

Rinse out one bottle with hartshorn and another bottle with spirit of salt; next bring the bottles together mouth to mouth; both will at once be pervaded with white vapors. The vapors in question are composed of sal ammoniac—a solid body generated by the union of two invisible gases.

TO REDUCE TIN INSTANTANEOUSLY TO WHITE POWDER.

Take a piece of tin foil—not tin plate, which is merely iron plate covered with tin—lay the foil in a saucer or upon a plate, and pour upon it strong aquafortis. Violent chemical action will at once ensue, ruddy vapors will be evolved, and the tin foil will crumble to white powder. Only one metal besides tin (antimony) gives rise to a similar result when similarly treated. Hence an action like that described points to either tin or antimony. But tin is a tough, and antimony is a brittle metal; wherefore the discrimination between them, even by the agency of this one test, is complete.

TO REDUCE METALLIC LEAD TO THE STATE OF POWDER, WHICH BURNS IMMEDIATELY ON COMING INTO CONTACT WITH THE AIR.

Dissolve sugar of lead in distilled water, and pour in a solution of tartaric acid, until a white powder ceases to fall. Collect this white powder, dry it, and when dry, pour it into a little glass bottle. Coat the bottle with clay, and dry the clay in an oven. Next lay the bottle amidst some unlighted charcoal, light the charcoal, and raise the heat to redness. Continue the application of heat until smoke no longer escapes from the bottle ; finally, dexterously stop the mouth of the bottle with a pledget of clay. Remove it now from the fire and allow it to grow cold. The bottle will hold a mixture of charcoal, resulting from the burned tartaric acid, and finely-divided lead. If the contents be poured out, they at once take fire. Several metals burn readily when reduced to the condition of fine powder. Iron is a notable instance of this, but the method of obtaining iron in powder is beyond the competence of a beginner.

TO MAKE A LIQUID WHICH FEELS COLD TO THE TOUCH, BUT WHICH RENDERS THE HANDS AND FACE LUMINOUS WHEN SMEARED WITH IT.

Immerse a piece of phosphorus, about the size of a pea, in an ounce or so of ether. After a time, portions of the phosphorus will dissolve, yielding an ethereal solution of that substance. If the hands and face be rubbed with this solution, which is perfectly innocent, the operator will seem on fire, and will pass for a very respectable ghost.

CRYSTALLINE BASKETS.

There is, as everybody knows, a substance called alum, which is beautifully crystalline, and always is seen shaped like double pyramids. This is a compound of an earth, *alumina*, and an acid, *sulphuric;* it is, in fact, the sulphate of alumina, and is put to many useful purposes. This substance is soluble in hot water, and in cooling, it crystallizes out on to anything that may be in the liquid, and the crystals will take any color,—thus indigo will color them blue, cochineal red, and so on. Now, bearing these facts in mind, take a quantity, say a pound of alum, and dissolve it in as little hot water as possible. Then having made a basket of wire, like Fig. 1, immerse

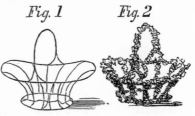

it in the hot solution, and put it quietly away to cool. Next morning you can take the basket out, and it looks like Fig. 2, all the wires being covered with beautiful crystals.

Should your first basket have given you some pleasure, here are directions to cut a nice one out of cardboard, one like that shown in the engraving, Fig. 2. Take your cardboard and draw one circle in the centre, and then a larger, just the distance apart you want the sides to be high. Then on these circles construct the hexagons that form the base and rim of your basket. Place the point of the compasses in

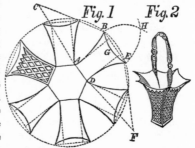

A, and afterwards in *B,* and draw with the pencil point two arcs

which intersect each other at C; this done, place the compass point at C, then describe the arc, $A\ B$, which will give the necessary curve to the side, and then from the points $D\ E$ draw arcs intersecting at F. From this point you obtain the side $D\ E$, then from the points $B\ E$ describe the arcs $B\ H$ and $E\ H$, and from H you get the curve G for the top; having done this with each side, on folding them up, they will form a very pretty basket, and any devices that suit the maker's fancy may be drawn or painted on the sides.

TO MAKE BEAUTIFUL TRANSPARENT COLORED WATER.

The following liquors, which are colored, being mixed, produce colors very different from their own. The yellow tincture of saffron, and the red tincture of roses, when mixed, produce a green. Blue tincture of violets, and brown spirit of sulphur, produce a crimson. Red tincture of roses, and brown spirits of hartshorn, make a blue. Blue tincture of violets, and blue solution of copper, give a violet color. Blue tincture of cyanus, and blue spirit of sal ammoniac colored, make green. Blue solution of Hungarian vitriol, and brown lye of potash, make yellow. Blue solution of Hungarian vitriol, and red tincture of roses, make black; and blue tincture of cyanus, and green solution of copper, produce red.

THE PHIAL OF THE FOUR ELEMENTS.

Take a phial, six or seven inches long, and about three quarters of an inch in diameter. Into this phial put, first, glass coarsely powdered; secondly, oil of tartar per deliquium; thirdly, tincture of salt of tartar; and lastly, distilled rock oil.

The glass and the various liquors being of different densities, if you shake the phial, and then let it rest a few moments, the three liquors will entirely separate, and each assume its place; thus forming no indifferent resemblance of the four elements, earth, fire, water, and air; the powdered glass (which should be of some dark color) representing the earth; the oil of tartar, water; the tincture, air; and the rock oil, fire.

CURIOUS EXPERIMENT WITH A GLASS OF WATER.

Saturate a certain quantity of water in a moderate heat, with three ounces of sugar; and when it will no longer receive that, there is still room in it for two ounces of salt of tartar, and after that for an ounce and a drachm of green vitriol, nearly six drachms of nitre, the same of sal ammoniac, two drachms and a scruple of alum, and a drachm and a half of borax.

TO PRODUCE METALLIC LEAD FROM THE POWDER.

Take one ounce of red lead, and half a drachm of charcoal in powder, incorporate them well in a mortar, and then fill the bowl of a tobacco-pipe with the mixture. Submit it to an intense heat, in a common fire, and when melted, pour it out upon a slab, and the result will be metallic lead completely revived.

SUBAQUEOUS EXHALATION.

Pour a little clear water into a small glass tumbler, and put one or two small pieces of phosphoret of lime into it. In a short time, flashes of fire will dart from the surface of the water, and terminate in ringlets of smoke, which will ascend in regular succession.

THE MINERAL CHAMELEON.

When one part of black oxide of manganese and three parts of nitrate of potass, both reduced to powder, and mixed together, are exposed in a crucible to a strong heat for about an hour, or as long as any gas continues to be disengaged, a compound of highly oxidized manganese and potass, possessed of some very curious properties, is obtained.—*Experiment* 1. A few grains of this compound, put into a wine glassful of water, produces a *green* color; an increase of the quantity changes the color to a *blue;* more still, to a *purple;* and a yet further increase produces a beautiful *deep purple.*—*Experiment* 2. Put equal quantities of this substance into two separate wine glasses, and add to the one *hot*, and to the other *cold*, water. The hot solution will be of a beautiful *green* color; the cold one of a *deep purple.* By using more glasses, and water more or less in quantity, and at different temperatures, a great variety of colors will be produced in this way from the same substance.

TO CAUSE FIRE TO BURN UNDER WATER.

You call for a pail of water, and having a certain composition in your hand, which you apply fire to, you throw it into the water, and to the great astonishment of the company, it will burn under the water till quite spent.

For the performance of this curious trick, by which many a wager has been won, take three ounces of powder, one ounce of saltpetre, and three ounces of sulphur vivum, beat and mix them well together; then fill a pasteboard or paper mould with the composition, and it will burn till entirely consumed, under the water.

TO CAUSE A STONE TO BE IN PERPETUAL MOTION.

This requires some hours' preparation, as may be seen by the explanation. When the necessary pains have been taken, the stone appears in a bottle continually moving.

Put very small filings of iron into aquafortis, and let them remain there until the water has taken off the iron requisite, which will happen in seven or eight hours. Then take the water, and put it into a phial an inch wide, with a large mouth, and put in a stone of *lapis calaminaris*, and stop it up close; the stone will then keep in perpetual motion.

FOUNTAIN OF FIRE.

Add gradually one ounce of sulphuric acid to six ounces of water in an earthen basin. Then add three-quarters of an ounce of granulated zinc, with a few pieces of phosphorus the size of a pea. Gas-bubbles will be immediately produced, which take fire on the surface of the effervescing liquid, and the whole surface of the liquid will directly become illuminated; fire-balls and jets of fire will dart from the bottom through the fluid with great rapidity.

ROTARY MOTION OF CAMPHOR UPON WATER.

Fill a saucer with water and drop into it camphor reduced to the form of coarse sand. The floating particles will commence moving, and acquire a progressive rotary motion, which continues for some minutes and then gradually subsides.

TO MELT A COIN IN A NUT-SHELL.

Take three parts of nitre, one part of sulphur, and one of dry sawdust; rub them together, and pressing down the powder in the shell, on which place a small coin of silver or copper rolled up; fill the shell with more powder and press it closely down; ignite the powder, and the coin will be melted in a mass when the combustion has been completed.

INSTANTANEOUS CRYSTALLIZATION.

Make a concentrated solution of sulphate of soda, or Glauber's salts, adding to it gradually portions of boiling water until the fluid dissolves no more. Pour the solution, whilst in a boiling state, into phials previously warmed; cork them immediately to exclude the air from the solution; place them in a secure place, without shaking them, and the solution will cool; remove the cork, and as soon as the atmospheric air becomes admitted, it will begin to crystallize on the surface, and the crystallization is complete.

COMBUSTION UNDER WATER.

Put a small quantity of hyper-oxi-muriate of potass and a bit of phosphorus into a wine glass; pour on them cold water. Take a glass tube and dip one end into sulphuric acid; press with the finger upon the upper orifice to retain it, convey the end to the bottom of the glass, take away the finger, and the combustion will take place instantly.

TO SET A COMBUSTIBLE BODY ON FIRE BY THE CONTACT OF COLD WATER.

Fill a saucer with water, and let fall into it a piece of potassium, of the size of a peppercorn (which is about two grains). The potassium will instantly become red hot, with a slight explosion, and burn vividly on the surface of the water, darting at the same time from one side of the vessel to the other, with great violence, in the form of a red-hot fire ball.

VIVID COMBUSTION OF THREE METALS WHEN BROUGHT INTO CONTACT WITH EACH OTHER.

Mix a grain or two of potassium with a like quantity of sodium. This mixture will take place quietly; but if the alloy of these two bodies be brought into contact with a globule of quicksilver, the compound, when agitated, instantly takes fire, and burns vividly.

TO MAKE A RING SUSPEND BY A THREAD, AFTER THE THREAD HAS BEEN BURNED.

Soak a piece of thread in common salt water. Tie it to a ring, not larger than a wedding ring. When you apply the flame of a candle to it, it will burn to ashes, but yet sustain the ring.

TO CAUSE WATER TO BOIL ON THE SURFACE OF ICE.

To effect this, first freeze a quantity of water in the bottom of a long glass tube, closed at one end, either by exposure to cold air, or by means of a *freezing mixture;* say equal parts of nitrate of ammonia and water. Then cover the cake of ice by a quantity of water, and hold the tube (without handling the part of it containing the ice) in such a manner over a lamp, that the surface of the water may be heated to the point of boiling; for this, the tube requires to be placed in a dragonal direction, which is such as allows the water at the top of it to be heated, while the ice remains unheated below.

TO MAKE WINE OR BRANDY FLOAT ON WATER.

To perform this seeming impossibility take a tumbler half full of water, and placing a piece of thin muslin over the top of the same, gently strain the brandy or wine through the muslin, and it will remain on top of the water.

CHEMICAL EFFECT OF LIGHT.

Wash a piece of paper in a weak solution of salt-and-water; dry, and then wash it with a strong solution of nitrate of silver; dry it in the dark, and, when dry, expose it to the sun's light; though colorless before, it will now soon become black. A picture may be made by placing a dried plant, bit of lace, etc., upon the paper, previous to its exposure to light.

COMBUSTION OF CHARCOAL.

Pour some dry charcoal, newly made and finely powdered, into a jar containing chlorine gas; a very beautiful combustion will take place.

TO PUT THREE LIQUIDS IN A GLASS AND DRINK EITHER WITHOUT DISTURBING THE OTHERS.

Make a strong syrup of white sugar and water, put it about a third up into a tall glass, then pour in carefully some milk which will float on the syrup, then on the top of the milk put some port wine, which will float on the milk. Now you may undertake to drink either of the lower liquids without disturbing the wine, by taking a straw and putting it carefully into either the milk or sugar, and sucking it up through.

DECOMPOSITION OF WATER.

Take a grain of potassium, wrap it up in a small piece of thin paper, and introduce it into a test tube, or small phial, inverted under water, and full of the same fluid. It immediately rises to the top, and, combining with the oxygen of the water, an equivalent of hydrogen gas is given off, which expels the water from the tube or phial, and occupies its place. A lighted match brought to the mouth of the tube will prove the presence of the hydrogen.

PRODUCTION UNDER WATER OF VIVID GREEN STREAMS OF FIRE.

Put two ounces of water into an ale glass or tumbler, and first add to it two or three pieces of phosphorus, the size of peas, and then forty grains of chlorate of potass; then pour upon the mass, by means of a long-necked funnel, reaching to the bottom of the glass, three teaspoonfuls of sulphuric acid. As soon as the acid comes into contact with the phosphorus and chlorate of potass, flashes of fire begin to dart from under the surface of the fluid; when this occurs, immediately throw into the mixture a few small lumps of phosphuret of lime; the bottom of the vessel will become illuminated, and an emerald green colored stream of fire pass through the fluid. The chlorate of potass yields oxide of chlorine, by the effusion of sulphuric acid, whilst the phosphuret of lime produces phosphuretted hydrogen gas, which, inflaming in the nascent euchlorine, gives the colored flame.

SUBAQUEOUS COMBUSTION.

Drop a small piece of phosphorus into a tumbler full of *hot* water, and force a stream of oxygen immediately upon it, from a bladder furnished with a stopcock and jet. The most brilliant combustion imaginable will be produced under water.

BOTTLED MOONSHINE.

Nothing in the world is more like "bottled moonshine" than phosphoric oil. A light without heat! Astonishing! But it is so. The light emitted by phosphoric oil is an unearthly spiritual kind of light. However near we are to its luminous influence, it nevertheless always appears to be at a distance. As it is probable that light from this source will have a practical application in places where the common artificial light would be dangerous, we shall explain the process of making it, for the entertainment of our young laboratorians, many of whom may perhaps live to see the phosphoric lamp used in dangerous mines. For experiment take a thin glass phial; about half-fill it with fine olive oil; then drop into it a piece of phosphorus the size of a bean; now place the bottle in boiling hot water until the oil is quite hot; shake it now and then, and the phosphorus will dissolve; keep the phial well corked; then let it get cold. Whenever you want a little moonshine, take the cork out of the bottle, shake the oil, and there will be light!

BRILLIANT LIGHT FROM STEEL.

Pour into a watch-glass a little sulphuret of carbon, and light it; hold in the flame a brush of steel-wire, and it will burn beautifully. A watch-spring may also be burnt in it.

SPARKS FROM TIN.

Place upon a piece of tinfoil a few powdered crystals of nitrate of copper; moisten it with water; fold up the foil gently, and wrap it in paper so as to keep out the air; lay it upon a plate, and the tin will soon begin to swell and afford a few flashes of light.

HOW TO STRIKE THE KNUCKLES WITHOUT HURTING THEM.

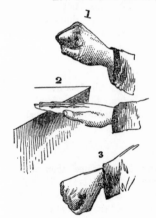

Select a marble mantel or any other hard surface, then tell the spectators that by a certain preparation you use, you have made your knuckles so hard nothing can hurt them, in proof of which you offer to strike them on the marble slab of the mantel. To do this, you raise your fist firmly clenched above the mantel, and as you bring it rapidly down open your fingers suddenly, and strike the marble, then close them again as represented in Figs. 1, 2, and 3; if this is quickly done, you will seem to have knocked your knuckles violently.

TO RAISE UP A HEAVY METAL MORTAR, OR THE LIKE, WITH A WINE GLASS.

Having inverted the mortar, spread on its bottom, or at least where the brim of the glass is to be placed, a little paste of flour and water. Then pour some spirits of wine into a small cup, set fire to it, and hold the glass over it, so that the flame shall ascend into the glass, and heat and dilate the air within. When the air is sufficiently dilated, place the glass without delay on the paste and press it tight against the bottom of the mortar, so that no air can pass in from without. Let it remain thus till the air within the glass is cooled; and then, if you lift up the glass, it will raise the mortar with it. You may use a piece of wet leather instead of the paste; but the latter is preferable, because the brims of common glasses are not always sufficiently level to press close to leather in every part, and a heated glass will be apt to crack when it comes in contact with wet leather.

THE TRAVELLING OF SOUND EXPERIMENTALLY PROVED.

There is probably no substance which is not in some measure a conductor of sound; but sound is much enfeebled by passing from one medium to another. If a man, stopping one of his ears with his finger, stop the other also by pressing it against the end of a long stick, and a watch be applied to the opposite end of the stick, or piece of timber, be it ever so long, the beating of the watch will be distinctly heard; whereas, in the usual way, it can scarcely be heard at the distance of fifteen or eighteen feet. The same effect will take place if he stops both his ears with his hands, and rests his teeth, his temple, or the gristly part of one of his ears against the end of a stick. Instead of a watch, a gentle scratch may be made at one end of a pole or rod, and the person who keeps his ear in close contact with the other end of the pole, will hear it very plainly. Thus, persons who are dull of hearing, may, by applying their teeth to some part of a harpsichord, or other sounding body, hear the sound much better than otherwise.

If a person tie a strip of flannel about a yard long around a poker, then press with his thumbs and fingers the ends of the flannel into his ears, while he swings the poker against an iron fender, he will hear a sound very like that of a large church bell.

TO PUT SAND INTO WATER WITHOUT WETTING IT.

A trick like this which is so opposite to the general nature of sand, may afford amusement. Take any quantity of fine, clean, silver sand, put it into a clean pot, and heat it until it will slightly brown a card which you may use to stir it; then for every quart of sand, put a piece of lard or tallow about the size of a walnut, and stir for two or three minutes, then when properly mixed and cold it is ready. By putting sand of this description carefully into water, it may be taken out hours after without being wet. When done properly, if analysed, no chemist could discern anything beyond pure sand.

THE MAGIC CUPS

Procure two tin cups without handles, quite plain, straight sides, with the bottoms sunk a quarter of an inch. On the bottoms spread some glue, and completely cover the glue with some kind of birdseed, only so as not to be seen when standing in an ordinary position. Have ready a bag filled with the same kind of seed as you used in covering the bottoms. Put the cups on the table; also two hats. Put one cup then into the bag, appear to fill it, and take it out turned bottom upwards, when it will look as if it had been filled. Put it in that position under one hat, in doing so turn it over. Then take the other empty cup, put that under the other hat; and, in doing so, turn that over, which, of course, must be invisible to the audience. Then remove the hat, and the cups will appear to have changed places.

THE MYSTERIOUS BAG.

Make two bags, about a foot long and six inches wide, of some dark material, and sew the two together at the edge, so that one may be inside the other, and it will appear the same if turned inside out. Next make a number of little pockets with a cover to them, which may be fastened down by a button and loop. Place these about two inches apart between the two bags, sewing one side of the pocket to one bag and the other side to the other. Now make slits through both bags about an inch long, just above the pockets, so that you can put your hand in the bags; insert your thumb and finger through the slits, and open the pockets. To perform the trick, articles should be put in the pockets, one in each, and the pockets covered over. The bag may now be turned inside out any number of times at pleasure, and it will appear to be empty; indeed, you can take it close to your audience and the trick will not be seen through. You can now cause to appear or disappear any number of articles which are of a light nature, much to the amusement of the company. This is the same kind of bag that Wyman, Blitz, and other magicians use to perform the celebrated eggbag trick.

THE REVOLVING SERPENT.

This illustration represents an amusing and instructive experiment, which proves the ascension of heated air by rendering its effects visible,

and it may also be used to test the direction of the currents in our rooms and dwellings. To construct one, a piece of card board is taken and cut in the form of a spiral as at A, and to give effect it may be painted to represent a serpent. Then prepare a stand as at B, having a needle in its upper end, and suspend the serpent from its centre on the needle, when it will assume the position shown at B. If this be now placed over a stove, or the tail of the serpent suspended by a bit of thread over a lamp, the heated air ascending through it will cause it to revolve in a very amusing manner. Two serpents may be made to turn in opposite directions, by pulling one out from the one side, and the other in the reverse direction, so that their heads may point towards each other when suspended

TO PASS A QUARTER INTO A BALL OF WORSTED.

Like all the best magical tricks, this is one of the most simple. A marked quarter is borrowed, a large ball of worsted is brought. Presto! the worsted is unwound, and out falls the money, that a minute before was in its owner's pocket. Here is the solution :—First, procure a few skeins of *thick* worsted, next a piece of tin in the shape of a flat tube, large enough for the quarter to pass through, and about four inches long. Now wind the worsted on one end of the tube, to a good-sized ball, having a quarter of your own in your *right* hand. You may now show the trick. Place the worsted anywhere out of sight, borrow a marked quarter, then taking it in your *left* hand, looking at it and saying " It is good," place the one in your *right* hand on the end of the table farthest from the company ; then fetch the worsted ; while so doing, drop the marked quarter through the tube, pull it out and wind the worsted a little to conceal the hole, then put the ball into a tumbler, and taking the quarter you left on the table, show it to the company (who will imagine it to be the borrowed quarter), say "Presto! fly! pass!" Give the end of the ball to one of the audience, request them to unwind it, which, being done, the money will fall out, to the astonishment of all who see this trick of legerdemain.

EXPERIMENTS WITH THE MAGNET.

Magnetism is the science that explains the several properties of the attractive and repellent powers in the magnet or loadstone. The ancients were acquainted with no other property of the magnet, than that which it has of attracting iron; but the moderns have discovered several others, such as its communication, its direction, declination. and inclination, to which we may add its annual and daily variation.

Magnetic attraction is both curious and interesting, and many amusing experiments may be performed with it; thus making the magnet doubly attractive to young people.

The magnetic attraction will not be destroyed by interposing obstacles between the magnet and the iron.

Lay a small needle or a piece of paper, and put a magnet under the paper; the needle may be moved backwards and forwards.

Lay the needle on a piece of glass, and put the magnet under the glass; it will still attract the needle. The same effects will take place if a board be interposed between the magnet and the iron. This property of the magnet has afforded the means of some very amusing deceptions.

A little figure of a man has been made to spell a person's name. The hand, in which was a piece of iron, rested on a board, under which a person, concealed from view, with a powerful magnet, contrived to carry it from letter to letter, until the word was made up.

The figure of a goose or swan, with a piece of iron concealed about the head, is set to float in water. A rod, with a concealed magnet at the end, is presented to the bird, and it swims after it. The effect is still more amusing when some food is put on the end of the rod.

The figure of a fish is thrown into the water, with a small magnet concealed in its mouth. Of course, if a baited hook be suspended near it, the magnet and iron, by mutual attraction, will bring the fish to the bait.

Put a piece of iron in one scale of a balance, and an equal weight in the other scale; bring the magnet under the scale which contains the iron, and it will draw it down. Reverse the experiment, and put the magnet in the scale, and balance it; bring the iron under it, and it will draw down the magnet. Suspend a magnet by a string, and bring a piece of iron near it, and it will attract.

If a magnet suspended by one string, and a piece of iron suspended by another, be brought near one another, they will mutually attract each other, and be drawn to a point between.

Suspend a magnet, nicely poised, by a thread, and it will point north and south, the same end pointing invariably the same way.

Rub a fine needle with a magnet, and lay it gently on the surface of the water; it will point north and south. Rub various needles with the magnet, run them through small pieces of cork, and put them to swim in water; they will all point north and south, and the same end will invariably point the same way. This mode of finding the north is sometimes of the utmost service at sea, when the compass is destroyed.

Opposite poles attract; poles of the same name repel. Take two magnets, or two needles rubbed with the magnet, and bring the north and south poles together, and they attract.

Bring the north poles near each other, and they repel. Bring the south poles near each other, and they repel. Rub a needle with a magnet, and run it through a piece of cork, and put it to float in water. Hold the north pole of a magnet near its north pole, and it will keep flying away to avoid it. It may be chased from side to side of a basin. On the other hand, an opposite pole will immediately attract.

Rub four or five needles, and you may lift them up as in a string, the north pole of one needle adhering to the south pole of another.

Put a magnet under a piece of glass, and sprinkle iron filings on it, they will arrange themselves in a manner that will be very surprising. At each pole there will be a vast abundance standing erect, and there will be fewer and fewer as they recede, until there are scarcely any in the middle. If the iron filings are sprinkled on the magnet itself, they will arrange themselves in a manner very striking.

Lay a needle exactly between the north and south poles; it will move towards neither.

Conceal a *small* magnet in the palm of your right hand under your glove, you can then borrow a watch, and by changing it from hand to hand the watch will stop and go again just as you will. In your right hand the watch stops from the action of the magnet on the balance-wheel; in your left hand it continues to indicate time as usual.

Place a magnet on a stand to raise it a little above the table; then bring a small sewing needle containing a thread, within a little distance of the magnet, keeping hold of the thread to prevent the needle from attaching itself to the magnet. The needle, in endeavoring to fly to the magnet, and being prevented by the thread, will remain curiously suspended in the air like Mahomet's coffin.

Place a common sewing needle on a smooth horizontal board, and move a strong magnet underneath the board, when the needle will revolve along the board, according to the peculiar motion given to the magnet.

Bore a hole three-tenths of an inch in diameter, through a round stick of wood; or get a hollow cane about eight inches long, and half an inch thick. Provide a small steel rod, and let it be very strongly impregnated with a good magnet: this rod is to be put in the hole you have bored through the wand, and closed at each end by two small ends of ivory that screw on, different in their shapes, that you may better distinguish the poles of the magnetic bar.

When you present the north pole of this wand to the south* pole

---

* For the more clearly explaining this, it is to be observed, that the two ends of a magnet are called its poles. When placed on a pivot, in just equilibrium, that end which turns to the north is called the north pole, and the other end the south pole.

of a magnetic needle, suspended on a pivot, or to a light body swimming on the surface of the water (in which you have placed a magnetic bar), that body will approach the wand, and present that end which contains the south end of the bar; but if you present the north or south end of the wand to the north or south end of the needle, it will recede from it.

EXPERIMENTS IN ELECTRICITY.

Electricity is a property which certain bodies acquire by friction, that is to say, the power of attracting or repelling light bodies which may be near them. If you rub, for example, a stick of sealing-wax with your hand, or rather with a piece of cloth or oiled silk, and then pass the wax within a few lines of small bits of paper or straw, you will see them rush towards the wax and adhere to it, as if cemented, until the virtue acquired by the friction is dissipated. The ancients had observed that yellow amber, when rubbed in this manner, attracted light bodies; hence the name of *electricity ;* for they called that substance *electron.* But their observation went no farther.

The moderns have found the same property in a great many other bodies; such as grey amber, and in general in all resins which can bear a certain degree of friction without becoming soft; as sulphur, sealing-wax, jet, glass, the diamond, crystal, the greater part of the precious stones, silk, woollens, the hair of animals, feathers, paper, and very dry wood. We give an illustration of a simple little electrical machine that can be made by any of our young readers. Take a board, A, and fasten to it four bottles of equal size, B, in the position shown. Into the corks of two of them place a wire ring so as to form a journal for a shaft on which is mounted a circle of gutta percha, C, which may be covered with lac varnish or not; to another of the bottles (an end one) attach a bent wire, E, and connect this to the ground or table by a chain. To this bent wire tie a silk cover, D. made of nearly two semicircles of silk sewn together, and also tie the other side to another bent wire, F, from which also some little spikes must project. If, all these things being prepared, the handle is turned so as to rotate the disk in the direction of the arrow, and the knuckle be held about an inch or less from F, a series of blue sparks will pass from F to your knuckle, each accompanied by a sharp cracking noise. What is this spark, and from whence does it come? are questions often asked and just as often left unsolved, for, to tell the truth, much as we have applied electricity to the uses of the arts, and well as we understand its laws, yet the fact is we know nothing of the thing itself, beyond that it is a *force*, and can be made manifest by friction and other means. The little machine we have described is a frictional machine, about the operation of which we know just this: that the friction generated between the disk and the silk causes the electricity which was *passive*

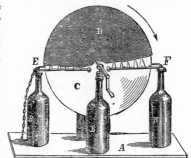

to become *active*, and it is attracted by the prime conductor, F, from which it flies to the nearest conductor, our finger, at the same moment more passive electricity passes from the earth through the chain (although were there no chain, it would be attracted from the atmosphere), and becomes by friction converted into active, and so the process is continuous, and the marvel is that this active and passive electricity are exactly the same. A pair of woollen rubbers, one on each side, may be substituted for the wires, E, which will improve the action of the machine.

A great many beautiful and entertaining experiments can be performed with glass tubes, sticks of sealing-wax and sulphur, when only small quantities of electricity are required. Glass tubes should be made as long as a person can well draw through his hand at one stroke, that is, about three feet, or something more, and as wide as can be conveniently grasped. It is not necessary that the glass be thick; perhaps the thinner the better, if it will bear sufficient friction, which, however, need be but very gentle, when the tube is in good order. It is most convenient to have the tube closed at one end; for the electric matter is not only thereby best retained on its surface, but the air may be more easily drawn out, or condensed in it, by means of a brass cap fitted at the open end.

The best rubber for a smooth glass tube is the rough side of a black oiled silk, especially when a little amalgam of mercury or other metal is put upon it. A little beeswax drawn over the surface of a tube will also greatly increase its power. In rubbing a tube, the hand should be kept two or three inches below the upper part of the rubber, otherwise the electricity will discharge itself upon the hand, and nothing will remain upon the tube for the experiment. When the tube is in very good order, and strongly excited, it will throw off many pencils of rays at every stroke, without the approach of any conductor, except what moisture may float in the common atmosphere. Our juvenile electricians should also be furnished with a rough glass tube, that is, such as has its polish taken off; though a cylinder of baked wood will do nearly as well. The best rubber for a rough glass tube or a cylinder of baked wood, as well as for a stick of sealing-wax or sulphur, is soft new flannel, or rather skins, such as rabbit or cat skin, tanned with the hair on, being much smoother, and having a more exquisite polish.

Having made these few preliminary remarks, we will proceed to describe a few curious experiments for the benefit of our young readers.

Electrify a smooth glass tube with a rubber, and hold a small feather at a short distance from it. The feather will instantly fly to the tube, and adhere to it for a short time; it will then fly off, and the tube can never be brought close to the feather till it has touched the side of the room, or some other body that communicates with the ground. If, therefore, you take care to keep the tube between the feather and the side of the room, you may drive it round to all parts of the room without touching it; and, what is very remarkable, the same side of the feather will be constantly opposite the tube.

While the feather is flying before the smooth tube, it will be immediately attracted by an excited rough tube or a stick of wax, and fly continually from one tube to the other, till the electricity of both is discharged.

Rub two pieces of fine lump sugar together in the dark, and a bright electric light will be produced. The same effect, but in a more intense degree, may be produced with two pieces of silex or quartz, the white quartz being best for this purpose. The same effect may also be witnessed by rubbing the pieces of quartz together, *under water*.

When grocers are sawing up loaves of sugar as samples, the sugar dust is beautifully luminous.

Lay a watch down on the table, and on the glass balance a tobacco

pipe very carefully. Next take a wine glass, rub it quickly with a silk handkerchief, and hold it for half a minute before the fire, then apply it to the rear end of the pipe, and the latter, attracted by the electricity excited by the friction and warmth of the handkerchief and

glass, will immediately follow it; and by carrying the wine glass around, always in front of the pipe, the latter will continue its rotary motion, the watch-glass being the centre on which it rotates.

Continuing our electrical experiments, we have, in the accompanying illustration, two pieces of apparatus that will serve to illustrate the principal laws which this force obeys. The first is a bottle, covered inside and outside, about three-quarters its height, by tinfoil, and having a metal rod passing through its cork, being connected by a piece of chain with the round ball or loop outside. It is called the *Leyden jar*, because it was supposed to have been contrived by M. Cunœus, of the city of Leyden, at the close of the year 1745; but Dr. Priestley ascribes its discovery to Mr. Von Kleist, dean of the cathe-

dral of Camin, who announced its phenomena in the same year. It acts as a reservoir of electricity. If the ball be presented to the prime conductor of the electrical machine, a series of sparks will pass from the machine to the jar, and will, so to speak, accumulate on the interior tinfoil. It would be more proper, perhaps, to say that the inside of the jar becomes in a higher state of excitement than the outside, and in consequence, if, after many sparks have passed into it, the outside is grasped in one hand and the finger of the other presented to the ball, a powerful shock will be felt, having just the force of the sum of the small shocks which have passed into it. The force being in a more active state inside than out, seeks, through the best conductors (your arms), to regain its equilibrium; and so powerful is the effort which electricity makes to be always equal, that should you go on charging a Leyden jar, without discharging also, it would discharge itself through the air, making that its conductor.

The little stand also in the illustration is for the demonstration of attraction and repulsion. A bent wire may be inserted in a piece of wood, and two pith balls connected by a bit of silk may be thrown over a hook at its extremity. Take a piece of sealing-wax and rub it on your coat-sleeve, then apply it to one ball, which will instantly fly to it, and then as suddenly fly away, and communicate its electricity to the other ball. The explanation of this is, that the sealing-wax, having more electricity than it wants, *attracts* the pith ball, and when that has got its fill of the same kind of electricity, *repels* it; thus demonstrating a great, if not the greatest law of this force, and which, with the simple apparatus we have described, our young readers can prove in a variety of ways; this law is, that bodies similarly electrified *repel* each other, while bodies differently electrified *attract* each other.

During exceedingly dry cold weather, when a north or north-east wind prevails, take two new silk stockings—the one black and the other white—and after having heated them well, put them on the same leg; the action of putting them on will electrify them. If you then pull them off, one within the other, making them both glide at the same time on the leg, they will be found so much electrified that they will adhere to each other with a greater or less force; indeed, they have been known to support, in this manner, a weight which was equal at least to sixty times that of one of them. If you draw the one from within the other, pulling one by the heel and the other by the upper end, they will still remain electrified, and you will be astonished to see each of them swell in such a manner as to represent the volume of the leg.

If one of these stockings be presented to the other at some distance, you will see them rush towards each other, become flat, and adhere with a force of several ounces. But if the experiment be performed with two pair of stockings, combined in the same manner, the one white and the other black, on presenting the white stocking to the white, and the black to the black, they will mutually repel each other. If the black be then presented to the white, they will attract each other, and become united, or will tend to unite, as in the last experiment. The Leyden jar may be charged with these stockings.

Take a piece of common brown paper, about the size of an octavo book, hold it before the fire till quite dry and hot, then draw it briskly under the arms several times, so as to rub it on both sides at once by the coat. The paper will be found so powerfully electrical, that if placed against a wainscoted or papered wall of a room, it will remain there for some minutes without falling.

If the paper be again warmed, and drawn under the arm as before, and hung up by a thread attached to one corner of it, it will hold up several feathers on each side. Should these fall off from different sides at the same time, they will cling together very strongly; and if, after a minute, they be all shaken off, they will fly to one another in a very singular manner.

Cut a bit of cork in the form of a spider, furnish it with eight white thread legs, and run through the body a long black silk thread, by which hang up the imitation insect. Excite a rod of sealing-wax and another of glass, both by means of the rubber, and hold them on each side of the spider, which will vibrate backwards and forwards. This experiment was invented by Dr. Franklin.

Warm two pieces of white paper at the fire, place them upon each other, on a table or book, and rub strongly the upper paper with India-rubber, when the papers will be found so strongly electrical, as to be separated only by force; or, if torn asunder in the dark, they will give out the electric spark. Silk may be made to produce the same effects.

Support a pane of glass, previously warmed, upon two books, one at each end, and place some bran underneath; then rub the upper side of the glass with a black silk handkerchief, or a piece of flannel, and the bran will dance up and down under it with much rapidity.

Warm and excite a piece of brown paper as before, lay it on a table, and place upon it a ball, made of elder-pith, about the size of a pea; the ball will immediately run across the paper; and if a needle be pointed towards it, it will again run to another part, and so on for a considerable time.

If a piece of paper be placed upon a smooth table, and then rubbed smartly with India-rubber, the electricity developed will be so power-ful, that two or three goose quills may be made to adhere to the under side of the paper, *after* it has been raised from the table.

Fix a stick of sealing-wax, W, and a rod of glass, G, upright, in a strong piece of wood, as shown in the engraving; then contrive a slender piece of wood, like that marked A, and from the end of its arm hang a very slender thread of white silk, with a light downy feather attached to its extremity; get some one to hold the board firmly while you rub the glass rod briskly with a dry silk handkerchief, and the stick of sealing-wax with a piece of dry woollen cloth. By doing thus, you have excited the electricity of the wax and of the glass; but the electricity in one case appears to differ in some respects from that

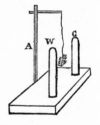

of the other, and, consequently, that of the glass is called *positive*, and that of the sealing-wax *negative;* one appears as if it had too much, and the other too little, and this state of things continues until an equi-librium is established. Accordingly, to effect this, you will see the fea-ther continue to move from the wax to the glass, and *vice versâ*, until the equilibrium is established.

Make a Torricellian vacuum* in a glass tube, about three feet long,

* A Torricellian vacuum is made by filling a tube with pure mercury, and then invert-ing it, in the same manner as in making a barometer; for as the mercury runs out, all the space above will be a true vacuum.

and hermetically sealed.* Let one end of this tube be held in the hand, and the other applied to the conductor; and immediately the whole tube will be illuminated from one end, and when taken from the conductor will continue luminous, without interruption, for a considerable time, very often about a quarter of an hour. If, after this, it be drawn through the hand either way, the light will be uncommonly brilliant, and, without the least interruption, from one end to the other, even to its whole length. After this operation, which discharges it in a great measure, it will still flash at intervals, though it be held only at the extremity, and quite still; but if it be grasped by the other hand at the same time, in a different place, strong flashes of light will dart from one end to the other. This will continue for twenty-four hours, and often longer, without any fresh excitation. Small and long glass tubes, exhausted of air, and bent in many irregular crooks and angles, will, when properly electrified, exhibit a very beautiful representation of vivid flashes of lightning. This experiment has been called the electric Aurora Borealis.

EXPERIMENTS IN GALVANISM.

Electro-magnetism, that is, magnetism produced by electricity, is a brilliant discovery of the present century. Dr. Franklin believed a connexion to exist between electricity and magnetism, from the circumstance that the poles of the compass-needle had been frequently reversed during thunder storms, and that the same effect could be produced by electrical discharges. To determine this connexion, Professor Oersted, of Copenhagen, made some experiments in the year 1807; but he did not complete the discovery until 1820.

The terms Galvanism and Voltaism are also given to electricity under a peculiar form; these being derived from Galvani and Volta, the discoverers. Chemical electricity would, however, be a fitter term for galvanism and voltaism, as well as for electro-magnetism, since the galvanic or electro-magnetism is excited by chemical agency, that is, by the action of acids on metals; and the electric power by friction, or by induction from the atmosphere.

Coat the point of your tongue with tinfoil, and its middle part with gold or silver leaf, so that the two metals touch, when a sourish taste will be produced. This simple effect is termed "a galvanic tongue."

* A glass is hermetically sealed by holding the end of it in the flame of a candle, til it begins to melt, and then twisting it together with a pair of pincers.

Ale and porter drink better out of a pewter or tin pot than from glass or earthenware, because of the galvanic influence of the green copper used to give the beer a frothy head.

Galvanic experiments may be made with the legs of a frog. A live flounder will answer nearly the same purpose. Lay the fish in a plate, upon a slip of zinc, to which is attached a piece of wire, and put a quarter dollar upon the flounder's back; then touch the quarter dollar with the wire, and at each contact strong muscular contractions will be produced.

Place a thin plate of zinc upon the upper surface of the tongue, and a half dollar or a piece of silver on the under surface. Allow the metals to remain for a little time in contact with the tongue before they are made to touch each other, that the taste of the metals themselves may not be confounded with the sensation produced by their contact. When the edges of the metals, which project beyond the tongue, are then suffered to touch, a galvanic sensation is produced, which it is difficult accurately to describe.

Place a silver teaspoon as high as possible between the gums and the upper lip, and a piece of zinc between the gums and the under lip. On bringing the extremities of the metals into contact, a very vivid sensation, and an effect like a flash of light across the eyes, will be perceived. It is singular that this light is equally vivid in the dark and in the strongest light, and whether the eyes be shut or open.

Put a silver cup or mug, filled with water, upon a plate of zinc on a table, and just touch the water with the tip of the tongue; it will be tasteless so long as the zinc plate is not handled, for the body does not form a voltaic circle with the metals. Moisten your hand well, take hold of the plate of zinc, and touch the water with your tongue, when a very peculiar sensation, and an acid taste, will be experienced.

Take a piece of copper of about six inches in width, and put upon it a piece of zinc of rather smaller dimensions, inserting a piece of cloth, of the same size as the zinc, between them; place a leech upon the piece of zinc, and though there appear nothing to hinder it from crawling away, yet it will not pass from the zinc to the copper, because its damp body acting as a conductor to the fluid disturbed, as soon as it touches the copper it receives a galvanic shock, and of course retires to its resting-place.

Plunge an iron knife into a solution of sulphate of copper (blue-stone); by chemical action only it will become covered with metallic copper.

Immerse in the same solution a piece of platinum; taking care not to let it touch the iron, and no deposition of copper will take place upon it; but if the upper ends of the metals be brought into contact with each other, a copious deposition of copper will soon settle upon the platinum likewise.

AN EATABLE CANDLE.

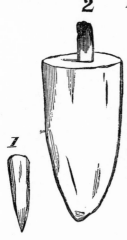

A good deal of amusement may be created by making and eating what is apparently the old stump of a tallow candle. This is done by cutting a piece of apple the shape required, and sticking into it a little fragment of nut or almond, like No. 1. You then have a candle stump resembling No. 2. The almond wick can be lighted, and will burn for more than a minute, so that the deception is perfect. You can afterwards eat it in the presence of the company.

THE PNEUMATIC PHIAL.

Provide a phial one-fourth filled with any colored water, and with a glass tube passing through the cork, or cemented into the neck of the phial, so as to be air-tight; the tube may reach to within a quarter of an inch of the bottom of the phial, so as to dip below the surface of the liquid. Hold this little instrument before the fire, or plunge it into hot water, when the air that is in the phial will expand, and force up the colored liquor into the tube.

RESIN BUBBLES.

Dip the bowl of a tobacco-pipe into melted resin, hold the pipe in a vertical position, and blow through it; when bubbles of various sizes will be formed, of a brilliant silvery hue, and in a variety of colors.

TO LIFT A BOTTLE WITH A STRAW.

Who would ever think that a bottle could be lifted by a straw? But it can be done in the following manner: Take a stout unbroken straw, and bend the thickest end of it, between the knots, into an acute angle, and put it in a bottle so that its bent part may rest against the side of the bottle, as in the engraving; then take hold of the end of it and you will be able to lift up the bottle by the straw, and the nearer the angular part of the latter comes to that which passes out of the neck of the former so much the more easy will be the experiment. In this case, the force being distributed in straight lines, the straw, if it be perfect, cannot break by compression, and there is no tendency to bend it.

TO MAKE A STRING APPEAR BLACK AND WHITE ALTERNATELY.

This puzzle is formed of a piece of elder, about three and a half inches long, with the pith removed: a hole is bored across near one end, and a pin fastened crosswise at the other end. A piece of cord is passed in at one hole, round the pin, and out at the opposite hole.

Knots being made at the ends, the cord is pulled through as far as it will go, and all the part exposed stained black; when drawn back this portion will be concealed, the cord seeming to go in black and come out white. A second cord is sometimes arranged at the opposite end, with a needle so attached as to be thrust from the end and inflict a slight puncture. The ends may be covered with velvet, and the rest bound over with silk.

LIGHT FROM THE POTATO.

Place a few potatoes in a dark cellar; when in a state of putrefaction, they will give out sometimes a light sufficient to read by. A few years since, an officer on guard at Strasbourg thought the barracks were on fire, in consequence of the light thus emitted from a cellar full of putrefying potatoes.

THE BOTTLE IMPS.

Our next is a little experiment illustrating the compressibility of air

:nd water, called the "Bottle Imps." Take a jar of glass, and fill it with water up to the neck; next provide a little figure having a hole in its centre that will contain sufficient air to make it buoyant. Put it in the water, and close the bottle with a piece of parchment or India-rubber tied tightly over the mouth. Now when the hand is pressed on the cover, the figure descends, and when it is removed, the figure quickly ascends, and so it may be kept dancing up and down for any length of time. The reason is this:—The water in the bottle is incompressible; when, therefore, you press upon the surface, it rises in the interior of the figure, and consequently by compressing the air into less space, renders the figure less buoyant; but no sooner is the hand removed than the inclosed air resumes its former volume, and expels the intruding **water;** in consequence, the figure regains its former lightness, and reascends.

TABLE TURNING.

"It does not follow," says Göthe, "that what is mysterious must necessarily be miraculous." We are accustomed to take so many facts for granted which science herself has hitherto been unable to explain, that the truth of this aphorism of the illustrious German cannot now be disputed. The most distinguished of modern experimental philosophers has left upon record a fact witnessed by himself, apparently quite as extraordinary as any of those phenomena about which the world is now puzzling itself. In Sir David Brewster's "Letters on Natural Magic," we find the experiment to which we allude was first performed before a large party at Venice, and afterwards repeated in his presence in England. This feat, apparently so marvellous, was the power of any six persons to raise a man of more than ordinary weight upon the points of their forefingers, and sustain him so suspended aloft for several minutes. It was done in this way. The lungs of the person to be raised, as well as of those who were to lift him, were inflated with air at the same moment. The person having been placed in a chair, a signal was given, at which each of the persons engaged draws a deep breath. When the inhalation is complete, there is a second signal; and in this simple mode a man of two hundred pounds can be lifted, as if he were no heavier than a feather.

This phenomenon appeared to be one which contained a direct contradiction of all the known laws of physics. Sir David professed himself wholly unable to account for or explain it; but a problem, which seemed so unintelligible to this practical philosopher, has received a very ready solution in our own times. And we mention the circumstance now, as a striking proof that phenomena the most startling and mysterious will occasionally occur, perplex the world for a time, and at length quietly pass away into that dreamy realm, the abode of shadowy and forgotten chimeras of the past. We are indebted to two young ladies

from Rochester, New York, for the notable discovery called table-turning. Margaret and Catherine Fox, whose names gained such celebrity in connexion with the spirit rappers, invented at the same time the rotatory motion of the tables, which they attributed to the influence of the spirits—a point which we believe is now altogether given up by professors of that mysterious art. From America the marvel passed into Germany, and so, *via* France, arrived in Great Britain. Some time ago the writer, chancing to be in Paris, found table-turning and hat-moving to be the evening's amusement of nearly every drawing-room he entered.

The first and the most simple experiment, which we quote from a work by Monsieur Roubaud, can be performed by means of a hat, because it is a subject easy to be operated upon on account of its lightness, while its size affords a surface large enough to contain five or six hands. This phenomenon may be produced by two persons, each facing the other; they cover the brim of the hat with their hands. There should be no pressure on the hat,—a simple contact is all that is requisite, and the wishes of the operators,—say those who believe in the mystery,—should be unanimous; that is to say, they thould desire the hat to turn in one particular direction. All being thus arranged, after a little delay, which may vary from a minute to an hour, during which the experimenters have liberty to talk and laugh as much as they please,—a sensation of heat and tingling is felt in the elbows, wrist, and fingers, and all along the nerves of the hands. Immediately after the manifestation of these symptoms, oscillations are distinctly perceptible. The increased application of the mind resulting from this, has a tendency at once to produce the phenomenon, did not the hands, by an organic contraction, exercised independently of the will, press the hat with greater force, and thus oppose a resistance which it cannot overcome.

This kind of spasmodic convulsion of the fingers does not take place with persons forewarned. When the hat is no longer under the influence of the will, the movement is always rotatory and continues with a velocity varying according to the physical or individual influences which act upon the fluid. When the motion is slow, it can always be increased by the power of the will, which can also alter the direction of the movement, and make the hat advance either backwards or forwards, to the right or to the left. If tried upon a table, this experiment will produce similar results. The floor, however, on which the table is to stand, should be perfectly even, so as to present no obstacle to the motion. The castors should be well oiled, and the weight in proportion with the surface, to correspond with the number of persons who are to take part in the experiment. In order to render the period of waiting as agreeable as possible, the operators should be of different sexes, in nearly equal proportions, and placed alternately. They must then lay their hands, with the palm downwards, on the table, and place them in contact with their neighbor's, by means of their little fingers, so that a complete chain of manual communication will be established all round the surface of the table.

As in the experiment of the hat, the wills of the respective persons engaged, must be unanimous. It would be better in the first experiments, to give no particular direction, but to wait until the table is actually in motion. Nor is it at all necessary that any particular attitude should be adopted by the hands. The effect will be produced if they are laid either on the back or edgeways; but the point of manual communication would appear to be almost essential. "This condition," says M. Roubaud, "is as necessary to give out the necessary fluid, as are alternate pieces of zinc and copper to the voltaic pile." The operators must also communicate with each other by that part of the body only which is in communication with the table. The phenomenon will not take place if any other communication exists, and the time for its production varies, as in the case of the hat, from a few minutes to an hour. Having thus given the outlines of this experiment, we shall not at present enter into an examination of the different arguments which have been adduced in support of the ingenious theories which have been started.

There may, or there may not be some subtile fluid hitherto unrecognised, by means of which mind can operate directly, not only upon animate, but upon inanimate matter. This suggestion of electricity is created and carried out by the union of hands; yet may not the same union contain a suggestion of a different character, but equally efficacious in producing the result, namely, having a multiplication of mechanical power? Although no force is directly used by any person concerned, and the pressure upon the table is confined to a simple touch, yet the touch, if applied in combination with the will, may be quite sufficient to produce a rotatory motion in a body capable of being easily moved. We have seen some persons blow upon the table to accelerate the result, just as a shoe-black blows upon a refractory boot he is endeavoring to polish. But it would perhaps astonish some of the operators, who are at this moment engaged upon these marvels, to be informed that even the touch, light as it is, which is applied to the surface of the table, if it were applied underneath, and if a signal were given and observed accurately, as in the experiment we have cited from Sir David Brewster's letters, the same weight which is merely moved could be lifted altogether from the ground on which it stands.

We revert, in conclusion, to the observation with which we prefaced our remarks, that what is mysterious need not be miraculous. An attempt has been made to invest this phenomenon with everything which could possibly attract and captivate the credulous public. We have endeavored to strip it of such character, and present it to our juvenile friends simply as it exists.

THE BOOK AND THE KEY.

When King James I. began to write his treatise on witchcraft, wherein he tells us " that the fearful abounding at this time, in this country, of these detestable slaves of the devil, the witchers or enchanters, hath moved me, beloved reader, to despatch in a post this following treatise of mine," of course with the benevolent intention of thoroughly awakening the reader's conscience thereon, the witches he so anathematized used divination by means of the key. By the time of the notorious John Prodgers, the witch-finder, it had descended to maid-servants, who, in cases of stolen goods, by placing the key in a certain chapter of the Book of Ruth, and pronouncing various names, declared that he or she at whose name the key moved was the thief. In a little French book on divination (" L'Art de connaitre l'Avenir"), we have the same under the title of " Cleidomancy," from *kleis*, a key; and the author declares that the custom is of great antiquity in Russia, where it is used for the discovery of hidden treasures. He gives two methods of divination; one is by attaching a piece of paper to the key with the name of the suspected person thereon; if the paper moves, the person is to be held guilty; but the other is as it is now sometimes done, and very little different from our illustration. Place the key in a book, then tie the book with a string; the person who consults it places the index finger (the first) of the left hand in the ring of the key, then she pronounces various places where she thinks the treasure is concealed. "Si elle s'est trompée la clef reste immobile, mais si elle remue son doigt, elle peut aller recueillir le trésor à l'endroit qu'elle nommat en ce moment." So says our little yellow book, for the truth of which we cannot by any means vouch.

It is held by two persons on the index fingers of the left hands, care being taken to allow space enough for the key to turn. In the choice

of a book, one must be guided by weight. The Bible we never experimented with from principle, especially as any book will do—a large dictionary. A thick octavo will do well for a moderate-sized door key. Held as in the cut for a short time, the key will turn half round, that is, it will become at right angles to its former position. Our readers must not suppose we think it to be magic, or anything else but a new and *probably magnetic fluid emitted from the persons, and influenced by their will;* if it be not the involuntary muscular action of the holders, as suggested by more than one savant. It is influenced by the will, as will be proved by the following experiments:—

Fix on a name which both parties know, say Eliza; repeat the letters of the alphabet at intervals, by the watch, of five seconds; the key will turn at the letter E. Replace the key, and by the same process the key will move at the letter T, the name Thomas being fixed on; the difference of time employed in the experiments being seventy-five seconds. If one of the persons only know the name, the key will turn, but more slowly and hesitatingly, proving that the influence of the will of two is more powerful than that of one; where neither, but a third person present knows the name, the key will not turn with certainty, thus proving that it is merely a scientific experiment, and, as every one but the most credulous must at once perceive, useless for purposes of soothsaying. Our readers will find some amusement in trying this, and especially in testing the strength of one person's will over another.

THE MAN IN THE MOON.

This is glorious fun for the long evenings, and will be found a valuable addition to the amusements provided at evening parties. In a room with folding doors, which will be best suited to the purpose—or otherwise it must be suspended from the ceiling—strain a large sheet across the partition. In the front room place the company, who will remain in comparative darkness, and in the back room put a bright lamp or candle, with a looking-glass reflector, or a polished tin one if it be convenient, on the ground. When an individual stands between the light and the sheet, his reflection, magnified to immense proportions, will be thrown forward on the screen, and when he jumps over the light, it will appear to the spectators in front, as if he had jumped upwards through the ceiling. Some amusing scenes may be thus contrived with a little ingenuity. Chairs and tables may be called down from above simply by passing them across the light; a struggle between two seeming combatants may take place, and one be seen to throw the other up in the air on the same principle. A game at cards, with pieces of cardboard cut out so as to represent the pips, may be played out, and beer poured from a jug into a glass, sawdust giving the best shadowy imitation of the fluid, may be imbibed during the game with great effect. Care should be taken to keep the profile on the screen as distinct as possible, and practice will soon suggest some highly humorous situations.

THE WATCH TRICK.

If a person will tell you the hour he means to dine, you can tell him the hour he intends to get up that morning. First ask a person to *think* of the hour he intends rising on the following morning; when he has done so, bid him place his finger on any hour he pleases on the dial of your watch, and to remember the hour he first thought of. To the hour his finger is on you now mentally add 12, and request him to retrograde, counting the number of hours you mention, whatever that may be, but that he is to commence counting *with* the hour he thought of *from* the hour he points at; for example, suppose he thought of rising at 8, and places his finger on 12 as the hour of dinner, you desire him to count backwards 24 hours, 12 he calls 8 (that being the hour he thought of rising), 11 he calls 9, 10 he calls 10, and so on (mentally but not aloud) until he has counted 24, at which point he

will stop, which will be at 8, and he will express his surprise to find
that it is the hour he thought of rising.

A DOUBLE-COLORED REFLECTION.

Pierce the centre of a circular piece of colored glass by means of a
common awl, well moistened with oil of turpentine, encircle the glass
with the fingers and thumb, hold it in the sunshine, or the strong light
of a lamp, and the following beautiful effects will be produced :—If the
glass be red, the luminous spot in the centre will be reflected green ; if the
glass be green, the spot will be red ; if blue, orange ; and if yellow, indigo.

THE FLUTE OF FANCY.

Take a good sound cork, with as few holes or cracks in it as possible.
By placing this against the teeth, holding it tightly between the lips, and
playing upon it with the bowl ends of two tea-spoons, a very singular
imitation of a piccolo or small flute will be produced. The tune should
be fancied by the player, and a quick air will be found most effective.

HOW TO BLOW OFF YOUR HAT.

Let the rim of your hat just catch the edge of the coat collar, and
then bending forward, the pressure will cause it to rise off the forehead. By making believe that your breath is causing it to ascend, you
will create considerable astonishment and diversion.

HOW TO PUT AN EGG INTO A SMALL-NECKED BOTTLE.

Steep the egg in vinegar for some time, when the shell will become
perfectly soft and pliable. It can then be forced into the bottle. If
water be afterwards poured into the bottle, the egg will regain its
proper shape and consistency, and will puzzle many as to how it got
into the bottle.

THE " TWENTY CENT " TRICK.

This ingenious deception, which appears so marvellous to the eyes
of the uninitiated, is thus performed. Borrow twenty cents from the
company, which display on a plate, having previously prepared five
cents in your left hand, which you keep concealed. Then take the
cents from the plate in the right hand, and mixing them with the concealed five, give them to one of the company to hold. Ask the
possessor to return five to you, which he will do, supposing he then
retains only fifteen, although, in reality, he of course has twenty.
Now, have another cent palmed in your right hand, so that when
giving the five cents to another person to hold, you may mix it with
that sum, and place the *six* cents in his hand. You may now ask him
as before to return *one ;* when you take it remind him he has only four

and you must now proceed with the most marvellous part of your illusion. Taking the one cent you have just received in the right hand, palm it, and pretend to place it in the left. Then striking the left hand with your magic rod, bid it fly into the closed hand of the person holding five, or, as he supposes, the *four* cents. On unclosing the hand, the cents will of course appear to have been transferred thither, and great amazement will result. Now taking the five cents, make a more dexterous pass into the left hand, whence you bid them fly into the closed hand of the person holding the supposed fifteen, and whom you now ask to return you the full sum of twenty cents, much to his own wonder and that of the company. If executed with care and dexterity, no illusion can be more effective.

THE VANISHING DIME.

This is a clever trick, and may be done with good effect in the following manner:—Previously stick a small piece of white wax on the nail of your middle finger, lay a dime on the palm of your hand, and state to the company that you will make it vanish at the word of command, at the same time observing that many persons perform the feat by letting the dime fall into their sleeve, but to convince them that you have not recourse to any such deception, turn up your cuffs. Then close your hand, and by bringing the waxed nail in contact with the dime, it will firmly adhere to it. Then blow upon your hand and cry "begone;" and suddenly opening it, and extending your palm, you show that the dime has vanished. Care must be taken to remove the wax from the dime before restoring it to the owner, if it should have been borrowed from one of the company.

TO BRING TWO SEPARATE COINS INTO ONE HAND.

Take two cents, which must be carefully placed in each hand, as thus: The right hand with the coin on the fourth and little finger, as in the illustration. Then place at a short distance from each other both hands open on the table, the left palm being level with the fingers of the right. By now suddenly turning the hands over, the

16*

cent from the right hand will fly, without being perceived, into the palm of the left, and make the transit appear most unaccountable to the bewildered eyes of the spectator. By placing the audience in front, and not at the side of the exhibitor, this illusion, if neatly performed, can never be detected.

TO CAUSE A DIME TO APPEAR IN A GLASS.

Having turned up the cuffs of your coat, begin by placing a cent on your elbow and catching it in your hand, a feat of dexterity which is easily performed. Then allege you can catch even a smaller coin in a more difficult position. You illustrate this by placing the dime half way between the elbow and the wrist, as in the illustration. By now suddenly bringing the hand down, the dime will fall securely into the cuff unseen by any, and seemingly apparently to your own astonishment to have altogether disappeared. Now take a drinking-glass or tumbler, and bidding the spectators watch the ceiling, you tell them the lost coin shall drop through the ceiling. By placing the glass at the side of your arm and elevating the hand for the purpose, the coin will fall from the cuff, jingling into the tumbler, and cause great marvel as to how it came there.

HOW TO MAKE A COIN STICK AGAINST THE WALL.

Take a small coin, such as a dime or a quarter, and on the edge cut a small notch with a knife, so that a little point of the metal will project. By pressing this against a door or wooden partition, the coin will remain mysteriously adhering against the perpendicular surface.

THE DISAPPEARING DIME.

Provide yourself with a piece of India-rubber cord, about twelve inches long, and a dime with a hole on the edge; attach the dime to the cord with a piece of white sewing silk, and after having done this, sew the cord to your coat sleeve lining, but be very careful and ascertain that the end upon which the dime is attached does not extend lower than within two inches of the extreme end of the sleeve when the coat is on. It is better to have the dime in the left arm sleeve. Having done this, bring down the dime with the right hand, and place it between the thumb and index finger of the left hand, as represented in the accompanying cut, and, showing it to the company, tell them that you will give the coin to any one present who will not let it slip away. You must then select one of the audience to whom you proffer the dime, and just as he is about to receive it you must let it slip from between your fingers, and the contraction of the elastic cord will make the coin disappear up your sleeve, much to the astonishment of the person who thinks he is about to receive it. This feat can be varied by pretending to wrap the coin in a piece of paper or a handkerchief. Great care should be taken not to let any part of the cord be seen, as this would, of course, discover the trick. This is one of the most surprising feats of legerdemain, and its chief beauty consists in its extreme simplicity. The writer has frequently astonished a whole room full of company by the performance of this trick.

THE KNIFE AND THE DECANTER.

To perform this trick take a decanter about half full of water, and place it before you on a square table, about three inches from the edge of the same, then procure a dessert knife and insert the blade between the table and the decanter, just sufficient to allow it to remain in a horizontal position, as represented in the cut. You can now inform the company

that you intend to introduce the knife into the decanter by one blow of the hand, and at the same time strike the handle of the knife a sharp blow with your index finger (as represented in the cut), and if skilfully done, you will cause the knife to fly upwards and descend into the mouth of the decanter. Like all sleight of hand tricks, this requires some practice before it should be attempted in the parlor.

HOW TO PASS A TUMBLER THROUGH A TABLE.

Place the spectators on the opposite side of the table to where you sit, having spread, unperceived, a handkerchief across your knees

Now take a drinking glass—a tumbler with no stem is preferable—and covering it with paper, mould the covering as nearly as possible to the shape of the glass. Whilst uttering some cabalistic phrases, drop the glass into your handkerchief unperceived, and, as the paper retains the shape, you will have no difficulty in making the lookers on believe the tumbler to be still beneath it. Passing the glass in the left hand beneath the table, you now crush the paper down with your right, when the glass will appear to have been sent through the table. It is needless to add, the spectators should be placed at some little distance on a level; and if a cloth is over the table, the trick will be more easily performed.

THE DISAPPEARING COIN.

To place a small coin in a pocket handkerchief, and wrap it carefully up; then to unfold the handkerchief, and make the coin disap-

Fig. No. 1.

pear. To perform this seemingly impossible feat, all you have to do is to take a half-dime and privately place a piece of soft wax on one side of it; then spread a pocket handkerchief upon a table, and taking up the coin, show it to your audience—being very careful not to expose the side that has the wax on it; then place it in the centre of the handkerchief, with the *waxed side up*, at the same time bring over the corner of the handkerchief marked A, as represented in Fig. No. 1, and completely hide the

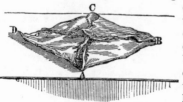

Fig. No. 2.

coin from the view of the spectators; this must be carefully done, or the company will discover the wax on the coin. You must now press on the coin very hard with your thumb, so as to make it adhere to the handkerchief; when you have done this, fold over successively the corners marked B, C, and D, and the handkerchief will assume the shape of Fig. No. 2.

Then again fold over the corners B, C, and D (Fig. No. 2), leaving the corner, A, open. Having done this, take hold of the handkerchief with both hands, as represented in Fig. No. 3, at the opening A, and sliding your fingers along the edge of the same, it will become unfolded, and the coin, adhering to the corner of the handkerchief, will of course come into your right hand; then detach the coin, shake out the handkerchief, and, to the great as-

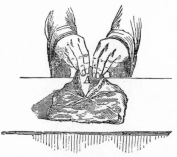

Fig. No. 3.

tonishment of the company, the coin will have disappeared. In order to convince the audience that the coin is still in the handkerchief after you have wrapped it up, you can drop it on the table, when it will sound against the wood.

This is an easy trick to perform, and, if well done, is calculated to create much astonishment at an evening party.

THE HAT AND QUARTER TRICK.

Place a hat, tumbler, and quarter, as represented in the cut; then, after making several feints, as if you intended to strike the hat upon the *rim*, give the hat a sharp quick blow upon the *inside of the crown*, and the coin will fall into the tumbler. This is a beautiful trick, if skilfully performed.

THE MAGNETIZED CANE

Is a very surprising little fancy, and is calculated to create much astonishment in the parlor or drawing-room. To perform this trick, take a piece of black silk thread or horse-hair, about two feet long, and fasten to each end of the same bent hooks of a similar color.

When unobserved, fasten the hooks in the back part of your pantaloon

legs, about two inches below the bend of the knees. Then place the cane (it should be a dark one and not too heavy) within the inner part of the thread, as represented in the engraving, and by a simple movement of the legs, you can make the cane dance about and perform a great variety of fantastic movements. At night your audience cannot perceive the thread, and apparently the cane will have no support whatever. The performer should inform the company before commencing this trick, that he intends to magnetize the cane, and by moving his hands as professors of magnetism do, the motion of the legs will not be noticed.

THE MAGIC COIN.

Although a purely sleight-of-hand trick, it requires but little practice to perform it with dexterity. Take a quarter of a dollar between the thumb and forefinger of the right hand, as represented in the accompany-

ing cut, then, by a rapid twist of the fingers, twirl the coin by the same motion that you would use to spin a teetotum, at the same time rapidly close your hand, and the coin will disappear up your coat-sleeve; you can now open your hand, and, much to the astonishment of your audience, the coin will not be there. This capital trick may be varied in a hundred ways. One good way is to take three dimes or quarters, and concealing one in the palm of your left hand, place the other two, one each between the thumb and forefinger of each hand, then give the coin in the right hand the twirl as already described, and closing both hands quickly, the coin in the right hand will disappear up your sleeve, and the left hand, on being unclosed, will be found to contain two quarters, whilst that which *was* in the right will have disappeared. Thus you will make the surprised spectators believe that you conjured the coin from the right hand into the left.

This is a toy made of about a quarter of a yard of pasteboard, cut round and covered with white paper. The outside edge should be neatly bound with gilt paper. The flat surface is ruled for mottoes, and all the lines meet in the centre. The writer should be very careful to draw a line of red or black ink between each, to make them distinct.

Exactly in the centre of the circle a wire is inserted, and on that is fastened a neatly-dressed jointed doll, of the smallest size. In one hand she holds a small straw wand, with which she points to the poetry beneath her. The wire is made steady by fastening it in the centre of a common wafer-box, covered and bound to correspond to the rest of the toy. The doll is just high enough above the pasteboard to turn round freely. When you wish your fortune told, twirl her round rapidly, and when she stops, read what her wand points to.